Composition for the 21st ½ century

Characters in Animation

VOLUME 2

Composition for the 21st ½ century

Characters in Animation

Thomas Paul Thesen

CRC Press
Taylor & Francis Group
Boca Raton London New York

CRC Press is an imprint of the
Taylor & Francis Group, an **informa** business

A FOCAL PRESS BOOK

CRC Press
Taylor & Francis Group
6000 Broken Sound Parkway NW, Suite 300
Boca Raton, FL 33487-2742

© 2022 by Taylor & Francis Group, LLC
CRC Press is an imprint of Taylor & Francis Group, an Informa business

No claim to original U.S. Government works

Printed on acid-free paper

DOI: 10.1201/b22147

International Standard Book Number-13: 978-1-138-74094-5 (Hardback)
978-1-138-74090-7 (Paperback)

Visit the Taylor & Francis Web site at
http://www.taylorandfrancis.com

and the CRC Press Web site at
http://www.crcpress.com

This book is dedicated to Alexandra Jäth and my parents Luise & Ludwig Thesen.

"Close your bodily eye, so that you may see your picture first with the spiritual eye. Then bring to the light of day that which you have seen in the darkness so that it may react upon others from the outside inwards"[1]

Caspar David Friedrich

[1] *The Romantic Imagination: Literature and Art in England and Germany* (1996) by Fredrick Berwick.

Contents

Contents

Acknowledgments

I would like to thank Katrin Albers for her patience in reading and critiquing the manuscript and Monika Horstmann for her invaluable input in typographical questions and cover design advice. Additional thanks go to Patrick Smith, Mia Goodwin, Melvyn Ternan, Emil Polyak, Giannalberto Bendazzi, Kinson Cheung, Park Seh Oh, William Kovacsik, Shinho Lee, and all my former students.

Author

For more than 20 years, Thomas Paul Thesen's career has been about learning and understanding the complexities of art, animation, and image-making, both in still illustration, drawing and photography and the moving image. He has worked in the industry as a character animator and visual development artist for companies like Pixar, DreamWorks, and Sprite Animation Studios. He has also taught for many years at universities across Asia, the United States, and the United Kingdom.

To know more about his professional and personal work, visit http://thomasthesen.art/.

CHAPTER 1

The Job of a Character Designer

What is character design?

The two words "character" and "design" obviously already define the two most important aspects of the tasks of a character designer. It seems fairly simple what the character designer does, but to fully comprehend the complex task one needs to first define those two simple words, which are explained in the first and second part of this book. Character is explained in the first section of this book, which deals with story and the character's relationships and personality. The second part of this book deals with the actual visual development of the character and what aspects we have to our disposal to not just draw the character, but to design it. The two aspects of character and design have to be equally and thoroughly covered in order to produce a believable and fully rounded character that convinces on every level. Obviously,

both elements strongly relate to each other and cannot exist on their own. This book clarifies those two parts of the task by not only explaining the technical side of the job, but also the intellectual side and the reasoning behind the artistic choices: the characterization and the development of a personality. Character design is a significant part of the visual development process for film and games, and also one that is the most difficult and misleading. It is not just the act of drawing the character, but creating the character based on a specific story. The final design needs to please on many different levels. Additionally, it needs to be engaging to the general public so they can easily submit to the escapism of the film.

There are literally thousands and thousands of characters being created on a daily basis and most of them lack an intellectual side. This is because a character is created without a story attached to it, which is *the* significant task in the creation of the character. The character of a rabbit (Figure 1.1) is obviously a character, but what is its purpose? A character only has a purpose if it is for a medium, like film, TV, commercials, or games. There always needs to be a reason for the character to exist. All media tell stories, which are the foundation for every character. Toys on the other hand, also presenting characters, can be rather vague as there is not often an actual story that the character is involved in, but most often merely a design. In the end, lacking the story side of the task creates characters for their looks alone and focuses rather on the technical bravura of the artist, than the creation of a unique character with personality. The audience connects with a character that has a story to tell. If the story is engaging the character can be weird and odd, but the audience will still connect with it. If there is no story, but just a fabulously designed character without an emotional connection, the audience won't connect with it and find the film pointless (although exceptions can happen). Story is always key!

Personality—story—design—audience

There are four aspects that define a character: personality, story, design, and target audience. If those four aspects are not covered the character is lacking its foundation, a foundation needed to allow the audience to connect. It doesn't matter if the character is technically executed with bravura and artistically stunning, what counts is how the four elements of story, personality, design, and target audience support

Figure 1.1

DOI: 10.1201/b22147-1

Figure 1.2

each other. A character is only then a true *character* by being unique and different; although not necessarily unique in all four areas of story, personality, design, and target audience. But one of the areas needs to be unique for the character to be interesting and not a total cliché. Everyone can draw a character like the one in Figure 1.2, which is a character that has a style—it's not a world-shaking one, but it's a style. However, without a story there is nothing that makes the character interesting, other than us remembering our own childhood drawings maybe (which is already filling the image with stories). A random photograph that we look at, depicting people we don't know is just that: a random photo. We don't really care about the people in the picture as we don't connect with them yet. What needs to happen is that we relate on an emotional level, which happens as soon as there is a story involved. One of the people on the picture, for example, just won the lottery. Immediately emotions start to evolve and we try to figure out who is the one that could be the millionaire. Every face is scanned by the viewer for clues that could give a hint of who it is that won the jackpot. Once we know who it is, it doesn't matter what the emotions of that person are. If they are laughing, crying, sleeping, yelling angrily, we will immediately come up with a story that fits the image and the actions on the picture, and we will be emotionally involved. Thus if a character

lacks a story and lacks a personality, the audience will be less drawn toward the character emotionally. Obviously there can be a connection toward a character that is cute, cool, adorable, sexy … but that does not mean that the viewer is emotionally involved. We can project cliché emotions onto the character and falsely believe we actually feel what we are supposed to feel. But what needs to happen instead is that the character is triggering real emotions in the viewer.

The characters in a film clearly draw all the attention and are usually driving the story forward, so they had better be very well designed to reflect their importance in the film. The characters themselves however do not only drive the story, but also set the design direction. They have to be unique enough to create a brand and a figurehead that can sell the movie and trigger the audience's interest in the film in the first place. Designing a character is a long and often tedious search for the character rather than just making one drawing and being done with it. The character should, like the story, be unique enough to surprise the audience with something new and fresh.

The difficulty is to find a design that actually IS unique, speaks a design language that is contemporary, and tells the audience that the film is new and worth watching (simply from a marketing perspective). Usually the audience doesn't care too much for something that looks old fashioned, unless it is based on a popular character like, for instance, Astro boy, who is an already established character and (hopefully) brings audiences into the theater because of his fame. Astro boy is a brand and clearly cannot be completely changed in his design if interpreted for a contemporary feature film, although it can be modernized and adjusted to today's taste and technological development. The changes made are commonly very subtle and keep the body proportions very much the same but stay in line with the overall look of the initial design to keep the recognition intact. Little changes in the shapes or small adjustments in the face often go a long way to translate a character from either one medium to another, or bringing the character up to date. All the other characters that are designed from scratch and not based on previous designs have to speak a design language that is contemporary and convinces the viewers they are watching something new and up to date.

Characters are designed for a purpose and, as mentioned earlier, that purpose is entertainment and the consumption by an audience that has a range of 0–120 years. However, a three-year-old toddler would not be able to appreciate character design for a target audience of 16 years and older, because the toddler does not intellectually grasp the complexity of that type of character. However, a 16-year-old is able to appreciate (not necessarily be entertained by) a character for a toddler. Not every character is for every age group and not every age group is entertained by just any character. The designer needs to always keep the target audience in mind while designing and also understand what age range is able to intellectually grasp the content of the story and character.

Finding the character

The process of finding that one specific character is a long and work-intensive one. For a feature or TV production, we don't just have to design a character that we enjoy and like ourselves, but a character that the target audience as a whole is convinced by and thus satisfied with. We cannot merely trust our own judgment but have to discuss the designs with the production team in order to find that one character that speaks to everyone. This of course is impossible because we all have different tastes and want to see different aspects of the character's personality to be dominant in the design, but we can at least try to steer toward everyone's taste. The outcome is a version of what the character can be, but it is never the only possible version. Once you realize there are other options and various interpretations of the character described in the script, you and the design team can discuss to what degree the personality traits should be visible in the design. You have many options in your visuals to describe the character and their likes, dislikes, behavior, and personality traits. Those options include shapes, textures, colors, expressions, poses, and attire. All these options help to define what kind of character the audience is dealing with. Some of this information is probably processed more on a subconscious level or not recognized at all by the viewer, but it helps the designer to come up with ideas and to develop an intellectual framework for the character. And even if the audience doesn't see the difference, they might feel it!

The job of a character designer

Everyone can call themselves a character designer as the title is not legally protected. Also, the success of being able to actually sell ones characters for productions does not make one a "true" character designer as the salability of a piece of art does by no means increase its artistic value. However, character design is a product as well as art and those two don't always walk on the same path. The question can be asked if the character of Jessica Rabbit from the feature *Who Framed Roger Rabbit* (1988) is art or a mere product. What is the definition of "art"—to push existing art forward and explore a new field, new visuals, and new "types" that have not yet been created or interpreted before? Popular characters seldom would cover the artistic side fully, but usually please the audience with appeal and personality. Artistic characters are usually more edgy and odd, exploring the graphic field rather than pleasing the audience, like the characters from Estonian animator Priit Pärn. That of course is not a judgment, as both directions have a purpose and are both equally important. In a feature film they can go hand-in-hand, like, for example, in Tim Burton's stop-motion film *The Nightmare Before Christmas*

Terms

Production bible, design bible, style guide:
There are many terms for this book that contains the rules for the style. It depends on the animation company how elaborate that guide would be.

Storyboard:
A storyboard is usually a wooden board, sometimes covered in cork, approximately 2 × 1 m in size, on which drawings are pinned in continuity to visually tell the story of the script. A storyboard drawing already takes composition, shot sizes, and staging into account; it relates the script with film language. The storyboards are usually rough drawings that don't give too many details, as their job is to quickly explain a facial expression of a character, or simple setup. Details are usually omitted.

Layout:
Layout is the refined composition of each scene in the movie. The layout department has the task to compose each scene in a way that helps the audience to easily read each image and know what is important in a frame.

Animatic:
The animatic is the drawn storyboard in a filmed version. Seeing the storyboard on actual boards is less effective than animatics to get a feel for the final movie and its timing. Animatics contain all the assisting compounds that make the actual movie: sound, music, dialogues, timing, camera-pans, editing, etc. It is recommended to produce an animatic as soon as possible as it is the only way to really judge if the storyboard works or not.

(1993) where the artwork of the character design is utterly unique and pushed the aesthetics of stop-motion feature animation to a new level in the beginning of the 1990s.

There are two different possibilities for the job of a character designer:

- The designer that is hired for his specific character style
- The designer that is hired for his ability to change styles and adjust to the needs of the project

What kind of designer one is will develop throughout one's career and some artists can change styles immediately while others cannot. However, what both artists need to be able to do is draw any kind of character—animals, humans, robots, or aliens, and be comfortable in every field. When on an assignment the designer needs to be able to quickly deliver the job without much delay and it needs to be artistically solid. That the client not always has the best taste is obvious and the designer has to accept what the client wants, whether it is logical or not. What is difficult for the artist is to figure out what the client *actually* wants in the first place and most clients are not able to clearly express that. The artist needs to be trained in figuring out what the project needs, but also what the client expects, which is more or less impossible if the client doesn't have any clear direction in their mind of how the project should look to begin with.

Often enough the character development is about finding the character and knowing what is the right or wrong direction when one sees it.

The character designer either works on a freelance basis and gets hired for producing artwork for inspirational purposes for a feature, TV production, a game or commercial, or works full-time for a company continuously delivering and designing characters. Whatever personal preference or the path destiny has intended, the work is usually very similar. The character is introduced to the artists, the needs of the production explained by a brief through the director, art director, or client, then the character is discussed in relation to the story. Once the artist has an idea of the direction of the project and has some knowledge of the character's personality, rough sketches are produced. Those are presented and discussed, and then based on the feedback either refined or a completely new direction is explored. Character design is mostly about exploration, not about "just" drawing a character. To find the final character takes usually dozens of possible characters to be tossed into the trash can. Eliminating the ones that don't fit brings one closer to the ones that do.

The financial side of the freelance character designer

Character design is not just the job that is done in that very moment of drawing the character, but the years and years of training that have led to the moment of being able to actually draw and design a character. Unfortunately talent comes in and also the ability to be creative and unique (or to be inspired by existing designs and claiming them as your own, which can be severely frowned upon).

How much would be charged for a character? Just because someone has been designing characters for 25 years does not mean that the result is any good, and neither does someone right out of school is not able to produce excellent work. In the end, it is the client that decides if they like the results and approve of them.

The rather delicate question is always the payment and how much a freelance designer can charge for the work provided. There are many aspects to how the pricing is determined and they are all very open and somehow not helping the new designer very much in setting a price, as there is no pay scale or list one can easily fall back on.

The idea to do work for free is still out there, and even experienced designers get asked to do work for free "because it will provide exposure." This is theoretically correct, but to think that every project one works on will actually be produced, end up in the theaters and then also be successful and get an award for best character design ever is foolish. Only a tiny percentage of the designs one does will be seen by the public. Therefore, the job of the character designer needs to be seen as an actual job, not a

hobby and not something that should be paid less because it is "fun" to do it. If charging too much the client declines, if charging not enough the work comes across as cheap and in the end will hurt future projects. But what is the middle ground? A private client that wants a character designed for a project or as a present for their friend obviously can't pay the amount of money a feature film company is able and willing to pay. Though the work might be the same or similar, the pay is very different. When determining the price charged, step back and ask yourself the following questions:

- What is the character for?
- Will I freelance or be employed?
- Who owns the rights to the character?
- How long will it take to develop?
- How many changes are included in the price?
- What is the final piece—a presentation piece or a sketch?
- What projects do I have on my resumé that might justify a higher pay?
- Is it just a one-time-job?
- Is the job beneficial to my entire career?

What is the character for?

Is the character for a feature film, TV animation, a commercial, a product, web page, or company logo? The bigger the scale of the distribution, the more should be paid for the job. However, the money is split into parts: part one is the actual work on the character, the amount of time needed to design it; the second is the copyright fee paid to the artist. The wider the distribution of the project, the more has to be paid for the copyrights. The actual compensation for the work of the design is not always the bulk of the income; what can be the bigger chunk of the pay is the copyrights for the character that the company has to pay. Design companies that work for a client (an animation company, for instance, that produces short films for a TV channel) but hire a character designer have already charged the rights of the character to the client. That money belongs to the designer, if they know how to get it and how much to ask for. This is obviously not transparent, so it is up to the designer to charge for the copyrights as the company probably will not offer a decent amount for the rights immediately (and that will depend on the company you are working for).

A character that is widely distributed and used as a national logo for a big toothpaste company, for instance, can go into tens of thousands of dollars. Therefore, the rights situation needs to be discussed in advance; in the case of bigger projects, there should always be an agency or lawyer involved to give the designer the rights and the compensation they deserve!

Will I freelance or be employed?

Big feature companies usually do not have the designer working freelance to design the final character/s but to provide inspirational work, then the final characters are designed by the character team within the company. The designer is paving the way with their style.

The more extensive the job is, the more likely it is for the designer to be hired on a term contract basis and then all the designs created during that period in the company will belong with rights and all to the company. The terms of the contract obviously depend on the scope of the project and the experience of the designer (all contractual work should be going through art agencies the artist belongs to assure the best deal for the artist).

If the job is on a freelance basis then the designer needs to look into the financial possibilities of the client. Small companies will obviously not be able to pay thousands of dollars for one character, even though the character might be distributed widely. One needs to calculate how much time would be spent on the designs and how much one needs to cover the monthly expenses and then decide what would be a fair price to agree on. Again: most designs are inspirational pieces and not the final designs. But the inspirational piece is still the one that contains the creative aspects of the character and thus needs to be compensated fairly. How much should be paid for the rights is again best decided with the help of an agency, and a lawyer if in doubt. It is however rather difficult which character out of the line-up designed is the one that will be used in the final project. Therefore, the designer is not being paid for "the one" but for the lot.

If the character is for a private client, then charging more than $500–$600 is pushing it, if it is for private use. But if the character might be used later on for wider distribution and possible television rights and such, then a contract needs to contain a clause that comes into place once the character's distribution situation changes.

Who owns the rights to the character?

Usually the character's rights belong to the artist. Just because someone buys a character does not mean they can do with it whatever they please. If the client wants to use the character for other than, for example, a one-time print advertisement, the rights need to be acquired from the artist. Once the copyrights are sold, the artist has no rights to the character anymore. However, that does not mean that a company can buy one character that has a certain unique style and then just design many other characters in that very style and not compensate the artist, as they still use his unique style. However, this is a rather tricky claim as style is often difficult to prove. A company that buys the rights has various options: either a short-term purchase (for one print advertisement for example) or for long-term use. The contract needs to state the length of the agreement and the scope of use.

The rights are usually divided into various sections of print, online use, TV, film, games, products, and general merchandise. Every section is again divided into subsections that then define, for example, of what kind of print, how many publications, national or international, the time frame of usage etc. It can become rather complicated and an agency or lawyer can help wading through the mess. Artists like to create, but we aren't always the most thorough business people.

How long will it take to develop?

How much is charged is obviously related to how long it will take to design the character. The first stage is usually the sketch stage where a couple or dozen (depending on the contract or personal speed and preference) of sketches are produced and then a direction for project or character is determined with the client. The chosen characters get either refined or changed depending on the comments. Some clients are immediately happy with the results whereas others are never pleased, and one change follows the next and it's a never-ending battle. For this to not spiral out of control the contract should contain a clause that clearly states how many adjusting stages are included in the work. Every additional change then needs to be added to the compensation. If this clause is not included in the contract the project can easily reach the point where the artist is turned into a pencil with no aesthetic decision-making power and is just there to change to the client's will (the client always has the last word, so our decisions are limited).

How many changes are included in the price?

Make sure that in the contract it is clearly defined how many changes in every stage of the production are acceptable and at what point the client would have to pay extra for further changes. Without this extra information in the contract the changes can easily get out of hand and the illustrator/artist is not compensated for the extra work. If for instance the final piece is already being worked on but the client then decides that changes need to be made in the design or the composition (changes that should have been mentioned long before the start of the final piece), there has to be a clarifying point within the contract that either prohibits significant changes and/or allows additional compensation.

What is the final piece—a presentation piece or a sketch?

It is one thing to develop a character through sketches, yet a very different one to create a final presentation piece that is painted with complex light and shadows, or even where a final style is to be developed. It needs to be clearly defined in the contract what the final piece consists of and what it is supposed to look like. Do mention which program or technique you are going to use to create the final design; also consider how some programs or techniques might take longer for the artwork to be produced, and add that to the compensation.

What projects do I have on my resumé that might justify a higher pay?

The longer you work in the industry and the more high-profile names you have on your resumé, the more you can charge for your designs. However, this can also backfire as you do not want to come across as arrogant with your work. Being humble and treating every client with the same respect goes a long way. Mentioning your past projects isn't always the right thing to do. The clients usually have a pretty good idea what you have done and pick you for your abilities or style, rather than the companies you have worked for.

Is it just a one-time-job?

A one-time job is higher paid than a job that is continuously providing you with projects. The longer the company supplies you with monthly work, the more stable a job can be. A good relationship with a company can be very beneficial and lowering the price can be a good start. Nevertheless, the company came to you for a reason because they liked what you have done in the past, so do not lower your price too much.

Is the job beneficial to my entire career?

Not every job is a great opportunity and a next career step. With some jobs you set yourself a path that is not always beneficial. Would you want to do campaigns for every product? If the campaign for the product becomes famous for whatever reason, do you want your name and style to be related? The work that you release into the public is the work that you will be remembered by. Make sure you morally and intellectually approve of the project.

Agency

Try to get an agent that represents your work and deals with contracts and legal issues, rights, compensation, and exposure. Having an agent is a situation that often makes things much easier as you can focus on what is important—your artwork, instead of dealing with contracts and the small print in legal papers. Find a trustworthy agency that fits your needs and your style, and do not just go with the bigger names. You want work to come from someone that appreciates what you are doing and represents it successfully. If the relationship with an agency is not rewarding, do not hesitate to find a new one that might be supplying you with jobs that you enjoy and that you are proud of. Be aware that some agencies have a clause in the contract that prohibits the artist from having other agencies represent their work, which means that you can only be with that one agency.

Exposure

What the character designer needs to keep in mind is that designing characters is their job, which means that the design has a value, not necessarily always a monetary value, but a value nevertheless. This value does usually not pay through social media pages and through "likes" of friends and people online. It is a job that needs to be taken seriously and needs to be treated professionally. Online exposure is obviously a hugely important mode of presenting your work, so having a well-designed web page with your best work is a given.

Never post work that has not been officially released by the client, unless you have clearly stated permission to do so. The tricky thing for working for feature or TV productions is the time it takes for the product to be released to the public. The artists are not allowed to post any of their work online until the film is released. As character design is done right at the beginning of the project, it can take sometimes years for the designs to be legally shown by the artist. Nondisclosure agreements prohibit the artist from showing the development work to the public. If this is ignored and the work becomes public, severe legal action will follow. Make absolutely sure that this is not going to happen! It not only can ruin one's reputation but also one's entire career.

The artistic side of character design

The client usually does not want the character designer to be overly artistic. They say they do, because they always want the project to be "unique" and not follow the work that has been done by other companies previously, but they often seek out the characters that are the least artistic and the least courageous. They generally pick the ones that are the most familiar and the most common because that's what they are usually comfortable with. The really unique and weird characters are not the ones that the general public is drawn toward and definitely not the ones that the art directors want to present to their clients (don't ask me why, I never understood it). Therefore, when presenting the newly designed characters, always consider if it is actually worth presenting all of them in the first place. Edit the sketches and take out the ones that aren't what you want the project to be (within reason of course). Is the designer comfortable with every sketch? Would they be happy if any of the characters presented is chosen or would it be better if some of the plainer characters are taken out, in order for the good ones to have the chance of being picked?

Successful life-long creativity

Character design is not just a temporary job, but a job that one wants to perform for a couple of decades. This reaches across fashionable styles that are en vogue at the moment. Design has to be understood in its core, which means the designer needs to know what actually makes a style and is able to lead their own personal style into the direction of what the job requires without sacrificing artistic expression. Never copy someone else's work for the job because the client wants you to; only use it as inspiration! Someone who can do great anime designs and nothing else isn't going to be a great asset in a company that might not do anime designs in 2 years' time, because the hype is over and a new direction is needed. Therefore, sticking with only one style or genre is not always the best way to go when it comes to a life-long creative job. If your specialty is drawing animals, once in a while also draw humans to expand your options on the job market. If you have a strong personal style however, stick with it and explore its options. Always try to expand your oeuvre and see what else you can do with it. Do not rest on laurels and fall into the trap of repeating yourself over and over, but explore new grounds and be *creative*. As the late singer David Bowie said about creativity and authenticity:

> Never work for other people in what you do; always remember that the reason that you initially started working in this is that there is something inside yourself that you felt that if you could manifest it in some way you would understand more about yourself and how you coexist with the rest of the society. I think it's terribly dangerous for an artist to fulfill other people's expectations. I think they generally produce their worst work when they do that. The other thing I would say is if you feel safe in the area that you are working in, you are not working in the right area. Always go a little further into the water than you feel you are capable of being in; go a little bit out of your depth and when you don't feel that your feet are quite touching the bottom then you are just about in the right place to do something exciting.

Interview with David Bowie in Michael Apted's documentary Inspirations, 1997

Lucky are those that achieve it!

Allow yourself to make mistakes

Creativity is not about redoing what you already know or can do, have seen before, or enjoy. Being creative is about exploring what has not yet been done and pushing yourself to another level, walking in a creative field that is unknown. It is like sailing in uncharted waters and finding islands here and there, not knowing what is living on them, but you have to step onto them to learn the mysteries that lurk in the woods. You have to continuously explore and challenge yourself with something new, otherwise you'll easily turn into a technician that isn't creative, but only technical. The difficulty in animation is that there is just so much to learn, so much to study, and it is impossible to know it all in a couple of years. It is not just learning how to draw, but how to use those drawings with purpose and meaning, additionally learning film language and composition, learning the subtleties of the trade and then on top of it being unique and having your own artistic voice. All of it is nearly impossible when one looks into the complexity of the subject of *animation*. Especially the creative part is a never-ending task that has no goal really. And because it does not have a goal, just a path that leads only to the next project, "exploration" needs to be the path's companion. When exploring new grounds no one knows what the outcome is, no one knows if the island one explores will be the one that is deadly or not. But you need to explore it anyway because it's all there is in art; and because you don't know what is there, you can fail. Your exploration can be miserably bad and people won't have a clue what you are trying to do with your art. You yourself sometimes have no clue, because you have not done it yet or not fully created what you wanted to. Only when it is done and finished you know if you were successful with what you wanted to create. It is about you yourself being content with your exploration, not anyone else. If you just redo what others have done before, that is just a simple technical practice of some sort. It teaches techniques, teaches form and shape language, and you can practice the trade. However, it is utterly uncreative as it is not your imagination, not your creativity, and not your background, historically or socially—it is someone else's. Most of us have to work in someone else's style in order to start the process, trying to explore who we are as artists. But at some point this is becoming old and you have to find your own voice. Allowing yourself to make mistakes and to even fail is what makes the creative field such an adventure, because you don't know the outcome.

CHAPTER 2

Visual Development Process

Visual development artwork is always created for a purpose. Either as the design for a feature film, a game, or a collection of visualized ideas to promote a project, its purpose is to tell a visual story that is easily understood, in the best case, with a design that is new and fresh. This type of artwork is not for its own sake; it is done for a project and is always strongly connected to the movie script, game concept, or project content. Therefore, all visual development artwork has to visualize those ideas and concepts and develop a world that only fits that specific content. If successful, it convinces the audience of the possible existence of the imaginary world created with its characters and environments. The visualization of any kind of project, interactive installation, game proposal, etc., needs to present its images in a contemporary fashion and exciting, new visuals to spur the imagination of the audience, and not repeat existing visuals the audience, has already seen before. Each project must develop its own unique design and look! The audience wants to be guided into a new world, a world they have not experienced. They want to be entertained, aside from a new story, with a new visual experience. The main purpose of development art would require it to be a fresh and new design with credibility that is strongly based on a concept and/or script and is, in the end, technically convertible.

The visual development process goes through several stages where the basic framework is more or less fixed. You first approach the topic by researching its possibilities, then develop the concept that works along the script, and finally design the characters and the environments. It is recommended that you follow this workflow, because it does help you to organize your work for the given project. Doing it step by step prevents you from getting lost in details before you have decided on the concept of the project. It is easy to lose the overview by skipping steps and working on the final artwork without finishing the concept stage or the foundation of the work. Due to the complexity and amount of work that needs to be done, you have to have a plan and follow it—a plan that assists you to not pay too much attention to the details in the beginning, but approach the topic from the overview and then work your way toward the details. It's like painting a tree: you don't start with painting each leaf and in the end think about the composition. You start with the basic shape of the tree and then develop, through thumbnail sketches, the composition, and color composition of your final piece; next you decide on texture and details, and only after all the planning is done and the whole concept works you start to paint the final piece based on your sketches and drawings

(and even with the final piece you have to again have a plan of how to paint it and where to start, etc.).

As mentioned, there are three steps in the visual development process that will all be discussed in this book:

1. Research and inspirational development
2. Concept and story
3. Design and final artwork

Overview of the production for an animated feature film (focus on CG)

The following is an "ideal" production; it does not claim to be **the** production of every feature in every company. Every animation studio has their own slightly different production pipeline and creative decisions, as also financial decisions, are made along the way that can alter the project's workflow.

To produce an animated feature film requires an amount of planning that is complex to say the least. The sheer amount of work a feature film requires has to be produced in a highly defined pipeline in order to have an efficient production flow. A big team needs to be kept busy with assignments and the workflow has to provide a constant supply of shots or artwork to be continuously refined by the different departments. Once this workflow stops, money is spent on the wages of artists without them finishing shots, which obviously would increase the cost of the movie. A well-thought-out production plan is crucial in this matter. This is where the line producer comes in and meticulously plans the work of each artist on the production, with the amount of time each will spend on every shot or piece of work. Hundreds of artists have to be included into the pipeline with their expected work productivity to keep the production efficient and afloat. To structure the production, the movie is roughly subdivided into three phases: Preproduction, production, and postproduction. The preproduction phase is the planning phase of the project, in which the initial story idea and the possible style direction is developed with script, storyboard, and initial designs. The production phase is the actual making of the movie (character modeling, scene building, and character animation). The postproduction phase is the final refinement— sound, music, and last changes, and once it is all done, the distribution of the film.

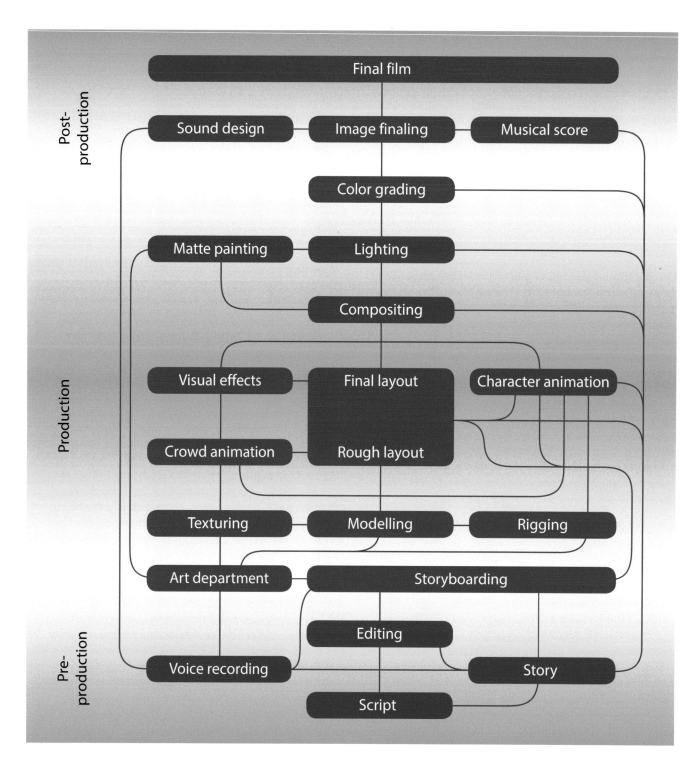

The preproduction starts with a rough treatment or a story pitch (see illustration above). This can consist of a short story or quick presentation to get the idea of the movie across, what the movie could be, not what the movie will be. Everything is still very open and just suggests a possible direction. There are, of course, movies that are based on existing stories or books. Therefore they already have a framework for the film, either in design direction or story direction. Examples includes *How the Grinch stole Christmas* (1966) and *Legend of the Guardians: The Owls of Ga'Hoole* (2010). Nevertheless, it still has to be refined and made fit for a feature film, which takes years in the making. It is by no means easier to have an existing story or design available in the form of a book as the question is how close does the film need to be to the book or can it be "artistically" altered?

If this rough treatment convinces on some level, the next step would be to get a writer/writers to develop story ideas and possible storylines, characters, locations, etc., and to explore the terrain of the topic.

The researcher or research department of the company starts to collect images and educational material for the various departments to be informed about the background of the story, and its historical or fantastical context. This research has to be done properly and meticulously to get all the facts right before the production starts. Any mistakes in the design or script, any flaws that derive from crude research, or faulty content deriving from a lack of expertise on the topic, can be disastrous and cause expensive changes.

Around that time the visual development department starts to explore styles, different character designs, and environments based on the script and story ideas. Where the writers explore the theme of the movie on a literal basis, the visual development artists on the contrary search for a visual representation of the movie's story and theme, and explore its visual effectiveness and range. The team is collecting visual styles, which might give a sense of what the movie's range is in terms of its artistic options. Once the style of the characters and the environments is approved (after usually a long process), they are developed further and refined. At one point of the design process when a very clear style has been approved, the production bible or style guide is written. This style guide contains, aside from the characters and all the information needed to define them (turnarounds, facial expressions, and shape language), the final design decisions, shape, and color language, compositional direction, usage of surfaces, patterns, textures, and materials. In short, the overall look of the movie with precise instructions of how to achieve that look in all its details.

Once the script is finished (hypothetically finished; most often the script is being worked on throughout the production) and it has been determined how many characters are necessary and how many locations are to be designed, the final voices and sounds are recorded (voices can also be recorded before to inspire the artists working on the project and/or seek funding if famous actors are involved). This helps everyone on the production to get a feel for the characters and "hear" who those characters are. The interpretation of the character by the actor and the character's relationships with each other are a crucial step in getting to know those characters.

The storyboard department starts early on in the production, roughly at the same time as the visual development team starts exploring. The storyboard artists take parts of the script, which is still in development, and turn them into working storyboards to give an impression of the film's direction in a rough form. That helps the writers and the directors to sense what works in the script and what does not. Though the script, a literary medium, already gives an impression of the movie, it is still the movie in a written form, which leaves lots of room for visual interpretation.

Film on the other hand is a visual medium, which mostly deals with images that drive the story. So turning the script into a storyboard at an early stage is highly beneficial and necessary for everyone working on the project to get a sense for the actual film. Storyboarding goes through many stages and lasts significantly into the production as it can be constantly changed and adjusted. Rewritten parts of the story also need to be boarded again. The storyboards are either drawn on paper or produced digitally and pinned on boards; they do not yet contain the aspect of timing, which is so very crucial for film making. The boards, therefore, are compiled into a film with sound and voices to judge the cinematic qualities. This storyboard reel (story reel) or animatic is slowly turning into the production reel as the boards are replaced by the rough layout. This gets replaced by the final layout, and then the finished character animated shots one by one. In the end, the result is the final movie as all the changes and improvements of the film will be cut into the production reel.

But back to the point where the storyboard is being made, the production of the film is finally greenlit if the company sees the project having value and being progressed enough to allow it into the next stage—production. Now the preproduction goes into the production phase, because at this point there is a story, a design direction, voices are recorded, and an overall solid concept is developed, which means that the foundation of the project is set. The entire creative staff of the movie is increased for the production, to fill in the demand for animators, riggers, background painters, clean-up artists, lighters, set builders, puppet builders, and anyone else needed in an animation production depending on the animation technique. At this stage, it is very difficult to make major changes in the design or script, because it would stop the workflow from one department to the next. Every delay in one department causes delays in every other department that follows in the process and therefore creates increasing costs. It is sometimes necessary to stop production or slow it down to improve certain artistic or technical aspects in the movie, but that is understandably avoided if possible to keep costs down.

Along with the main characters' design the backgrounds are also invented and planned, and once approved by the directors, producers, and art directors, get handed over to the modeling department which models the characters and sets, which are then rigged and textured. At this point, the layout process starts, which is the compositional and technical refinement of the shots the storyboards suggested. Where the storyboard is very rough and rarely contains details, the layout department is responsible not only for putting all those details in to create a well-arranged composition, but also furnish the backgrounds with objects and "stuff." Additionally, layout deals with the technical setup of each shot (type of lens, camera position, length of the shot, character position, quality control, and accuracy of the shot). The layout department has to deliver shots on a daily basis to the character animation department.

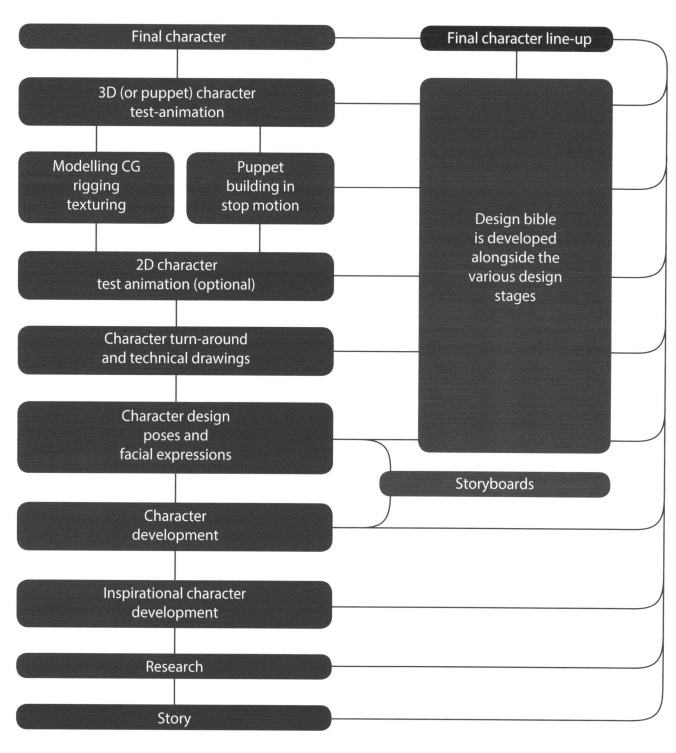

The directors are judging in daily meetings (dailies) all of the creative output of each department and give comments and suggestions on how to improve the models, layout, character animation, etc. Shots are improved over and over again until they are on par with the rest of the film so there is a consistent quality. The animated shots are then sent to the special effects department to add fire, smoke, water animation, simulations, or other special effects, and the crowd department adds needed background characters. Once all the moving characters and effects are included the shots go to the texturing department, then the lighting department, and then back to editing to put the finished shots into the production reel.

The postproduction begins when the fine tuning of the images is worked on; the colors are corrected, some reediting might be necessary, some of the animation might have to be adjusted or redone, the sounds are added, there is image-correction of rendering mistakes, the title and final credits are added, and the sound and music are finalized and synced. Title sequences for each language have to be produced and the film is then finally, after about 2–3 years, ready for distribution.

The production of a 2D hand-drawn production or stop-motion production works in a similar fashion in terms of the production flow. However, certain departments are replaced or added due to the different needs of every technique.

Character design (see illustration on the left)

Character design is part of visual development and usually at the beginning of the entire design process. The characters start in the story department with the definition of the characters, their personalities, and impact they have on the story. As the story is still changing at that point the characters in the script are also evolving and any design direction is still open. The descriptions of the main characters go into the design/art department first and inspirational character development suggests how those characters could look and what style direction they could be covering. This is done not only by in-house artists but also by freelance artists to create, in their personal style, inspirational work or inspirational character development. Alongside this process, the visual research is being covered to educate and inform the artists of what topic they are dealing with and what needs to be known about the material and theme covered. The inspirational artwork not only has to cover the main characters, but often covers a wide range of characters to get a sense of the visual options in general. In the end, a full range of characters is to be designed. Nothing at this point is final and definite; everything is still open and continuously discussed. Temporarily approved designs might go back into the story department for idea development and for the story artists to get inspired by the character suggestions. The inspirational designs help the directors and art directors to slowly approach a style that the film seems to ask for. At some point, the inspirational phase goes into the character development stage where the character designers officially start with the design of the main characters. This process can last from a couple of months to a year or more, depending on how long it takes until the main characters are "discovered." In weekly or monthly meetings, the newly designed character suggestions are presented to the directors and producers and further steps are decided on. Once a character is approved, it is drawn in various poses and expressions to explore its possibilities as the main character and its ability to carry the feature film through 90 minutes. The finished designs are again presented to the team. Once approved the technical side of the design starts, which is defining the dimensionality and final look of the character in drawings. To get a feeling of the dimensionality, maquettes are sculpted (or already sculpted in digital form) and the translation from the 2D drawing to the 3D character starts. The bigger animation companies have 2D traditional

animators that take the main characters and create hand-drawn test animation to see how the character would move and act, how far it can be exaggerated, squashed, and stretched, how the acting in relationship with the character's recorded voice is expressing the personality. The character then is sent to the modeling department to translate it into a 3D, CG sculpture. In this stage, there is a strong relationship between the character designer and the modeler, as the designer usually has to explain how the drawings of the character should be interpreted and what aspects in the design are important and need attention (this is also true for the maquettes being sculpted). Alongside this process, the character's facial expressions are being designed and it is decided how extreme the character animation is going to be in terms of timing, exaggeration, and squash and stretch. Those expressions and mouth shapes are also going into the modeling and rigging department to be discussed on their feasibility and practicality. More test animation is done to see how the character is actually animated and what changes need to be done to perfect its look from an aesthetic and also a technical side. After that, the character is finished and can be released into the pipeline for character animation, where the character animators start practicing with the character and learning its controls and artistic possibilities.

This entire process is obviously different in every company and also depends on the kind of project that is being developed. Every project is different and requires a slightly different approach.

The different jobs in animation production

Animation director

The animation director is the head of the production from a creative perspective and is usually involved from the beginning of the project, shaping it with creative vision. There are two different types of directors in animation: the auteur or director that not only makes creative decisions but also affects the film's stylistic direction, with a style they already bring into the project. This kind of director is more often dominant in short subjects rather than feature films; however, Hayao Miyazaki, Satoshi Kon, Alain Gagnol, Jiří Trnka, or Jan Švankmajer, for instance, all come with a specific style in their work. The second type is the director that also makes creative decisions, but follows the style of the studio so the work is usually less personal and more geared toward mass consumption. One needs to always keep in mind that very few feature animation directors have the freedom to really shape the project and follow only their very own vision. Everyone in film has someone they have to work for and report to, so creative decisions

Book on producing animation:

Winder C, Dowlatabadi Z. (2011). *Producing Animation*. Waltham, MA: Focal Press.

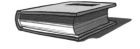

are usually made not by a single person, but the group. Most projects have a set direction or formula from the beginning that the film has to follow (kid's movie, family entertainment, specific target audience, etc.). Reinventing the wheel is commonly not the goal for feature animation; however, there are exceptions like Alê Abreu's *Boy and the World* (2013) or Michaël Dudok de Wit's *The Red Turtle* (2016).

Most of the time, big productions in feature film or TV animation have not just one director but two, to cope with the amount of work that has to be dealt with, each according to their strengths, deal with a specific area of the production or they both share the workload. If the production requires even more people to take leading positions there can be a supervising director that then distributes responsibilities to a group of sequence directors (which often was the case in the older Disney features).

As mentioned before, the director is usually involved in the project from the beginning. This can include overseeing and shaping the project already in the preproduction stage (writing, storyboarding, and visual development) and accompany it until the end of the production—and even further, during the promoting of the film. Although the director has creative power, this by no means assures that every creative decision is implemented. Because of the responsibility of overseeing a project that is spending a multimillion dollar budget, there are many more people involved in final decisions. Sometimes the directors are replaced because their vision does not match the vision of the studio, so the studio pulls the plug and hires a new director that more closely follows what the studio expects. People who also shape the production are the head of the studio, producers, art directors, directors of cinematography, editors, analysts, and various departments that have demands that shape the project in terms of its feasibility, finances, or sometimes even creatively. At the end of the production, test screenings with questionnaires for the viewer's opinions can also have an impact on the film's outcome. By no means is the director the sole decision-maker in the production.

The day-to-day job of the animation director is to see the vision of the project through to all departments and to make sure everyone on the team knows where the film is going, what is to be expected, and where issues need to be solved creatively and economically. The animation director communicates with the head of writing, director of photography, art director, head of editing, animation director, head of sound, composer, and producers. However, the core team from the beginning is usually the director with the art director and producer. Throughout the production, the heads of various departments will join and leave the process.

For example, the director meets with the art director and discusses the possible visual style of the project, who himself then communicates this to the visual development team. Their produced artwork is then discussed again with the director and producer who decide on the next steps. The character animation

progress is also discussed in meetings (or "dailies") with the animators present and critiqued in miniscule detail to achieve the highest possible consistency and quality on screen. In fact, every department's output is continuously reviewed in meetings with the director to make sure the project has the highest quality and is creatively on track.

There is yet another job the animation director is often responsible for: promotion of the project. This means acting as spokesperson for the production and raising awareness for TV, commercials, investors, presentations of any kind, or just general in-house presentations to the staff. After the production is finished, there may be a requirement to give interviews for DVD releases, TV infomercials, or informative presentations.

Overall one can say that the animation director is the communicator between the various departments from the beginning until the end of the production. The artistic and creative input depends on the common practice of the studio or the animation director's talent, knowledge, experience, and ability.

Animation producer

The job of the animation producer is multilayered and touches upon many fields in the production. Where the director is the creative voice of the production, the producer is responsible for the financial aspects and the smooth running of the production in terms of staff, schedules, and budget. The producer is also responsible for the production following its initial path and not running into creative or financial issues.

The producer oversees the entire production so has the responsibility for outsourcing material to other studios or freelance artists, thus guaranteeing the project's timely completion.

There are many titles for producers depending on their rank and job: the producer is usually the highest rank (but does not necessarily have to be), the executive producer is responsible for finances, development, or production, then there may be the coproducer (assists the producer but has less control over the entire production), the associate producer (also has a key role in the production but has less control than the coproducer), and the coexecutive producer (again less control than the executive producer). Confused? Relax, so am I!

All these titles however depend on the demands of the production. What this role contains varies greatly and what title is being used in the credits not only depends on the actual input into the movie, but also on rights, seniority position, experience, etc. A successful feature film, for example, that has a follow-up TV show being produced might have the executive producer of the original feature also as the executive producer on the TV show. The actual job might not be extensive, but the role for the feature can be extended toward the TV show (but does not have to be).

The line producer is another type of producer who is responsible for the precise scheduling and work distribution, the daily handling of the bureaucratic side of production. This includes, for instance, being in charge of calculating the amount of time each artist is supposed to take for a given task. Then, how much time it should take to finish the entire project can be planned alongside the budget, although this is on a smaller scale and involves smaller units of the project compared to the producer.

Art director

"Art director" or "production designer" are two terms that can be interchangeable, and sometimes one is superior to the other. Because of the often confusing use of the terms, I will use the term art director.

The art director is responsible for the translation of the director's vision (or the studio's vision) into visuals, and deals with everything that is design related. This is not just characters and background, but also input into the overall creative interpretation of the script into a film. Because a film is a complex system of interlocking artistic fields, every aspect needs to follow the overall concept to create a piece of art that is consistent in its artistic language. The art director makes sure this language is interpreted correctly, following the style guide, in every visual on screen. Character design and background design need to be congruent in their vision, but the character animation, the texture, lighting, editing, or sound has to strengthen that stylistic and creative direction, not weaken it. The art director takes the advice and critiques from the director and communicates it to the visual development staff, being responsible to make sure this vision is kept throughout the entire production on every visual level. How far these responsibilities expand depends on the production and the studio.

CHAPTER 3

Storytelling and Drama

One central character struggling with a strong need which is being thwarted but who manages, one way or another, to resolve that need by the end of the play, leaving him or her a changed person.

(McLaughlin 1997, p.20)

Creating a character

Developing a character is a very tedious and complex process that one can easily get lost in. There is never a point when the entire character is completely developed as every new task or challenge the character is exposed to require a new decision of how the character would react. Just because a character had the same situation before doesn't mean they are going to react in the same way again, as since then they have had other experiences that might have affected them in such a deep way that they now choose to react differently. The development of the character is always based on past experiences and also general personality, whether extroverted or introverted, honest or corrupt, etc. Every new situation the character is exposed to requires a new evaluation of their actions. Every decision is based on past experiences and is therefore rooted in a reason. In animation, those experiences and the character's personality have to be translated into visuals that clearly show who that character is. Each little detail of the design has, exactly like the character's actions, be there for a reason. Without the reason there is no need for it to exist as it does not bring the story forward. And in film and animation: everything goes back to story!

There are extraordinary character studies that explore the characters not just in a feature film but also in longer formats that allow a character to grow and bring in complexities that the time restriction of features do not allow. The TV shows of Vince Gilligan's *Breaking Bad* (2008–2013) and *Better Call Saul* (2015–) show an exceptional development of a character whose complex decisions are explained in miniscule details during the length of the show. The character has reasons for their actions, and have decisions to make that are not simply explained by "the character is honest" but many aspects in their environment contribute toward dealing with the situation and affects the character's final decision. The audience witnesses the gradual change of the character's personality due to circumstances. Can this complexity be achieved in animation or games? Absolutely! We just need to steer away from the general belief that both media are for entertainment purposes only and not fit for

complex character development. A perfect example is the stop-motion animated feature of Charlie Kaufman and Duke Johnson, *Anomalisa* (2015), in which the protagonist's complex emotions are explained in great details and the film makers successfully shy away from animation clichés creating an outstanding animated feature that is a true character study. A film like this is very rare in animation where the general direction is light comedy. However, complexity is also found in comedic pieces. The relationship between Daffy Duck and Bugs Bunny, for instance, is following strict rules that cannot be broken if the goal is to keep the character's personalities intact. Personality is what makes a character interesting and what attracts the audience to follow the character's journey. Chuck Jones talks in his book *Amuck* about him having a cat at a young age that wore the rind of a

grapefruit on his head one day and it was a particularly odd cat, not at all like all the other cats. He goes on explaining:

> If you see a cat, you do not necessarily see all cats. He was not every cat, in other words, any more than any of us are really every man, or every woman. We do take that for granted, too. That laid the groundwork, so when I got to doing things like Daffy Duck, or Bugs Bunny, or Coyote—that's not all coyotes, that is, THE particular coyote. "Wile E. Coyote, Genius." That's what he calls himself, at any rate. He's different. He has an overwhelming ego, which isn't necessarily true of all coyotes.[1]

It is the unique quirks and interesting personal oddities that make the characters memorable. In stories, we do not really want to see someone that is just average. Everyone has something in their personality that is unique and that needs to be exaggerated to make it clearly visible. However, if the character is supposed to be bland and absolutely average, then they need to be the most average character that has ever lived, it needs to be pushed to the extreme, so that the audience believes this character is so extraordinarily average this actually makes him an original. His blandness has never seen a higher level in society's history—that is a unique character right there!

What makes a character interesting in fiction?

There is the important difference between empathy and sympathy. What we need to evoke in the audience is empathy because only empathy makes us feel the emotions of the character ourselves, whereas sympathy makes us feel for the character. We would pity the character and feel bad for them but not feel their emotions ourselves. Empathy evolves when knowing something about that character, their background, personality, and the reasoning behind the happenings in the story.

A simple story will clearly demonstrate what makes a character interesting in the first place, and how we as an audience start to be involved in the story.[2] In the following examples, pay attention to the point in the story where you are being emotionally involved with what is happening:

1. *A man goes down the street and picks up a cat.*
   The randomness of the situation does not affect us emotionally at all.
2. *A man goes down the street and picks up a small cat.*
   Now we are a little bit more involved as we know that the cat is small and probably not yet able to take care of itself. We feel compassion growing.

3. *An old lonely man goes down the street and picks up a small and helpless cat.*
   We have two characters that work well together as they fill a need in each other's life. The old lonely man needs company and the small cat needs help. What still makes this story boring is that there is not yet a problem that would make it difficult for either of the characters to reach their goal. This would create tension and involve the audience in hoping for a positive outcome, which might or might not happen.
4. *An old lonely man goes down a dark street and picks up a small cat that is threatened by a vicious dog.*
   Now we are fully involved in the story. The mood is further defined and there are two characters that are in need of something or someone to improve their lives. But there is also an obstacle in their way prohibiting them to attain their goal easily, which in this case is the vicious dog, the antagonist.

A character in any well-developed story has to have a goal. Just reaching that goal easily lacks interest and the story would be over before we know it. A story and character are only then interesting when there is an obstacle that prevents the character/s from reaching their goal with no effort. This obstacle is present in the physical world (external) as well as in the character's personality (internal). The internal obstacle usually directly affects the character's life and is often the reason that keeps them from reaching their goal; internal and external struggles are directly related and affect each other. The character needs to address this internal problem first and change, which then allows them to deal with the external one. A strong and stable personality has no internal struggle and is therefore not in need of change, and thus has little to offer in terms of traditional storytelling, which is about the character learning from experience through the told events to reach a higher level of personal growth. Change however is required for a story worthy of being told. The character that doesn't change their personality (beliefs and thoughts, feelings, and behavior) during the period of the story lacks interest. There needs to be some change or realization of why a specific behavior is not giving the intended results of the character reaching his goal. Change is often the reason for the story to be told in the first place. A character that just goes on a holiday trip and enjoying it is not very interesting, but it becomes interesting for the audience once the character experiences something in this new environment that affects them in such a deep way that they are forced to reevaluate themselves. This is the basis of storytelling: to explore the changes in personality or behavior needed for the character to be successful in their search. It is about a study of the character. This is much more interesting and engaging than solely presenting a character without the intellectual framework that is responsible for why their actions were happening in the first place.

---

[1] Interview with Chuck Jones, June 25, 1993. *The Academy of Achievement.* http://www.achievement.org/achiever/chuck-jones/#interview (retrieved January 23, 2016).

[2] I read this kind of example in Marks D. (2009). *Inside Story: The Power of the Transformational Arc.* London: A&C Black Publishers and thought it incredibly effective and convincing.

A character needs internal struggle, which leads to conflict, and conflict is the essence of storytelling. If, in the unlikely instance that the character is a perfect character with only positive traits, a stable and strong personality, conflict still can develop if the character struggles to make the right decision caused by external events. The external affects the internal and the struggle starts. For instance, the protagonist's brother killed someone for whatever reason. Would the protagonist help him to get rid of the body and become involved in the crime because he loves his brother? Or would he hand him over to the police and get him locked up forever? The conflict would be the struggle between wanting to help someone he loves but also following what is right according to his moral code. It is very difficult to answer for the character and decide what he would do. Does he love his brother more than he believes in the moral code that keeps society functioning, or would he accept his brother's mistake, throw all his beliefs overboard and also step into illegality, a step that is irreversible? If the decision is made about what the character decided to do, then what are the reasons for him making this choice? Why does he choose to save him? What does he gain? Is there some unresolved issue between the brothers that leads him to this extreme? Is the reason buried in their shared childhood? Has there been an incident in their childhood and the trauma was the cause of the brother's murder? Any decision is based on a complex network of experiences and upbringing. All of this is exactly the struggle of the two characters Jean Valjean and Javert in Victor Hugo's novel *Les Misérables* (1862). Both try to make the right decisions from their perspective, but both have very different reasons and experiences that affect their actions and reactions, which are diametrically opposed.

As everything in visuals is based on a story, we need to first understand the traditional story structure and how the characters develop with the story or the story out of the characters.

Story

Every story being told (excluding the experimental ones) follows the main character on a path or partial path of their life. The audience witnesses a moment in the life of the protagonist that had a significant impact on how they continue on life's path. We observe this life-changing situation through which they learn a lesson that will affect them in a profound way. The first aspect of a story is, therefore, a timeline—a partial path of the protagonist.

As we have seen in the example with the old man that picks up the small and helpless cat, the moment we introduce an obstacle into the story we start to significantly care about the characters and are emotionally engaged. Emotions are the key for engagement! The obstacle, therefore, is the second aspect of

story that goes alongside the goal of the character. The obstacle is prohibiting the character from easily reaching that goal or task that they set out to accomplish. In Disney's *Pinocchio* (1941), for instance, the main character's goal is to become a boy; however, he needs to learn to behave like a human before he reaches his desired transformation. He has to go through three stages of obstacles until he finally understands what it means to be human. The first obstacle is trusting and following Honest John and Kitty, the second is being lured into Stromboli's puppet theater, and the third obstacle is going to Pleasure Island. On the island, he learns the lesson that one has to have a conscience, and that his selfish ways are not leading him to understand what it means to be human, but they turn him into a foolish donkey. By leaving Pleasure Island with a tail and donkey ears he understands the point of having done wrong, but has not yet fully internalized it. Once he decides to rescue his father Geppetto from Monstro's belly and selflessly jeopardizes his own life to save Geppetto, he has fully transformed and grasped

what it means to be human: to be selfless. This is the point where he truly changes and is now worth being also transformed physically, because the emotional and mental change has already occurred. The obstacle, therefore, is not only a physical obstacle in the form of the antagonists (Honest John, Stromboli, and Pleasure Island), but also a psychological and emotional internal obstacle that he has to overcome. Pinocchio needs to learn to act like a human first. Without this reevaluation of his former behavior and the slow learning curve, the story does not have much to offer as the plot would be emotionally empty and we need emotions if the audience is to be involved. Also, if the story lacks reasons for the character's actions, which are supported or driven by his emotions and personality, the actions seem random and unrelated to that character and the journey. The outcome of those actions caused by the emotional struggle can go both ways: the character can either learn a lesson that then helps them to reach a higher level of self-awareness or they don't learn the required lesson and therefore become a tragic character who does not reach the goal. Pinocchio does reach his goal because he changes and does learn his lesson, even if it is a simple one. A film only then drags the audience into its story when the characters have comprehensible emotions that have plausible reasons.

Not every film has the main character learn an important lesson as clearly as in *Pinocchio*; there are exceptions to the rule and they still work.

Three-act structure

The typical film structure is based on a division of the story into three acts that clearly show the development of the happenings, and with it the emotional development of the characters. The division into three acts goes back to Greek stage plays, where the distinction between the acts served as a framework for the most basic building blocks of the story: beginning, middle, and end. Early cinema, developing out of theater practice, also followed the same structure of acts 1 to 3. The term "story" means the development of events and situations from one point in time to another. Without a development, there is no argument for the narrative to exist in the first place other than creating a mere mood. But even a mood piece like Disney's *The Old Mill* (1937) has an evolution in its storm-battered location. Even in this simple short there is a development in the location and the characters as they are exposed to the events (yet in a very simple way without the characters having defined personalities but only rudimentary ones!).

There is of course the artistic value of film as an art form that doesn't necessarily have to follow this typical three-act formula (e.g., Matthew Barney's Cremaster Film Series), but this kind of film is more a museum piece rather than fitting into the traditional entertainment formula with easily accessible narratives. But for an entertaining story structure, the following is a helpful guide.

First act

The first act is the exposition, the introduction of characters and locations, and the audience is slowly led into the world of the slowly sprawling story. The first act introduces not only the characters and locations, but also exposes the characters' (protagonist's and antagonist's) goals, what they are seeking, and why. Those goals can be materialistic, ideological, emotional, or intellectual goals. The character strives for this goal, but does not yet know how to achieve it. Likewise, the value system of this world and its inhabitants needs to be announced. We need to know what is important for the people living in this world in general, and how their beliefs and morals relate to the protagonist's own values. Only then does the audience know how the goal of the protagonist relates to the surroundings and if this goal is actually achievable. Pinocchio wants to be a real boy. He is a talking wooden puppet that was brought to life by the magic of a fairy. In Pinocchio's world magic exists, so his being turned into a boy is actually a possibility. Indiana Jones wants the Covenant of the Ark, which is an extremely powerful and valuable historical artifact that has been searched for over thousands of years. But Indiana Jones is one of the best archeologists out there which we have seen in the first scene where he skillfully removes the Golden Idol from a temple in South America in 1936, an idol that many others have failed to acquire. Because we know that Indy is one of the best we also know that his goal of getting the Ark is also a possibility. What pushes every story forward however is always conflict. So the first act exposes the characters to the conflict that will drive the events. The most important event that happens in the first act is the inciting incident, which draws the main character/s into the conflict. This incident can either be caused by the character or by an external occurrence the character is not actively involved in, like witnessing a car accident. This event will have an impact on the character's life and/or emotional state that they then try to resolve. Every story is dealing with a progress of some sort—a continuous series of events—therefore, the story in the beginning is in need of this inciting incident that forces the character to react and starts this chain of events to unravel. At the end of the first act, another event happens that causes the conflict to swell dramatically. This so-called first turning point raises a dramatic question, which will be answered at the end of the third act and is the dramatic force behind the action and suspense: will Indiana Jones get the Ark of the Covenant and will his complicated relationship with Marion be resolved?

Second act

The second act has the character struggling to obtain his goal, but he continuously fails to do so. Something or someone (external forces: antagonist; internal forces: emotional struggle) prevents him to reach that goal easily. There are obstacles on the character's path that have to be overcome. The first part of the second act has the character being confronted with these obstacles in not only the form of physical obstacles like the antagonist (Nazis), but also in the form of psychological obstacles like old beliefs and habits (the way Indiana treated Marion years ago), that clearly present themselves at this point in their ineffectiveness. The character tries to solve problems the way he has always done, but this time it does not prove successful (the Nazis are too powerful and also Marion has grown up and can see through Indiana's problems). The struggle starts to wear the character out and the continuous failure pushes the success further away than ever. It is obvious that change has to occur for the objective to be achieved! This realization of what needs to change is not solely coming from the protagonist, but can also come from coprotagonists or mentors that lead the main character on their path. Halfway through the second act the character starts to realize his faults and flaws, and a change is starting to be possible. From the beginning onward, coprotagonists can point out the protagonist's faults, but he himself would not be able to see or accept it. He needs to go through the disappointments of the second act to fully grasp his wrongdoings and shortcomings. The second part of the second act deals with what has to change, but the character is not yet ready to fully commit to the change (psychological and thus emotional change) and therefore the goal is still not in reach. He has not yet learned his lesson of how to solve the problem in a different way. His old ways still prove to be inefficient. The problem will continue to increase in significance until the

climax, which is the second turning point of the character's struggle to succeed. This climax is an event that is so intense that the character finally succumbs to the change. He realizes that transformation is crucial for the next stage to happen, which then leads into the third act. Pinocchio realizes only when he himself turns into a donkey that change must happen. Indiana takes all his skill and prowess and gets the Ark back from the Nazis. He fights dozens of them and succeeds, only for the Ark yet again falling into their hands.

Third act

The impact the second turning point has on the character is dramatic. It is what Dara Marks calls "the near-death experience" which fiercely changes the character's beliefs. The third act resolves all the issues and struggles, and offers a final resolution for the characters. The protagonist has permitted the change to happen and now the problem can finally be solved in a climactic scene, which then releases the protagonist with the sense of accomplishment physically and emotionally, having reached a higher level of self-awareness.

There are nevertheless two options: the main character either makes the right choices and has the transformation, thus evolving emotionally and stepping out heroically; or refuses to change and fails in the quest, and the story ends tragically

without the character reaching the goal. However, even when failing in the quest it is mostly the emotional success that counts, as we empathize with the character on an emotional level. Pinocchio fights Monstro, which is one of the most climactic scenes in animation not only from a story point of view but also, and especially, from a technical perspective. Pinocchio learned to be selfless and gives his life for rescuing his father Geppetto. Indiana understands that he cannot stop the Nazis, but he can prevent himself and Marion from succumbing to the allure of the Ark and not glancing into the mysteries it contains. He fights his urge of unearthing the truth, the urge of exploration that has driven him into archeology in the first place. Indy does not succeed in having the Ark being exhibited publicly as it is being stored in a warehouse, hidden once again, but he succeeds in solving his emotional problems with Marion. In the end, he does succeed, not in what he wanted as a goal, but what he needed in his emotional life.

Throughout the three acts the tension is continuously rising to show how the characters are struggling more and more to achieve their goals. The climax has the highest tension toward the end of act three and the protagonist hopefully walks away from the events with more emotional strength and wisdom.

This three-act structure can of course be altered and played with; it is not as rigid and solid as it seems. There are myriads of options and interesting changes that make this seemingly inflexible formula a solid basis for a creative playing field.

Plot and subplot

A typical bad horror film has a story, in which the characters get chased by something/someone and in the end they are either slaughtered or they escape. What is usually missing is an emotional attachment to the characters. If we do not care about the characters in the first place, why would we seriously care about them dying? We would have sympathy for them struggling of course, but the empathy is missing, the true feeling of the emotions felt by the characters. Emotions are needed to make the audience care. In Roman Polanski's classic psychological horror film, *Rosemary's Baby* (1968), he gives us exactly that: emotions and empathy. In the actual feature film not that much is happening when it comes to chases or gore, but we learn about Rosemary and her husband, their happiness and soon to be born baby, their struggle as a young couple to establish a life for themselves in New York City. The film tells the story of the couple moving into a new apartment, meeting neighbors and decorating their new home. Rosemary however develops fears of her neighbors seeking her baby for the Devil. It is the close relationship between Rosemary and the audience, learning so much about her inner feelings, anxieties, and hopes that we care about her deeply, because we get a glimpse into her topsy-turvy emotions. This emotional level is necessary because it not only tells us about her fears and thoughts, but also because it is relevant to her actions and reactions to what

is happening around her. Without knowing her personality, her actions, and reactions are much less meaningful or believable. It is the emotional level that makes the actions understandable and in the case of Rosemary, also frightening. The fear she experiences is shared by the audience because we empathize with her. Therefore, the film works because of its emotional level, not only because of the happenings. The successful script usually has two levels: the plot and the subplot. The plot deals with the action in the film, the active events the characters are involved in. The subplot contains the emotional life of the protagonist evolving, changing, or developing. The active events represent the exterior world of the protagonist, the emotional level the interior. An overall rounded story has to have both elements, plot and subplot, to be successful. The plot contains the actions and obstacles that hinder the protagonist from reaching the goal and being the reason for them having to address the inner emotional struggle. They either overcome them by changing and reaching the goal in the end, or by not changing and succumbing to the road blocks, and ending tragically. Plot and subplot are the two elements that contain external and internal actions and reactions, and both need to relate to each other in order to create a complex and convincing whole.

Story and animation

Animation is obviously a form of filmmaking and therefore can follow traditional storytelling in a linear narrative way: exposition with the introduction of the character/s and the conflict, to complication, to crisis and climax, to resolution; or it can go to the opposite side of the spectrum and abandon conventional story lines to focus on its visual characteristics or exploration of movement. It can also replace a traditional story with pure emotion and perception, like a stream of consciousness approach or even an abstract animated piece where story is replaced by abstract visuals that convey emotion or intellectual ideas, represented by just colors or shapes.

Animation is usually separated into two different fields: character animation and experimental animation. Character animation is the feature film type of animation that is mostly driven by characters that evolve through the storyline. This can be either hand-drawn animation (2D), stop-motion, or 3D animation (and all the other animation techniques used for feature animation that allow a broad range of emotional expression in the characters). This story-driven animation usually follows the traditional storytelling technique with a narrative plot. Experimental animation does not necessarily use that approach, though of course it can. Experimental animation, as the term suggests, deals with an experimental playfulness that explores animation in all its forms and techniques. Movement is a basic building block of animation, and experimental animation can freely play with movement itself or with the timing of the movement (movement being

information contributes to the entire experience of the film and has to follow its lead and always support it. Everything is story!

Simplicity is always the key for story (and everything else in the film for that matter). The audience has to understand what is happening on the screen. If the story is too complex it does not come across and the audience will start to get bored. Usually there is not a whole lot of time to explain long back stories or how an invented society functions and there are limits of what can easily be explained on screen. For the screenwriter, a phrase like "and then he stepped into the busy streets of eighteenth-century Berlin" is easily created in the reader's mind. For the animator and the animation designer, it is a very heavy task. Everything has to be designed, every house, all the characters are to be historically accurate, which of course is rather costly and time-consuming. It is, therefore, advised to determine which part is significant for the story to be understood and which part might not be needed because it does not really bring the story forward. One has to be cost-effective and know when to cut a shot or scene because it is too expensive, too time-consuming, or just not important enough for the overall development of the characters. Animation is one of the most costly film techniques exactly because everything has to be created from scratch.

Storytelling in animation design

Animation design is all about storytelling, though not literally but visually as every image, composition, color, character, attire, shape of a tree, or even the size relationship between the characters are all part of visual storytelling. In every image, there is a story embedded and the animation designer has to learn which characteristics of that image are the main aspects that tell the story. How do all the various design characteristics contribute to the main storyline, and how can we push that information in our design to give the audience the correct information about a specific scene, character, mood, or environment? Why does Disney's Tarzan have big hands and feet? Because he is a character that explores his environment through his tactile senses. Making the hands and feet bigger puts emphasis on them and informs the audience that there is a strong connection between his hands and his environment. In animation design, every little aspect of the character or the environment is of importance for the successful interpretation of the literal script to the visuals on screen. Without the story as the foundation, visual development is not possible since it is of utmost importance for the information and emotion from that script to be transported to the audience visually. Story in this regard is the foundation of everything we design, and vice versa everything we design tells a story, even just a dot in an otherwise empty frame tells a story through its size, color, and composition.

In experimental animation, this approach is a little different as the personal artistic expression and interpretation of design and

not just character, but every part of the image). Experimental animation can also be abstract and invent new visuals that follow abstract rules and hence can completely lack traditional storytelling. It focuses on a nonphysical visual language and uses the basics of image-making like color, shapes, composition, etc., to create films, scenes, or shots completely devoid of nature. As already mentioned above, the narrative therefore is substituted with intellectual ideas and emotions rather than easy-to-follow storylines. Since the broad use of 3D/CG animation in feature films, all other forms of animation are considered experimental animation or experimental techniques. In the beginning of the 1960s, CG animation was itself experimental animation but since the early 2000s has become the leading technique, pushing all other techniques into the background. Things obviously shift with popularity. There are of course always projects that close the gaps between the two animation directions.

However, story is not just the sequence of actions that we follow on screen, it is much more than that. Story is everywhere on screen, it is what each image tells us, all the information that we receive when watching a film. The characters and their look, the colors, shapes, moods, compositions, relationships between the characters themselves, and the environment, all the objects and their design—everything on screen tells us something. All of this story is more important than the use of easily understood design solutions, which are the already proven, successful design norms of the general animated feature.

Digital arts and storytelling

Digital arts has a very wide scope. From phone applications, to computer games, to art installations and interactive projects, digital arts is not easily definable as one specific and solid group as it is in the nature of digital arts that it rapidly changes on a daily basis due to the technical innovations that the medium brings with it. Digital arts, aside from the visual experience and the use of sound that it shares with film and animation, can also play with interactivity and even bring physical stimulation, like gustatory and olfaction stimulation, the vestibular sense or thermoception as possible building blocks to the table. This starts a communication between project and user, a communication that goes beyond what traditional animation or film is capable of. But in terms of storytelling, digital arts follows a similar structure to animation. It has the full range of storytelling in a computer game or the lack of narrative in an abstract installation. Phone applications and games include many projects with interactivity where the user can interact with a device or project and actively change the progression

of the experience; therefore, a linear narrative can turn into a nonlinear narrative with the user controlling the outcome of the story/game. This of course is the case in all kinds of digital games where the narratives are not fixed, but a free flowing entity that can develop into every direction.

However, the look and design of every part of digital arts projects is part of the narrative or sometimes the narrative itself. It is rather tricky to talk about narrative in this context in the traditional way, because there is often no narrative but rather an exchange of emotions and knowledge, an exchange between artist, artwork, and user/audience. This exchange of emotions and knowledge is based on the viewer's history and changes constantly as the interaction forces the user to reinterpret what they experience at every moment of the project. So the storytelling aspect, or more accurately the emotional exchange, opens up toward what the user contributes to the project and their willingness to participate. Although the more abstract the project is, the more the information conveyed through all aspects of design or interactivity are just placeholders for the actual meaning of the project, and it is up to the user to find their own interpretation of the meaning or the narrative of the piece. It can be either intentionally clear or offer countless interpretations depending on the user, and of course the artist's willingness to what extent they want the message to be read. Traditional storytelling usually tends toward someone that tells the story to the one that the story is told to. This traditional, rather one-way approach to story, is replaced in digital arts projects by an emotional exchange that happens between artist, audience/user, and the art project itself. In certain interactive projects, the project itself learns from the user and adjusts itself to provide what the user might want or need. Storytelling is replaced by active communication that goes in every direction.

Genre and design

The term "genre" means a story or location-theme that movies share. Sci-fi, western, or fantasy are genres and so are superhero films, romance movies, musicals, or sport films. Animation however is technically not a genre but a technique as it deals with any kind of theme and is absolutely not confined to a specific story type or location—quite the contrary. But it always appears as a genre for the convenience of the audience and because it is still most often seen as "for children." As much as one might not like the idea of a genre as it has the tendency to stereotype the film, it has its benefits on some level. Certain genres come with conventions that the audience often expects. A sci-fi film is supposed to come with spaceships, aliens, and such and if it does not, then it might be more difficult to sell the film to a public that has genre expectations. These are obviously very superficial, nevertheless more often than not they have to be considered. A genre also can come with a certain design language which is not easy to break as again, the audience expects a certain look. Many viewers want the same or a similar experience when they choose a film from one genre. For instance, a Disney feature animation comes with so many expectations and restrictions that it is not easy to please everyone. Also, the design of a Disney feature follows a direction of stylized realism. So the conventions have to be kept in mind, but constantly just supporting an existing style is the opposite of creativity and in the long run will bore the audience. Innovation and creativity is required to push the design forward and explore its possibilities. *Alien* (1979) by Ridley Scott, for instance, was truly a game-changer for sci-fi design and how space can look dirty, oily, and dangerous. The design of *Alien* touches upon our inner fears in terms of organic black and dark shapes that mimic bones, spines, and sexual organs. David Lynch's interpretation of Frank Herbert's famous book series *Dune* (1984) is another example, where the conventional spaceship and sci-fi design was turned upside down and introduced images that were unique and different, and did not follow the so popular original *Star Wars* series (1977, 1980, and 1983) direction that has dominated the style of sci-fi movies until today (which in turn took Kubrick's *2001: A Space Odyssey* as an example). And *Star Wars* itself is technically not part of the genre of science fiction movies, which deal with futuristic science. The *Star Wars* story plays in the past, not the future as it states in the beginning "A long, long time ago ...." So genre is not always a clearly defined categorization of film.

It is recommended to look into genre conventions and take them as an example. That does not mean to replicate the design, but to know about what is expected from that genre and then deciding which direction to go: to follow the given conventions or not. An animated feature film that is not geared toward a blockbuster summer audience does not, of course, have to follow a genre cliché at all. But knowing the genre the film is covering is a more than recommended task, especially when it comes to films that cater toward an already existing fan base.

Books on screenwriting:

Egri L. (2009). *The Art of Dramatic Writing: It's Basis in the Creative Interpretation of Human Motives*. Rockford, IL: BN Publishing.
Marks D. (2009). *Inside Story: The Power of the Transformational Arc*. London: A&C Black Publishers.
McLaughlin B. (1997). *The Playwright's Process, Learning the Craft from Today's Leading Dramatists*. New York: Back Stage Books.
Wells P. (2002). *Genre and Authorship*. London: Wallflower Press.

CHAPTER 4

Personality

> We go down twice into the same river, and yet into a different river. For the stream still keeps the same name, but the water has already flowed past.
>
> **Seneca: Epistulae, Letter 58, p. 23**

What makes the character interesting?

It is developing the character and fleshing out the details that then as a whole define who that character is and why he reacts the way he does. You will see that the following character is becoming more and more interesting because there are more details and also conflicts within the character:

1. *A young woman that wants to study science.*
   Nothing too unusual yet ....

2. *A young woman in the mid-1980s wants to study science because she wants to become an astronaut.*
   This is already a little bit more interesting as it's usually the boys that get the privilege in stories to want to be astronauts. So the woman now has a unique direction already. As for the obstacle we are not sure yet as it isn't yet clearly expressed.

3. *A young woman in the mid-1980s wants to study science because she wants to become an astronaut. Her mother was always interested in science but never had the social encouragement during her youth to pursue a career in science. She was the one that nurtured her daughter's passion.*
   Now, we have a reason for the character being interested in science, but there isn't yet a struggle within the character.

4. *A young woman in the mid-1980s wants to study science because she wants to become an astronaut. Her mother was always interested in science but never had the social encouragement during her youth to pursue a career in science. She was the one that nurtured her daughter's passion. In class, everyone was making fun of her because she was interested in science and mocked her that she will never get a job in the field precisely because she is a woman. But it was also her sexual orientation as a lesbian that forced her to define not only her role as a woman but also her sexual position in society. This defining of her role in the work field and in society led her to strive for the most difficult position in the field as a woman. To literally reach for the stars. She struggles with finding a balance in her life with work and sexual orientation, dealing with* the HIV crisis in the 1980s in which many of her male gay friends die of AIDS and she can see the stars as a neutral space, devoid of political struggles, and a new frontier representing a new beginning, a metaphor for much in her life. The stars represented her deceased friends, purity, new grounds, and a new direction for society, a light to strive for.

You can see how the character, even in this simple example (and partial cliché), becomes more and more interesting and the growing complexity allows the interest of the audience in the character and story to increase. We understand the reasons behind her decisions; the complexity of her decisions is derived not only from one level of her life but also from various levels that are intertwined.

DOI: 10.1201/b22147-4

Character with personality

What is personality? The Oxford Dictionary describes it as:

1. The combination of characteristics or qualities that form an individual's distinctive character.
2. Lively, engaging qualities.[1]

The important word for creating a character is "distinctive." A character that has qualities that are engaging and lively, is the basis for an interesting character who is not solely a cliché but unique. The character needs to be intriguing enough for the audience to be involved into getting to know that new personality. Being engaging and lively does of course not exclude negative traits as those are also part of someone's personality. To create a believable personality with a full range of traits involves a long process of dissecting the character into their actions and reactions in given events. How do the character's actions/reactions relate to their personality traits and are they logical within the framework of those traits? The character needs to be consistent in personality and cannot be a hothead in one situation but an understanding and quiet person in another, *unless* there are solid reasons that cause the character to act like that. Those reasons can go back to an incident that is rooted in the past or present, nevertheless reasons are needed to make the character's behavior not just logical but also comprehensible.

Personality is on the one hand based on genetics (nature), but also affected by upbringing and social exposure or the lack thereof (nurture). Every trait has some reason for being there and for having developed in the first place. A character is not just happy or angry (which are not personality traits but short-lived emotions). There are reasons that need to be explored, defined, and possibly discussed. If the character is genetically sad or angry, the root might be depressive tendencies which are not always caused by a negative social environment, but sometimes are a chemical imbalance in the body itself. This then would be a reason for the character to be depressed. A character however is much more complex than being described in only one or two words and he has many more shades of emotions that surface depending on the situations given. The character in the story is on a journey of emotional transformation and experiences events that challenge his beliefs and personality and he is either changing throughout the story and then gaining a higher level of self-awareness and probably fighting emotional demons, or staying the same and failing in his quest. If he changes his beliefs and learns from the challenges he will reach his goal and finally succeed. His new gained self-awareness and subjective judgment of his former self allows him to improve emotionally. There are the two already mentioned levels to the character: external actions and internal struggle. Without it the characters and the story will most likely fall flat and lack the driving forces that bring the characters from one point of the story to the next as the external and internal world push each other forward. Characters are driven not only by actions but also by emotions; however, emotions also cause actions and vice versa. A character does not just act, there is a reason for each action, as tiny as that action might be. Every subtle blink of an eye has to have a reason! And many of those reasons lie with the personality of the character. In animation, we need to consider the details in order to clearly visualize the personality and all the miniscule movements in body language assist us in creating a unique personality that precisely describes who this character really is, a character that the audience will believe in.

Personality models

First, one needs to understand that the study of the human personality is extraordinarily complex and not at all clearly defined yet in its entirety as the research is still ongoing and has not been able to clearly define personality at this point. The so-called Big Five are five factors that define personality; there is various other personality models (Cattell and Hexaco) and they are all valid sources for getting an idea of how complex the human personality can be and how various elements relate to each other. It is clear how understanding the personality affects the story as the character's decisions are leading the story. But how does all of this connect to the design and the appearance of the characters? During the design process not just one or two

---

[1] http://www.oxforddictionaries.com/definition/english/personality; (retrieved October 5, 2015).

drawings are produced, but a myriad of possibilities are being suggested. In this timely process, all designs get eliminated one after another until one character evolves that contains all the character traits of the earlier literal description of the script. The visual version of the character is never just one perfect one, but a version that comes close to who is needed for that specific story. Character design is never really finished as it can be tweaked and changed forever. Character design does not follow reality but supports theatrical reality, an artificial reality on screen. The characters can be stylized and sculpted not only in their personality but also in their looks. Aspects that seem more important than others are highlighted and others are visually downplayed. Though at some point, the decision has to be made of which design is the best fit, knowing that not each single aspect of a character's personality can be included into the design, but it can be approximated. What is usually the factor that decides which design is the one chosen is the character's personality. If the personality traits do not come across in the design then the character does not convince yet. For this to happen, the personality needs to be clearly understood first. This is where the personality models can come in, to grasp what personality can be:

The Big Five

1. Openness to experience: (inventive/curious vs. consistent/cautious). Appreciation for art, emotion, adventure, unusual ideas, curiosity, and variety of experience. Openness reflects the degree of intellectual curiosity, creativity, and a preference for novelty and variety a person has. It is also described as the extent to which a person is imaginative or independent, and depicts a personal preference for a variety of activities over a strict routine. High openness can be perceived as unpredictability or lack of focus. Moreover, individuals with high openness are said to pursue self-actualization specifically by seeking out intense, euphoric experiences, such as skydiving, living abroad, and gambling. Conversely, those with low openness seek to gain fulfillment through perseverance, and are characterized as pragmatic and data-driven—sometimes even perceived to be dogmatic and closed-minded. Some disagreement remains about how to interpret and contextualize the openness factor.

2. Conscientiousness: (efficient/organized vs. easygoing/careless). A tendency to be organized and dependable, show self-discipline, act dutifully, aim for achievement, and prefer planned rather than spontaneous behavior. High conscientiousness often perceived as stubborn and obsessive. Low conscientiousness are flexible and spontaneous, but can be perceived as sloppy and unreliable.

3. Extraversion: (outgoing/energetic vs. solitary/reserved). Energy, positive emotions, surgency, assertiveness, sociability, and the tendency to seek stimulation in the company of others, and talkativeness. High extraversion is often perceived as attention-seeking, and domineering.

Low extraversion causes a reserved, reflective personality, which can be perceived as aloof or self-absorbed.

4. Agreeableness: (friendly/compassionate vs. analytical/detached). A tendency to be compassionate and cooperative rather than suspicious and antagonistic toward others. It is also a measure of one's trusting and helpful nature, and whether a person is generally well-tempered or not. High agreeableness is often seen as naïve or submissive. Low agreeableness personalities are often competitive or challenging people, which can be seen as argumentative or untrustworthy.

5. Neuroticism: (sensitive/nervous vs. secure/confident). The tendency to experience unpleasant emotions easily, such as anger, anxiety, depression, and vulnerability. Neuroticism also refers to the degree of emotional stability and impulse control and is sometimes referred to by its low pole, "emotional stability." A high need for stability manifests as a stable and calm personality, but can be seen as uninspiring and unconcerned. A low need for stability causes a reactive and excitable personality, often very dynamic individuals, but they can be perceived as unstable or insecure.

Hexaco personality model

- *Honesty-Humility (H):* sincere, honest, faithful, loyal, modest/unassuming versus sly, deceitful, greedy, pretentious, hypocritical, boastful, and pompous

- *Emotionality (E):* emotional, oversensitive, sentimental, fearful, anxious, vulnerable versus brave, tough, independent, self-assured, and stable
- *Extraversion (X):* outgoing, lively, extroverted, sociable, talkative, cheerful, active versus shy, passive, withdrawn, introverted, quiet, and reserved
- *Agreeableness (A):* patient, tolerant, peaceful, mild, agreeable, lenient, gentle versus ill-tempered, quarrelsome, stubborn, and choleric
- *Conscientiousness (C):* organized, disciplined, diligent, careful, thorough, precise versus sloppy, negligent, reckless, lazy, irresponsible, and absent-minded
- *Openness to Experience (O):* intellectual, creative, unconventional, innovative, ironic versus shallow, unimaginative, and conventional.[2]

Personality traits: Thoughts, feelings, and behavior

Personality traits are based on a genetic (nature) and environmental (nurture) base that either are stable over a life-time or change. The stability of the personality is partially based on the stability of a life-situation or the continuous change of it. To what extend do genetic and environmental factors affect the stability of the personality?

The latest opinion is that personality is mostly based on the genetic factor and that environmental influences have an effect but do not significantly contribute to the personality's stability, neither do environmental influences completely change the personality. They affect, but do not turn around. Nevertheless, severe life-experiences like psychological trauma, major social events, or death can have a sizable impact on the shift of one's personality. The theory of Social Maturation by Robert Kegan suggests a correlation between the genetic basis and the environmental influence in the development of the personality as experiences either trigger and stabilize elements in the personality or subdue them. The environment has influences on personality throughout one's life and the personality can always be affected depending on the stability of the life-situation. Then there is also the debate on how stable a changed personality due to severe events is or if the personality slowly shifts back to its former stage. A person goes through various stages in life[3] and each has an effect on the outlook on life itself. Those newly developed opinions and experiences one goes through in one's life shape the personality. However, because of the usually increasing stability

during maturation (job, marriage, and wisdom), the personality has the tendency to also stabilize and be less prone to change. Significant life events like moving out of the parental environment, entry into the job-life, entry into a romantic relationship, the death of one's parents, grasping one's own mortality, all affect how life is seen and lived. So living life itself affects how we think, feel, and behave in the various stages in life. Every experience, big or small, has an impact and can reshape our beliefs.

Physiology, sociology, and psychology

To make the process of developing a complex personality, a bit easier one needs a plan of some sort to not get lost in details. Playwright Lajos Egri developed in his book *The Art of Dramatic Writing*[4] (Egri 2008, 54–55, 132) characters from three different dimensions that he divides into physiology, sociology, and psychology. Those three cornerstones define the character's personality. In order to develop a well-constructed and thought-through character, all of the three fields of physiology, sociology, and psychology must be covered for the character to be whole and in the end not just a cliche but a logical character that acts and reacts through reasons. The question of "why?" has priority number one, being the force that drives the constant refinement of the character's personality by not just stating, but explaining. No person just "is," but "develops into" due to causes.

Physiology[5]

1. Sex
2. Age
3. Height and weight
4. Color of hair, eyes, and skin
5. Posture
6. Appearance: good-looking; overweight or underweight; clean, neat, pleasant, untidy; and shape of head, face, and limbs
7. Defects: deformities, abnormalities, and birthmarks; and diseases
8. Heredity

Sociology

1. Class: working, ruling, middle, and petite bourgeoisie
2. Occupation: type of work, hours of work, income, condition of work, union or nonunion, attitude toward organization, and suitability for work
3. Education: amount, kind of schools, marks, favorite subjects, poorest subjects, and aptitudes
4. Home life: parents living, earning power, orphan, parents separated or divorced, parents' habits, parents' mental development, parents' vices, neglect; and character's marital status

---

2 Ashton MC, Lee K. (2007). Empirical, theoretical, and practical advantages of the HEXACO model of personality structure. *Pers Soc Psychol Rev.* 11(2): 150–166.

3 Erik Erikson (1902–1994) was a German-born American psychoanalyst who divided human life into eight stages which influence one's personality. In every stage, we are exposed to experiences that shape and affect our outlook on life and how we see ourselves in society and the world.

4 Egri L. (2008). *The Art of Dramatic Writing.* Rockford, IL: BN Publishing.

5 Egri L. (2008). *The Art of Dramatic Writing.* Rockford, IL: BN Publishing, pp. 55–56.

Primary Factors and Descriptors in Cattell's 16 Personality Factor Model (Adapted From Conn & Rieke, 1994).

Descriptors of Low Range	Primary Factor	Descriptors of High Range
Reserve, impersonal, distant, cool, reserved, impersonal, detached, formal, aloof (Sizothymia)	Warmth	Warm, outgoing, attentive to others, kindly, easy going, participating, likes people (Affectothymia)
Concrete thinking, lower general mental capacity, less intelligent, unable to handle abstract problems (Lower Scholastic Mental Capacity)	Reasoning	Abstract-thinking, more intelligent, bright, higher general mental capacity, fast learner (Higher Scholastic Mental Capacity)
Reactive emotionally, changeable, affected by feelings, emotionally less stable, easily upset (Lower Ego Strength)	Emotional Stability	Emotionally stable, adaptive, mature, faces reality calm (Higher Ego Strength)
Deferential, cooperative, avoids conflict, submissive, humble, obedient, easily led, docile, accommodating (Submissiveness)	Dominance	Dominant, forceful, assertive, aggressive, competitive, stubborn, bossy (Dominance)
Serious, restrained, prudent, taciturn, introspective, silent (Desurgency)	Liveliness	Lively, animated, spontaneous, enthusiastic, happy go lucky, cheerful, expressive, impulsive (Surgency)
Expedient, nonconforming, disregards rules, self indulgent (Low Super Ego Strength)	Rule-consciousness	Rule-conscious, dutiful, conscientious, conforming, moralistic, staid, rule bound (High Super Ego Strength)
Shy, threat-sensitive, timid, hesitant, intimidated (Threctia)	Social Boldness	Socially bold, venturesome, thick skinned, uninhibited (Parmia)
Utilitarian, objective, unsentimental, tough minded, self-reliant, no-nonsense, rough (Harria)	Sensitivity	Sensitive, aesthetic, sentimental, tender minded, intuitive, refined (Premsia)
Trusting, unsuspecting, accepting, unconditional, easy (Alaxia)	Vigilance	Vigilant, suspicious, skeptical, distrustful, oppositional (Protension)
Grounded, practical, prosaic, solution orientated, steady, conventional (Praxernia)	Abstractedness	Abstract, imaginative, absent minded, impractical, absorbed in ideas (Autia)
Forthright, genuine, artless, open, guileless, naive, unpretentious, involved (Artlessness)	Privateness	Private, discreet, nondisclosing, shrewd, polished, worldly, astute, diplomatic (Shrewdness)
Self-Assured, unworried, complacent, secure, free of guilt, confident, self-satisfied (Untroubled)	Apprehension	Apprehensive, self doubting, worried, guilt prone, insecure, worrying, self blaming (Guilt Proneness)
Traditional, attached to familiar, conservative, respecting traditional ideas (Conservatism)	Openness to Change	Open to change, experimental, liberal, analytical, critical, free thinking, flexibility (Radicalism)
Group-oriented, affiliative, a joiner and follower dependent (Group Adherence)	Self-Reliance	Self-reliant, solitary, resourceful, individualistic, self sufficient (Self-Sufficiency)
Tolerated disorder, unexacting, flexible, undisciplined, lax, self-conflict, impulsive, careless of social rues, uncontrolled (Low Integration)	Perfectionism	Perfectionistic, organized, compulsive, self-disciplined, socially precise, exacting will power, control, self sentimental (High Self-Concept Control)
Relaxed, placid, tranquil, torpid, patient, composed low drive (Low Ergic Tension)	Tension	Tense, high energy, impatient, driven, frustrated, over wrought, time driven. (High Ergic Tension)

5. Religion
6. Race and nationality
7. Place in community: leader among friends, clubs, and sports
8. Political affiliations
9. Amusements and hobbies: books, newspapers, and magazines read

Psychology

1. Sex life and moral standards
2. Personal premise and ambition
3. Frustrations and chief disappointments
4. Temperament: choleric, easygoing, pessimistic, and optimistic
5. Attitude toward life: resigned, militant, and defeatist
6. Complexes: obsessions, inhibitions, superstitions, manias, and phobias
7. Extrovert, introvert, and ambivert
8. Abilities: languages and talents
9. Qualities: imagination, judgment, taste, and poise
10. Intelligence quotient (IQ)

Character and change: The transformational arc

Every character changes because life in general is continuous change, there is no constant. The emotional development of the character, or the transformational arc, is the actual story in its core elements. Situations affect us and let us grow in

strength or become weaker. Every struggle or difficulty that we have to endure in any moment of our life is part of the overall development. Our "self" is never stable but in constant flux (though I shall repeat, it is still debated how much a personality can actually change and if the change is permanent). We grow up and are unavoidably exposed to situations, people, physical changes, environmental changes, or changes in our bodies, mental changes through learning experiences, and the accumulation of knowledge. "Everything changes and nothing stands still"[6] is what the Greek philosopher Heraclitus of Ephesos (535 BC–475 BC) stated.

This philosophical idea is the cornerstone of many a philosophers and religions. Change happens in the most insignificant detail up to the universe as everything is in fact in a state of constant transition. Therefore, defining a character as "that is how this person just is" is neither enough nor reflects reality. The character behaves like that in this specific moment in time with their present physical and psychological state, and sociological standing. A couple of years later they might react very differently because of experiences that caused a shift. Even if the shift is miniscule, it is there. No one lives without being affected by change. A character description therefore can only be a moment in time and not a solid truth devoid of transformation.

The characters of Hayao Miyazaki's movies are exceptional examples in animation of characters changing and growing due to the challenges they are exposed to, as Miyazaki's characters are very well defined in their personalities—not just being clichés but living and breathing. Sen of the feature *Spirited Away* (2001), for instance, is a cowardly little girl in the beginning of the film who is lazy and childish. Through the tasks that she is given in order to rescue her parents, she grows emotionally and becomes more responsible: she grows up. She takes on the challenges and fights to get her parents back. Looking at the characters in many older Disney films their growth is not as strong as Sen's as they often do not have to fight for their position but either regain the position they had previously or get into a position that they are supposed to have to begin with. Aurora in *Sleeping Beauty*, for example, is such a weak character. She does not grow as a character at all as she isn't particularly active in the film, she is actually absolutely inactive, there is no change in her personality, she does not learn anything. The ones that do the job for her are the three fairies and the handsome prince. They are the ones fighting for Aurora's position as a princess, not her. A strongly developed character is in a different emotional and psychological place before the events of the film compared to the end of the film. There is change happening that elevates the character onto another level, a level that improves their situation and relationships if the character is a heroic one, or does not if the character is a tragic one. However, there needs to be change

---

6 Quoted by Plato in Cratylus, 402a.

for the story to unfold. Without change there is no need for the story to be told. But that change needs to come from the character. They have to understand what needs to be improved in their behavior to allow the change to happen.

Cause and effect

Without a logical and proper reason there is no personality trait that "just is." Every single trait has a base that it developed from. However, there are traits that are genetic and others that developed, nevertheless the basis needs to be explored. If it is genetic, how did this trait affect the members within the family group or the character over time?

Emotions have a cause and affect not just in the physical expression but also in the mind. Someone that is angry has constant psychological problems, which will seriously affect their sociological standing and, of course, their physiological state. Anger itself is usually a short-lived emotion, not a personality trait. If it is an emotional expression that occurs frequently, then the emotional stability of the character might be low (the primary factor in Cattell's personality model that can relate to anger is emotional stability). Anger has a source and that can be a low ego strength, where reality is too difficult for the individual to cope with. The result is anger and/or avoidance. The angry character will have a different posture, their expressions will change, their overall appearance will express anger or the possibility of it easily happening. But anger alone means nothing if the source of the negative emotion is not explored and understood. What made them angry to begin with? Is it still a natural response or is it fits of anger that go beyond a healthy level? Describing a character as "angry" therefore does not do the personality justice and it has to be refined. Not only the

source of the emotion has to be found but also the effect it has on all three dimensions—physiology, sociology, and psychology.

Happiness is the trait that most students mention when it comes to a character's personality and the one that is the most impalpable. Happiness is like anger—an emotion, not a personality trait; it is the emotional result of an event. It is not easy to define what causes happiness. If we would claim that those who achieve their goals are happy, this would mean that someone who wants to be a pilot is happy once they reached this goal. But there is so much more in his life than being a pilot. Happiness must be more than just that. We need to first define what happiness actually means and then look at our developing character and determine how happiness is found in this description. Happiness is not a constant emotion that once achieved never changes, but a "state of well-being and contentment"[7] that is in constant motion. Happiness is part of overall well-being and positive human health. The attainment of a gratifying life is part of the field of positive psychology that deals with the various aspects in life that contribute to overall well-being, which by itself contains life satisfaction, morale, self-esteem, and happiness. In Ryff and Singer's study on positive human health, well-being is based on six different elements:[8]

- Self-acceptance
- The establishment of quality ties to others
- A sense of autonomy in thought and action

---

[7] http://www.merriam-webster.com/dictionary/happiness (retrieved December 6, 2015).
[8] Ryff C, Singer B. (1998). The contours of positive human health. *Psychol Inquiry*. 9(1): 1–28.

Perspective

Perspective always depends from which side the character is presented and then understood by the audience. A murderer whose action is only shown from a neutral position is, in the eyes of the audience, a cold-hearted monster that seemingly kills for pleasure or out of insanity. We cannot understand the action and thus the character turns into an emotionless monster. However, if we tell the story from the perspective of the murderer and follow them on their journey toward the murder, we might even empathize with them because we understand the reasons why this murder had to happen. This does not of course justify the action of murder, but it makes us understand why it happened. The monster turns into a tragic human.

For example, the very difficult topic of pedophilia: for most of us, the idea is so foreign and evil that we do not even want to understand what goes on in the mind of someone that finds children sexually attractive. However, if we would have a story where we follow the protagonist on a journey on which they obviously suffer from their sexual orientation, but cannot act on it because they know it is wrong and that the consent of the child can never been obtained, thus the sexual release will never happen. The only release is either child pornography, which would push them into illegal action, or castrating medicine, which takes away their entire sex life. Both are obviously difficult decisions. The character will be pushed in the story to their emotional limits. Events will happen that make it necessary for them to make a decision. What makes this perspective so difficult to endure is us finding empathy with the character. We know that what they feel physically and mentally is wrong, but they are still shown as a human being and thus have emotions, even if they are difficult to grasp. Or we can simply show them from the perspective of the child that gets molested as a sick and twisted monster that needs to be locked away forever.

What is the perspective that the character is presented from? Black and white is simple, but characters are not.

In the TV show *Sons of Anarchy* (2008–2014), we follow the illegal actions of a motorcycle club and their murderous lifestyle of retaliation and gun trade. During the course of the series the characters get hurt and struggle with their own wrongdoings. It is very difficult for the audience to really empathize with the characters as one feels "they did deserve this emotional pain as they inflicted so much pain on others." The moral code of the group is very twisted and does not follow the code of the "common citizen." Is it right to make the audience actually empathize with disturbed personalities? It obviously is as long as the moral perspective of the entire show is clearly saying that murder is morally wrong.

The different types of characters

The two different types of characters in the traditional narrative feature are the protagonist (and coprotagonist) and the

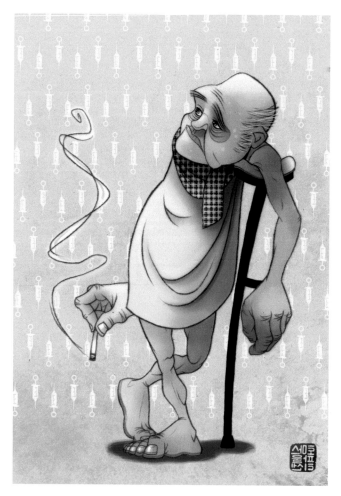

Figure 4.1

- The ability to manage complex environments to suit personal needs and values
- The pursuit of meaningful goals and a sense of purpose in life
- Continued growth and development as a person[9]

Happiness is a result of the sum of various positive elements in one's life, it is "the by-product of a life that is well lived."[10] What needs to be examined in the character's life to be valued as "happy" is not the momentary pleasures indulged in and the resulting short-lived emotions of joy or happiness, but the various elements that contribute to the overall well-being. And those go beyond "a good marriage" or "standing up for oneself" or "having tons of money" but need to cover the three aspects that give physical, social, and psychological gratification. These two examples of angry and happy show that defining a personality and exploring it through the character's actions can be a very complex endeavor that is not easily done. It does take time and effort but will benefit the overall logic of the story.

9 http://www.liberalarts.wabash.edu/ryff-scales (retrieved on).
10 Ryff C, Singer B. (1998). The contours of positive human health. *Psychol Inquiry*. 9(1): 5.

antagonist (and coantagonist). Every story has to have both elements of pro- and antagonist to get the story flowing and keep the characters, their relationships, and development interesting. Only if there is a conflict which is represented on both sides does the story have a flow, and is developing. The protagonist is the main character, whose quest the audience follows, whereas the antagonist is the initiator of the conflict and is hindering the protagonist from succeeding in their quest.

Protagonist

The story should always have only one main character whose story is being told. There can, of course, be more side characters who help the main character along on his path, but their story is neither the main nor the subplot. The dual relationship of plot and subplot is important for the protagonist to be defined as such, it is their emotional development that is important for them to be considered as the main character. "The protagonist holds the goal of the plot and the subplot"[11] is the purpose of the protagonist's position in the story.

> The pivotal character (protagonist) is a driving force, not because he decided to be one. He becomes what he is for the simple reason that some inner or outer necessity forces him to act; there is something at stake for him, honor, health, money, protection, vengeance, or a mighty passion.[12]

A hero in our mind is the perfect specimen: handsome, smart, attractive inside and out, that performs heroic deeds far beyond what the common human being is capable of. Their status of being the protagonist is visualized by simple attractivity. The "hero" does not have to have all the positive personality traits available and does not necessarily have to be the most beautiful or handsome character in the lineup. However, perfection has the tendency to be plain and boring as there is no room for development. Conflict is lacking within their personality that creates issues and problems with other characters. A famous example is the character of Snow White. She never goes through a transformational arc in the film. She is fleeing from the evil queen, but never faces her own fears but relies on the help of others. In the end of the film when she is awakened by the prince, she has not really learned anything, other than her stepmother is now dead and she herself is safe in the arms of the handsome prince. The plot of the film contains lots of action, but the subplot lacks an emotional arc for her. We never really care too much about Snow White because there is no emotional change for her other than her being a damsel in distress, but we care about the dwarfs as they experience an emotional development. First of all they get quickly used to the new "house rules" and we are especially emotionally involved in Grumpy's emotional reaction toward Snow White in the famous scene animated by Bill Tytla. The animation shows clearly the emotional

growth in his facial expression when Snow White kisses him. This leads to his extraordinary action toward the end of the film when he leads the group of dwarfs toward the witch. Snow White never really learns to stand up for herself as she always relies on the help of others. She is truly the damsel in distress, requiring the help of a hero to save her and carry her away to a happy ending. Technically this makes Grumpy the protagonist, but unfortunately the story is not told from his perspective. In contrast to Snow White, Pinocchio is a protagonist that does have an emotional change: he goes from being a selfish and naïve puppet to being a selfless, altruistic hero with true human feelings, giving his life for his father's rescue. He has to go through the trauma of the metamorphosis into a donkey to finally realize his wrongdoings and rescue his father Geppetto even if it will cause his own death. This act gains him not only the gift of becoming a real boy, but also the empathy of the audience. Emotionally, in that regard, Pinocchio is the much more successful character. "Snow White, Cinderella, and Beauty are all being acted upon rather than acting, and waiting for the prince to come along rather than changing their own situation."[13] Pinocchio is however

Figure 4.2

[11] Marks D. (2009). *Inside Story: The Power of the Transformational Arc*. London: A&C Black Publishers, p. 69.
[12] Egri L. (2008). *The Art of Dramatic Writing*. Rockford, IL: BN Publishing, p. 132.
[13] Hayes D, Webster C. (2013). *Acting and Performance for Animation*. Waltham, MA: Focal Press, p. 91.

one of the few early Disney characters that has that emotional arc (alongside Dumbo who learns that it is in his own power to fly and change his fortune), whereas Cinderella or Aurora follow the simple structure of the hero fighting to regain their former position for them or to gain a position that they should have had in the first place.[14] There is not much of an emotional development.

The plot is a metaphor of the subplot's theme and the protagonist is the personification of that theme. In Hal Ashby's feature film *Harold and Maude* (1971), the protagonist's emotional journey turns 180 degrees from suicidal obsession toward enjoying life. The theme of the film could be "live your life to the fullest." Harold, an 18-year-old man, has suicidal tendencies that he expresses by staging his own death in various gruesome forms. He is stuck in his emotional development as he enjoys the idea of dying. The coprotagonist of the film is Maude, a 79-year-old woman. She believes in life despite its sometimes harsh realities; Harold on the other hand does not. The antagonist is society in the form of Harold's mother, his uncle a military officer, a psychiatrist, and a priest, but they all do not live life to the fullest—they perform a duty. They all strongly oppose Harold's relationship with Maude, the free spirit, as they see it as highly inappropriate. The theme of the story, "live your life to the fullest" is represented both in the plot and the subplot. Harold's transformational arc is from being obsessed with death in the beginning of the story toward a stronger and more self-confident young man that faces life in all its shades at the very end of the journey. The theme is also present at all times in the plot, with Maude teaching him about life and how to enjoy it despite its tragic moments. Maude's tragic past is just hinted at with: she is a Holocaust survivor and still she is full of life and hope. Her surviving the Holocaust stands

in a stark contrast to Harold's suicidal behavior in a very rich and spoiled environment. In the end of Harold's journey, he learns the lesson of fighting for his own happiness and confidence. The film's metaphor is represented by Harold learning to play an instrument in order to play the famous song *If you want to sing out, sing out* by Cat Stevens with the lyrics expressing the theme very clearly.[15] The theme needs to be represented by metaphors or metaphorical actions in the plot to correlate with the subplot's equal developments. Both can contradict each other as long as they strive for the same goal. A film is a piece of art, not a piece of reality, and theatrical reality is not equal to regular reality, therefore can be strengthened in its elements!

Many of the animated side characters or antagonists are more interesting than the main characters, exactly because of their obvious flaws and problems. Personality traits that cause frictions with other characters, force the protagonist to follow their transformational path. In Sony Animation's feature *Cloudy with a Chance of Meatballs* (2009), the main character Flint Lockwood is a rather dysfunctional young man. He is on the one hand brilliant mentally and also capable of creating his outrageous inventions physically, but both his exterior and interior are flawed. He is not able to express his emotions very well, neither toward his father nor to Sam Sparks, the weather intern he is falling for. It is his internal emotional journey to learn how to express his feelings that enables him to fix the problem of the faulty food processor

---

[14] Booker MK. (2010). *Disney, Pixar, and the Hidden Messages of Children's Films.* Santa Barbara, CA: Praeger, p. 11.

[15] *You can do what you want*
The opportunity's on
And if you can find a new way
You can do it today
You can make it all true
And you can make it undo...

The Very Best Record of Cat Stevens

FLDSMDFR (Flint Lockwood diatonic super mutating dynamic food replicator), the invention that lets gigantic food items rain from the sky, not on his own, but with the help of his friends. He has to learn to let others help him on his journey. The character is interesting because of his faults and because of us being able to relate to most of his issues. It is the faults that make a character exciting, not their perfection.

Secondary Characters

The secondary character helps the protagonist to achieve their goal, and pushes the plot forward. In order to be regarded as secondary, they need to care for and share the goal of the subplot, the emotional transformation of the protagonist. Otherwise their importance in the subplot is diminished. If they would have their own emotional arc, the audience would have to empathize with two characters' emotional arcs. The audience easily loses interest as it becomes rather complicated to follow. The subplot, or the emotional arc, is solely reserved for the protagonist. They might share the same goal as the protagonist in terms of the plot, but their emotional arc is not as pronounced (which does not mean that they would not have one). The secondary character is the one that stands by the side of the protagonist and leads, guides, or supports them on their path toward the goal. The secondary character often has the knowledge to teach the protagonist, but cannot solve their problem. The protagonist needs to learn the lesson alone via the emotional transformation. The secondary character doesn't have an answer for the resolution of the protagonist's issue,[16] but is encouraged to find their own, and maybe even go on their own emotional path (which again would be hinted at but would not be the center of attention within the subplot).

Sidekicks

The sidekick is a version of the secondary character and is contrasting the protagonist and through their divergent personality and physical traits, points out the qualities of the protagonist. Usually the sidekick has their own qualities that add to the qualities of the protagonist, and fill the gaps the protagonist requires to solve the problem ahead.

The sidekick is also the protagonist's "voice"—not only the one to talk to, but also the one that expresses what the protagonist does not or cannot talk about yet.

In animation, sidekicks are often the comic relief as the protagonist is usually a character that is more reserved. The sidekick is either intellectually incapable of grasping the situation and needs it to be continuously explained, or is the one that

explains it to the protagonist and thus to the audience. The mere fact that the sidekick is listening to the protagonist's monologues is important for the protagonist, to just have someone to talk to.

The protagonist's ability to have friends and social relationships is also proven by the existence of the sidekick as the audience can witness how the two relate to each other and solve social problems. Often this leads to the audience being able to relate to the sidekick more easily than to the protagonist, if the protagonist is too distant or emotionally cold.

Sidekicks are generally less attractive and intelligent than the protagonist, again strengthening his traits and looks. However, there are of course exceptions.

Dumbo would have not learned to fly without the help of his friend Timothy Q Mouse, Pinocchio would have failed without his conscience Jimini Cricket, Simba without Timon or Pumbaa, Marlin without Dorey, Aladdin without the Genie, Mister Incredible without his family, Ariel without Flounder, Scuttle, or Sebastian ... the list is endless, as most Hollywood animated features have a strong relationship between protagonist and sidekick.

The idea of the sidekick character in animation is often pushed to an extreme where a sidekick is invented to just accompany the protagonist or secondary characters even if it is not helping the story along at all. Morph in Disney's *Treasure Planet* (2002) accompanying John Silver or Rapunzel's chameleon friend Pascal in *Tangled* (2010) are rather questionable characters whose necessity within the story is weak to say the least. There should always be a strong reason for the character to be there and that reason needs to be within the story. Without a strong reason what's the point? And why would Rapunzel have a chameleon in the first place? The randomness breaks the logic of the setting and its central European fauna.

Antagonist

The antagonist is usually the character whose goal is contrary to the protagonist's, oppose, and stand in the way. The objective creates the path of obstacles that hinder the protagonist and thus the antagonist challenges, with their actions, the progress of the protagonist. We see the antagonist often as the bad guy because we see the story from the perspective of the protagonist. The antagonist does not necessarily consist of only one character, but can be more than one, as long as they share the same goal. As important as the antagonist can be, it is not required for the film to have one that is an actual character. It can also be society itself, an idea, or a problem that not necessarily has to be impersonated by a character. For example, a woman tries to overcome cancer. She is fighting for her life: so her goal is to survive. The cancer itself is the antagonist. However, the cancer is a rather abstract, intangible concept, which makes it difficult for the audience to be fully emotionally involved.

16 Dunne P. (2006). *Emotional Structure: Creating the Story Beneath the Plot.* California: Quill Driver Books, p. 41.

his actions, and also he would then have an emotional struggle, due to his personality disorder, which makes it difficult for him to function socially on a daily basis.

Contrary to most Disney villains are the antagonists in Hayao Miyazaki's features. They are often compelling because of their true emotions and their humane depiction of character. His villains are never just evil, they never seek power for no reason. Every villain in Miyazaki's films has emotions and reasons that are understandable and go far beyond simplicity. Their goals are as complex and emotional as the goal of the protagonists, which makes his films so extraordinary as both sides struggle and there is no real good or evil. Even the protagonists have flaws and make mistakes, and the villains also show love and understanding. Miyazaki creates antagonists that do have their own goals and objectives, and they stand against the main characters of course. However, once the audience has actually accepted the fact that they are the villains, Miyazaki surprises us with their human side, that goes far beyond black and white. His villains are never one-dimensional characters that are just "bad." Especially the main antagonist of his feature *Princess Mononoke* (1997) Lady Eboshi, the leader of Irontown, is an extraordinary character. Miyazaki not only shows her as the dark villain that destroys the forest to smelt iron, but also explains to us why she is doing it: to help prostitutes and outcasts, or people with leprosy to have a place to live. This exceptional human touch turns the initially just dark character of Lady Eboshi into a character that has a reason for her actions and thus she becomes human and we empathize with her on a personal level. All of Miyazakis "villains" show this human side that prevents them from being one-dimensional.

As much as the protagonist needs a reason for their actions, an antagonist also needs reasons, otherwise they are just "evil," which lacks believability and intellectual depth.

The antagonist does not always have to be "the bad guy." They are obviously the character that opposes the protagonist, but can also have a change of heart at the end or during the film's plot. Director Frank Capra[17] called his character Anthony P. Kirby in *You Can't Take it With You* (1938) a "villain-hero" as he is the antagonist in the film, a rich and ruthless banker that wants Grandpa Vanderhof to be kicked out of his house, where he lives with family and friends in a kind of alternative commune. However, at the end of the film Kirby changes his mind and he realizes that he himself is friendless, just as Vanderhof had told him before. Kirby does not take the house off Vanderhof and he is actually the one that learns a valuable lesson in the end, realizing that friends are important. He turns from side character to main character in the end, because he is the only one that really learns a lesson and changes his emotional status from being ruthless to being less money-driven.

The involvement could be intensified if the woman is fighting cancer, but her insurance denies her the treatment she needs due to bureaucratic and pedantic reasons. The insurance then stands for the antagonist and is more graspable than the cancer itself. Antagonists are narrative devices that strengthen the opposing side of the protagonist and facilitate the audience's emotional involvement.

The emotional foundation of a villain is usually very simple in animation. Jafar in Aladdin just wants to be in power and take the position of Sultan, and marry Princess Jasmine. However, it is never really mentioned why he wants that power. What does he want to do other than "being in power?" Change the political landscape or change the social order, built hospitals, or start an economic revolution? It is never even mentioned why he wants to marry Jasmine other than the typical semireason: she is pretty. Jafar is not a very complex character as the reasons for why he wants what he wants are rudimentary. Therefore, there cannot be a complete emotional development in his case as there is no emotional basis other than the will to power. If he should achieve this power, what would he do? Just sit on the throne and be "powerful," worshiped by thousands, and that's about it? If Jafar is really portrayed as a psychopath or narcissist then he would be a much more interesting character as then there are reasons for

17 Capra F. (1997). *The Name above the Title*. Boston, MA: Da Capo Press, p. 241.

Minion and henchman

The henchman or minion is the sidekick of the antagonist and usually less developed in their personality. Their less-defined personalities, or often clichéd rudimentary personalities, demonstrate the inability of the antagonist to maintain meaningful relationships, which stands in stark contrast to the strong relationship between protagonist and coprotagonist or sidekick. The henchman is usually looking up to the antagonist and is submitting to them, being clearly the "muscle of his master." The henchman needs to be overcome by the protagonist to get closer to the antagonist or the antagonist's goal. The lack of personality in the henchman makes them often expendable soldiers for the antagonist's cause that the audience does not care too much about, but that express the physical strength and sheer prowess of the antagonist.

The development of character personality

Of course, character personality was not just born in a single moment in time but was a development within the animation industry over an extended period. The development of personality animation was only possible at Disney. The company was one of the only ones that actively strived for more realism in their work and continuously refined the quality of their visuals and characters. Their work was always based on realism, creating a believable version of reality, whereas other studios were less keen on recreating an interpretation of reality. Studios like Warner Brothers or Fleischer Studios had a slightly more surreal approach to their productions, as had most other companies in the animation industry that could not or did not want to produce Disney's complexities (or did not have the finances to spend on lavish productions like Snow White or Pinocchio).

In the 1920s, animated characters were seen as surreal and cartoony drawn vaudeville actors, not yet as living creatures with thoughts and true emotions. Felix the Cat, Koko the Clown, Betty Boop, Flip the Frog, Oswald the Lucky Rabbit, and even early Mickey Mouse were the most famous characters in the 1920s and early 1930s and they did have rudimentary personalities, but it was by no means a thoroughly developed one that showed emotional depth. The characters' personalities slowly developed from the end of the 1920s into in the mid-1930s. If one looks into the development of the live-action characters of Buster Keaton, Harry Langdon, Charlie Chaplin, Stan Laurel and Oliver Hardy, or Harold Lloyd they did not exhibit deep personalities in their short

subjects, but had developed them for their feature films to some extent. Their characters also grew over time into more complex personalities once the creators became more familiar with their creations. Animators in the 1920s and 1930s used these live-action characters' movements, jokes, and personalities as inspiration and also as learning tools for their own developing trade. Also, sound film in animation assisted the characters on screen to express themselves differently and more realistically; the acting style changed from the 1920s to the 1930s onward and became less theatrical and more "realistic" for the screen. The early characters' acting style in the 1920s is defined as *figurative acting* where the character lacks emotional depth and presents a mere figure that, with the help of poses, music, sound, etc., expresses a cliché of an action or emotion rather than making the audience believe in the character being alive. Figurative acting often falls back to the use of standardized poses that are universally understood and accepted as representing a specific emotion.[18] At the Disney Studios from the mid-1930s on, animators developed the characters' personalities more and more and refined them to achieve believable personalities that could compete with live-action performances. They needed to because the first feature

Snow White and the Seven Dwarfs (1937) demanded a higher complexity of the characters that went beyond the short subject and kept the audiences interested for 83 minutes in a feature film. Nevertheless, Walt Disney himself made it clear that he never wanted to replicate reality but to create his own cartoon reality where the characters are stylized, yet complex in their behavior—he wanted caricatures that would be founded on fact. An acting style that exaggerated and interpreted reality, but did not imitate it was needed to push the short films on another emotional level. However, certain stepping stones needed to be crossed first in order to reach the point where the character animation could be truly believable in its performance and stylized realism. In order to being able to technically allow the characters to act more realistically, the 12 principles of animation needed first to be defined as such and then mastered. By the mid-1930s, those principles had been discovered and were clearly explored in the short films and thus more complexity in the characters' performances could take place.

The real need for more personality in the characters started actively with the development of the seven dwarfs for Disney's first feature *Snow White and the Seven Dwarfs* (1937) in 1935–1936. Walt Disney saw the need for each of the dwarfs to have a distinct personality that had to come across clearly for the audience to be able to distinguish them from

---

[18] Crafton D. (2013). *Shadow of a Mouse: Performance, Belief, and World-Making in Animation*. California: University of California Press, p. 25ff.

another, and to believe in them not being just a group of dwarfs, but a group of individual personalities. Also, the visual design that Disney had pushed further and further toward stylized realism, based on European story books from the nineteenth century, runs alongside the development of the characters' more complex personalities. The more the backgrounds became convincing in their composition, color handling, and depth perception the more they also needed characters that could literally stand their ground. Slowly, the characters steered away from figurative acting and developed into characters that perform through *embodied acting*, which has the character express believable emotions and have a personality that is fully convincing, coming from an emotional being with complex reasoning. Emotions are presented as complex interactions between pose, facial expression, timing, and performance that all go back to the character's unique and well-defined personality. The goal is a realistic character that the audience empathizes with, not only sympathizes with.

While the characters developed slowly from figurative toward embodied acting, there was still plenty of poses and actions used deriving from stock poses from 1920s cliché characters like the "boxer" or the "bully and yahoo" and also simple, generic poses that express "anger," "happiness," or "shyness." Up to today, these clichés are used in less sophisticated productions or to refer to the beginnings of animation. Those generic poses do clearly express their emotions and are understandable, but they avoid a unique personality.

There are stepping stones in Disney's *oeuvre* that show how the characters did make the needed steps from rather cut out entertainers to actual thinking and feeling living beings. The characters did have individualized movement before and came across as unique; however, their performance was still generic in parts. The following examples are of course excellent pieces of animation and the negative points are made to only compare them with what came afterward.

1935: *The Tortoise and the Hare*

The characters clearly have personalities and beautifully express them in their character animation. The principles of animation are well incorporated and are also played with creatively, but the poses, despite being exciting, are very much standardized and remind one of live-action comedies and vaudeville acts where the actors act for the audience on a stage. The composition and action mainly happens on the x- and y-axis and not much in the z-axis, which accentuates the flatness of the stage and contributes to the feeling of a stage performance.

March 1936: *Elmer Elephant*

The character of Elmer has already believable emotions, but still also uses stereotypical poses and performances. The animators,

for instance, often fall back on stock expressions like Elmer being shy in front of Tillie, the birthday tigress, who is in love with Elmer. There are, however, moments of more believable emotions especially when Elmer is crying at the river. This is a very personal and intimate occasion where one starts to feel a hint of empathy for the mistreated elephant rather than just feeling sorry for him. Nevertheless, the emotion to Elmer's outburst is never fully empathized with by the audience as it is repeatedly interrupted by little visual jokes spread throughout the performance. Much in this shot can be contributed to the stronger background composition and mood, which comes back similarly in a much stronger and emotionally gripping fashion in *The Ugly Duckling* in 1939.

October 1936: *The Country Cousin*

The animation for the two mice in this short was done by Art Babbit and Les Clark, two of the masters of character animation. The character of the country mouse is convincing not only in its movements and demeanor but also in its personality as a country bumpkin that is unrefined, yet zestful and truly enjoying the feast in front of him. The personality of the country mouse and city mouse is stepping away from just being cute and adorable to something more complex as the mice do have movements, habits, and personalities that are complete opposites. The country mouse is gullible and excited about the feast yet tries to not be too noisy and behaves clumsily and crudely, whereas the city mouse is refined, arrogant, and sophisticated in all its movements. This is a step up from the simplicity of Elmer who is only showing one clear emotion at a time that isn't unique or personalized. It could be performed in the same way by any other character in the short. The two mice however are opposing each other and neither could use the actions of the other.

1937: *Snow White and the Seven Dwarfs*

Grumpy's animation is done by Bill Tytla, who started his career at Disney in 1934. Out of the seven dwarfs, it is the performance of Grumpy in some scenes that shows what can be done emotionally in animation, and that animated characters do have the same abilities to move audiences as their live-action counterparts. When Snow White kisses Grumpy on the forehead when he is leaving for the mines, the change in his attitude is something that had not yet been done in animation. One can witness on screen the feelings that Grumpy has for Snow White and how he himself tries to fight them unsuccessfully. Animation at this point has now truly discovered how a character made of lines and paint can express subtleties and move the audience.

1939: *The Ugly Duckling*

The true character performance of the duckling goes hand in hand with the image's mood and the music. The character of the Ugly Duckling is fully convincing in its emotions and the animators play effortlessly with the character, having learned the full scale of emotional depiction. The characters do not seem to play for the audience on a mere stage anymore, but the camera is freely exploring the space. The moments of the duckling in the forest and at the lake are magical and convincing as the emotions are now continuous, not sporadic.

1940: *Pinocchio*

In *Pinocchio*, it is not just the main character that has a fully developed personality, which shows naïvety and innocence, but also the other characters—Stromboli, Honest John, Geppetto, and Jimini Cricket—are personalities in their own right. The practice of the seven dwarfs' unique personalities is clearly expanded now to every main character in the lineup. Some of the moments of Pinocchio's performances are bringing tears into the eyes of the audience, when, for instance, Pinocchio is petrified by Stromboli's outburst of anger, a scene that is utterly chilling. Again, it was Bill Tytla's abilities that made the performance of Stromboli such a convincing and emotionally gripping highlight of the film.

1941: *Dumbo*

Bill Tytla again animated the most moving scene in this rather modest feature. The moment when lonely Dumbo is cradled in his mother's trunk and then has to leave her again is heart-wrenching. The subtlety in the animation, the expressions, and the timing is emotionally moving and Tytla seems to play the characters with ease.

There are obviously many more stepping stones in the list of shorts and features that Disney produced at the time, but the mentioned examples give an idea of how the transformation from figurative to embodied acting can be seen. Also, many more artists besides Bill Tytla did animate noteworthy performances but the scope would be too great to name them all.

At the Fleischer Studio, the characters continued with their figurative acting approach and even Popeye, one of the most famous characters at Fleischer, never reached a level of complexity in his performance or personality that goes beyond the simple character that acts out of impulses. Not even in his later performances did he seem to live outside the confinement of the screen, but rather act for the audience on screen (that does not limit the entertainment level of those shorts of course!). In Fleischer's first feature film *Gulliver's Travels* (1939), the characters had no more than rudimentary personalities and standardized performances which is prevalent in every scene. In Fleischer's next feature however, *Mr. Bug Goes to Town* (or *Hoppity Goes to Town*) (1941), there is a clear development toward more refined and complex characters that are unique and, despite many clichés in their foundation, do have some unique personality traits. In his extraordinarily successful series *Superman* (1941–43) however, Superman himself or Lois (or any of the villains) never were explored in their psychological possibilities. They do move,

and move quite well and convincing (and the design of the shorts is gorgeous!), but the characters never act convincingly, have no psychological reasoning for their actions that keep the audience guessing. One knows beforehand what the characters are going to do as they fall back to stock ideas and actions rather than let the personality of the character lead the action. Superman is clear; he is perfect, which leaves no room for him doing anything else than just the right thing. Because we never get to know the character, never know anything about him other than being "super" and "fast as a speeding train" there is no goal other than catching the villain, no emotional obstacle that the hero struggles with.

At Warner Animation, the situation was different in the 1940s as their famous characters started to appear with each other in their shorts in various scenarios. They interacted with each other and therefore the new situations that the characters found themselves in demanded a discussion among the directors and animators of how each character would act and react in given situation. Slowly, over time, complex relationships developed and those were visualized in the refined performances of Bugs Bunny, Daffy Duck, Elmer Fudd, and many others. Especially the relationship between Bugs and Daffy revealed the clearly opposing personalities of Warner Brother's animation stars and their constant bickering. Their egos were diametric opposites and because of their differences the storylines became interesting and a new type of animation started to evolve very different from Disney's, with different characters, different character animation and very important: different personalities, which were closer to the dark side than Disney's tendency toward sweetness and emotional pleasantry.

Once UPA started their production at the end of the 1940s the stylization of the design also meant a stylization of the characters, and with it, their personalities. Complex characters were replaced by character types with a dash of uniqueness that did have depth in personality but their character animation did not allow the realism that made Disney's characters so convincing. But UPA's goal was to stay away from this realism and constitute a new field of animation that incorporated modern art and a modern sensibility into the art form of animation. Disney's realism seemed out of fashion in the beginning of the 1950s and the simplification of the design required a simplification of the animation process on every level (except UPA's short *The Tell-Tale Heart* from 1954). That doesn't mean that the characters were flat and unrefined—quite the contrary—but their performances lacked the convincing subtleties of realism that made Disney's characters so emotionally convincing. Embodied acting can only be convincing at its full scale if the character animation is striving for realism in its physical actions. The more the movement itself is stylized, the more the emotional expression is being sacrificed (this is a tendency and not a rule!).

Interestingly enough, many of the contemporary features also play heavily with stock performances, as much as in the old days.

There are certain actions and visual gags that appear over and over in features, producing repetitive clichés rather than unique actions and reactions. It is a learned behavior copied from TV shows and feature films, games, and popular entertainment rather than real life—a copied triviality, devoid of true emotions but projecting an image or movement on top of the character's personality. One can see this trend in many American productions where a character type is expressed by a specific body language, by a certain fashion style, and suitable physical attributes. Many lineups of characters are so clichéd they appear to be constructed and generated at the drawing board by checking certain parameters rather than creating an interesting and unique assemblage of "normal" characters, not ideal types. The development of character personality is still ongoing and its complex possibilities in animation can be seen in Charlie Kaufman and Duke Johnston's feature animation *Anomalisa* from 2015. The characters are as complex as in any live-action film and perform in a believable way without being stereotypes. The personalities of the two main characters, Michael Stone and Lisa Hesselman, are the most complex in animation so far.

For more on character performance, see Barrier (2003), Crafton (2012), Hayes (2013), and Hooks (2011).

Visual imperfections

The protagonists are usually the heroes and heroines and as such are often considered as having to be physically perfect or close to perfection for the audience to see their might, their endless possibilities in terms of achieving their goals, and going even further. This can make it a bit implausible once in a while that the pretty ones are also the ones that succeed (which by the way is a questionable message for children's films to begin with, and they are mostly the target audience). Characters need to be relatable and convincing in their personality *and* physicality. Their personality is often flawed and the very basis of the problems of the character. Having a character that looks good but just has to learn a lesson in his or her personality to then achieve the level of happiness, luck, and wealth that destiny has had in mind all along, might lack convincing power for some viewers. As much as it is appreciated that many of the characters on screen have broadly above-average looks, which is going back to the beginning of cinema, it is a must to also think of the opposite and suggest characters that do not follow the supermodel formula. Little flaws in the character's body can go a long way to make them appear one of "us" instead of one of the unreachable and very lucky few. All of us have flaws and it is often the flaws that make us unique and give us a look that is different from the rest. For instance, Hogarth's little chipped tooth in Brad Bird's brilliant feature *The Iron Giant* (1999) gives the boy literally a bit of an edge. He seems more playful and less "proper," more active, but still very much a child. It is not much at all to add an imperfection

to the character but it does have benefits in facial expressions or poses. Phoebus, the Captain of the Guards in Disney's version of *The Hunchback of Notre Dame* (1996) (a very different character from Hugo's original novel) is the typical good-looking hero, tall and muscular, but he also has a rather big nose, surprisingly big for a character of his position. Very similar to Phoebus's looks is the character of Kristoff in Disney's *Frozen* (2013). He literally looks like a CG version of the shaven Phoebus and he also has a rather big nose. Both characters are very manly and adventurous, lovable, and positive, rather down-to-earth types. The big nose does bring them actually down to earth and they feel like they are solid and strong, able to stand up and fight for what's right. It is obviously not just the nose that gives out that message, but with the long blond and slightly messy hair, their outfits and everything else a character is developed that expresses the "normal" rather than the "extraordinary" even just in a hint. Very often when characters are designed, in the beginning of the design process they are meant to be "normal" in order for the audience to connect with them more easily, but then through review after review little things here and there get changed, the characters are often pushed more toward "sexy" and attractive in order to be that special hero or heroine. This is a common procedure that can give out the wrong message for children if they are exposed to the typical Barbie-ratio over and over again. Having a flaw needs to be the norm, not the exception and having only the villains and sidekicks being the flawed ones also expresses a world view that is questionable.

Why, for example, is the character of Sadness in Pixar's feature *Inside Out* (2015) the chunky one with geeky glasses? The message is clearly that fat people are sadder than skinny ones. And to substantiate this message, the character Happiness is visualized as the sexy, skinny, and pretty one. Why is anger a male character, but disgust is female? These are stereotypes that do show imperfections in characters or what is seen as an imperfection (not that this is always a correct view), but show them in a clichéd character that circumstantiates questionable stereotypes.

Books on performance and acting in animation:

Barrier M. (2003). Chapter 1: Cartoon Acting. *Hollywood Cartoons: American Animation in its Golden Age.* Oxford: Oxford University Press, pp. 8–285.

Crafton D. (2012). *Shadow of a Mouse: Performance, Belief and World-Making in Animation.* California: University of California Press.

Hayes D, Webster C. (2013). *Acting and Performance for Animation.* Waltham, MA: Focal Press, p. 91.

Hooks, Ed. (2011). *Acting for Animators.* London: Routledge.

CHAPTER 5

Relationships

Relationships are important to make the audience feel that the character relates to their social and natural environment, reacts to it, acknowledges it, and is part of it. The environment, both social and natural, has always an impact on the character in the form of shaping habits or emotions as much as the character in turn has an impact on their environment, shaping it after their liking, needs, or just by living there. Relationships assist tremendously with storytelling as stories evolve through additional visual information and are intellectually enriched by them. For example, Miyazaki's *Princess Mononoke* (1997): San grew up in the forest and was raised by wolves, which is obvious in her outfit that is different from Ashitaka's, which follows the traditional outfit of the Emishi, an indigenous tribe from

northern Japan. Both characters however loosely relate to each other because they share a similar height, age, and features (the face shape is similar, their entire facial structure shares a similar direction). The viewer does not necessarily see the relationship, but feels it. These relationships are tremendously helpful in touching upon the subtexts of a story, the little details that are not mentioned in the film but are still important to not only make the viewer understand the relationship but also feel it. It is also clear from the visuals who belongs where. Ashitaka wears the Emishi tribe's practical garb of a hunter connecting him to a social setting, whereas San wears a fur cape, a necklace of teeth (or bone), and a white shirt, which in its color relates her to the wolves she lives with. The teeth around her neck obviously do the same

and also give her a natural fierceness and strength. It is the materials of fur and teeth that relate her to the natural world!

There are two different relationships that are important: the relationship between the various characters and the relationship the characters have with their environment in the form of objects, architecture, nature, and general surroundings.

Character relations

There are plenty of options between the characters, how they relate to each other and also how the characters relate to the viewer. All of the mentioned possibilities can of course be overwritten by a story.

One character

- Figure 5.1—The character is by himself: he is unaware of being watched. This gives the character the possibility to be completely himself and act/react in a very private manner.

- Figure 5.2—The character communicates with the viewer: he is aware of being watched and is emotionally reacting to the viewer. This breaks the fourth wall and allows the character to be part of our world and vice versa.

Two or more characters

- Figure 5.3—The characters have eye contact and face each other: this is the strongest relationship between the two (aside from touching each other).

- Figure 5.4—The characters acknowledge each other, but do not have eye contact. Each is looking somewhere else.
- Figure 5.5—One character is not acknowledging the other and is obviously turned away from the one that is

directly looking at him. It is obvious who is disrupting the communication.
- Figure 5.6—Both do not interact with each other visually, but know each other.
- Figure 5.7—Both clearly disregard each other. There is a gap in their relationship. Because of their closeness, it is nevertheless still possible for them to reconcile with each other.
- Figure 5.8—There is no relationship at all; the distance between them could be an indicator of either being unfamiliar or that the gap in their relation is irreconcilable.
- Figure 5.9—The characters visually communicate with the viewer. This again breaks the fourth wall and brings the three, viewer and characters, in visual and intellectual contact with each other. Each becomes part of the other's reality.

In the typical character design presentation, the characters are usually by themselves and not grouped or interacting with others; the focus lies on that specific character's personality, not on the relationship between multiple characters, despite more often than not much of the personality is about how the character interacts with others socially. However, there are some instances when there needs to be a visual connection between the main characters if their relationship is crucial to the story. For example, the friendship between Tulio and Miguel in Dreamwork's *Road to Eldorado* (2000) is so strong and important to the entire story that it would be beneficial for the character design process if the characters, from the inspirational development stage till the final character design stage, always interact with each other to explore their relationship in its full range. Producer Bonne Radford says about the friendship between the two: "The buddy relationship [between the duo] is the very heart of the story. They need each other because they're both pretty inept. They're opposites—Tulio is the schemer and Miguel

Figure 5.1   Figure 5.2   Figure 5.3   Figure 5.4

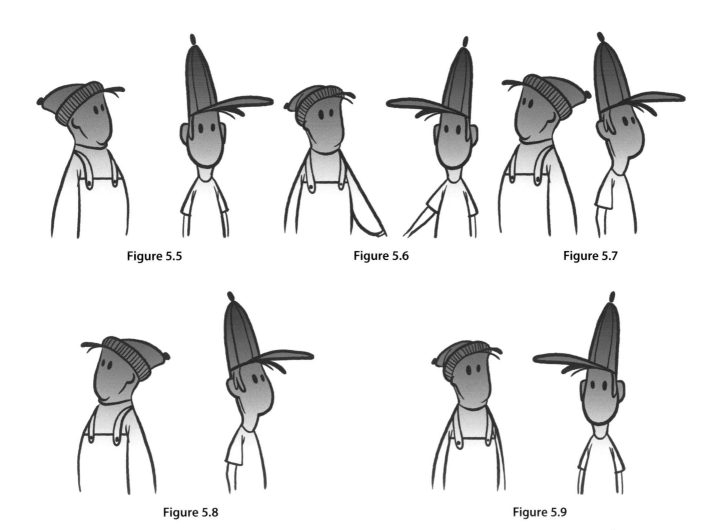

Figure 5.5   **Figure 5.6**   **Figure 5.7**

Figure 5.8   **Figure 5.9**

the dreamer. Their camaraderie adds to the adventure; you almost don't need to know where they're going or what they're after, because the fun is in the journey." Because the characters are opposites in their personalities (they might even fill each other's shortcomings), their looks need to express their differences exactly and the importance lies in them juxtaposing each other, and with it accentuating each other's uniqueness. It is easier to design this discrepancy if the characters are always presented as a couple where shapes, colors, forms, body ratios, etc., can oppose each other from the very start.

As we have seen in the options of two characters interacting, the relationship between two characters does not have to be a close one where they look at each other and have a friendly relationship. The opposite also makes a strong point: two characters do *not* acknowledge each other. Relationship does not only mean a close positive connection, but can also be a negative one or the lack of one altogether. Communication is never only one-directional! If A does not respond to B, then A has to have a reason for not responding, which is already the

beginning of a story. There needs to be some social element that makes the audience care through the characters' interaction with each other. It is much easier for the viewer to feel the characters being "alive" if there is already a social component of some sort in the image that shows that they live a relatable social life within their own universe or pictorial realm.

Two characters that are friends or lovers actually do not necessarily have to be opposites, because "opposites attract." However, it does help if there is some trait in their personalities that does differentiate one from the other. How do two characters that are friends or lovers fill each other's gaps in their personalities? Do they complete each other or are they actually very much the same? Do lovers slowly equal each other in looks? Do they share the same values and likes or are they totally opposites and that is why they fit each other? These are the questions that need to be asked while designing characters that are believable in their differences. Not all differences in personality balance each other out. Some combinations are a gunpowder barrel just about to explode. It already starts with the simple shape language of

Figure 5.10

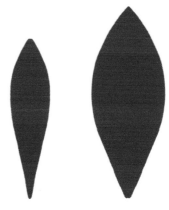

Figure 5.11

the characters that can either, like in Figures 5.10 and 5.11, be very similar in both characters or can oppose. There is no right or wrong; there is only a decision that visualizes the character's direction.

A relationship can also include someone who is never visible in the story at all, someone who is the role model for the character. For example, a young girl's role model is Jane Goodall, the primatologist and anthropologist. How can this be made clear in the design of the girl's habitus? Of course, one needs to know Jane Goodall and/or what she actually looks like in order to make the connection. So the image of her needs to be, or could be, displayed at some point to make it clear to the audience who the girl looks up to. From then on the similarities in clothing, body shapes, hairstyle, etc., all reiterate that relationship again and again. The very idea of the girl worshipping the primatologist is then constantly apparent and fuels the story.

Apart from the intellectual relationship between the characters, there is also the physical connection between them, which is expressed through poses, vectors, and mostly through arm- and eye-directions and glances. Giambattista Tiepolo's painting of *The Death of Hyacinthus* from 1752 (Figures 5.12 and 5.13), for instance, shows the complex interaction between the characters that surround the corpse of Hyacinthus, who despite being dead still interacts with the group. Apollo, Hyacinthus' lover, is mourning over his death caused by a disc being blown to his head by the jealous wind god Zephyros. Even the marble herm in the back is looking

down at the dead young man. The parrot's tail is also pointing directly at Hyacinthus' head. All the characters are related to each other and thus create a manifold system where the eye wanders through the picture and is in constant movement. One can feel the stir and commotion in the group due to the drama that unfolds in front of them.

Relationship with the environment and objects

Characters also need to relate to their environment, to make it clear that they are not just pasted into the scene, but are part of it, that is, they live and breathe in it. Characters need to interact with someone or something, which can be their surroundings (visible or invisible), on- or off-screen space, or a prop or an object. As long as there is an interaction or a focal point for the character's attention, the action in the pictorial realm invites the viewer in and allows the character to be an illusion of life, because the character is part of the realm the viewer is participating in. Figure 5.14 has the character looking at their buddy's hat. The hat itself reminds us of the friend. There is a close bond between character and hat. Figure 5.15 however has the character holding the hat, which creates the already mentioned connection, but also has the character looking off-screen, telling us that he is looking for a friend who is outside our visual field. Including the off-screen space already starts an interesting story because it keeps us guessing and there is suspense. The simplest way the environment can

Figure 5.12

Giambattista Tiepolo *The Death of Hyacinth* (Courtesy of Wikimedia Commons).

Figure 5.13

Figure 5.14

Figure 5.15

Figure 5.16

be included is in the form of light and shadow to suggest that there is something in the off-screen space, but I prefer not to show it like in Figure 5.16. If there is a shadow, then logically there has to be a light source and an object that casts the shadow. It gives the image depth and expands the on-screen space.

The relationship between character and environment is always a very close one. The character fits into the environment, is part of it, or is not at all. A horse in a cinema, for instance, does not seem very realistic, which is exactly why it is interesting. The relationship between the two makes the situation unique and the question is apparent—what does that horse do in the cinema?

The environment also shapes the character of Robinson Crusoe. He looks like he is living off nature, creating his clothing out of plants and animal skin, and also from tattered remains of the ship's salvage. The relationship has to be clear not only in what that character is actually doing in his environment, how he fits and relates to it, but also how the environment in turn affects the character. This is a crucial relationship as it often touches upon the basics of the story and reiterates its very foundation.

The character that relates to the off-screen space is also showing a social awareness even if it is a negative one as in the picture of the man with the umbrella (Figure 5.17). The character looks at the umbrella and holds it similar to a weapon. But he turning his head to the left, but glancing to the right, makes it seem like he is up to something. One would expect outside the frame is his victim, who is not yet aware of the tragedy that will unveil. If the character would just look into empty space, the impact of the image would be a very different one. But because there is focus and concentration on the umbrella, his evil thoughts do come across. The relationship between man → umbrella → off-screen space (possibly the victim) creates a sentence that one can read from left to right: angry man + and umbrella that is held upside down = probably a bloody mess.

Figure 5.17

CHAPTER 6

Emotions

Story in animation is the basis of everything. All is story—however, emotions are the foundation for a story and it draws upon the audience's empathy, and characters' actions are always based on their emotions. Everything we do in animation and image-making is about emotions. It is not only that we evoke emotions in the viewer, but we also use emotions to create our artwork. Every brush stroke and line, every color and shape is a visualization of an emotion that the artist felt at that very moment in time or tried to convey through their art. The artist's job is to interpret a specific moment of a story or an aspect of a character's personality and visualize it in a new and unique way that the audience may not have seen before. By remembering the emotions from the past or by putting oneself into the mind of the character, the artist's felt emotion is then interpreted into lines, colors, and shapes. The outcome is turned into the medium of drawing, painting, or film and is spawning that same emotion in the viewer in reverse, if things go as planned. By being able, as an artist, to translate the felt emotion into lines, shapes and forms, colors and story, and inventing a personality for the character, those characters are able to start breathing on screen and turn into unique and convincing living beings that the audience believes in. I'm using the word "inventing" as it is so much easier to copy an existing cliché personality instead of looking into the character's true psychological complexity and inventing a visual interpretation instead of recreating an existing one. The same is true for not only the characters but also the environment as it comes with a personality. The character and their environment always coexist and affect each other. For example, the scene requires a sunset because the character is at the end of one difficult task; the evening stands as the successful end of one task. One could easily create a sunset with the typical red sky and would be done with. That would obviously work—the audience would get the point and everything is peachy. However, is the color of the setting sun, its shape, the composition, and overall mood exactly visualizing the emotion that the character is going through? Is it the *right* interpretation of the emotions instead of just a representation of a common sunset? The audience can only reconstruct what the character is truly feeling if it is shown on screen. We cannot just explain in words what the character is emotionally going through; therefore, the only way is to show it in the character's movements and of course the design of the background, plus music and sound. For example, if the character is happy during the sunset to have successfully finished the given task, but there is also a hint of sadness because of the price they had to pay to finish the given task (by losing a friend on the way, for instance), then the sunset should also include this sadness and express that "every success comes with a price." The typical color of deep red for a sunset could maybe shift to a slightly different tone that isn't expressing pure happiness, and obviously needs to be expanded through all the other aspects of design. This enlarges the character's emotional

Figure 6.1

DOI: 10.1201/b22147-6

starts talking. The moment is ruined and the emotion becomes cheap and disappears. The words interrupt the audience's very personal connection with the characters on an emotional and visual level instead of on an intellectual level. Why did the film makers interrupt this lyrical scene with dialogue? What happened is that the emotions that were already doing their job were rationalized and ruined, instead of allowing the image to speak for itself and let the audience enjoy the moment.

Much of animation is fixated on the action of the storyline and what the characters are doing. Often the thoughtful moments in between are missing or are, like in the scene just described from *Wall-E*, ruined by too much verbal information. The audience does not necessarily have to be spoon-fed in order to understand what is happening on the screen. Quite the contrary: if there are some points left open that keep elements of the character's personality a secret or even question the character, it can be exciting, because the audience's mind is kept awake with questions. The audience is actually an active part in the experience, not just a passive observer. Not everything needs to be fully explained on screen to the last detail; the audience isn't usually stupid.

Characters and emotions

Emotions in characters are often contradicting themselves and are seldom one-dimensional. A current situation that evokes an emotion in the character is filled with past memories of happiness and loss, anger and shame, all mingled together in an amalgam of feelings. To make it even more complex, it is also infused with future wishes and fears. The visualization of those complex patchworks of thoughts and dreams, memories, and wishes that the character is going through is one aspect that makes film such a powerful and strong tool. Film can interpret and can freely play with all of the aspects of graphics, timing, editing, music, and sound. Additionally, in animation anything is possible and any kind of emotion can be interpreted (not truly represented, but interpreted through exaggeration), and thus it can affect not only the consciousness of the viewer but also the subconsciousness in the perfect instance.

Emotions take time to evolve and spread within the viewer. It is not too difficult for the emotions to be superficially recognized as what they are, to be understood in terms of what the character at that very moment is feeling. It is, however, not enough to just understand that the character is going through those emotions, but time needs to be given to the viewer to feel these emotions themselves and become one with the character on screen, to develop empathy, not just sympathy. Much of the animation usually does not allow this time and thus the viewer often just watches the happenings on screen, is blinded by the never-ending action, and does not fully immerse in the emotional complexities and subtleties of the characters' true and complex personalities. The silent moments in a film, the quiet frames where nothing happens, where characters just stare, stand,

range not only through the story but also through the design of the background, which reflects the emotional depth of the character. The complex emotions are then infused into the setting and the entire mood of the shot, which is not only expressed by the character, but also through everything else in the image. The mood of the scene has a huge impact on the emotions felt by the audience, emotions that are not always easy to portray through the character alone.

However, one needs to be very careful with expressing emotions as just little things here and there can totally ruin the perfect mood. In Pixar's feature *Wall-E,* we see at one point Wall-E and Eve flying and dancing through space, being watched by a couple of humans from a spaceship. The emotions of this scene are stunning and without words the audience clearly understands the connection between the two robots and their joy. We are sharing that special moment with the two and it is a visual feast that connects the viewer intensively with the characters on screen ... until one of the humans in the spaceship glance, and communicate quietly with each other; moments of nature, clouds, or an overall simple mood push for these emotions to become real in the viewer because these moments allow the viewer to think and reflect on the character's thoughts. That does not mean that the image itself needs to be quiet, it can still be an action-filled image. Silence and contemplation can come in many forms. What is needed is a quiet or surreal moment that elevates the film image onto a level that allows the audience to feel, to think, to inhale the emotions and be enveloped in them, and to let them breathe. The moment in Katsuhiro Otomo's *Akira* (1988), when Tetsuo turned into this gigantic blob of meat and body fluids, the action is at a high point. Afterward, to contrast this thrilling scene, Akira appears to take Tetsuo with him and the action is mostly quiet as it is the moment when we understand the relationship between Kaneda and Tetsuo—how they met, and their troubled yet intense friendship. Because the visuals are so overwhelming at times in those action scenes, the silence or near silence helps tremendously to focus on the emotion between the two characters instead of just the action. The silence has an impact on the moment itself, which is heightened and clearly marked as being important, being a moment of life-changing significance. But it is also leaving room for the mind to wander and not being overwhelmed by sound that clearly connects with the action on screen and drags most of the attention. Having non-diegetic sound (sound that does not originate from the source on screen) can make the scene feel surreal and create room for the mind to wander and also for emotions to be felt.

The films of Terrence Malick are an exceptional example of these quiet moments being spread throughout the film constantly. Scenes are often compiled of silence and mood, resulting in films of philosophical and spiritual grandeur. Malick does not rely on what people say and do, but the moments in between in which they think, stand, contemplate, and just are, which are equally significant if not even more so. Additionally, he intersperses his scenes with moments of nature and environment, which in their silence and serenity not only add a level of spiritualism and lift the scenes from the real to the surreal, but also provide the needed space for the viewer to feel and immerse themselves in the moment. Malick often stops time and invites contemplation with the characters for a precious moment. Everything turns into shared emotions.

Those quiet moments are important to follow the character's true emotions in their complexity, not just their superficiality. A character, a headhunter, for instance, takes a train from Moscow to Harbin to find someone he needs to eliminate. The question is, however, what happens in between Moscow and Harbin and what is the emotional drive of the character to actually go from Russia to China to find that someone. How does the long trip change him, how does it affect his emotional foundation? At the end of the trip does he still need to find that someone or has the trip and with it his emotional journey made that goal obsolete because the headhunter has changed for the

better? What is important is that his emotions are visualized, not just the action. Emotions not just in a simple way but in a complex way portray him as a character with a believable personality, a past with probably meaningful social connections, and not just as a simple thoughtless killing machine. There is often one significant moment in a story that is the culmination of the character's understanding of not what he wants, but an understanding of what he needs for him to reach a higher level of being. Those moments are obviously extremely important as they express the realization of his own flaws and are often the turning point in the story; they are loaded with emotions that need to be visualized. The seemingly empty, yet crucial moments invite the viewer's mind to rest and step into the emotional turmoil of the protagonist. Those moments do not necessarily have to be fully explained, but the audience can understand what the character is thinking and feeling if the visuals lead the way and time is given that allows the emotions to settle in. Through those quiet moments an important connection between audience, character, and environment is established,

with the character, we need to create believable personalities and with it emotions that the audience can relate to. We know that killing someone is obviously wrong. We assume that if the headhunter kills someone, there must be some kind of emotional reaction on his side for him to appear human and not like a mindless, monstrous robot or seriously disturbed psychopath. Small additions in his personality or in the story itself can trigger thoughts in the audience that linger on for the entire film if fuelled once in a while. For example, he kills a 35-year-old man with a moustache. Whenever he sees another man with a moustache, the camera just stays on the hunter's face a little bit longer, maybe slightly zooming in, in order to suggest him thinking, remembering … the audience assumes that he is now feeling regret for having killed a man. The killer is shown as having some kind of emotion, which opens up a huge box of story points and also makes the character more relatable because he is now slightly more human. However, if any time there is a man on the street that has a moustache and the camera shows him and follows him just for a moment, then cuts back to the face of the headhunter who does not react at all, does not even register the young man, then his emotions are not affected at all, which means he is emotionally empty. It is the little additions in between that stir up the thoughts of the audience and keep the suspense.

Emotions during the drawing process

Emotions are crucial! When drawing a sad character you need to feel that sadness, indulge in the emotions that the character is feeling. You need to know why that character is sad and how in that very moment the character deals with their sadness. It is not just "sad," it is the reason behind the sadness, the extent of it, and the relationships that lead to that emotion in the first place. When I draw the character, I am the character at that moment and I get into the character's emotions to the point where it really hurts, where you are really happy or strong, weak or courageous. You feel it yourself and then translate those feelings into lines and colors. This does not mean that every drawing one makes is successfully expressing those feelings felt that the audience clearly can feel themselves the artist's grief, happiness, or joy. But it is an important tool on the side of the artist to *be* the character and, while drawing, have a flow of ideas that support that mood.

which lasts and gives a movie grandeur and a cinematic scope that goes far beyond the scale of much of animation's often universe-shattering action scenes chasing each other. True emotions are not created by explosions, guns, and never-ending action scenes but through comprehensible and human relationships that are always based on emotions.

The character that is a headhunter and kills for a living is one that people probably have problems relating to as most of us have not taken a life for no reason other than money. In order to make the audience believe in the story and the protagonist's emotional journey, and maybe even identify

CHAPTER 7

Message or Theme

Most film is entertainment and entertainment is in the first place a product (whether we artists like it or not), which costs money and needs to make money back. And animation is unfortunately not the exception—quite the contrary, it is extremely expensive. In its most positive outcome, animation can also turn into a piece that not only entertains but also expresses a sophisticated opinion or message. Film is an art form and thus has in its developed form something to say, a moral, a message, or a thought. But it also has a theme on which the whole story is based—and there can be more than one theme in a film. There is a difference between a theme and a message. The theme is what the story is about, its topic, a recurring idea (e.g., in music), whereas the message is what that topic expresses and means on a personal case study, what conclusion the audience can draw from the piece. The message or moral is at the end of the fairy tale and wraps up with what the listener has learned from the story; the theme, on the contrary, is continuous throughout the story being pointed at again. The message does not necessarily have to be blunt and obvious—it can be subtle and unassuming. If the artist chooses for the film to have a message, it is obviously a personal decision. It would be advantageous if the message is a humane one and represents a positive moral. *E.T. the Extra-terrestrial*'s theme, for example could, be "love," whereas its message is "friendship overcomes everything." The theme appears throughout the film and Elliot grows up in a household where love is absent. The father has left, the mother is too busy with herself and overwhelmed, which is juxtaposed with the love that Elliot develops toward *E.T.* Neither theme nor message is always positive; there have been controversial pieces of film produced whose messages are less than satisfying from a moral perspective, however their fame derives from technical and artistic accomplishments. For example, Leni Riefenstahl's features *Triumph des Willens* (1935) and *Olympia* (1938) are considered technical achievements (and also artistic and aesthetic) of the highest level. The content and theme they deal with, the celebration of the Nazi party in Germany in the 1930s or the Berlin Olympics in 1936, are nonetheless dubious to say the least. There can be a significant gap between the art and its message. However, a message and theme greatly assist the production and the overall logic of storytelling and design if all elements express one idea and follow one theme (or more if that can be controlled). Both help to organize the flood of ideas to be controlled and reduced, by throwing out those ideas that do not support theme or message.

"Add not a single component to the mix which cannot contribute to your central character's dilemma, further the conflict, or intensify his or her struggle."[1] This statement, written for screenwriting, also fits very much the process of visual development. The more ideas, the easier it is to find the ones that make the project unique. Too few ideas and one easily gets stuck with clichés. A theme and message make it much easier for those ideas that bring the story forward to crystallize and then represent what is needed, instead of what is distracting for the overall clarity of the story and design.

Every story should contain a message that sums up what the story is *actually* about. The events are there to bring the plot forward and get the protagonist closer toward the goal.

---

[1] McLaughlin B. (1997). *The Playwright's Process, Learning the Craft from Today's Leading Dramatists.* New York, WA: Back Stage Books, p. 26.

DOI: 10.1201/b22147-7

If the actions are not related to the character's path, why include them into the story? The most popular word for students to use when describing plot ideas is always the word *just*: the character is *just* experiencing it. But what is the reason for the character either being exposed to a specific situation or reacting to it? The reason for any event to be included in the story and the character then being exposed to it has to relate to the theme of the story and, subsequently, how the events affect the progress of the character's journey. All events will affect the emotional struggle and have to have a purpose for their existence. How does an event push the story forward and push the character toward the goal or away from it? The theme and message determine the reasons for these events to be included so that the character will be forced on this path. It also gives explanations for why it is important for the character to go down a certain path instead of choosing another.

Pinocchio's theme, for instance, is "growing up." Everything that happens in the story is Pinocchio being exposed to simple temptations that he has to learn to avoid, which he doesn't of course because the point of the story is for him having to learn the lesson the hard way. He has to fail the first temptations in order to learn what the moral of the story is: only selflessness means truly being a human.

It is sometimes difficult to decide what action the character should take and where it all leads toward; but when the theme and message are established, it does make it easier to decide *for* the character, as both can demand a certain action that needs to happen for the character to stay on the path leading toward the moral. If the reason is a highly intellectual framework or just a simple statement does not matter as long as there is a thought or statement. For example, the message of a film is

"War is pointless." The theme would be set during World War II. The story that develops and grows out of this statement will express the beliefs of the writer(s), director, and artists that make creative decisions to develop the story (as long as they consciously and thoughtfully developed the characters and their actions follow the theme). They will have to make decisions for the characters whether to perform the right or wrong actions. Those actions will naturally follow their beliefs and the resulting story will hopefully express "War is pointless." If the characters join the army excitedly and their actions in the story, as well as their emotional development, are pro-war, the initial theme might not come across, but the opposite theme—"War is actually pretty awesome." To let the characters perform against the theme could of course be an artistic device to let the audience question the impact that the excitement of war itself can have on a young person and therefore question the system of war in general. This in turn can again lead to "War is pointless" if the actions of the main character are morally questionable or destructive to themselves and/or their surroundings. Therefore, having a theme from the beginning will shape the characters and the development of the story.

During the writing process, of course the theme can change because the characters will develop in their personalities and might no longer fit the initial theme. One might realize what the story is *actually* about after having dealt with it for weeks. The theme and message not only shape the story and the characters, but will also shape the design of the characters and the design of the world itself. In the case of "War is pointless," there are various options:

- The design shows the catastrophic side of war and presents the war machine in a negative and destructive way. An example is Roman Polanski's feature *The Pianist* (2002) with slightly desaturated colors and strong contrasts, giving the images a clearly negative tint.
- The design shows the thrilling side of war and how the characters are excited about joining, then the war machine could be shown in a strong and forceful way. In the end, however, the story needs to express the message clearly that "War is pointless" without the design being so exciting and thrilling that it threatens to overwrite the actual message. An example is Paul Verhoeven's *Starship Troopers* (1997), a sci-fi satire that uses fascist design and aesthetics for its theme of "War makes fascists of all of us."[2] The design is exciting and the look is stimulating the viewer in supporting the cause; however, it is pushed so far that an uncomfortable feeling creeps in that then makes one question one's initial approval.
- The design shows the war machine in a neutral way and allows the audience to follow the story without being too affected by the design, thus making up their own mind.

2 Verhoeven P. (1997). *Starship Troopers*, DVD Commentary.

An example is Oliver Stone's feature *Born on the Fourth of July* (1989), which has visuals that steer toward realism (somehow) to allow the audience to feel the brutal reality of war.

- It is therefore the spanning theme and concluding message that affect the entire universe of the film, story, and design. The theme or message does not need to be the subject of the discussions between the characters, but can be an overall blanket that covers the film yet is never mentioned as such. Nevertheless, no other topic should ever take over and dilute the theme!

- The characters and those personality traits they are struggling with are often contrary to the theme, to create tension. If the theme is "fight for your own self-confidence," the main character would most likely have a lack of confidence and will discover their self-confidence and learn to stand up for themselves throughout the story.

CHAPTER 8

Research and Concept

The three steps of the visual development process

There are three different fields for visual development: character design, environment design, and effects design. All three need to follow the same design concept and speak the same design language in order to create a world that is believable in itself. There is however, in all three fields, a process of three steps that help to streamline the production: research—concept—design. The first two, research and concept are dealt with in this chapter. The rest of this book will focus on design.

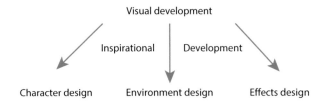

1. Research and inspirational development

In this first and very important step you build the fundament for your following work. In order to learn something about the topic your film is based on, you have to research it. Take this step seriously, since it provides you with the most important tools for the visual development process: ideas. It doesn't matter how creative we are, at some point we have to widen our knowledge about the world that surrounds us. Our mind is not big enough to keep and store all the possible images and information needed to create inspirational artwork for any topic. The vast amount of landscapes on earth, the amount of fauna and flora, the sheer endless variations of characters are impossible to remember in detail by one human mind. Therefore, every time you start a new project, use the research time to study thoroughly. It will strengthen your work and provide you with valuable ideas. Without the proper research you will fall back on ideas that are clichés rather than unique artwork, and you definitely want your images to differ from other projects and/or artists.

Make searching for unusual images, compositions, color-combinations, characters, animals, architecture, landscapes, artwork, and so on a habit of your daily work. Every time you see something that strikes you in one way or another, copy the image and create a folder for it on your computer. Name your folders so it is easy for you to find the images again when you need them. Having a library of unique visuals is immensely helpful.

Explore the topic through research

As I mentioned above, research is essential in the beginning of every project. We don't know all the details of the project's topic and we don't know about the specifics if we don't research them. Don't just assume that you know everything about the given task! Make yourself acquainted with the surroundings that are mentioned in the script, the characters, the flora and fauna, and educate yourself in every possible way. Read about the topic, collect images, listen to music that fuels your creativity, and watch movies to enrich your knowledge and visual library. If it helps you creatively to eat the food of the country you base your designs on, do it. Everything that spurs your imagination and creativity is worth exploring. This is a very important step, because everything that follows is based on your research and how thoroughly you dove into the topic. If the foundation is weak, the house you build on top is not going to be very stable either. Use your curiosity and research for a couple of days or more if necessary. It will help the whole project by not just giving you knowledge but by helping you with shapes and colors, textures, and so on. Use the research as an exciting task, where you find something interesting in even the driest of topics. It is your job as the artist to sell the topic visually to the audience and if you are not interested in creating that world, how could you make the audience care?

Examine multiple styles and designs to cover the broadest range of design options. Search for comics, illustrations, movies, books, paintings, and artwork of all kinds to broaden your range of design and style possibilities for the project. After a couple of days of dealing with the topic, you will get a feeling of what would actually fit the project and what would not.

All of us draw and design a certain way which is mostly limited to one style we like or one that we are used to (or even one that is right now in vogue). Out of habit, we have a range of images in our mind that we always fall back on. It is therefore crucial to expand that source of images before every project and consciously design in various styles. Searching for styles, of course, doesn't mean to copy the style of other artists, it means to use it as inspiration for the possibilities that are out there. It is the task of the designer to develop a style that looks new and takes the latest movies into consideration, yet doesn't copy them! You don't want to design a film that looks like it's 15 years old. That would defeat the purpose of getting people to want to see your film (however, using old design as the basis can sometimes be part of the overall concept of the film). Also copying the look of existing movies or artists seems pointless. If it has already been done and the audience has seen it, why do it again? Why not try something new?

DOI: 10.1201/b22147-8

Explore styles in your artwork

During your inspirational development phase you should create different designs that explore the various stylistic possibilities of the topic, rather than presenting just one design or one style. In the first stage of the design, the artwork is created for inspiration. It is not just the search for the final characters' or locations' look, more the search for options of its personality, attitude, or mood. So use the time and have fun exploring. The first drawing might be the one you will finally use, but that happens very rarely and often you find the right character by chance. It is better to have various characters to choose from, as that gives you options to see which one is right for the project and what style fits the story. By exploring the character you actually think about their personality—past, present, and future. Every new drawing you make opens up another personality trait or side of the character that you might want to use in your final piece. Sometimes, you need to go through hundreds of characters to find the right one; one character suggestion is just that: one. Multiple characters open up a discussion of which one is "the one."

The goal of this part of inspirational development is to have a new and unique design. It is not recommended to settle with a look that reminds you of existing designs. From the beginning, you should always aspire to create a new look that only fits this one project. Of course, it is difficult to come up with a completely new look that no one has seen before. We always base our artwork on something that we like and admire. Yet it shouldn't be a blunt copy of that style, but an interpretation of it. Put in your own personality and be unique.

Literal and visual approach of research

Find words that describe the character and its environment: those terms might help you to come up with design ideas (the character or the landscape might be described as old, new, wet, big, tiny, rough, tasty, green, tight, leathery, slippery, hairy, nervous, hesitant, etc.). Once you have a couple of terms that describe one side or personality trait of your character, think of images that remind you of those terms. For example, "wet"—I can think of water, ice, rain, a wet cloth, a mop, a wet street, an aquarium, mold, and so on. Assuming your character is "wet," you can use those images that came into your mind and combine them with the character. They might have mold everywhere, because of being moist all the time. They could have a couple of snails crawling on them at all times or they are constantly standing in a puddle of water, or smell like an old mop (it is tricky to depict "smell," yet not impossible); use the look of the old mop, for instance, and its colors and combine them with the character. Maybe their clothes have some "mop quality" to them in terms of their textures. The possibilities are endless. What is so important when you deal with images is that one image connects to another and another, and so on to infinity. With just one term you can create an infinite number of visual connections, a network of ideas that will definitely enrich your designs.

Terms

VisDev:
Visual development

Inspirational character development:
Sketches and artwork that suggests what the look of the characters could be. Those drawings are often just quick sketches that give you an idea of the character. They have the purpose to spur the imagination and serve as inspiration for the film team.

Inspirational sketches:
Character sketches, background sketches, sketches with gags, or situations that are inspirational for the team and enrich the project visually and storywise.

Visual development artwork:
All the artwork that is done for the movie, including the inspirational artwork.

Character design:
All the artwork that is done for the design of the characters, including turnarounds and facial expressions.

Character development:
All the artwork that leads to the look of the characters.

Find images that contain the look, the mood, color, or any other quality that might represent aspects of the character or environment you are working on: whatever you find could inspire you to make a connection between the project and the image. But don't limit yourself to the obvious. Try to be creative in this stage and look for images that not just show the obvious but also represent an intellectual idea. Many images are not just about what you see, but there is a subtext in the image that can tell a totally different story of what you might expect at first sight. Start thinking about what the final film could feel like and how you could enhance its content, but never just think of this final image as the only option. Be open to changes and creative solutions!

Examples:

The character is supposed to be "fast"—look at racing cars, motorbikes, racing outfits; some of those designs could be used in your character to describe them as fast. Use, for example, design ideas from racetrack suits and integrate them into the character's clothes. Most people know the look of racing cars and racing outfits and this might help them to quickly grasp that side of the character. The audience has to understand immediately that the character is fast. There is not enough time for them to figure things out slowly, because the next information for the story is just a cut and another shot away.

The character is "old"—look at objects that are old and how they changed their appearance with age. They get scratched, are dusty, they lose parts, the colors fade, they sound different, etc. Research old architecture and understand what it is that makes it look old. Why does Angkor Wat look so ancient? Imagine which of those qualities you could use for an old character and how they become more and more interesting and exciting as a personality by adding more visually. The advantage of it is also that you create a character rather than produce a cliché of an already existing one.

Be creative with your mind

When you do the research for a tree, for instance, don't just look for trees but look for something that might resemble a tree: a broccoli or a strangely shaped snow crystal. As I mentioned above, make connections and combine images in your mind that might not fit each other immediately but they will surely spur your creativity. The broccoli tree looks already delicious in my mind and the snow crystal tree looks cold. You have to train your mind to make connections and let your imagination explore the possibilities. Train yourself in combining various aspects of images and see what happens with them once you connect them.

For example: Try to see with your inner eye the combination of the two words "skyscraper" and "fur" … what does a furry skyscraper look like? Close your eyes and concentrate on that image. Let that image evolve, and really see and feel it. What kind of fur did you use to dress the outer surface of the skyscraper with? Is it just on the outside of the building or inside, too? Is it fluffy fur or short fur, dry or oily, short or long, smooth or rough, is the fur dark-colored at the shaft of the hair and light colored on top, warm, or cold, does it smell clean or dirty?

Once you can actually feel the image, change the shape of the skyscraper in your mind: recall famous buildings you know and cover them with various kinds of fur. When you have in your mind the building you like, then just add details to it—colors, moods, furniture, or elements like water or earth. Imagine yourself walking through that furry place and how this would feel on your naked feet. How soft is the ground, how does it feel to touch the walls, how does it smell? Practice the use of your imagination and just change the details once you are walking through that imaginary world in your mind. Maybe the walls are alive and are slightly moving, breathing … an endless stream of images is going through your mind once you let that movie play and develop itself. Animation is a medium that knows no visual boundaries: use it!

Aside from the visuals, emotions are a very important part of this exercise. They are essential in every stage of image-making and should never be forgotten. Every environment and character gives us a specific feeling based on experience, and all those emotions can be used in the images that we create. It's up to the designer to bring those feelings to the surface and use them as ideas in the artwork. Emotions, though, are obviously subjective and easily allow critique.

The only necessary setup for this practice is a quiet space where you can relax and forget the environment around you.

You have to be able to close your eyes and see the images with your inner eye. Every distraction can prohibit you from concentrating and thus you lose those connections between images that are so important for creativity. With some practice you don't even have to close your eyes anymore, you can just see it.

This stream of consciousness approach is another valid source for you to explore the visual options. When you have thought about your project for quite a while and you feel visually stuck, it is helpful to step back and let the brain just go wild a little. It can be fascinating what your brain comes up with on its own without you interfering with logical thoughts.

The goal of this exercise is not to get exactly the image you imagined onto paper, but to get a feeling for the environment and collect ideas. The end result might be different from what you expected, but it made you look at the project from a different angle and perspective, and that is always beneficial.

Scientific accuracy or the lack of it

Read about the topic from a scientific standpoint to comprehend its complexity. Too much information can hinder creativity, but no knowledge at all can also be dangerous for the outcome. There has to be a balance of both and the final product should

show that you acquired some knowledge about the topic you have been working on. You don't want people in the audience to question your interpretation and teach you about what is wrong in your work. If you should make the decision that you want to ignore the scientific truth for whatever reason, that of course is absolutely valid; but always have a reason for why you do that and give hints in the movie that show that. Without that reason the audience might not be convinced of your decision of neglecting scientific accuracy. If you decide that your character can breathe in outer space or underwater—show why. You don't have to go into elaborate explanations and long storylines; the right character design might already tell you the abilities of the character and the explanation is visually there. Most movies deal with Earth or suggest places we can imagine with the physical laws already imbedded within our own. If gravity is turned off all of a sudden, you would have to give some clue of why that is. If magic suddenly happens, you have to tell the audience why and where it came from. It is not always sufficient to have the "magical glowing stone" solve the problem.

All visuals that you created seem obvious to you who is familiar with the world, because you already have it finished in your mind. The audience has no clue yet and needs plausible explanations to fully understand the scope of your world. Otherwise they will not grasp the story or the characters. There are certain stories though where everything is possible and the scientific truth just doesn't exist. No one really asks why there is a seashore and a beach in Bikini Bottom in SpongeBob's crazy world. It's a shore underwater, which of course doesn't make any sense whatsoever. But we already know that a talking sponge, who works in a burger joint on the bottom of the ocean doesn't make any sense from a scientific standpoint to begin with, so we do know that in this show the world is upside down.

Searching for correct information is not as easy as it seems. The Internet is a huge source of information, which does not mean it is always the correct information. Be careful which web pages you use for your research. Many pages seem informative, but don't always contain scientifically correct information. Just be careful and use sources that are trustworthy. The same of course is true for libraries. Always double check every point! I personally love Wikipedia. I know that not everything on it is correct, but I can double check and it gives me a good overview that I can then build my research on.

Other creative possibilities
Every artist has different methods of spurring their creativity. Try out different approaches and practice your very own creativity. Ideas are seldom a product of the moment, but a result of visual thinking, that, practiced every day, evolves into a habit. Some people practice seeing shapes and characters in spots on the wall or clouds, other artists like to search for ideas while drawing or painting in sketchbooks, others like to roam through libraries or make collages with magazine cutouts.

There are many ways of practicing your creativity and over time you will learn what helps you to be creative, and you will use it to its full capacity. Wherever you go, look at shapes and colors, objects, and people. Go through your daily life while exploring your known surroundings anew and see the world in a different way. Try to find the extraordinary in the ordinary and lift reality to a new level. See the world from a different perspective, literally—climb under the table and discover how the room looks like from underneath. Be playful and allow yourself to be a child!

You can use all these discoveries in your own work and make your art more interesting and personal. Visual artists should present the world that surrounds them in a different light and question the environment and its people, its politics and morals, and create artwork that makes the audience think and see their environment anew.

Story and research
While doing the research always have your story in mind and imagine how you could use those inspirational sources you are studying to improve the very story you are working on (if of course you are in the job position to do that). When you look at the actual environments in your research, they might give you clues for new story developments or in reverse, question parts in your story that are not convincing yet. Your story should not be a fixed chunk of concrete that you have to turn into images at all costs. If the script just doesn't work because of some visual problems that occur, think of creative ways to either solve the problem or make changes in the script accordingly. Get rid of the parts in your script that don't make sense or don't seem to fit in either the characters or the location. It is very easy to fall in love with elements you have created and therefore not be able to change them or get rid of them entirely. If it doesn't work, cut it out or change it! It can be very, very liberating!

Be personal
Always aspire to personal work. There is the time to appreciate the quality in other artists' work. Using qualities of their art in your own helps you to grasp design and through it, learn. But there is a difference between being inspired and copying. You can only develop as an artist if you think like an artist, which means that aspiring to the extraordinary and new is a goal you should set for yourself. Always seek out the images that bring something new to the world, a new view onto life, be it reality or fantasy, something people have not yet seen. In my opinion, art is only then art when it tries to create a direction that gives the known imagery a twist into the unknown or unexpected, and explores new visual and intellectual ground. Many artists produce huge amounts of work and every piece looks exactly like the work of another famous artist. Every image is stylistically a copy of someone else's work. There is the danger that there is nothing personal in their work. It is all technically perfect and the visuals look beautiful, but there is no personal statement in the work, no development that shows an intellectual

debate—the work is all surface, but no content. Do strive for personality and uniqueness. Unfortunately we cannot all be unique. There is always a struggle between, on the one hand, learning the trade of animation and its different techniques and using all that knowledge in a production, and on the other hand, developing your own personal expression in art where you explore your own personality and position in society. Both are very difficult tasks that take years of training and learning, thinking, and creating. Only if you explore the unknown will you have a lifelong task in front of you that keeps you creating and producing. If you copy a style or imitate a fashionable trend you will at some point run out of possibilities, since this trend will surely pass as a new trend is always around the next corner. That is why you have to learn how to be creative and how to develop a direction instead of copying a design. You have to learn the foundation of design and how to control it instead of relying on the visuals of others to provide you with inspiration. How to keep your own interest in the field of animation and art alive and how to explore and continuously create is not an easy task at all. Visual development, because of its complexity, needs to be practiced and learned, needs to be constantly adjusted anew to its time and to the development in art, film, comics, etc., and of course to your own interests and where you stand with your artistic opinions at that point in your life. The other possibility is that you don't care about all of that and you just create what you want to see despite what everyone else thinks. It's supposed to be art: so go for it!

2. Concept

The difficulty in a feature project as much as in a short film is to not get lost in details. There are so many scenes and characters, a vast amount of backgrounds, and keeping the overview is a real task. Furthermore, to develop a look that is consistent throughout the scenes and consistent in every detail is yet another matter. In order to achieve that successfully, you need to establish rules that set the tone of the film and the direction of the design. This is the role of the concept, which establishes ground rules for the film in a very simple and basic form. The concept is used for an early pitch in an animation studio, to get the idea of the film across. It is accompanied by some artwork, some character descriptions, and a short storyline containing the main characters' paths and challenges. But it also contains the purpose of the film, the message and the "why." Why is this film being made? What is the purpose of the character's journey? The concept will be refined further during the early stages of the development. It explains in more detail what the film would contain, the locations, the main characters, the stylistic direction, and its overall look (nevertheless, later on the design bible, style guide, or design book will contain the final list of rules of the film's design and how to achieve it—how the composition works, how the characters are to be designed, what the props look like. With the design bible in hand one should be able to design the entire feature). As the concept is just the starting point of your

design process, those rules of course are vague and not set in stone yet, but possible options. The concept contains only a framework of what the world that you will create needs. After you have researched the topic and narrowed down your choices of visuals, you decide on a couple of images that you think are a good starting point for the look and mood of the film. Dissecting those images and finding out what makes them feel right is the first step toward the concept. The purpose is to see the film as a whole project with its stretching arc, not just its single scenes. What is the overall mood of your film? What is the broad direction? These are very simple questions, but they have to be answered in order to set up a foundation for your design: the style for the whole film. Having a concept supports the decision-making on every level of the production. It helps to channel your ideas and form one solid and logical plan, which is based on an intellectual groundwork. It mainly deals with the intellectual content of your story and how you can visualize it. In this stage, you question every part of your story idea and find explanations for all the questions arising. You try to create a world, which makes sense in itself and is a logical creation. The concept should be solid and help you to avoid flaws in your content, which are difficult to correct later on. It should serve as a guideline for your work, in which everything fits and where everything follows the rules you established for your film.

Things to consider for the concept:

- What is your main idea? Find one idea/moral/sentence or theme that is representative of what you want to say with your work. Cut everything else and concentrate on that one idea. For example:
    1. Pinocchio: Selflessness leads to being truly human.
    2. Spirited Away: Grow up and find your true self.
    3. ParaNorman: Accept people for who they are.
- Create an intellectual basis for your idea: think about your work not just in a visual way. Remember that all images contain, aside from the obvious, other levels of information. The same is true of course for every other aspect in a film.
- Channel your thoughts: go through all your initial ideas and your research library and find those ideas which are the strongest, which fit together, and make sense in their relations.
- Ask and answer questions about your story idea: the main question is always "why?"
- Create characters that make sense in their personality and their actions.
- Find reasons for these actions.
- Find visual explanations for your story and for your characters; how would the characters/environment look and why? How does the environment influence your characters and vice versa?
- Constantly ask questions and base your concept on logic that follows the logic of that specific world you are creating (even if your main idea is to have no logic, then that is your concept).

- Make connections between visuals, storyline, and characters.
- Have visuals that help the story to be understood and try to keep things simple.
- The look of the environment should reflect the action and/or mood in the scene.
- Use environments and their habitats to support the mood of the story point.

- Think about the suspense of the storyline (climax) and how you could represent that climax visually.
- Go through all your story points and check them for necessity. Are they really important for your story? Do you really need them to get the idea across? Maybe another story point would be stronger and easier to understand?
- Technical aspects: aspect ratios, technique, length (approximately), budget, etc.

CHAPTER 9

Design Scale

The visual basics

Character design is one of the more difficult and complicated parts of the visual development process, as the characters of course draw all the attention and are usually driving the story, so they had better be very well designed to guide the audience into the plot. The characters often set the design direction and have to be unique enough to create a brand and a figurehead that can sell the movie and make the audience interested in the film in the first place. Designing a character is more a search for the character than just making one drawing, therefore you should use all options in design to create a unique character, and mold and shape it according to the script. The character should, like the story, be unique enough to surprise the audience with something new and fresh.

The predicament is to find a design that actually IS unique, speaks a design language that is contemporary and tells the audience that the film is new, exciting, and worth watching (simply from a marketing perspective). Usually the audience doesn't care too much for something that looks old-fashioned, unless it's based on a popular character like, for example, Astro boy, which was turned into a CG feature in 2009. Osamu Tezuka's character had already been an established brand for decades and brought audiences into the theater because of its fame. Nevertheless exactly due to this very fame, it cannot be changed completely in its design if used for a contemporary CG feature film. Though it can be modernized and adjusted to today's taste and technological development, the changes need to be very subtle and keep the body proportions and details very much the same. Little changes in the shapes or small adjustments in the face often go a long way in order to translate a character from either comic to CG or in Astro boy's case, a comic and TV show to CG. The audience is familiar with the look and they watch the movie with the expectation to see Astro boy, and not a very different version of him.

The process of finding that one specific character is a long and work-intensive one. For a feature or television production, the design team does not just have to design a character that they like themselves, but a character that the audience as a whole is convinced by and thus satisfied with. We cannot just trust our own judgment but have to discuss the designs with the production team in order to find that one character that speaks to everyone. Unfortunately this of course is impossible, considering we all have different tastes and want to see different aspects of the character's personality to be dominant in the final design. The outcome is one version of what the character can be, but it is never the only possible solution. Once you realize there are other options and they give you various interpretations of the character described

in the script, you and the design team can discuss to what degree certain personality traits should be visible in the design. You have many options in your visuals to describe the character and their likes, dislikes, behavior, and personality traits. Those options include shapes, textures, colors, expressions, poses, attire, and even the physical hygiene of the character. All these options help to define what kind of character the audience is dealing with. Some of this information is probably processed more on a subconscious level and not recognized by the viewer. But even if the audience doesn't see the difference, they can always feel it!

Example for game characters

Cliché soldiers are fighting alien enemies on a distant planet in the desperate attempt to survive as the last remaining humans. The focus is a highly exaggerated militaristic one, depicting the characters as überhuman soldiers that are beyond any realistic scope. The characters are very much pushed into hyperrealism to exaggerate their abilities. They are mere clichés of humans. Being overly manly, overly muscular, the soldiers are carrying guns and equipment that would drag every bodybuilder into the ground. (You get the direction: this is full cliché!) Their facial expressions are mostly an angry frown, to underline their toughness and eagerness to slay the alien villains. The point of all this is obviously to make them appear so strong as if they are actually capable of defending the entire human race on their own against the evil threat. The overly exaggerated look tells us the story of their intense military background; the scars speak of past battles and the resulting expertise in slaying, fighting, and their exceptional strategic capabilities; and their physical strength and physique is beyond a natural human body and thus excites us to see ourselves in those characters. We don't really care about the characters' subtle memories of their childhood or their love toward opera. This would be information that is distracting and out of place. The characters just present to the audience the image that fits the story and help it along, making it exciting and helping the viewer to be involved in the action. Obviously this exaggeration is a little tricky as there is no emotion involved and the characters are just there for the action, not for their emotional presence. The point is, after all, action, as banal as that might seem. However, any small hint of emotion drags the audience into the action and we start to care. If we don't care about the characters emotionally, not vote for their survival with our hearts, then we don't really care for their cause either.

Imagine one of the characters carrying a delicate bag and how that would completely change the character's personality and also the direction the story would take. Or if they would hold up a small dirty doll. The story would be a completely different one. All of a sudden we'd expect them to want to rescue a child or avenge its death, or are reminded of their own traumatizing childhood. Small details can be very significant in giving an image an edge and leading the audience into a different direction, away from the mere cliché. This is what makes characters interesting and unique, which should always be the goal.

Visualizing temperament and personality

Generally, characters are meant for animation, games, commercials, TV, or feature films and therefore will have to act, move, speak, and communicate ideas and thoughts through movement or facial expression. Characters for logos or as product mascots don't necessarily have to do that; they are designed as moving characters but not as acting characters. An acting character has to have a personality and emotions to engage. Most of the information of a character's personality will be presented by its habitus and behavior on screen, the way it is dressed and animated, its voice, timing, facial expression, etc. This is where a dilemma lies: we design a still character and need to imagine it moving, because that is what it will be doing on screen. Otherwise we'd design a bunch of corpses (the immobile kind, not the zombie variation). Showing all the different personality traits of the character in one design is obviously not possible, which doesn't mean that you as a designer should accept that some of the more specific and complex aspects of its personality can be rather tricky to translate into visuals. It is not easy to show in the character's design traits like "slightly hesitant" or "overly cautious" without presenting a cliché. You should aspire to find an interesting and unique visual representation for those personality traits that you consider important enough to be dominant in the character's look. Developing the character's personality on a literal level is helpful in the beginning of the process and asking questions about the character is crucial:

- Who is the character?
- What are its personality traits and why does it behave the way it does?
- What affected its personality?
- What is their background and how did the background shape its ideas and ideals?
- What kind of friends does it have, what kind of people does it spend time with?
- How does its personality show in its clothing?
- How does its personality show in its behavior and actions?
- What are the reasons for its actions?
- Where is it from and how does this show in its looks?

At the beginning of a production, very often the character's description is not very detailed and you have to find a direction that might fit at that point of the film's production and then develop the personality along the way. Personality is per se the actions and reactions of people to their social environment, their general genetic basis, their thoughts and beliefs, their former personal experiences, and how those affect their present actions. To check off all those points doesn't necessarily give you an interesting personality; the character itself has to be unique to spark an interest in the audience that lasts at least the amount of time they are on screen.

The challenge is to express complex personality traits of the characters in visuals. How does one express a conservative outlook on life or honesty visually without being banal? That is where an endless supply of ideas comes in handy. However there is also a rather logical approach that helps with developing ideas.

First one has to define what this actually means. Is it a conservative outlook on marriage, job, lifestyle, religious beliefs, or all of it? This does not only mean to show a bright signal that immediately points out this specific personality trait. It can be a metaphor that stands for this trait, like a color or a shape, attitude, clothing, physique, expression, poses, hairstyle, symbols, movement, personal objects, texture, or cleanliness that tells the audience who they are dealing with. Film allows to describe a character's personality through mentioned design, but also voice and dialog, music, light, composition, editing, and all other filmic possibilities to explain what is left unsaid. It is the task of the character designer to show the audience quickly who the character is and the quickest way of course is the look and feel of a character. With subtle hints here and there in the design, you can give a subliminal and subtle message. The design team has to decide which personality traits and aspects of the character need to be dominant on screen.

Shrek, for example, is an ogre that lives in a swamp. His clothes therefore are very rough and rustic and mirror his home perfectly in texture, style, and color. His hands are big and bulky, he is overall very burly, which suggests a lack of subtlety and refinement. His lack of hygiene might be suggested by his green skin color. Those combined visuals express a personality of someone that rejects change, likes his old-fashioned ways in the swamp, and is overall rather conservative and antisocial. Not only because everyone is scared of and by him, but he also just doesn't have anything in common with any of the other folks. All of Shrek's design details underline this personality and describe a character that is very different from the rest of the inhabitants of Far Far Away.

Animation is about exaggerated visuals! Exaggeration is one of the essential ingredients in animation design, to accentuate elements deemed important. Often clichés are pulled up to replace exaggeration and find an easy way around of being unique and developing a character where exaggeration follows the needs of the story. Clichés are described as "a sentence or phrase, usually expressing a popular or common thought or idea, that has lost originality, ingenuity, and impact by long overuse."[1] It is fine to use clichés as a starting point for the character and it can be helpful for quick comprehension to do so. Though if your character is just a cliché, it is uninspiring. The audience is neither surprised nor excited about a character they have seen various times before. They prefer to see a character they do understand quickly yet still has aspects in its personality and appearance that are unforeseen and uncommon. This will grab and most importantly hold their attention. The task is to find a character that is compelling and has a more complex personality than the mere cliché would provide. Clichés lack reasons, they just pretend. People are not just angry or happy or mischievous. Those personality traits are based on reasons that might be buried in the character's past. No one is angry for no apparent reason (other than the ones that are psychologically imbalanced—and even for those, the reason is that they are psychologically imbalanced). Always find the reasons for why a character acts like it does. Explore the character's personality instead of just scratching the surface. Once the reason is discovered there might be the possibility of visualizing it in the design. Nevertheless, do be careful to not get lost in too many aspects of the character's personality. Too much information is overwhelming for the audience and they might not grasp what exactly it is you want to portray. If there are parts in the character design that contradict each other that can be interesting if it fits the personality, but it shouldn't tell two conflicting stories at the same time. A character with a unique and believable personality and design is Coraline. It is obviously not just the style direction that makes the character interesting and uncommon, but the choice of shapes, clothing, colors, and textures. Everything in her character speaks of her being an independent mind, not following the conventions. She has a lot of self-made knitted clothing which gives her a comfortable warmth and familiarity. Her unique hair color and hairstyle interestingly frames the face. The blue color of her hair invokes the night sky and suggests a dreamy and wondrous side. She is skinny and has thin tubes for arms and legs making her a lanky girl that has not yet reached the first steps to adulthood, though her expression and the way she carries herself show an already developed and strong personality. Coraline's design is all very clear and subtle and none of the visual information is pushing itself into the foreground. Too much complexity overloads the character with information, so it has to be condensed into the most important aspects of the character's personality. The two characters above (Figure 4.1 and Figure 4.2) have personality traits that all go into one direction. The chain-smoking guy's facial color, paleness, clothing color, pose, his crutch, the expression, and focus on the cigarette all define his personality. The background color and the print of a syringe say hospital and unhealthy. The old lady on the other hand (Figure 4.2) has much brighter colors, the facial expression is happy, her skin color is healthy, her clothing brighter yet still

subtle, her pose is relaxed and the fox around her neck is a weird addition that suggests her fashion sense of the past (did she actually shoot the fox herself?). The background color shows her being soft and sweet.

Example

You have to design a character that is usually calm and quiet, but sometimes goes into an uncontrollable rage. If you would design the character as a regular quiet guy but you give them a bright red sweater to wear to express the rage they sometimes go into, this would take away the idea of them being calm in most situations, because the color red would be so dominant that it contradicts the calmness that you want to describe. You have to find a way to show that they just sometimes go into a rage. Dress the character in clothing that expresses their usual calmness with, for example, a cooler color, but add a subtle design or a zigzag line on their shirt with a strong color, that stands out just enough to give a clue about them sometimes getting very angry. You could use an elevated sinus rhythm as a pattern on their shirt. What is important in this case is the fact that his character is usually calm and the general calmness needs to be the dominant design element. The secondary element is the rage aspect that only sometimes occurs and therefore must not dominate the design.

In the case of *Stressed Eric*, a British TV series, Eric has a vein that pulsates whenever he starts to freak out. At the end of each show, when he is completely stressed the vein actually strangles him. When Eric is somehow calm, the tiny vein on his forehead is a visual clue and information enough to not disrupt but stand as a reminder for the audience that Eric can explode at any given moment.

Conflict leads to storytelling

We have seen in the description of "personality" in Webster's dictionary: "The combination of characteristics or qualities that form an individual's distinctive character." Again, the word "distinctive" is what needs to be looked at. Distinctive means what separates one from the other and elevates the character from the group, makes them unique and different. Therefore if one sticks to the cliché, the character is everything but distinctive. But what is it that makes a character distinctive? Character design at its very core is storytelling and storytelling as we have seen has conflict as its core element. If we now apply conflict to the character's personality, we are actually getting somewhere. Conflict is what makes the personality struggle and fight with itself and thus create the ground for a story that is worth telling. A character that is plain and just goes to work and home afterward to read has no passions or internal struggles. But a character that has a reason for reading because their life and job is so plain and all their passions are internalized and lived out in adventure novels is much more interesting. There we have the struggle between the external boring world and the internal rich imaginative world that is full of passion. This clash within the

[1] http://dictionary.reference.com/browse/cliche (retrieved December 1, 2015).

character's personality is so interesting that a story immediately takes shape. Contrasting elements in the personality are common; we all have various sides to our personality and are not simple and straightforward. We are complex creatures with many contradictory opinions and beliefs, which only surface when a situation points them out as *being* contradictory. The question is how do we visualize conflict in the character design? By simply using elements in the design that suggest a contradiction in the personality and thus allow a story to develop. For example, we have the character of a little baby girl. She is adorable and cute, she is a little chubby and has some cute curly locks on her head. Her dress is light pink and she is giggling. To this point the character isn't much of a surprise, there isn't anything distinctive about her. We need that spark that starts the fire of the story to grow. How about we add some dark rings under the baby's eyes to suggest a darker side underneath the rest of the cuteness? We can give the baby a hand gesture that adds a weird touch. Anything that describes the character's personality in a unique way is worth exploring. But this distinction is not limited to objects or attire but can also be explored in colors, shapes, and body ratio, and in the relationship and exaggeration between the characters in a full character lineup. If all characters are gray, but one character has red cheeks, then that one character appears special and is—because of the simple use of red cheeks—unique and distinguishable from the rest of the characters in that lineup.

Character consistency on the design scale

A character that is cartoony, has to react and act cartoony. It has to be designed cartoony in all its various elements—the skin texture, the shape, language, the facial expressions, the clothing, character animation, the personality, etc. Every detail in the character needs to say "cartoony" otherwise the persuasiveness of the character is in jeopardy.[2] There are five different levels of design that can be distinguished from each other (see Figure 9.1):

Hyperrealism

The design aspires an even more realistic look that actual reality provides. Characters are "perfected" and pushed to an even higher level of reality. Nature is enhanced and "improved."

Realism and fantastic realism

Realism needs to be split into two different sections. Realism itself copies our reality without deviating from the source; there should be no artistic addition that pushes the character away from reality (of course that includes a dream-like reality where there are fantastical creatures and surreal moments; however,

Design-scale

Figure 9.1

---

2   For feature animation with traditional storytelling and continuity style that is . . . short films can have a much more open approach as the emotional believability of the character in short films does not have to be as complex as in feature films.

they also need to be "realistic" in their looks and animation). The other side is fantastic realism, in which reality is dealing with characters and creatures that are not realistic but designed, rendered, and also performing in a realistic fashion.

Cartoony and artistically stylized

This level also needs to be split into two as cartoony is more of a style direction that comes often with a certain look (big eyes, exaggerated design with bigger hands and feet, round shapes are often dominant, pushing of body ratio and shapes). The same level of stylization however can also be achieved by staying away from the cartoon formula and moving into the area of "artistically stylized." This is a more personal artistic approach, more unique in its use of all the elements mentioned before (e.g., most films by the company Folimage which would be artistically stylized, whereas Bugs Bunny is cartoony).

Heavily stylized

A character that goes toward abstract is an abstracted character (not an abstract character), meaning elements within the character have been simplified and/or their shape and form language is getting closer and closer toward basic shapes like circle, oval, square, triangle, or trapezoid. These characters then are heavily stylized. A famous example would be the animation of UPA (United Productions of America) where character animation and design go hand in hand on the design scale.

Abstract

Abstract is not fully connected to the design ladder, as abstraction is per definition not part of the realistic world but wants to create its own realm devoid of any connection to nature. Logically there cannot be a "character" in fully abstract design as a character is a living being that is always part of nature itself. Even a character that is just a circle is part of nature if its character animation attaches human emotions to the circle. An abstract character therefore is an oxymoron, but it can be an abstracted character, which would fall under heavily stylized, not abstract.

Figure 9.2 roughly places various features and short films onto the design scale and there is a clear distinction between realism and fantastic

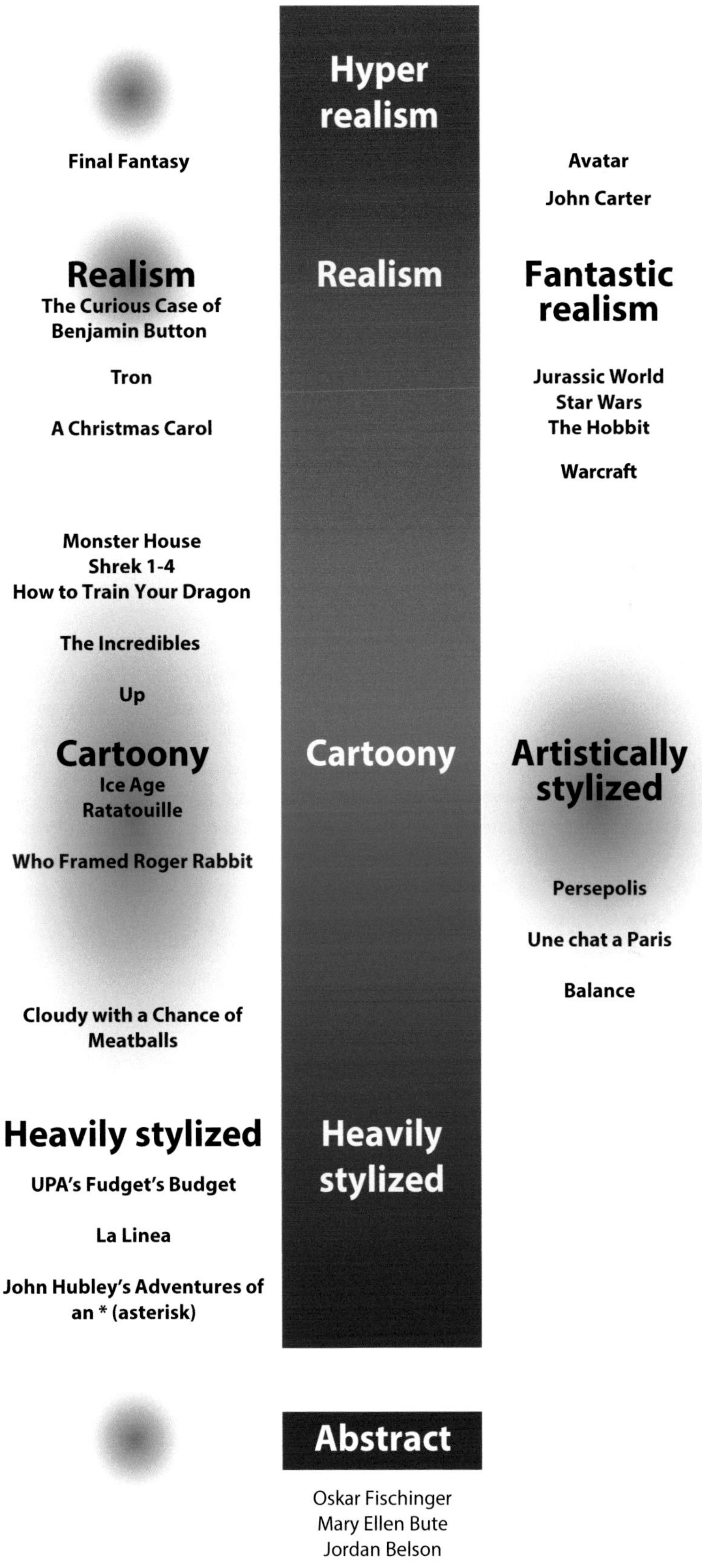

Final Fantasy

Realism
**The Curious Case of
Benjamin Button**

Tron

A Christmas Carol

**Monster House
Shrek 1-4
How to Train Your Dragon**

The Incredibles

Up

Cartoony
**Ice Age
Ratatouille**

Who Framed Roger Rabbit

**Cloudy with a Chance of
Meatballs**

Heavily stylized

UPA's Fudget's Budget

La Linea

**John Hubley's Adventures of
an * (asterisk)**

**Hyper
realism**

Realism

Cartoony

**Heavily
stylized**

Abstract

Avatar
John Carter

**Fantastic
realism**

**Jurassic World
Star Wars
The Hobbit**

Warcraft

**Artistically
stylized**

Persepolis

Une chat a Paris

Balance

Oskar Fischinger
Mary Ellen Bute
Jordan Belson

Figure 9.2

realism, and also between cartoony and artistically stylized. The radius of realism has the smallest range as it is so very much defined by our daily experiences and the further one steers away from realism the broader the possibilities become. The question now is: is it possible for a character to have its various elements of design (shape and form, color, etc.), personality, and performance freely shift from one design level onto another and thus have the different elements occupy different places on the design scale within one character? For instance, the character design is cartoony but the character animation is hyperrealistic. Would this work? The answer is in my opinion: absolutely not, if one wants to follow the contemporary story structure of continuity style film and create characters that are believable in their own theatrical reality.[3]

In 1970, the robotics professor Masahiro Mori described the phenomenon of getting uncomfortable with humanoid robots that mimic the human look, though do not match precisely the human counterpart. Mori used the by now very popular term "uncanny valley" to describe the gap between believability, disbelief, and rejection. Since then the term uncanny valley has often been used for the described phenomenon of the "nearly" realistic human character or robot being rejected by the viewer due to its lack of persuasiveness. The uncanny valley however has never been successfully proven as a scientific fact and is still a theory. Since the 2000s, the term has also been used for the production of CG animation, triggered mainly by the release of the sci-fi film based on a computer game series: *Final Fantasy*. Its goal was to create realistically rendered and realistically performing characters, with unfortunately a less than convincing outcome despite the (for the time) technically often stunning visuals. Since then the uncanny valley has been discussed when it comes to CG animated characters. Notwithstanding, the term uncanny valley is always still only used for characters that come very close in look and movement to a real live humans. The rejection is based on being uncomfortable with what is presented in it not being convincing, or not "correct." This rejection can be strange or outright creepy which in turn then destroys or questions the believability of the character and thus exposes them as fake. But what about creepy cartoony characters? The phenomenon of the uncanny has never been discussed in characters whose design is less realistic. The audience's emotional reaction to the uncanny in animation is in the author's opinion detectable on every level of the design scale, from hyperrealistic to realistic, cartoony, heavily stylized, and abstract as it always deals with a lack of believability. The uncanny valley is set off by unconvincing design and animation of the character: certain elements in the animation are not as they should be in order to give the character full "life." The character does not fully fit into the realm of its own artificial environment, and lacks the emotional depth and accuracy one would expect from the character performing in its very own theatrical reality. The following tries to discuss this rejection by the audience of characters on the entire design scale that lack the believability needed to convince, therefore tries to show the current description of the uncanny valley is just a small segment of the lack of believability in characters. This can range from hyperreal all the way down to abstract and is not just a phenomenon that is related to realistically performing ones.

Realism, style, and persuasiveness

The protagonist Okuyama says in Hiroshi Teshigahara's feature *The Face of Another* (1966)

> The face is the door to the soul. When the face is closed off, so too is the soul. Nobody is allowed inside. The soul is left to rot, reduced to ruins. It becomes the soul of a monster, rotten to the core.

Okuyama, the main character in *The Face of Another*, has lost his face in a chemical accident in the company he is working for, which left him severely disfigured. His psychologist helps him to a new face that Okuyama can wear allowing him to explore life with a very convincing and realistic mask instead of bandages. What makes this feature interesting is that it raises many questions about who we are, what we are, how our self is not just our face and looks, yet the face is the door to the soul as it is the only "open" gate that gives us a glimpse into the true thoughts, emotions, and reactions of a human. Does the new face of Okuyama change the former person that is now wearing it? Is crime nonexistent if the person committing it can change his face right after? What Okuyama is afraid of is the changing of his personality through the new face; however, this is also paired with his excitement of being able to get away with actions that his older self would have never dared to perform. How much is the face and physique related to our "self?" In animation into the lifeless puppet or drawing, a "soul" needs to be breathed in. The goal of the animated character is to make it seem as if the character has a soul and a face that is not closed off, allowing the audience to peek inside. Without it, the illusion of life is missing and the character never steps out of our reality of actually being a puppet or a drawing into its own theatrical reality on screen.

There are six points that assist the creation of a believable character in animation:

- Concept and position on the design scale
- Character design (the look and aesthetics in relationship with the story)
- Character personality
- Character's relationship to their environment
- Character's objective and goal (story)
- Performance and character animation

(All of the mentioned points have to go hand in hand with the film's mood, editing, etc.) All of these points, contrary to most live-action

---

[3] If however the goal is to create the highest level of "oddness," then it is a creative decision that comes with an artistic goal, which then of course can work.

characters, can be enhanced or exaggerated by stylization, which strengthens the important personality traits of the character for better understanding and a stronger impact, or simplifies it. The performance and character animation however is what brings the character really to life and hopefully makes their actions and reactions believable. Performance itself also has various aspects that are all equally important for the character's believability:

- Artistic interpretation of the situation, action, and reaction, and its translation into motion (level of stylization)
- Technical aspects of forces, weight, timing, and movement also in relationship to stylization
- Facial expressions and poses that reflect the given story point and also the emotional and psychological state of the character, again in relationship to the level of stylization

All of the three points are strongly connected to each other and cannot stand on their own, and neither can they go into different directions in terms of their stylization. All aspects need to follow the character's position on the design scale, which determines the degree the character is stylized.

Real humans and sculptures and the uncanny

Might there be a similar emotion like the uncanny valley when we deal with living humans? I would say that there most definitely is. I feel the strong urge to observe people that look unusual, especially people with facial surgery. The enhanced features are fascinating on many levels as they present something uncommon and even inhuman sometimes. This makes me uncomfortable and the natural curiosity kicks in, and therein lies the attraction. There are plenty of examples of surgically altered faces online that show features that are just not "right" and one can easily find faces online that most definitely fall under the term uncanny and creepy. It is the face's falseness that we can very easily detect. Our natural curiosity is turned on and we enjoy to just observe. It is the curiosity of the bizarre, the strange and different that attracts the eye. When I meet people wearing masks on a carnival I am extremely uncomfortable because I do not know who is in front of me. I cannot fully judge the person, who are they, and what they might do. I'm always on high alert as the safety net of facial recognition is gone. The person in front of me is beyond my social skills of being judged. I cannot read their expression and what they are about to do is beyond my understanding. Something similar is true when people wear sunglasses. The most important part of the face that speaks and carries the core elements of communication is the eyes. Talking to people for a longer period of time while they wear sunglasses makes one question the sincerity of the conversation. The relationship between me and my conversation partner feels much weaker if the eyes are covered. The person with sunglasses feels less emotional compared to the one without them. The reduction

of the emotional range reduces the person's "humanness" and pushes them slightly toward the artificial. I remember a baroque church close to my home village in southern Germany that had in the back a display case with waxen feet and hands, given by those that were thankful for the healing powers of God; they were tokens of gratitude. As a child they were rather unpleasant. They were not just waxen representations of limbs in my mind but were actual limbs being displayed. It of course depends on one's imagination and emotional response to those objects if they are seen as real or not. I did know they were artificial, but nevertheless they were still real in their own reality, their display case. It is one's ability to question what is real and what is not; to what extend is the viewer able to see the life in an otherwise dead object or character. Artists like Duane Hanson, Ron Mueck, or Robert Gober play with the audience's reaction to realistic or hyperrealistic sculptures and the outcome is astounding. Seeing one of Mueck's pieces is a surreal and mind-opening experience that is only possible if the sculptures are observed in person and in a very intimate closeness, which allows the eye to wander and explore the miniscule details of the character's surface without a time constraint. One cannot stop exploring because one cannot believe that they are NOT real. The detail is intoxicating and lures one into a different reality where people are tiny or huge, where time stands still and our innermost urge to just stare at others without being caught and exposed to embarrassment is fulfilled. Duane Hanson, one of the star artists of Pop Art, created hyperrealistic glass fiber sculptures of people in day-to-day situations that often blended into the visiting crowd of the museum exhibition. The separation between sculpture and audience started to be blurred and one could always see people staring suspiciously at Hanson's sculptures, not because they appeared creepy, but because they did not move at all and therefore seemed trapped in a single moment. Those sculptures are not creepy because of their design or their lack of reality, quite the contrary as they are as real as they could be. What makes them creepy is THAT they are so real, but do not move. This is their only flaw but then again is also their biggest strength, because it allows us to shamelessly stare. We expect them to move and because they don't, they seem to defy our understanding of reality. Another artist that makes one often cringe is Robert Gober. Especially his waxen pale and hairy legs that come out of walls, for example his piece *Untitled* from 1991 in the Whitney Museum of American Art, put a surreal element into the exhibition room that the audience is taken back by. It is obvious that the leg is not real, because the material clearly says that it is wax. But exactly because of its paleness it does look uncomfortable and utterly creepy, carries the visual aspect of "death" in its body, very much like the waxen token in the mentioned Catholic church. The audience knows that it is artificial but that does not make it less creepy. They still believe in the odd possibility of it being real, despite its falseness. The leg is of course touching upon the uncanny valley or is it just convincing in its own artificiality and its artistic impact? Gober's work is close of being realistic, because it has a perfect human form, has hair, pants, and shoes, but also has the surrealness that withdraws it from the reality and the setting of the museum. The museum setting makes it very obvious that it is part of an exhibition and not a real leg. It is the perfection of the sculptures of Hanson, Mueck, or Gober that make them appear haunting, the knowledge that they are sculptures has a very strong impact on the audience as the constant demand comes to mind: they should move! The sculpture Inochi of Takashi Murakami, showing a hybrid between human boy, alien, and robot, is obviously very unrealistic and only distantly resembles a human being. Pushed and stylized, it asks the question about beauty and the future of the human idealistic features. The piece is very creepy because of its surreal design, yet also very attractive because of its technical bravura. It speaks to our sense of curiosity and keeps us staring at it because it is unrealistic and pushes the boundary of design, uses our curiosity toward the bizarre to drag us into its own reality. Why is a sculpture like Murakami's Inochi also making us cringe? It is not realistic at all and thus should not make us uncomfortable or reject the character as being creepy; however, it does. There is no closeness to reality and the character is not hyperrealistically rendered. It is the bizarre design that is responsible for its reaction in the audience. The idea that the uncanny valley (if it does exist at all) only appears in characters that are close to being realistic is in my opinion questionable as very similar emotions of rejection toward any kind of characters come up despite them not being realistic at all. In the following I will refine this with examples of every level on the design scale.

Performance, movement, and aesthetics and the uncanny

The human brain is perfectly capable of detecting the slightest mismatch between the body's locomotion and emotional actions and reactions of an actual human being—the reason why botox faces look unreal. The uncanny started with the movement and looks of robots, so they should be the starting point. Movements of photorealistic or hyperrealistic robots that try to mimic those human actions, if not perfectly matching the tiniest details, are immediately discovered as unreal. We are so acute in especially reading emotions in faces that much of the understanding of the facial expressions and body language, and the resulting acceptance of the person, is happening instantly and often on a subconscious level. Communication is a continuous flow of information of emotional changes and subtleties that need to be grasped by the viewer in a split second. We have learned through socialization to recognize what the other person is feeling—or hiding and lying about. It is not just the simple emotion of "happy" or "sad" that is expressed, but a multitude of expressions are possible with 20 different facial muscles whose subtleties are extremely difficult to replicate in an artificial character. The micro muscle movement gives us subtleties that robots are not (yet) capable of performing. Therefore a robot is not at all convincing as the technology has not yet reached

a level of true make-believe. They might be convincing as an advanced robot, staying within the cluster of robots, but they most definitely do not reach into the cluster of human motion. In much of the research that has been done about the uncanny valley the visual stimuli that are used to prove the existence or nonexistence of the uncanny valley are by themselves creepy to begin with. Visuals are so extremely complex, that trying to prove a point with subpar visuals is a rather pointless endeavor. Only excellently crafted visuals with high-end design can be the basis for a study, not visuals that are poorly crafted from a design perspective. And even presenting excellently crafted examples like the test robots of high-profile companies and projects, are unfortunately not yet convincing on any visual level. It is the lack of accurate movement, the lack of correct upper facial expression that makes those robots look creepy from the beginning. Hiroshi Ishiguro's Geminoid HI-1 and Geminoid-F, or Henrik Schaerfe's Geminoid-DK, or David Hanson's robotics are not even coming close to being convincing in their mere locomotion. Their looks are also not at all realistic enough aesthetically to prove the point of believability. They are technically spectacular achievements but from an artistic perspective not at all what they should be. It is the hardware of joints and motors, the quality of skin and wrinkles that still cannot produce realistic human motion, nor all human emotions. Those robots immediately show their artificiality in looks, movements, and expressions to the acute eye. The tarnished hair, the pale skin color, the lack of realistic surface, the lack of subtleties in the eyes' moisture and depth paints the robot as unreal. If then the movement is also lacking the subtleties that are needed to produce realistic emotions, the result will logically be unrealistic, thus can be seen as creepy. The robot obviously wants to be something that it is not: a realistic human being. It is pretending to be something different than it is. Computer animation compared to robotics is slowly but steadily catching up with its own persuasiveness, but still has some way to go to really make us believe in the artificial facial expressions of realistic human characters. The audience will have to accept an artificial character not knowing that the film is computer generated. The visit to a movie that is already advertised as being fully CG or having CG characters will always make the audience look twice as hard to detect the faults. This, as we have seen in the steady technological evolvement and artistic achievements in the last decade, will change and the CG characters in future projects will undoubtedly leave the disbelieve to be an issue of the past when it comes to mimicking realistic characters. Obviously the animators need to have a much greater understanding of emotional expressions, microexpressions, and the true visualization of the psychological state of the character. The audience's learning curve rises with what they are exposed to. The more CG characters they see that all strive for believability and realism, the more quality the audience expects as they are able to detect subtleties that would have not been an issue years ago. As much as Jurassic Park's dinosaurs were praised at the time and are still fully convincing in the film, they are not as complex as the dinosaurs that appear in *Jurassic World*, which was released 25 years after the initial film. Much of the muscles and skin texture of the original dinosaurs are just not persuasive enough for contemporary CG visuals. There is an obvious difference between a dinosaur and a human, the latter being much more difficult to animate and thus less likely to be undetectable as being artificial. There have been great artistic and technical advances that pushed the envelope further and further and there is no reason to believe that it will not continue and give us artificial humans that are fooling even the most doubtful critic. There are various techniques in character animation that bring convincing realistic results but they all come with their very own complexities and also different results. It depends on the goal which technique is the one that supports the story.

Keyframe animation versus motion capture and rotoscoping

There are two different types of approaching realistic animation: one is the type where movement and timing, poses, and composition are the tools for the animator to create an individual piece of animation, where every single element is designed for its most artistic impact. Pose and facial expressions work together. This is the type called keyframe animation. The other type is the motion capture type where the actor creates the character's performance and the animator adjusts the timing and action based on the motion capture information (however, this also can include the slight adjustment of the poses with all its artistic aspects like silhouette, reading direction, vectors, directions, negative and positive space, line of action etc.). An example of artistic animation is Disney's Pinocchio, where every shot is sculpted to the highest artistic standard. Every key pose is perfection and is composed in relationship to the focal point, the background design, the accompanying characters, the reading direction of the image, and the overall movement in the frame. The result is a highly complex artistic product that can never be produced by an actor as it is a unique piece of art following hundreds of years in art history. The opposite would be Bakshi's *Fire and Ice* (1983) in which one can immediately recognize that the movement of the characters is rotoscoped. The character's poses performed by the actor do not follow the complexity of the design of poses with all its creative decisions that are made by the animator following the keyframe animation style; The animator approaches the design of the frame from a very different perspective compared to the actor. This is because the keyframe approach considers each single keyframe in terms of its readability, its understandability, its aesthetics, and also its best impact from a two-dimensional perspective: the flat frame. The actor does not care about all these details as they do not break the shot into frames neither do they see their three-dimensional acting space as a two-dimensional graphic plane. Of course the actor also considers silhouette and readability, but not to the degree the animator does. Rotoscoping these

performances, like motion capture, translates another artistic field, acting, into animation and adjusts it, cleans it up to get rid of little issues here and there to make the movement into a fluid performance that expresses what the realistic shot needs; the emphasis is on the realistic as the rotoscoped shot is realism translated. It also adjusts the actor's looks to the character's design. Both types, keyframe animation and motion capture/rotoscoping need artistic decisions, but only the latter has the little subtleties and unconscious movements in it that make it very realistic. Yet is has the disadvantage of being less artistic in terms of the compositional adjustments of silhouette and pose. Even though it is often adjusted, the overall realism is usually kept intact in its timing and lack of artistic accuracy of silhouette. I am not claiming that one is better than the other, but traditional handmade animation is surely more artistic by using movement as a tool for an artistic goal that is fully handmade, which is very different in its result compared to using recorded human motion as a basis that is then adjusted. One type creates human motion from scratch and the result is a highly complex piece of motion art, applying a myriad of rules and artistic decisions to the movement, the other uses human motion with the adjustment (and often artistic improvements) of the animator and then creates a movement that is more realistic. It is the miniscule subtleties that animators cannot replicate on their own without the use of the rotoscope or motion capture systems. It depends on the need of the feature film which system is more practical and also more convincing. Bakshi's feature *Fire and Ice* can be critiqued on many levels, but its style is very close to the fantasy art of Frank Frazetta that the film is based on. Traditional hand-drawn keyframe animation might not have given the images as much of Frazetta's flair for realism as rotoscoping did. Since the early 1920s the technique of using human motion for the simplification of the complex and difficult task of traditional character animation, was discussed by the audience. Already Max Fleischer's Koko the Clown, rotoscoped from live-action footage (where Max Fleischer filmed his brother Dave in a clown costume) was realistic compared to other contemporary animation, so much so that it very much distinguished itself from, for example, Felix the Cat. The first shorts showed Koko as a mischievous character that caused trouble for Max Fleischer, who acted as the master of the little clown, that always either climbed out of the inkwell or was drawn by Max onto an animation board and then causing trouble in the hand-drawn realm of the board. Once more characters were introduced into the short films and the character's design was changed by Dave Huemer, the rotoscope technique was abandoned, and also Max Fleischer stopped acting as the character's master. There is a significantly different feel between Koko's rotoscoped character and the frame-by-frame animated one. The latter has a distinctive animated (or illustrated) feel to it and his unique world is consistent in design and animation, whereas the one based on live action relates much more to Max Fleischer and is an animated character in our world. In the deliciously surreal short *Koko's Earth Control* (1928) Koko and his dog Fitz are pulling the Earth's destruction lever, which causes the entire planet to be incinerated. The entire planet of Koko's world, not yet our world. Once Koko's animated world shakes violently he gets catapulted out of his reality and lands in our reality, or the 1920s Hollywood, which then starts to violently shake. But there is a clear distinction between the two worlds. The rotoscope shots in Disney's *Snow White and the Seven Dwarfs* or *Sleeping Beauty* that are heavily and recognizably based on live-action footage stand out as being oddly different and it was seen by the audiences at the time. It does not matter if the shots were incredibly difficult to produce as for the audience, it is the result on screen that counts. But over and over again the technique of rotoscoping was used to either bring more realism to the screen, as a stylistic decision and/or to cut costs (like in Bakshi's *Lord of the Rings*). And the result is not always an artistic disadvantage as long as its realistic movement fits the realistic design of the world that surrounds the characters and fits the design of the characters themselves. Then rotoscoping is a convincing technique, like in Bakshi's *Fire and Ice*. Nevertheless, Snow White dancing realistically with the dwarfs, that are heavily cartoony, yet also dancing realistically, is not very convincing as the two designs in relationship to their locomotion is too discrepant. One can see the underlying live-action footage driving and dominating the animation, yet can also see the cartoony design covering it up. The end result feels like humans wearing costumes. The very same happened in Zemecki's *Monster House* where the characters were slightly stylized but the character animation was heavily based on motion capture, also resulting in human characters with oversized heads that lacked realistic human facial expression. The discrepancy between design and character animation is the cause of disbelief.

Animation and the uncanny valley in realistic characters[4]

One of the directors that frequently explored the field of motion capture and pushed its limits for many years is Robert Zemeckis, directing the *Back to the Future* series and the feature *Who Framed Roger Rabbit* (1988). Robert Zemeckis' *The Polar Express* from 2004 was the first feature that used the motion control system for its entirety, which by itself is an achievement in its own right. The story of the film was well received and even the design in its detail and mood was praised, however it was frequently critiqued on stepping quite often into the uncanny valley in the character's animation, which look photorealistic (somehow) and they move in a photorealistic way (somehow) but the result is just close to the actual human motion. There is some stylization in the design and also some exaggeration in the movement, but overall the film tries to be realistic (or hyperrealistic) but it isn't. Unfortunately the achieved realism in the design does not match the subtleties of the facial expressions, especially in the eye movement, which was the point that was quite often critiqued. Thalia Wheatley, a neuroscientist at Dartmouth says "Think of horror movies—zombies, vampires, or even clowns, because they have faces painted on that don't move. It looks like a person's face but it doesn't move like one. A conflict arises in the brain, which is unsettling."[5] In Robert Zemeckis' following film *Beowulf*, produced three years later in 2007, the issue of the creepiness was less dramatic though still very obvious. It continuously drew the attention away from the story and toward it being unreal and awkward despite the convincing design of the rustic setting. The believability of the characters however was higher than in the previous attempts. There was a huge amount of work being done for especially the eye movement in *Beowulf* to overcome the issues of dead eyes. However it did not persuade fully. Fair enough: the latest examples of photorealistic animation are reaching the point where the audience is asking themselves: "Is this really animated?" as the images are so perfect. But not yet perfect enough for the audience to not ask the question at all. The film that convinced in most of its parts in terms of the character animation was *Avatar*, though one needs to remember that the characters were not humans, just human-like, which is a very important point as we still give human-like characters more leeway than actual human characters. Audiences worldwide did accept the characters' look and movement as realistic and convincing. The motion capture was precise and elaborate, and caught even the small muscle movements in the actors' faces. This led to a mostly convincing animation that did not distract often and kept the audience's attention focused on the story. There were though some shots where the characters felt unnatural in their movement and physicality not matching the intended "hyperrealistic" perfection (the first shots of Jake Sully running out of the lab into the garden in his avatar body; those shots feel very forced and unrealistic as the actual run does not match the physicality of the body 100%). This then can break the escapism and remind one of the artificiality of the happenings on screen. However, it only breaks it if the audience member has the eye to actually detect the mistakes. The most convincing CG characters are still dragons, tigers, and aliens whose animation is mostly convincing and the audience accepts them much more often as being real (e.g., the Tharks in Disney's *John Carter*). As humans we are obviously specialists in detecting other humans' behavior and movement, however we are not specialists in

---

[4] Brenton H, Gillies M, Ballin D, Chatting DJ. (2005). *The uncanny valley: Does it exist?* Paper presented at the 11th International Conference on Human–Computer Interaction, Las Vegas, NV. Brenton et al. (2005) suggest in their paper four working hypotheses for further research and debate, as those points frequently come up in the discussion on the uncanny valley:
  a. The uncanny valley response related to presence
  b. Increasing realism heightens sensitivity to cues indicating falsehood
  c. Perceptual cues indicating falsehood are especially potent in the eyes of faces
  d. The uncanny response is culturally dynamic and subject to change over time.

[5] Talbot M. (2014). Pixel Perfect: The scientist behind the digital cloning of actors. *The New Yorker*, April 28 Issue. http://www.newyorker.com/magazine/2014/04/28/pixel-perfect-2 (accessed 27 October 2017).

the movement and behavior of dinosaurs, dragons, tigers, or aliens which benefits those characters immensely. There is, for instance, already 60 facial expressions on anger that Paul Ekman has determined.[6] Within those emotional groups of expressions the subtleties between honestly showing the expression and only pretending the emotion is yet another level of complexity. When it is already difficult to create emotions that are honestly portrayed, it is even more complex to portray emotions that conceal lies and betrayal. Leakage in facial and vocal expressions (through the aforementioned microexpressions) show the actual feeling that one subconsciously reads. And with the facial expression of course comes also the reaction of the entire body. As Ekman states: "Occasionally, head movement—down, back, forward, or to the side—has been in expressions of sadness, fear, interest, or disgust." It is therefore also the ability of the animator and/or actor to recreate the emotion believably. But in a film we have snippets of information (shots) that are like puzzle pieces assembling an entire character's personality. Some of those snippets are convincing and others are not. Then there is the question of whether the actor is actually able to control those muscles in the face that are by most people not controllable if the emotion is not honestly felt. Faking an emotion is therefore often seen within the facial muscles that cannot be deliberately controlled. The animator who uses self-shot footage might not be able to produce a realistic and thus fully convincing performance and neither might the actor. The produced shot will be an artistic interpretation of the emotion, not a realistic representation. Referential expressions are showing emotions that are not felt at that very moment, but refer to emotions having been felt or will be felt in the future. For those emotions the muscles that cannot be controlled, the so-called reliable muscles, should be inactive to clearly show to the viewer that this emotion refers to an event past or future. Then there is also the question of the individual intensity of the facial expression, the duration of the expression and the variants in the expressions. Animators tend to use simplified clichés for expressions that quickly convey the needed emotion. Creating personalized emotions for the specific characters is obviously done, but the complexity of inventing believable expressions for a fully realistic human character is, as we have seen, a rather scientific task going beyond what science has discovered as of yet. What motion capture can do is record the surface of the emotion, but it cannot look into the mind of the character. I assume it is similar to figure drawing where the drawing that only replicates the surface image of the model is not as convincing as the drawing that incorporates the knowledge of skeleton, muscle structure, weight, movement, etc. The animator that needs to create a realistic character performance therefore needs to look into the "soul" of the character: its eyes and complex facial expressions, which as mentioned before is so often the trap that leads into the uncanny valley. To recreate these subtleties from scratch realistically is for the animator more or less

impossible if they cannot rely on an actor's groundwork either in video footage or motion capture.

What could only be semiconvincing with motion capture for human characters, the motion capture or reference footage for animals performed by human actors is also tremendously helpful in a convincing performance. Even characters like the velociraptors in *Jurassic World* are based on the skills of actors portraying those vicious dinosaurs. The subtle movements of the different personalities of the actors give each raptor its own variant in movement, adding not just personality but also emotions and a thought process to the shots, are what makes those scenes with the velociraptors so convincing. The animators are not copying, but creatively using the framework of the actors for their work (obviously this varies from shot to shot). It is usually emotions that we as the audience relate to and even dinosaurs are more convincing with some kind of emotion, even if it is pure imagination and has nothing to do with the actual animal, realistic or not.

The trouble with eyes in realistic characters

Audiences' mostly critiqued aspect when watching Zemecki's *The Polar Express* was the issue with dead eyes, which made them uncomfortable, reject the characters, and even describe them as creepy (however the film was still a very big financial success). The eyes are the most delicate parts in the expression of the human face and are the parts that are scanned the most by the viewer. Research shows how important eyes are for the understanding of personality. Rauthmann et al.[7] for instance demonstrated, how gazing and eye movement is linked to the five personality traits (the Big Five[8]). The findings were, for example, that people with high openness as a personality trait, fixate longer and more deeply on visual stimuli. "Open individuals have been found to be 'deep,' thoughtful, intellectual, culturally interested, and creative."[9] A longer fixation on a target helps to accumulate deeper information and insight into the fixed target. If the eyes of an animated character do not just express the character's emotional state at that very moment and in relation to their personality traits, they will lack the full scale of persuasiveness. The entire character then fails in being believable as a representation of an actual human character. It is not at all enough to just come close to realism if the design is realistic. Realistic characters have to provide an insight into the character's very soul (or personality). The closer the design therefore goes toward realism or in the most extreme form wants to perfectly copy realism, the more detailed the

---

6 Ekman P. (1993). Facial expression and emotion. *Am Psychol*. 48(4): 384–392.

7 Rauthmann JF, Seubert CT, Sachse P, Furtner MR. (2012). Eyes as windows to the soul: Gazing behaviour is related to personality. *J Res Pers*. 46: 147–156.
8 The Big Five are openness to experience, conscientiousness, extraversion, agreeableness, and neuroticism.
9 Rauthmann et al. (2012, p. 153).

animation has to be. Ergo, the further away the design goes toward cartoony, stylized, and abstract, the less detailed the eyes need to be to convince. How about a character that has realistic eyes, but a slightly unrealistic body and movement such as *Madame Tutli-Putli* (2007)? This is an extraordinary stop motion short film produced by the Film Board of Canada and directed by Chris Lavis and Maciek Szczerbowski. Madame Tutli-Putli herself is an exceptional character in every perspective as in her design she has realistic eyes and eyebrows that are composited onto a stop motion puppet. Actress Laurie Maher was recorded and then only her eyes could be seen in the final film. "It's the first time such a painstaking feat has been pulled off, giving Tutli-Putli's metaphysical adventure extraordinary impact."[10] The eyes are extremely convincing, as they are real, but the rest of the body is slightly stylized in its movement, due to the stop motion technique. This creates a very weird emotion in the audience as we get the opposite feeling of the creepiness in CG characters' dead eyes, by being presented a character that is very much alive because of the real eyes, but less so in the body. The directors give us a human thinking and feeling soul that is trapped in a puppet. The realistic eyes not only create a sense of life, but are haunting in their own right.

Aesthetics

It is not just the complexity of the movement and emotions that are so difficult to replicate in artificial characters, but also the aesthetics that are often just not "right" and can easily push the character into disbelief. The audience rejects characters not only because the character animation is off, but also because the design is often unpleasant. As humans, through aesthetics and a selection process we can immediately detect healthy and attractive humans (who is attractive to whom is obviously a very personal opinion). However, what we can also determine is if someone is just slightly "off" aesthetically. For the basic survival of one's genetic code, health, attractiveness, and pleasing features are of great value for choosing a partner (there are of course more complex biological actions going on than just the visuals!). Aesthetics therefore play a significant role in who we are attracted to and who we are not. Most tests, that want to find the existence of the uncanny valley, just do not present aesthetically pleasing visuals but, for instance, morph one image into another, without adjusting the images to create a pleasing visual.[11] Aesthetics are a very tricky thing … for example: someone with a prosthetic leg pulls up the pants and shows the slightly flesh-colored artificial leg with socks, shoes, and all. The visual is weird and we try to look away. A prosthetic leg however that is

beautifully designed with intricate metal work and wood inlay mimicking tattoos, is a piece of art and we are fascinated by the advanced technology and the "cool" design. The huge difference between a traditional prosthetic leg and a cool design is that the cool prosthetic leg does not hide the fact that it actually is an artificial leg, whereas the old-fashioned artificial leg wants to hide the fact that it is artificial. The same is true in animation: the slightly stylized character does not hide the fact that it is an artificial character, that it is handcrafted, whereas the realistic one wants to be something that it's not: the image of a human being. And that makes us suspicious. The logical conclusion is that the feeling of discomfort is just a natural occurrence where the mind knows that what it is looking at is not what it pretends to be, and thus the mind is cautious. When communicating with people we need to figure out if someone is sane, honest, helpful, or dangerous. We judge them on their appearance, their health, sanity, and how they express themselves in actions and reactions. Are they believable in what they are saying? Are they trustworthy? Meeting new people is always a test: how far can we trust them, are they honest, are they benevolent … for this we need their body language, their facial expression, and their habitus. Anything that steers ever so slightly away from what we are used to or expect (not just physically, but also social norms or cultural differences) might cause us to take a step back and question the person in front of us. So the slightest hint of lack of reality is already enough for us to be on alert. Many tests that try to approach the infamous uncanny valley deal with subpar visuals and robots that are questionable in their aesthetics. For example, the test performed by David Hanson et al.[11] uses an image of Princess Jasmine from Disney's feature *Aladdin* (1992) and morphs it into the photography of a beautiful real girl. What the researchers completely ignore is that a 2D image, a graphic image, with its shape-oriented flatness and lack of 3-dimensional form, is morphed into a photo with light and shadow, texture, and all that realism has to offer. This is mixing two completely different media: 2D and 3D. The final image in the mentioned study has the realistic face of the girl on the body of the cartoon character with the hairdo of Jasmine. The body ratio of the girl is obviously very different from that of the cartoon character and thus the overall design of Jasmine fits in all its details the cartoon style, whereas the altered image of the final pretty girl looks like it's been cut out and glued on. The study itself cannot be trusted if the base is already using images that are from an aesthetic point of view more than questionable and grotesque to begin with. Another study with morphing images is done by Juni'ichiro Seyama and Ruth S. Nagayama[12] using puppets and drawings that are also morphed into girl's/women's faces (why does it always have to be women when it comes to those experiments?). The puppets have a very different quality to them as they have in their eyes a rather uncomfortable stare, due to the iris being

[10] McQueen A-M. (2007). All eyes on animated pioneer. www.canoe.com (retrieved January 18, 2016).

[11] Hanson D, Olney A, Ereira IA, Zielke M. *Upending the Uncanny Vally*. Hanson Robotics Inc, Fedex Institute of Technology, the University of Texas at Arlington Automation and Robotics Research Institute, and the University of Texas at Dallas, Institute for Interactive Arts and Engineering.

[12] Seyama J, Nagayama RS. (2007). The uncanny valley: Effect of realism on the impression of artificial human faces. *Presence.* 16(4): 337–351.

shown completely, without the upper eyelid covering parts of them, ultimately making them look scared or crazy. The results of those experiments can only be doubted. What seems to be the case however is the growing discomfort in relation to the growing discrepancy between the design elements. The closer one gets to realism the more complex the creation of the character becomes.

Animation and rejection in cartoony and less realistic characters

A film's goal always is to get the audience to believe in the characters actually being alive and behaving in a convincing way. The audience wants to be fooled in that they accompany the characters on a journey. If that is the case then the audience believes, even if it is just for the length of the feature, that those characters' adventures and perils are real and that the characters are not just in actual and real danger but that their emotional reactions are also very real. However, this does not mean that the characters have to be photorealistic to make the audience believe. Daffy Duck is very much stylized but still we believe in him being real in his own cartoony world. And that is the important point: the design of the entire world has to be convincing in itself. If it is heavily stylized or realistic, the characters still have to convince on the level of the rules of that specific world. The character is always part of that world, so naturally they have to speak the same design language. Because of the enthusiastic output of realistic characters since the very start of computer animation, the entire field of animation has been pushed into the real or even hyperreal, which before the dawn of CGI was technically extremely difficult. If the designed world is stylized, the characters and their movement also need to be stylized. The more the characters perform in a realistic world, the more they need to be realistic and we expect them to be as convincing as real people on the street that we communicate with daily. And that creates a huge challenge: to be accurate enough to match the original. We do not spend too much time conversing with cartoon characters, but spend time all day long with other humans. For most people it is very difficult to distinguish one squirrel from the other, as they look all the same. The more time one spends looking at squirrels one finds the differences and after a while each single one has its own personality and movement. Continuous observation allows the differences to stand out. That is the reason why it is so difficult to recreate human motion and emotion artificially in CG, because we are so familiar with our own species and can detect the miniscule faults. We have to look for characters that do not fit into their assigned world and try to figure out the reason for the mismatch. Figure 9.3 explores the design discrepancy in various feature film characters and which element of their design is the mismatch in the overall design rule.

- *Shrek:* The body ratio of Shrek is 1:4¼ whereas Fiona's ratio is a realistic 1:6. They both are the same species.

- *Monsters vs. Aliens:* The skin texture is way too realistic for the cartoon characters.
- *The Good Dinosaur:* There is a stark discrepancy between very cartoony character design and hyperrealistic backgrounds.
- *Monster House:* There is a discrepancy between realistic character movement and the lack of pushed facial expressions.
- *Snow White and the Seven Dwarfs*: There is a discrepancy between very cartoony body ratio and character design in the dwarfs and the realistic movement of Snow White.
- *The Boxtrolls:* The skin texture is way too painterly for the cartoony characters.
- *Toot, Whistle, Plunk and Boom*: There are very stark discrepancies in the overall design of the film.
- *Fantasia: Toccata and Fugue in D Minor:* The concept is abstract, but there appear realistic elements in the film (musical instruments in the sky).
- *The Thief and the Cobbler:* The main characters are cartoony and mostly smooth in their outlines, whereas the brigands are rough and follow a different character style altogether.

As can be seen, the disbelief of the character within its own theatrical reality can be caused by many different aspects, but they are all caused by some mismatching element within the character or character and environment.

Inconsistencies in the design: *Monster House*

CG features have often made the mistake of stylizing their characters but using realistic character animation that is based on motion capture, for instance, Sony Pictures Animation's *Monster House*. The idea of using a shortcut for the character animation is going hand in hand with the lack of understanding that handmade character animation is an art form with a visual style that has developed over not just 100 years, but is based on aesthetics of thousands of years of character poses and compositional arrangements of characters. It comes with a quality that motion capture doesn't have if it is not adjusted heavily in its composition and poses. In *Monster House* the characters are stylized, the body ratio is pushed, the facial ratios, forms, and shapes are very much exaggerated, but the animation is weirdly focusing on the realistic movement of the motion capture performance. Contrary to the body however, the facial animation is extremely reduced in most characters (not so much in the character of Nebbercracker's facials, but even there the muscle movement is very limited). This extreme discrepancy within the body's movement is what makes those characters look unreal and artificial. For example, the head itself is moving realistically, but the facial features often move just slightly and therefore look dead and mask-like. The actor's performance is not following the compositional guidelines for artistic poses of exceptionally crafted feature animation and thus the character staging has the look and feel of a simple stage production, or just poorly executed animation. It lacks some of the key

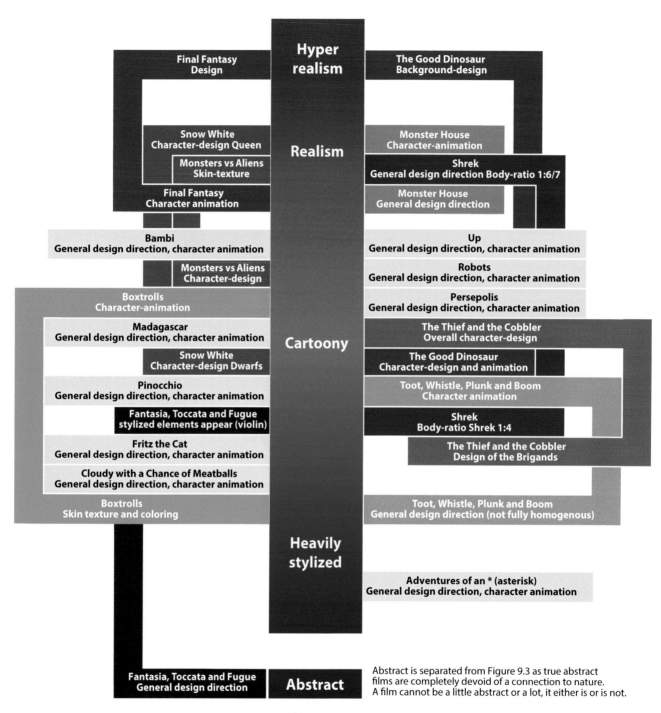

Hyper realism

Final Fantasy Design

The Good Dinosaur Background-design

Realism

Snow White Character-design Queen

Monsters vs Aliens Skin-texture

Final Fantasy Character animation

Monster House Character-animation

Shrek General design direction Body-ratio 1:6/7

Monster House General design direction

Bambi General design direction, character animation

Up General design direction, character animation

Monsters vs Aliens Character-design

Robots General design direction, character animation

Persepolis General design direction, character animation

Cartoony

Boxtrolls Character-animation

The Thief and the Cobbler Overall character-design

Madagascar General design direction, character animation

The Good Dinosaur Character-design and animation

Snow White Character-design Dwarfs

Toot, Whistle, Plunk and Boom Character animation

Pinocchio General design direction, character animation

Shrek Body-ratio Shrek 1:4

Fantasia, Toccata and Fugue stylized elements appear (violin)

The Thief and the Cobbler Design of the Brigands

Fritz the Cat General design direction, character animation

Cloudy with a Chance of Meatballs General design direction, character animation

Boxtrolls Skin texture and coloring

Toot, Whistle, Plunk and Boom General design direction (not fully homogenous)

Heavily stylized

Adventures of an * (asterisk) General design direction, character animation

Fantasia, Toccata and Fugue General design direction

Abstract

Abstract is separated from Figure 9.3 as true abstract films are completely devoid of a connection to nature. A film cannot be a little abstract or a lot, it either is or is not.

Figure 9.3

elements in animation which are silhouette, directions, vectors, and especially a strong line of action. The actors that portray the characters are not giving them a presence that is unique, but just create rather plain personalities and consequently the lack of interesting movement very much enhances the artificial feel of the characters (there are exceptions of course). The facial features never enhance the character's overall direction, there is no aesthetic unity within the character, no vectors or line-of-actions that dominate the entire pose and go with the facials, in short, to present well-crafted character poses for animation. The characters never seem to look at each other or an object/direction properly as the eyes do not lead the movement and the eyebrows never open up the facial expression toward the focal point. The characters move like humans with giant carnival heads. Their artistic composition is a mismatch and is not homogenous at all. This is not to be blamed on the uncanny valley as so often stated but just an inconsistent overall design with mismatching character animation. Realistic characters need realistic animation, stylized characters need stylized animation. There is no exception in entertaining feature animation (as of yet).

An exceptional example in creating CG animation where design, character animation style, and layout speak the same language is DreamWork Animation's *Madagascar*. The entire film's design follows a geometric style where angles are even seen in the character animation and the layout. The flow of the character animation is slightly interpreted through a more edgy character arc that gives the characters a Warner Brothers timing that is tight and edgy. Because of the unity of all its design elements, the feature works in its visuals extremely well.

Pushing the design into emotions and personality

The next step in the design would be determining the extent of the emotions (visually and psychologically) and facial expressions in relation to the position on the design scale. *Monster House* mostly lacks strong facial expressions which makes the faces look dead and mask-like (which would obviously be fine if this is part of the concept of the film, which it isn't in the case of *Monster House*). We already have two different design elements that don't match each other: realistic character animation and slightly stylized character design (Figure 9.4). Are the facial expressions following the stylized design, or the realistic movement? Or something in between? The characters in *Monster House* actually have their very own direction of stylization where the expected magnitude of the expressions is reduced tremendously, thus once more spreading the design on the scale instead of reducing it. The more stylized the characters are, the more stylized the emotions should be to create a design that's in all its elements consistent. In *Monster House* the facial expressions need to be pushed much more to match the design. This does not necessarily mean to push them

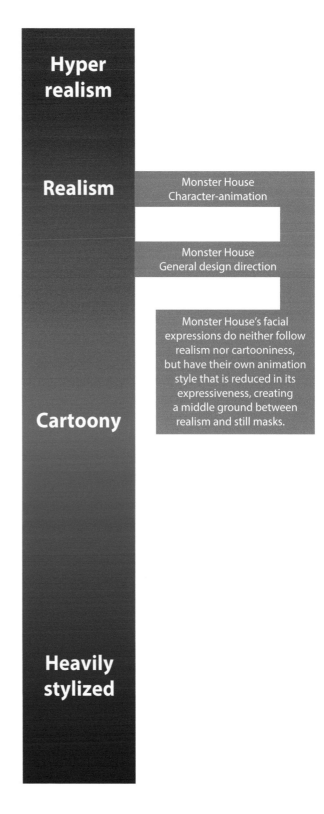

Figure 9.4

in their character design, but to push them in their extremes in the character animation. The animation principle of exaggeration is the most dominant in cartoony characters, which are destined to have their expressions, emotions, and poses pushed to the extreme. The simplification of cartoony body shapes go hand in hand with the stylization of the emotional expressions. It would be rather odd to have a 2D character that is heavily stylized to act with realistic expressions, as they would need much more detailed line quality to express those complex expressions. To achieve realistic emotions in the facial setup the details in eyes, brows, forehead, mouth, etc., would break the simplicity of the design of a very cartoony and stylized character (again: there are of course exceptions). The level of stylization is then not on par with the representation of the emotions (however the future will tell if that is really the case). This is the visual representation of the emotions. There is also the psychological representation, which follows the same rule of homogeneity. The extent of the character's exaggeration in terms of psychological traits also goes hand in hand with the style. Roger Rabbit has, because of his exaggerated cartoony character design, pushed and exaggerated personality traits. He reacts to everything much more extremely and his emotions are always pushed to the limits, but his entire personality is so hyped up and over the top that it is a pleasure to watch. Only because of the homogeneity in all his character elements in relation to his design is he really believable as who he is.

Discrepancy in the character elements (Figure 9.3)

The discrepancy in characters that are creepy or don't fully convince on a visual, performance, or psychological level does not necessarily show constantly throughout the character's performance, but often just in little glimpses here and there and smaller movements or actions; however, they are often felt subconsciously. There are in a feature film maybe just a couple of moments that feel very weird and strange depending on which element of the design or the character animation the discrepancy touches on. In *Shrek*, for example, it is the design that reminds us constantly of something not being right (aside from the character animation[13]). Shrek himself has a body ratio of about 1:4¼ (four heads ¼ in height) whereas Fiona as an ogress has a realistic body ratio of 1:6, which fits her general body type realistically. All the other characters are also realistic in body proportions, it is only Shrek himself that does not fit into the design. It is unfortunately enough to be distracting and especially in the shots with both Shrek and Fiona interacting—the discrepancy is very dominant as both are supposed to be from the same species: ogres, but

Shrek's hands are gigantic (Fiona is cursed, so she appears as a human by day but turns into an ogress by night). If Fiona would not be in the film, then there would only be humans and Shrek himself, which would work slightly better as there is no character that compares to Shrek. But because Fiona is the link between human and ogres the discrepancy is so very obvious. Therefore the slightest deviation from an assigned design direction can point out the character as artificial and therefore stop the needed logic of the film to be fully, 100% convincing. This can also happen with a concept not following general expectations that the audience has about specific characters. The often-applied scene or shot where the characters breakdance or join in popular music tracks most of the time feel contrived and not only out of place, but out of character. Most of the characters are not the type to do or be able to breakdance, or follow any other contemporary trend. The result is grandmas twisting their hips to Beonce's or Britney Spears' music and the audience is slightly embarrassed as the scene is pandering to the audience's taste instead of following the character's personality. It is not just the design and the character animation but also the personality and action that can make or break a character. In DreamWorks Animation's film *Monsters vs. Aliens* (2009) the characters are cartoony and the world is likewise stylized to the same level; also, the character animation is a perfect fit. However, the skin of the characters is overly realistic. One does not expect realistic skin like that on a cartoony character; it breaks the illusion of unity and is therefore confusing or creepy. The characters in the close-ups, when the texture is especially dominant, look uncomfortable. The character appears as something that it is not, claims to be on a level of realism that it is not. One does not expect a rather realistic skin with freckles and blemishes on a stylized character. It is unfortunately the urge of many CGI artists to push the visuals to an ever higher degree of realism without realizing that the uncanny valley's effect can happen on every level of stylization. The uncanny valley does not just run horizontally through realism, but runs vertically along the stylization graph from hyperreal all the way down to abstract.

For Pixar's *The Good Dinosaur* (2015) the rather unique decision was made of separating the level of stylization dramatically between background and characters. The background was so heavily realistic that it shifted into the hyperreal, creating images that are even more real than nature itself. It is not a replication of reality, but a perfection of it. The water animation of the raging river was making the audience wet! The background visuals were stunning to say the least. The characters on the other hand were very cartoony, some more than others (the raptors were the most cartoony, not fitting into the style of the film at all). The different style made the characters look like toys that were left out in a beautiful and stunning landscape. Hyperrealism and cartooniness fight each other in every shot. If the characters were actually toys, then there is a reason for this shape-oriented and simplified character design and it makes sense, ergo the design would work. But the characters are supposed to be real dinosaurs

---

[13] Considering that the first *Shrek* film was done in 2001 it was a wise choice to use keyframe animation for the characters instead of motion capture, which wasn't up to the task yet and also to keep using keyframe animation due to design consistencies throughout the entire series.

and humans, so their design needs to match the level of stylization of the world they are living in. They are part of nature and nature itself created them, so there is the requirement for unity. Either nature needs to be more cartoony or the characters need to be more realistic. The human boy however was also stylized and cartoony, but had a convincing and stunning animation which made him by far the most interesting character in the film. However, his design did not fit the dinosaurs level on the design scale as the latter were much more simplified and stylized in terms of their shape language.

Abstract aesthetics

An example for the abstract section on the design scale is Disney's *Fantasia* (1940) and its segment of Johann Sebastian Bach's Toccata and Fugue in D Minor. Walt Disney invited the famous animator Oskar Fischinger to work on the piece as he was one of the key internationally acclaimed artists in the abstract animation movement. Unfortunately Fischinger's expertise and sensibility toward abstract art was not only not understood, neither was his development work for the short section of *Fantasia* followed by the Disney artists and thus the initial concept of creating an abstract piece was destroyed. It is obviously the misunderstanding of what abstract actually means that makes this segment very difficult to endure. Abstract is the total lack of relation to the natural world. Abstract art creates a world of shapes and forms, colors, and compositions that do not relate to the natural world. Disney's segment has an abstracted superficial look to it, but integrates musical instruments that fly through the sky interpreting the musical movement. Realistic objects per definition break the realm of abstract. The outcome can only be kitsch despite its technical bravour. Disney's *Fantasia 2000* (2000) with its segment after Ludwig van Beethoven's Symphony No. 5 falls into a very similar trap but this time there is a discrepancy between character design and character movement. The characters are a geometric placeholder for "abstract" but do not have the same level of abstraction in the character animation, which is cartoony and represents the movement of butterflies. It is neither abstract in its lighting nor in the storytelling; every element refers to a realistic image or action. Thus the outcome is an uncomfortable mishmash of misunderstood artistic terms and visual realism, and ends up once more as kitsch.

Conclusion

As mentioned before a discrepancy or mismatch in these six aspects can make the audience question the character's believability:

- Concept and position on the design scale
- Character design (the look and aesthetics in relation to the story)

- Character personality
- Character's relationship to their environment
- Character's objective and goal (story)
- Performance and character animation

I personally do not see much of a difference between my emotions toward the realistically dancing Snow White and the very cartoony dwarfs or a character in the slightly stylized *A Christmas Carol*. Both times there are moments where the characters look wrong and I do get the feeling of it being uncomfortable because it is not giving me what I expect to see.

The same is true for the characters in any CG film that are supposed to be convincing, but are not because of something in their movement or design not following the initially assigned position on the design scale. But because the CG character is much more realistic, we tend to focus more on the eyes (it would be an interesting study to see how the eyes scan an image that is rendered flat, compared to one that is rendered photoreal); however, the rest of the body can be "wrong." Daffy Duck can be as convincing as a living and breathing character as much as a hyperreal CG character has the ability to do, one just needs to see Daffy Duck perform in *Duck Amuck* from 1953, where no one would argue that he is not real. The idea of a character being rendered photoreal and therefore being more convincing is a false one in my opinion. The question is to what extent one believes in the character on screen actually being real. Is Roger Rabbit an actual, real character that the audience believes exists? Of course he is. That is why the film works. If he was not, if the audience would just for a moment during the film think that Roger is merely paint on a sheet of acetate, the film would have failed. So why would the uncanny valley then not appear in cartoony characters that are not fully convincing because of the design not matching the character animation style? I would argue that it can, however it depends on ones susceptibility to accept cartoony characters as being "real" which is the goal of anyone who creates characters: to make them real in their own world. A hyperreal character has to fulfill exactly the same requirements as a cartoony character: to be convincing and fool the audience into the belief that they exist. However, the more real a character is supposed to be the more the details need to be correct and match human looks and behavior (which as we have seen in the realistic style needs to penetrate deep into scientific terrain). Brad Bird said when *The Incredibles* (2001) was released: "The character design was difficult ... CGI looks plastic without detail, but beyond a certain point with the stylized deformed people, it starts to look creepy."[14] The question is, how susceptible and trained the viewer is to recognize this discrepancy. Therefore, the uncanny valley isn't strictly connected to realism, but to any kind of discrepancy between character design, character animation style, and environment.

[14] Butler M. (2009). *Final Fantasy or The Incredibles*. journal.animationstudies. org (retrieved June 12, 2016).

So the uncanny valley is not limited to realism, but just a general discrepancy in the overall character design which causes various levels of discomfort in the audience. Overall character design includes: aesthetics, color, shapes, facial expressions, body ratio, clothing, personality, character and personality, goals and aspirations, abilities, character animation, and relationship to the environment. The rule to avoid the issue of the uncanny is whether the believability of the character in the environment is to be maintained. Then every element of the design and the character animation has to stay in the same range of stylization unless there is a story, a design, or an artistic reason why they should not. That seems to be a rule; however, rules as always need to be broken to push art forward. So I want to see a character that breaks this rule and is still convincing.

CHAPTER 10

Pose and Communication

The human body has three major ways of communication:

- Language
- Facial expressions
- Body language

Language applies to character design insofar as it can serve as inspiration for the designer to imagine the character via the voice. However, we usually deal with drawings and 2D imagery without the voice being provided. Nevertheless, the first time Hugh Harman and Rudolph Ising's character *Bosko* was presented to the public in *Bosko, the Talk-Ink Kid* in May 1929, it was one of the first characters with a synchronized talking voice in animation. Bosko talks to his "creator" and introduces himself to the audience. Adding a voice to a character gives them a stronger presence and adds believability in their being alive in their very own reality. Bosko's first short film was never seen by a broad audience but was only meant to be a presentation piece to promote Bosko, who became Warner Brother's first cartoon character and started the famous *Loony Tunes* series with *Sinkin' in the Bathtub* in 1930. Language is a crucial part of animation and obviously carries a significant aspect of the character's personality, not only for the audience but also for the designer. Having the voice of the character while designing is tremendously helpful in visualizing who they are (if one has the luxury of being provided the voice, that is). Next to language there are the facial expressions and also body language to communicate with. Those two express the inner emotional state of a character and how they relate, or not, to their environment. The time-based physical communication (as mentioned, facial expression and body language) can be simplified into a series of poses (or keyframes, key poses in animation), which are artistic body compositions that express the action in poses and communicate nonverbally the story or the thoughts of a character. Poses generally have three distinct goals:

1. Express the character's emotions
2. Express the character's actions and the story
3. Express a message or theme

The first two points always have to be covered if the character is supposed to be a fully believable personality that not only acts, but acts for a reason (see embodied acting). The reason and the character's emotional state need to be visualized for the pose

to make sense and be understood in its complexity, not only in its action. This doesn't mean that the complexity of the inner emotional life of the character is fully comprehensible to the audience, but its visualization needs to be strived for.

The third point of expressing a message or a theme is more difficult to achieve in animation and much easier accomplished in sculpture or painting, which deal with one visual instead of the time-based medium animation, where many poses combined make the character move. The theme touches upon the meaning of the piece and how the audience can interpret what they see additionally to what the story and visuals already present to them. The works of Yuriy Norshteyn are excellent examples of how to use animation as a tool for complex storytelling that goes far beyond entertainment and leaves the audience with many questions, by evoking moods and emotions aside from a mysterious story. His work, including the very popular *Hedgehog in the Fog* (1975) or the magnificent *Tale of Tales* (1979), are masterpieces in animation that are neither easy to understand nor to interpret. But it is exactly this that makes those pieces a pleasure to watch again and again. The poses are sometimes not clear, but imply various interpretations that open up the meaning to an array of options. Clarity is sometimes avoided.

All three mentioned goals of poses express the personality and temperament of a character, show their introversion and extroversion, show the relationship between people in a group, and express who is dominant and who is submissive. Poses are crucial for images or sculptures in the interest of conveying the story and/or theme to the audience with the character's body as the tool of communication. We have the possibility for:

- One character, who is not explicitly communicating with anyone but self-reflecting (Auguste Rodin's *The Thinker* (1904) in sculpture or Yuriy Norshteyn's *Hedgehog in the Fog* (1975), where the character of the hedgehog does loosely communicate with the other characters, but is much more thoughtful and observant than social).
- One character who is communicating with someone/ something that is inside or outside the realm of the sculpture/ character and/or unseen by the viewer (*Augustus of Prima Porta* (1 AD) in sculpture or Jiří Trnka's *The Hand* (1965) or Peter Lord's *Adam* (1991) in animation).
- Then there is the group arrangement, where many characters interact with each other (*Laocoön and his Sons* (~27 BC–68 AD)

DOI: 10.1201/b22147-10

in sculpture or Brűder Lauenstein's *Balance* (1989) in animation.

- Some characters may also reflect on their own within the group (Auguste Rodin's *The Burghers of Calais* (1889) in sculpture or many of the works of the Brothers Quay) in which the characters do not communicate with each other in a traditional sense, but go through the escapist setting on their own or weirdly communicate nonverbally.

For the purposes of character design, the pose has to reflect the personality of the character and show what their position is in the story in very simple and obvious visuals. Naturally, the pose has to describe the character from the script, usually with the intent to portray a unique personality that the audience will be excited about. As we only have the pose to sell the character in their personality to the director or art director, the pose itself has to be unique and specific enough to captivate their interest, but also recognizable enough as a character cliché to be immediately understood. It is not just the habitus of the character that is of interest, but the basis of their personality which in turn is what makes the character unique and needs to be visualized. The personality is the center of the character and should always be the core information throughout the design process and integrated into every step and every detail of the design, and of course the character's pose. Personality and appeal have to show immediately and should not leave any questions open, but quickly explain who the character is and who the audience is dealing with. With a clear and easily readable pose, the audience has fewer problems understanding the message and he character is less likely to be misinterpreted.

What is a clear pose?

- A clear pose is when all the body parts, facial expressions, and apparel speak the same language and express one thought or story point.
- Most poses concentrate on one action, have one direction, and don't confuse the viewer with several ideas. There is clarity in the movement and a simplicity in the flow of all lines in the body.
- All body parts strengthen the line of action and go with its flow, not against it.
- The silhouette is clear and the expressions comprehensible.
- Nothing covers up parts that are important for the character to be understood.
- A good pose always has only one focal point. Several focal points confuse and ruin the comprehensibility of the pose (very few exceptions apply).

For a pose to be fully understood one needs time. The more time there is to observe the character the more complicated the pose can be. Details and intricate connections between character

and story require time to be grasped. In animation, this time is usually not given and the pose has to be read in a split second. In sculpture and painting there is plenty of time to observe the sophisticated and artistic tour-de-force of vectors and content, so those poses can be much more complex. Animation has to reduce the complexity of its poses in order to be clear and immediate in its message. This does not mean that it has to be banal! One always wants to create unique poses in order to evoke interest in the audience and avoid stock poses.

Poses in the character performance

Another very important point in animation is to create interesting poses throughout the character animation and not only focus on one main pose, but make every keyframe pose count. Each pose needs to be designed with the same care and eye for detail. There can be one main pose that describes the entire shot or action and all the other poses either lead toward that pose or away from it, but are enhancing the main pose's set direction. In longer shots though, the poses need variation in order to give the shot contrast and the composition of the frame different options to not appear stagnant. The Warner Brothers' short films directed by Chuck Jones are packed with exciting and interesting poses throughout the shorts and never allow the audience to lose their interest toward the characters because the poses never repeat themselves and always keep the character alive. Repeating poses show the audience that the character is handmade and it clearly shows a lack of imagination. The poses of Daffy Duck in *Duck Amuck* (1953) or any short film with Wile E. Coyote are constantly changing and are always pushing the idea to the extreme, yet keep the storytelling element as the priority. The characters are never stuck in one area of the compositional field but always vary their physical action and their position in the frame, which makes the shorts appear as extremely well crafted as their characters. This kind of quality for exquisite poses can only come from extensive study of the character and also an animator or director that

explores in his drawings the possibilities of the shot and the creative exploration of the composition and pose.

Creating poses does take time and lots of pencil mileage (however, like always there are artists that just make amazing poses magically appear, others have to work hard on getting decent poses). When drawing poses it is very helpful in the beginning to have a checklist at hand that can quickly be looked at to see if all the points that should be considered are actually applied. All the points are mentioned in this book and can just be compiled into a list.

Technical aspects of poses

To create the right pose for a character there are many different aspects that need to be checked one by one to result in a pose that has the clarity needed to be read immediately. Those aspects are explained in the following chapters.

Case study: Pose and facial expression in Disney's *Tarzan* (1999)[1]

During the 1990s, Disney pushed in various feature films toward more realism in its traditional drawn animated features. The tendency to realism started with the success of *The Lion King* (1994) that not only had rather naturalistic characters but also, with the use of blurry shadows, rendered them even more realistic (for 2D animation standards). This added a level of dimensionality and with it a complexity that was new to hand-drawn animation. The digital coloring allowed blurry shadows that were not possible, or not to this extent, in earlier cell animation. This came with a price, literally. But not only the costs of the feature rose. Adding shadows to characters and taking them out of their two-dimensional plane makes it more difficult to address their graphic qualities in favor of the ever rising appreciation and fashion toward a more form-oriented computer graphics look in animation (the first CG feature film *Toy Story* was released in 1995). Traditional Disney animation (from Disney and other companies that followed its aesthetic lead) felt the urge to compete with CG animation visually, and instead of focusing on the graphic advantages of its own tradition, often succumbed to the realistic rendering of a perfect dimensional world. Especially *Treasure Planet* suffers from this urge to produce form instead of shape, though the result is often quite impressive from a technical perspective. One of the most complex characters during that phase is the character Tarzan due to his anatomical accuracy and realistic

(-ish) physical action. The complexity and also the difficulty of bringing a character like Tarzan onto the screen requires all the other characters to follow the same level of stylization of course. The other characters in the film however are more cartoony or even very cartoony (Jane's father, Professor Porter for instance), not fitting the lead of the main character in their character design and animation. Creating a cast that is that different can have its drawbacks.

Tarzan himself follows anatomy[2] to a degree that was new to hand-drawn animation of human characters which usually emphasizes simplicity, exaggeration, and cartooniness. In his character design he is the clean-cut athletic hero with dreadlocks that resembles more a sports magazine *Tarzan* than a man growing up without the knowledge of physical hygiene, a shave, or a toothbrush. It apparently reflects his upbringing in the jungle and his relations with animals instead of humans. Nevertheless, the character design and also the animation focuses on his jungle background by constantly referring to his very own way of dealing with his environment. It is this tactile exploration that is reflected in his big hands and feet, which he uses to feel and grasp his jungle world, very much like an ape does. Because of his semi-naturalistic physique and nakedness, the animation had to rely on accurate anatomy and intense study of musculature, which had been done before successfully for the animals in *Bambi* in 1942 but never to the extent needed for Tarzan in a human character.

---

[1] Due to the fact that the Disney Company did not release the copyrights for images of the feature *Tarzan* to be used in this educational section, which would have tremendously helped the understanding of the discussed compositions and poses, it is necessary for the reader to check and compare the images from the movie via the provided time-codes alongside the text to fully grasp the compositional intent.

[2] A character that was likewise based on rigorous anatomical studies, animal instead of human anatomy, was of course Bambi, from the Disney feature with the same name from 1942. But generally, intense anatomical studies on such a complex level is not the norm in cel animation.

Supervising animator Glen Keane designed Tarzan's character and based his work on Auguste Rodin's sculptural group *The Citizen of Calais* (1884–1889) and also Aimé-Jules Dalou's statue *The Triumph of the Republic* (1889) on the Place de la Nation in Paris. Tarzan's design includes a contemporary sensibility in the face and hair, but also keeps the complexity and drama in the poses that can be found in Dalou's sculpture. Tarzan's movements are a combination of human and animal behavior, suggesting that he is neither man nor animal. The exploratory curiosity of an ape with their awkwardly half-upright walk, the flexibility of a cat combined with the speed and tree-climbing abilities of monkeys create a unique character that has human and also animal traits without him feeling like a patchwork of both. He comes across as a believable character that has one foot in each world. The side characters clearly distinguish from Tarzan. The clash between Jane's Victorian behavior and Tarzan's uninhibited curiosity is a continuous source of comedic release in the film. And Clayton's character is in its ruthlessness and determination an other side of clichéd manliness that contrasts Tarzan's in most parts.

The sensibility in some shots of Tarzan's character animation are so well animated by supervising animator Glen Keane that they truly make one forget that it is animation that one watches. Especially the moment of the first meeting between Jane and Tarzan has an emotional impact that is as convincing as any live-action film. The scene takes time to evolve and allows emotions of empathy to develop, which does not happen very often in 2D animation as a slow pace is so difficult to achieve. The scene plays quietly and is rather long with a strong focus on the emotional development of the main character, who is mostly silent. It is pure animation and movement, and has all the strength it needs to move the audience in a moment that is unique in its emotional persuasiveness. The emotions are not bluntly shown but we can see in Tarzan's face and especially in his eyes the thought process he is going through during the recognition of another human in front of him. Glen Keane explains his emotional approach to this very scene:

> These scenes for me are often the most difficult because you are trying to express such emotions that you feel yourself and you experienced in your own life. And I remember animating these scenes feeling the same emotions Tarzan was going through and all you can do sometimes is just press harder on your pencil to try to make the drawing express what you are feeling in your heart and you hope that the audience can feel it as they are looking at it. The scene where Tarzan meets Jane face to face is a moment where he discovers someone like him. You have to express it in the eyes and I tried to find a moment in my own life when I had seen and discovered somebody like myself for the first time and I remember my daughter Claire being born, 30 seconds old, the doctor puts her in my hand and I looked and it was like a mirror I could see myself. And I told Claire: When you see this scene Claire, that's not Tarzan looking at Jane that's me looking at you.[3]

The scene works so very well because it takes its time to allow the character to express complex emotions through his face. Tarzan's eyes, the subtle movement in the eyebrows, the poses, the composition and focus are all perfectly composed to create the very emotion that is so moving and so incredibly difficult to achieve.

The whole scene with its two characters falls somewhat into two parts: Jane's and Tarzan's. Both characters do not fully speak the same design language as Tarzan is marginally more realistic in most shots, especially in the close-ups, and Jane is rendered slightly more cartoony. Only at the end of the scene when Tarzan is listening to Jane's heartbeat he is rendered again more cartoony and both characters fit each other in their design. The difference of the anatomical approach of Tarzan compared to Jane is very obvious in this scene as Tarzan is built up from the inside out with muscles and skeleton as a foundation, whereas Jane is built up from her shape and form language. One can very much feel the anatomical structure underneath Tarzan's skin. His animation is just movement and subtle action/reaction. Jane's constant talking and verbal reaction of what is happening however is somewhat distracting and not necessary as the excellent animation explains very much what is going on. One can claim that it is her personality to be verbal and express her thoughts and emotions, but still it interrupts the flow and extraordinary subtlety of Tarzan's outstanding character performance. What is often forgotten in animation (and also live-action feature film) is that film per se is a visual medium, which is its strength. It does not need verbal explanation in order to work and be understood. Quite the contrary: often sound and dialog distract from the "art of movement" that animation can be. Sound is crucial to open up the artificial screen of animation and give it a wider space outside the frame, though too much sound and it adds another level of artificiality. The scene with Tarzan is not about Jane's character trait of rambling, but about his recognition of another human being and *the* pinnacle moment of the movie (maybe even Tarzan's life, as it is the moment that will change everything for him). From now on he is seeking the company of humans. Would silence in a scene of this emotional caliber be stronger in it allowing the emotions to run more fluently and uninterrupted?

The way the scene is planned out is perfectly following Tarzan's thought process of going from the glove and hand of Jane to the comparison of both their hands, to Tarzan's eyes that show the recognition and then the comparison of their heartbeat: one step at a time. In this scene, Glen Keane gives us a character in all his complexities and the character animation perfectly allows us to not only see the character in his skin and bones but also provides an important glimpse into his mind and emotional world.

Time-code 00:38:23: The setup of the scene is established: Jane occupies the left and Tarzan 2/3 of the frame, a position that each will keep until they start to know each other in the middle of the scene. A strong push toward the left through

---

[3] Glen Keane in *The Making of Tarzan*, DVD 2013, Disney's Tarzan (1999).

Tarzan's pose and line of action pushes Jane left. She in her pose is succumbing to his push, bends, and tilts left. The horizontal tree-branch's upwards curve creates a strong vector, that with Jane's yellow skirt makes her the focal point of the image. Everything seems to push toward her. because of Tarzan's darker skin color he blends slightly more into the background and also occupies most of the frame as he is the one that dominates the action. Jane is the passive and defensive one, Tarzan the active. Behind him everything is open and free. This allows of course the interpretation of him actually being "free" and her being "restrained," not only physically but also socially through her uptight behavior in England's Victorian society (Figure 10.1).

Time-code 00:38:31: The focus shifts from Jane to her glove, and Tarzan inspects it. In order to compositionally strengthen this point, her hand is part of a compositional triangle with his back and hairline, arm, and shoulder as the opposing side. The triangle appears mirrored and upside down in Jane's pose (elbow–head–glove). Tarzan's facial expression is very easy to read in its depiction of curiosity toward Jane and her clothing. He reacts to her with animalistic and uninhibited wonder. The composition of his poses underline the connection between him and Jane in the entire scene and Tarzan always opens up his face and body toward Jane and the action is mostly kept in the middle of the frame.

Tarzan's character in this shot compositionally reads toward the left. His eyebrows open the face toward Jane and the dreadlock that falls down on his left shoulder closes the intimacy between the two as much as Jane's hair closes it from the opposite side. The tree behind Jane prevents our eye from leaving the image to the left. He has a greater range of movement which Jane does not have. Both characters in this scene are not only demanding their physical space in the composition, but also their emotional space. Tarzan is curious and has no hesitation to examine Jane, she however (unsuccessfully) demands distance. He is constantly pushing toward screen left whereas Jane is restricted to a small space (Figure 10.2).

Figure 10.2 (Time-code 00:38:31)

Time-code 00:38:33: The triangular shape of Tarzan's pose is maintained and the gloved hand serves as a vector toward his facial expression. The background keeps a negative space open for the vector of the glove to visually elongate along Tarzan's head (Figure 10.3).

Time-code 00:38:39: In this shot we have Tarzan pulling off Jane's glove to reveal her hand and compare it with his own, realizing that they are both the same. When he lifts the glove his eyes move upward with the tip of his finger and his eyebrows lift up from the right, which visually intensifies the movement of glove and hand upward. The eyebrows follow the movement of his left hand and open the face toward the tip of the finger. This very subtle movement is intense enough to be felt. In this shot Tarzan is still, despite being in the center of the frame, occupying the right side as this is his position in the entire scene. Tarzan is always on the right in the scene, whereas Jane is on the left. We focus now solely on Tarzan exploring the hand and glove, and his slow realization of another human in front of him. Jane is obviously still in our mind in this shot, but she isn't in the frame allowing the intimacy of Tarzan's reaction to be fully played out. This shot is about Tarzan, not Jane (Figure 10.4).

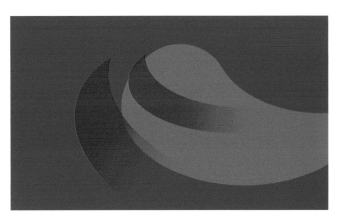

Figure 10.1 (Time-code 00:38:23)

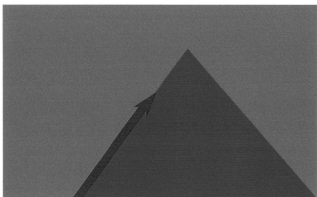

Figure 10.3 (Time-code 00:38:33)

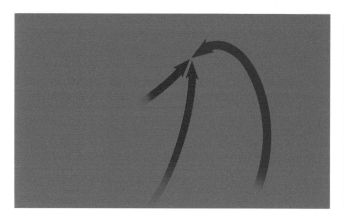

Figure 10.4 (Time-code 00:38:39)

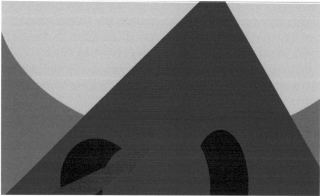

Figure 10.6 (Time-code 00:38:43)

Time-code 00:38:40: The glove is pulled off the hand and its movement is accentuated by the background. The leaves on the right have the visual strength to lead the eyes upward; nevertheless, two twigs with leaves are pointing toward the glove. Again the triangle appears with Tarzan's hand and Jane's forearm.

She is still very much positioned in the left corner, which underlines her still being pushed by Tarzan to the left (Figure 10.5).

Once the glove is off her hand (00:38:42), Jane immediately looks back at her naked hand. This is now where the focus lies.

Time-code 00:38:43: Cut to the new focal point still being maintained in the exact same position. Again a triangular composition with Tarzan's eyes on the same level as the fingertips of Jane. His hands are bent inward bringing movement toward Jane's hand, whose forearm serves as a vector into his face. The leaves in the background bulge downward, emphasizing his head's position (Figure 10.6).

Time-code 00:38:51: The frame is divided into the two sections, still giving Tarzan more space than Jane. The background accentuates the position of the hands with its movement by bulging in the middle upward, creating an interesting combination of compositional elements (Figure 10.7).

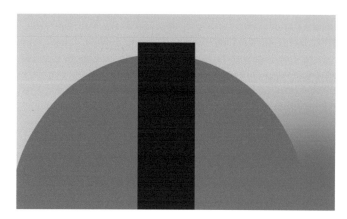

Figure 10.7 (Time-code 00:38:51)

Time-code 00:38:53: His upper body is inscribed into a trapezoid shape, a masculine geometric shape, within rests a circle that contains his arm and shoulder and is also exactly on the level of his eyes, therefore accentuating their position (the circle can also include his trapezoids, the lower muscular wings of his back-muscles). He is positioned with his eyes and face in the middle of the frame, though his overall body is positioned slightly to the right. The positive space of his knee is balanced by the negative space of the arms on the left side. The width of his knee on the right and the distance of arm on the left to his side is the same. The background gives a subtle negative space to Tarzan's position and envelopes him rather than him just overlapping the background (Figure 10.8).

Time-code 00:38:57: This is the moment of the realization that there is another human in front of him. Hands are slowly lowered to give way to the connection between the eyes. Emphasis is shifting from the former focal point of the hands to their eyes by lowering the hands and taking them away from the audience's attention, replacing their importance with the new focal point of the eyes, where the change in his mind is made visible. There occurs a very clear step-by-step approach to Jane: glove–hands–eyes.

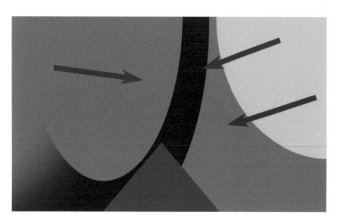

Figure 10.5 (Time-code 00:38:40)

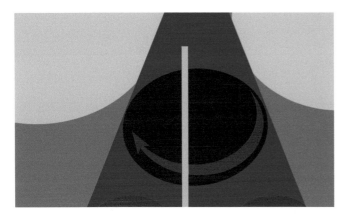

Figure 10.8 (Time-code 00:38:53)

Time-code 00:38:59: Jane's head is counterbalancing the hands on the lower right which sets both parts off as being not only prominent, but also relating to each other. The leaves behind her flow on a straight line downward right into the hands, making a connection between her eyes and the hands, despite her looking at Tarzan. Compared to the shot before she is occupying the negative space left of Tarzan in this shot; their bodies do not overlap from one composition/shot to the next yet. The next shot introduces this connection very clearly by overlapping their eyes (Figure 10.9).

Time-code 00:39:02: This shot has Tarzan's extremely subtle facial expression in a choker shot or extreme close-up. That the mouth is nearly cut out by the frame puts the emphasis onto the eyes and eyebrows, which is where the emotions are the most obvious. The audience feels as if they are looking into his soul, or at least his mind. Compared to the shot before, his eyes are on the same level as Jane's, making the connection between them easily visible (Jane's left eye is actually in exactly the same position in the previous shot as Tarzan's right eye in this shot).

Time-code 00:39:07: This is the moment where Tarzan discovers Jane's heartbeat and puts his ear toward her chest. His whole pose is moving toward her and he now very much gets into Jane's personal

space. However, his line of action is not curving toward Jane but rather away from her, making it a hesitant and respectful approach. The composition moves all the way to the left being only pushed back again by the tree behind Jane. Tarzan's whole pose subtly moves toward Jane: his leg, his whole upper body is leaning left. His line of action forces Jane back and his leg in the right lower corner accentuates his tilt.

The overall image feels solid on the left and open toward the right. Jane can't escape. This intense intimate moment is beautifully reduced in his rather strong compositional force through his subtle facial expression that is just tenderness, trust, and curiosity. His eyebrows again open up the face toward Jane. The falling dreadlock is again closing the view toward the right locking the intimate focal point into the area of the upper left screen (Figure 10.10).

Time-code 00:39:11: By cutting into this extremely intimate moment between the two in a close-up, which she obviously does not enjoy, the audience is adding to her discomfort and the discomfort of being part of this rather rude penetration of her personal space.

Her hand is positioned in a way that accentuates the horizontal of his eyes and eyebrows. In addition, the shape created by her hand and bust is juxtaposed by the negative space created in the upper right.

His hair is positioned in a way that creates a curve that leads upward making it a vector to her facial expression which is important to keep in mind, not as the center of attention, but as side information that is still crucial (Figure 10.11).

Time-code 00:39:19: Now the two characters have the same distance from the frame, which suggests that now they are equal because it is understood by Tarzan that they are the same, having the same heartbeat. Her body shape and line of action is leading directly into his face and both lines of action are confronting each other, being both convex though from different perspectives: his because of presenting his heartbeat

Figure 10.9 (Time-code 00:38:59)

Figure 10.10 (Time-code 00:39:07)

Figure 10.11 (Time-code 00:39:11)

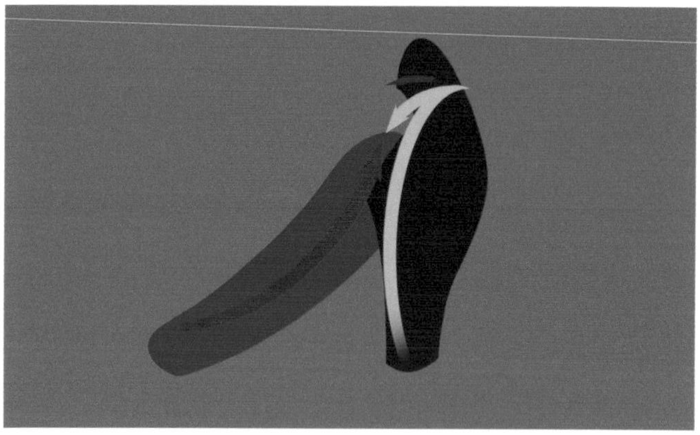

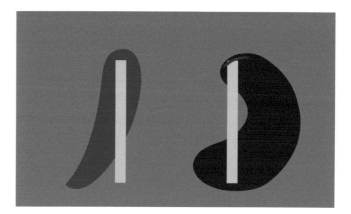

Figure 10.12 (Time-code 00:39:19)

to hear and her being pulled over. His very strong straight pose, chest stretched forward, leads into his head which is positioned in a strong downward angle. The horizontal eyebrows show determination and also relaxation (Figure 10.12).

Time-code 00:39:22: In this shot she is still somewhat rigid and defensive, however more relaxed than before, whereas his manly pose is very open and focused, occupying much space. His concave body shape exposes much of his back which is a relaxed pose, not expecting any threats from her or his surroundings. It is a pose that reflects his comfort level in this situation. His eyebrows are tilted toward Jane's face, accentuating their connection. The focus is on the invisible thread between the two, which the background leaves assist by opening up a large negative space. Both characters are in the same position in the frame as Tarzan has now accepted her as an equal. She is not pushed against the left frame anymore (Figure 10.13).

Figure 10.13 (Time-code 00:39:22)

CHAPTER 11

Thumbnail Drawings

Thumbnail drawings are small sketches of about 3–5 cm in size, and in the first stages of the design process should always be considered as the essential starting point. Due to their small size they force the artist to focus on the basics of the drawing, its foundation. For instance shapes, poses, line of action, and composition are much better understood in their content and design direction on a small scale. In character design, thumbnail drawings allow you to explore the character's main body shape more easily in as much as the size of the drawing does not allow drawing details in the first place. The scale of the thumbnail drawings does not allow the smaller parts and/or decoration of the character, which at this stage of the design are insignificant. Bigger drawings focus more on facial expressions, details in the clothing, or the line quality. In small drawings there is just not the space to add those details, so one is only able to draw the character's basic shape or pose (or what else needs to be focused on). The importance of thumbnail drawings cannot be overestimated. Their ability to spur creativity without the restriction of the complexity of bigger drawings is their utter strength.

Do as many thumbnail drawings as you can to get a feeling for the character and its shape (at least a few dozen of them). Explore which shape might work and which one would not, and slowly approach what kind of character or type the shapes suggest. In order to get a sensibility for the character's shapes and to "feel" them you have to explore them in many drawings over and over again and clearly focus on the drawing process. At some point you will feel how the shapes of the character make sense on an emotional level. To reach that point you need to concentrate on the drawings and allow yourself to be in the drawing instead of just superficially drawing it. *Being in the drawing* means to step inside the drawing itself and feel what the character is feeling, to see the environment, and feeling its emotions. This will only happen when the concentration and imagination is focused on the character and its shapes. In that stage, being concerned about how to draw the character from a technical perspective will take away much of the concentration that is needed for feeling its personality and unique shape language. However, thumbnail drawings are also very helpful when exploring perspectives of characters or figuring out specific complexities in poses.

Thumbnail drawings are about testing the field of possibilities and approaching the character from all sides. Through the exploration you search for the look and feel of the character instead of just drawing one version and being done with it. It is a constant trial-and-error process in which you investigate what shape suggests a certain type that fits the character description. Don't be satisfied with your first drawings, because they might not contain the strongest solution (sometimes they do, but you only know that in the end of the process once you are finished exploring). Do not work on the final character drawings until you solved all the basic anatomical, pose, and design problems in thumbnail sketches. Rushing this process just allows mistakes and awkward designs or poses to be carried along until the end.

Do your thumbnail drawings with as much variation as possible. The more variation you have on the paper the better it is for finding the *one* character that does fit.

The main focus in character thumbnails should be:

- Shape/form
- Line of action
- Weight (of body and fabric)
- Balance
- Contrapposto
- Character type
- Tension and compression
- Clothing in its simplest form

Finding a character

The thumbnails in Figure 11.1 are variations of the same theme to "find" a character rather than just drawing it. This method provides a variety of options and also a feel for the character and their body physique. By changing body proportions, shifting the height of clothing, the size of arms, shoes, hands, head, the line of action, and the bend of the spine, a whole lineup of different characters can easily be created in a very short amount of time.

Yet another technique is drawing silhouettes and exploring the possibilities through that. This is a very popular technique when it comes to more complex characters with lots of gear and equipment, like robots, soldiers and such, or fantastic creatures, or especially architecture or mechanical objects/vehicles.

Figure 11.1

DOI: 10.1201/b22147-11

Figure 11.2

These thumbnail drawings of an imaginary animal living in a fantastical forest is drawn with an initial vague idea of what the character should be like. The shapes and rough details are changed constantly from one sketch to the next to really explore what possibilities and even rough personalities the character allows. Quickly done, they already give you many characters that it becomes actually easy to find the one that fits the story.

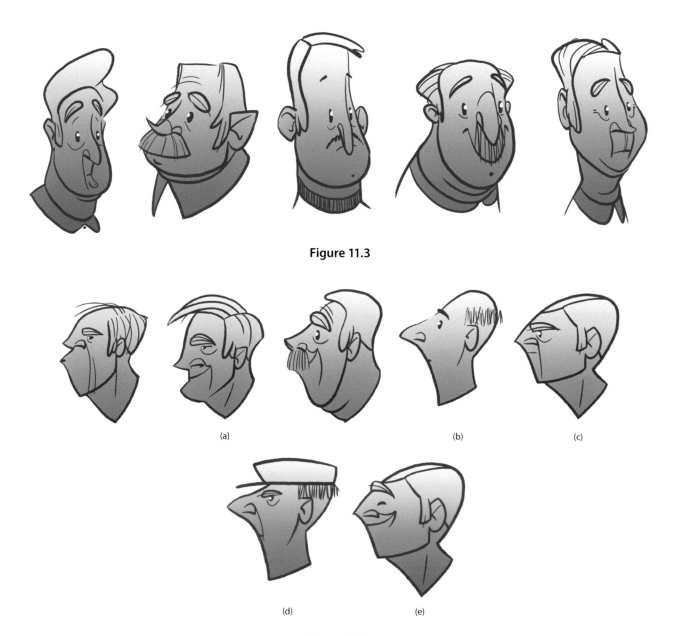

Figure 11.3

(a)　　　　　　　　　　　　(b)　　　　　(c)

(d)　　　　　(e)

Figure 11.4

Silhouettes can assist in finding extravagant shapes of clothes and gear. Silhouette explorations are part of thumbnail drawings but focus on another aspect. The thumbnail drawings in Figure 11.2 focus on the look of the character and its possible form; Figure 11.1 focuses on the overall posture and weight of the character and its shape. Silhouettes however focus on the character's outlines mostly created by the clothing and gear but are not very helpful in really finding a personality that is based on weight and posture. All do have overlapping areas, for instance they all contain various shape options or body ratios. The three are obviously closely related, yet do differ in their outcome and purpose. I personally find silhouette explorations for character design not very helpful.

Inspirational sketches

Where thumbnail drawings are usually only seen by the artist and are tools to understand the character's most basic aspects, inspirational sketches are the ones that the production design team will see and discuss.[1] Those sketches don't show exactly

---

[1] Some artists use thumbnail explorations as the basis for their inspirational sketches and others don't. It is up to one's ability and preference which work method leads to the most convincing outcome. One should not forget that knowing shape language by heart and being able to control it without elaborate thumbnail explorations becomes second nature to the experienced draftsman. That does not mean eliminating that step is recommended.

what the character will look like, but suggest options. Style options, shapes and personalities, attire and all other variations that the character could develop into, are suggested in inspirational sketches. Some animation productions also employ illustrators to paint full illustrations as inspiration for the artists on the team. The point of inspirational sketches or illustrations is to give as many options as possible, as they might trigger ideas within the team and help to carve out the characters. The more ideas there are, the clearer it is what does not fit! Inspirational sketches do what the name implies: they are there to inspire, not to pin down already.

Finding the character

We have seen that characters can be developed through thumbnail drawings because the miniscule size lets you focus on the foundation of the character, rather than the details. This is a very useful technique to come up with characters and get a feel for their shapes and the general physique of their postures. However, what counts is the result, not the way the character has been developed. Any process is valid as long as the result is good. There is also the technique of just sketching character's faces in a ¾ view (Figure 11.3) and getting a feeling for how the face reflects the character's personality. Drawing a whole bunch of faces, picking the adequate one and adding the body to it is

of course another valid technique. A further creative path is just drawing side views of the character (Figure 11.4) and through the silhouette finding out who that character is and how he or she looks. The side view makes it easier, for example, to consider verticals and horizontals in the composition, round shapes versus geometric shapes, and how all of them interact with each other (example (a) having mostly round shapes and lines, (b) having a very "empty" design with lots of empty space, (c) many edges and straight lines). The possibilities here are compositionally endless.

One has to be careful though to avoid falling into the false opinion that certain shapes or forms are always a sign for a specific personality trait or "type." Simple adjustments in the design can significantly change the character's personality (d and e, which are a variation of b and c).

Front views in general are not a good starting point as they neither show perspective nor the relationship between the protruding forms of the face like nose, chin, or any angle of the skull other than the jaw. Front views should be avoided in the development of characters! However, they are obviously very important in the understanding of the character's forms.

The ¾ view provides the widest information on form, the side view with the widest information on the silhouette.

CHAPTER 12

Shape

Shape is one of the most important aspects in character design and also one of the most difficult to not only comprehend but also to incorporate and master. Everything in character design goes back to shape and its impact on the design is significant from the very beginning of character design itself.

Shape refers to an area in a two-dimensional space, defined by a line or color, by contrast, light and shadow, texture etc. *Form* on the other hand refers to the same idea in a three-dimensional space. Furniture, sculptures, or 3D objects have forms. Paintings, drawings, prints, and any other 2D planes have shapes (though one obviously can render form in paintings and drawings). Form can only then be achieved when there is light and shadow or another aspect that gives the form its dimension in a three-dimensional space (like a CG wire-frame model suggesting a form). Shape on the other hand can exist without light and shadow as it never needs to break away from the two-dimensional space (it is a bit more complex than that, but more later on).

Dealing with character shapes is the most important step in the first stages of designing characters, objects, and environments. They not only define the silhouette, but they also establish a personality foundation or type for the character. The shape is the first impression we get when we look at someone or something. Whether they are big, small, thick, thin, top heavy or bottom heavy, strong or weak, the shape immediately gives us a hint of the character's foundation. That impression is mainly a cliché,

Figure 12.1

being a very quick and simple judgment, but nevertheless an important one. The shape of a man is usually different from that of a woman or a child. The shape of an old person is different from that of a young person. With it you express the character's physical strength or weakness, abilities or disabilities, even clothing and hairstyle. Different shapes create different characters and personalities.

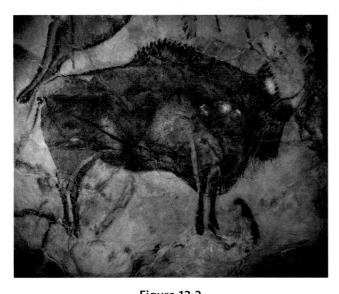

Figure 12.2

Altamira Bison: ~ 22 – 13 000 years old (Courtesy of Wikipedia Commons).

Figure 12.3

Venus of Hohle Fels: ~ 38 000 years old (Courtesy of Wikipedia Commons).

DOI: 10.1201/b22147-12

95

Figure 12.4

The body shape should always be distilled down to represent the essence of the character, be the visual core statement for the character. Finding this core statement is a laborious task as the possibilities are infinite. The original shape needs to be stylized and strengthened by pushing its essence—it needs to be exaggerated. Exaggeration is one of the key elements in animation or the graphic arts. However, there is never just one solution as every artist would interpret the character differently. Picasso's endless sketches of bulls show his search for the perfect stylized shape of this specific animal that is not just a representation of a bull, but an interpretation of it. It is this very search that allows the artist to find a new solution to an old problem: the human and animal shape and form, and its artistic interpretation which goes back to the dawn of human art. When it comes to very early two-dimensional depictions of animals dealing with shape, the paintings in the Spanish caves of Altamira (22–13,000) or the Cave of El Castillo (40,000) have animal paintings that are about 40–13,000 years old (Figure 12.2 has a painting of a bison in the Altamira cave with an age of 13 000 years). They base their style on the stylization of the original animal's shape, which is their most significant feature. The Venus of Hohle Fels (Figure 12.3), found in southern Germany, is around 35,000–40,000 years old, making it the oldest piece of art interpreting the human form yet discovered. The interpretation of its form is stunning, considering its age. It is exactly the same treatment that early twentieth-century art struggled with: finding the essence of the stylized form of the human body. It is difficult to really judge the piece as its content is shrouded in mystery, but from a technical perspective it exaggerates elements of the body that seemed to be important for the artist 35,000 years ago, who found a solution for not just representing but interpreting the female form. The way of dealing with shape and form of prehistoric art is nothing short of spectacular, and focuses on the stylization of the natural shape and form in the very same

Figure 12.5

Figure 12.6

A small change in shape in those thumbnail drawings of a Santa Clause already changes the character drastically and gives you a very different personality. It is not just the main Shape that is changed, but all the small shapes, too like moustache, eye-brows, beard, hat, coat-design and shoes.

manner as twentieth-century art does from a technical perspective. Art itself started with the stylization and exaggeration of shape and form, and its importance cannot be overestimated!

In Figure 12.4, you can see the shape of a dustball squashed and stretched into various different shapes. I just played with the main shape and explored what I could do with it. This exploration gives me many possibilities to choose from. If you observe each shape, it suggests a slightly different personality than the one right next to it. Some are hesitant, some bold and others afraid, some are hiding, peeking, or being disappointed. Every shape has a story to tell and if you start to explore them and read their meaning, you can find characters and personalities you would usually not think of. It is one way of helping you to be creative. The "playing" with the shapes is of crucial importance when it comes to designing characters. It allows you to *find* characters and playfully explore the character possibilities in personality and aesthetics. In the case of the ball, I just played with the body shape. There are still all the shapes inside the body I can change and be creative with. In the case of the fluffy ball in Figure 12.4, I can just change the shapes of the eyes and the pupils. In other characters I can change the mouth, nose, ears, the shapes in the hairstyle, the neck, clothing, hands, nails … all the different shapes that in combination create the final character and its personality, like the Santa Clause in Figures 12.5 and 12.6. It is up to you and your sense of design what fits and what does not, that lets you develop interesting combinations of shapes. For the character studies of the dustballs I chose a very simple shape, and squashed and stretched it to see what I can do with the character and how I could make it more interesting. When you look at the shapes without the eyes, you already get an idea of how the character's personality could be just based on their silhouette. With the eyes there is even more personality to be found in all the examples. With a very little work I have already 28 different characters based on one simple idea. When trying to *find* the character always start out simple and basic before going into complicated details, which are more decoration than basic information. And the most basic information is the body shape.

When the character is more complicated than just a dustball, a simple thumbnail drawing that focuses on the silhouette and body shape gets you started if you don't already have a direction for the shape. Observe all the possibilities in the beards, the brows, mustaches, buttons, etc., the possibilities are indeed infinite. Play with a range of possibilities first before settling on a character too early, and don't draw a character without understanding its basic shape. You can "find" the character by drawing various thumbnails and searching for a shape that fits the description of the character. By exploring body shapes you find the types that don't work and slowly develop the character that does.

Shape, and relationship to elements surrounding it

Shape does not only relate to the character itself but also how the character's shape relates to its surroundings, either in its

composition or its content. In Figure 12.1, we have a sparrow on a falconry glove. The sparrow's body shape stands in a strong relationship with the glove's shape, connecting both and playing with positive and negative shapes. The juxtaposing shapes make it obvious how both sparrow and glove relate to each other and create a sense of belonging. They also clearly show who has the upper hand. It's the proud shape of the sparrow that dominates as its shape shows strength. The glove is submissive to the sparrow's bulging chest. Another example is the painting *The Cactus Lover/Der Kaktusliebhaber* (after 1850) (Figure 12.7)

Figure 12.7

Carl Spitzweg Der Kaktusliebhaber (after 1850) (Courtesy of Wikimedia Commons).

by the German Biedermeier painter Carl Spitzweg (1808–1885). We see the cactus lover adoring his plant in front of him. The ironic visual statement being the man having the same shape as his plant, having the same colored coat as the cactus, and both bend toward each other. Even the shape of the man's head is resembling the cactus's. Spitzweg uses shape to make a visual pun.

The five aspects of shape

To fully understand shape one needs to dissect one into its elements first and know about their strengths and weaknesses for any further successful exploration.

The five elements as seen in Figure 12.9 are:

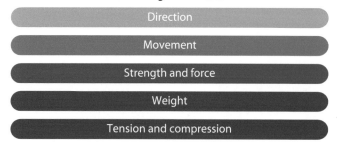

Direction

Movement

Strength and force

Weight

Tension and compression

Once one can feel those five elements when drawing a shape and senses them during the drawing process, the shape expresses itself in a dialog with the artist and demands to be strengthened and improved upon. For that to happen however, one needs either a natural sense of shape or lots of pencil mileage and concentration.

Case study: Simple shapes in Cartoon Network's *Foster's Home for Imaginary Friends* character Blooregard Q. Kazoo

Foster's Home for Imaginary Friends (the title exactly describes what the show is about) was a TV show on Cartoon Network from 2004 to 2009 with an immense amount of characters. Literally hundreds of imaginary friends are living in Mrs. Foster's foster home, which is a maze of corridors and rooms all inhabited with an array of left-behind imaginary friends. Out of the whole ensemble the simplest and also most dominating character is Blooregard Q. Kazoo (Figure 12.8), the imaginary friend of the protagonist Mac,

an eight-year-old boy who created Blooregard as his imaginary friend. Bloo is nothing more than a single cylindrical shape with a rounded top and despite his lack of anything else than his body shape, eyes, mouth, and sometimes two simplified shapes that serve as hands, he still has an extraordinary amount of expressiveness and personality. His selfish, narcissistic, egotistical, and often jealous character drives the main story points in each episode and also everyone else in the foster home nuts. The character designer and

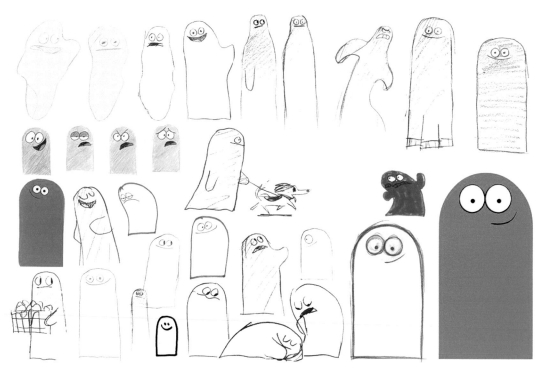

Figure 12.8

Tomm Moore: *The Secret of Kells* (2009); character-design.

The 5 Aspects of Shapes

Direction

Which direction is the shape facing and how does that impact the character of the shape?

Movement

Which movement is the dominant one in the shape depends on the direction and flow. It usually is going from the smaller to the bigger parts of the shape; however, it can also be the other way around if the final character is planned with this movement in mind.

Strength and Force

The outer and inner forces struggle with each other and affect the shape. The outer forces (gravity for example) is either stronger than the shape and dragging it down or the shape is stronger than the outer forces and holds itself upright.

Weight

Where is the main weight located within the shape and how does the shape react to its own weight distribution? Is the weight evenly distributed or is it low, so dragging the shape down or high up, so the shape is having enough strength to keep the weight up?

Tension and Compression

Where in the shape are the acting forces that compress and stretch the shape? How does the shape react to outer and inner forces?

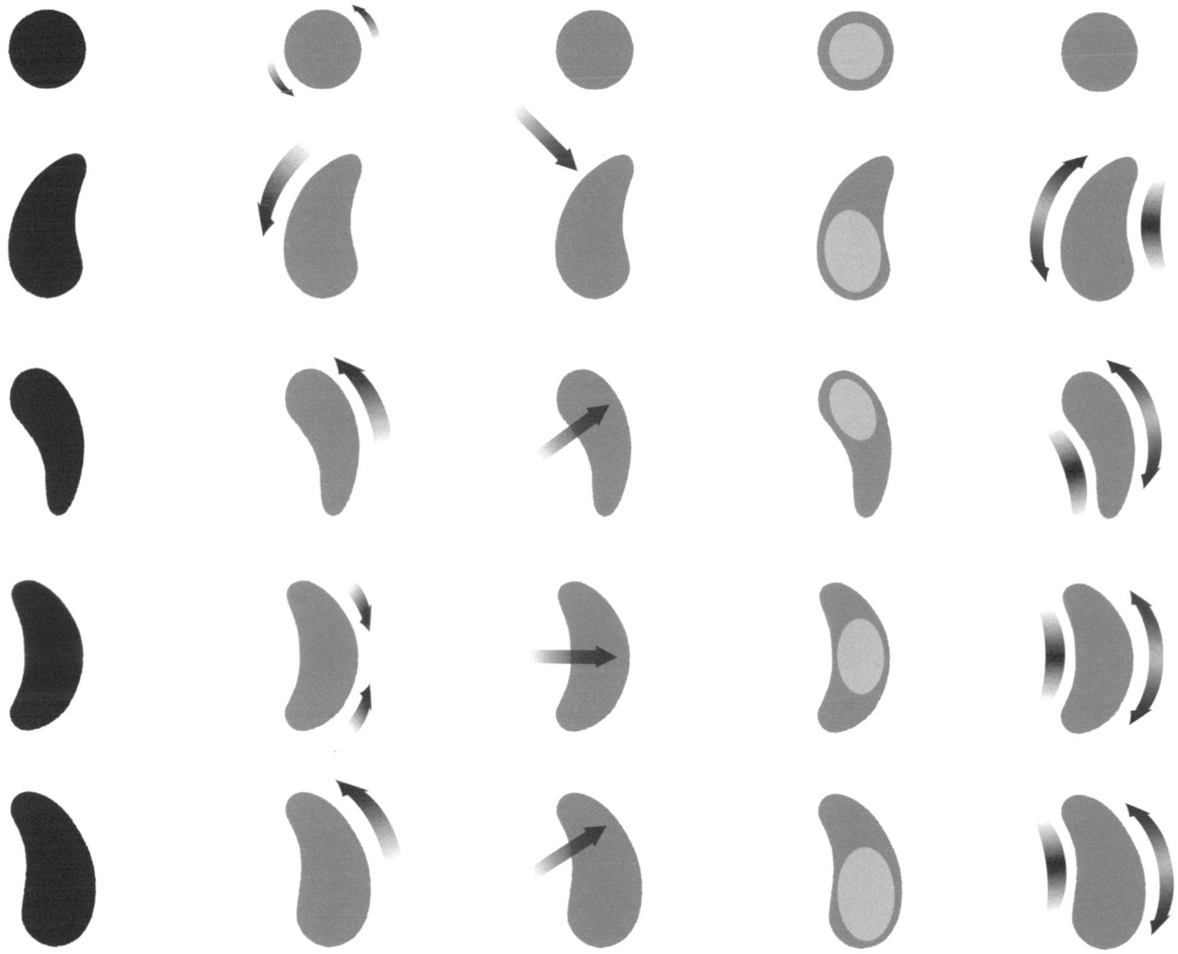

Figure 12.9

creator of the TV show Craig McCraigen (Cracken) writes about the development of Bloo on his blog:

> I know it's hard to believe that there was actual visual development on a character as simple as Bloo, but it's true. He first started out as a transparent nebulous shape then became solid and got shorter and shorter. It's almost as if the character was literally coming into focus the more I thought about him.[1]

What makes Blooregard appealing is of course his voice and personality, but also the simplicity of his design. Because there are no details the character's pose and line of action plus the simple facial expression carry the entire emotion of Bloo. Poses, so very much based on shapes, have to be precise and immediately recognizable. Because of the limitation in his design, more emphasis is given to those few elements that allow him to express himself and they become the key elements. To achieve a great character, a simple shape is sometimes all that is needed.

[1] http://fosterstv.blogspot.hk (retrieved December 1, 2016).

From simple shape to character

As I mentioned before, there is not just one way of exploring a character, so any approach is of course valid as long as one understands basic shape. Thumbnail studies help you to come up with an idea that you might not have had in the first place, they also teach you in a simple manner the idea behind shape and how to "feel" it in your drawing. Much of what happens on the page is due to chance and imagination, happening in the instance of the drawing process. It is the dialog between artist and drawing in that very moment. Thumbnail drawings are just another way of being creative and solving basic problems of the character's shape, its anatomy or clothing, and type. Once you have a thumbnail drawing that you like from your simple lineup (the first drawing of the line-up in Figure 12.10) of tiny drawings you need to push their shapes with their arrangements (Figure 12.11) and get a feeling for the overall body shape; squash and stretch them and change the body ratio in order to get the essence of the character even more clearly into the thumbnail. Exaggeration is the key and pushing all the various elements of the character. Do that several times with either transparent paper that you can put on top of the drawing or with different levels in your digital program,[2] and see how the character gets stronger and stronger in its design every time you exaggerate it again. This can be done several times to really feel the shape and the character within it. At some point in this process you'll realize that

Figure 12.10

the character actually loses appeal and starts to look weird or just doesn't represent the personality and/or type that you were going for in the first place, then you might have gone too far; though there are some possibilities for the shapes to be altered and pushed.

Once we do this step from the thumbnail drawings to actually "finding" the character within those suggested shapes, the shape aspects of direction, movement, strength and force, weight, and tension and compression already describe a rudimentary type (Figure 12.11). However, those mentioned five aspects of shape need to be in relationship with the character's intended personality and type; obviously, they cannot go against it otherwise the character would be contradicting itself. So let's explore what qualities the five aspects of shape have in the actual character.

Interpretation of the shape

A shape by itself cannot be defined per se as representing a certain personality but merely a type. It depends on the interpretation of the shape and from which angle it is being seen, or how it is being "refined." The shapes in Figure 12.12 are both the same, but the characters underneath are exact opposites because their direction is seen differently. Shapes always allow various points of views and thus interpretations.

The character's body shape

We are usually dealing with not just one simple shape in character design, but a complex arrangement of shapes that, when compiled, describe a body. The five aspects of shape need to be seen from a more defined angle and have to be seen in relation with the physical forces the human body is exposed to, to understand in turn how the body reacts.

Figure 12.11

---

2 Reduce your drawing layer in your program in its opacity so that you can only slightly see the drawing. Then add another layer on top and draw over your thumbnail drawing. Make sure not to trace, but to use the underlying thumbnail as a guide that needs to be exaggerated.

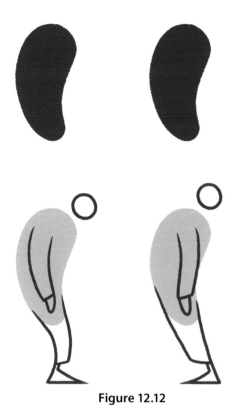

Figure 12.12

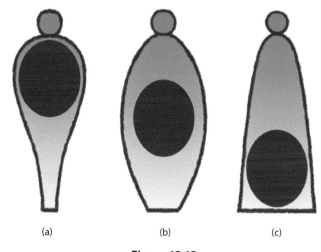

Figure 12.13

Weight

Where the weight is located in the body shape is crucial insofar as it determines the overall ability of the body to either fight gravity or not. This is not only related to the *actual* strength of the character but also the body's ability and the character's will to hold themselves upright. There are two different weights that need to be considered:

1. Physical weight
2. Visual weight

The physical weight is the actual weight of the character, how much they weigh in their entire volume. The visual weight

on the other hand is determined by various factors that make the character *feel* heavy/heavier without them necessarily being so. Those determining factors can be any of the aspects of design like color, contrast, shape, form, texture, light and shadow, size, and the relationship to other characters or objects around him. A huge baroque wig might not weigh too much, but it looks very heavy because of its big shape and form. A black top hat looks much heavier than a white top hat because of the visual weight of black itself, which is much heavier than white. When doing the thumbnail explorations on body shape, it needs to be considered if the character is dressed or naked as the shape of the clothing can dramatically change the character's visual weight.

Figure 12.13a is top heavy, but because most of the weight is located in the upper part of the body, they feel lighter, defying gravity, as if the weight lifts the character up from the ground. Imagine a balloon being within the upper body and wanting to go upward; however, it could also be a big heavy ball that the skinny legs then have to carry and balance. Both directions need to be clear in the design: is the character *actually* heavy, or just looks heavy? Examples for this type of character is Archibald

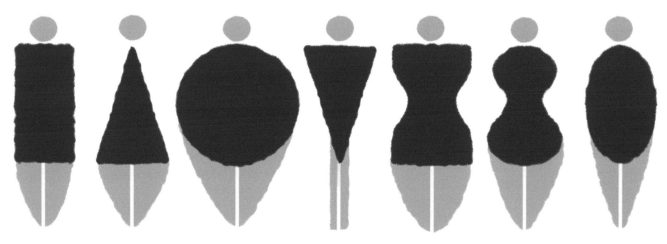

Figure 12.14

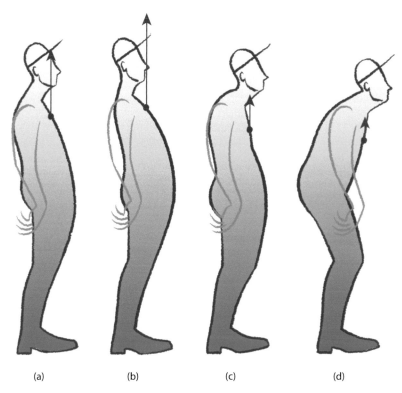

(a) (b) (c) (d)

Figure 12.15

Snatcher in *The Boxtrolls* (2014), or Sergei Alexander Bobinsky in *Coraline* (2009), or Neil Downe in *ParaNorman* (2012).

Figure 12.13b is also very heavy, but the main bulk of the weight is lower in the body and more evenly distributed, creating a stronger connection to the ground (e.g., Norman's grandmother in *ParaNorman* (2012) or Miss Spink and Miss Forcible in *Coraline* (2009)), which makes them bottom heavy.

Figure 12.13c has the weight very low, so the ground connection is the strongest. The actual weight is less as we don't expect the legs to be oversized and heavy (e.g., Wybie Lovat in *Coraline*). However, the visual weight of the cloak can feel heavy and drag the character down. The weight depends on the material of the cloak or dress. Emily, the murdered young woman in *Corpse Bride* (2005), for instance, has this shape; however, she feels very light because her dress is made of silk and is transparent, therefore shows the delicate body underneath. Clothing can exaggerate the physical shapes of the human body and can create visual weight where there is no actual weight. The weight distribution is of course not confined to those three examples mentioned but can be distributed in any way imaginable. Coraline's main weight, for example, is in the head, not the body.

Figure 12.14 shows the different body types in their most simple form. Already in this stylized shape one can detect some form of character type. Gender in this simple example however isn't yet possible to determine if one does not want to fall into the cliché. Even the typical hourglass female form could be drawn as a man if the style allows it. In terms of personality however this is still

just blunt cliché. This simple example presents a body type, not a personality. The danger is to put too much emphasis on the relationship between body type and personality; just because someone has a certain body, has nothing to do with their personality and how they behave or act. Someone who is athletic can still be a couch potato and someone that is overweight can still love sports and practice it every day. Avoid blunt clichés and be more unique with your character.

The suspension point

For the sake of simplicity and to understand weight in the human body more clearly, one point can be seen as the suspension point of the entire body being pulled up. This point determines the inner strength of the body to keep itself upright if strong enough, or lack of strength, and then the body succumbs to its own weight, being dragged down by gravity. Obviously the force of the suspension point is just a theoretical idea, in reality this force comes from the core and leg muscles to keep the body in its pose. When this point is considered and especially felt in one's own body, the standing pose is understood more deeply and can be implemented in the designs. The illustrations show how the body could react to that imaginary force pulling it up:

In Figure 12.15a, the body is standing relaxed.
In Figure 12.15b, the chest plate is pushed out and up, slightly raising the entire body; the legs are straightened.

(a) (b) (c)

Figure 12.16

(a) (b) (c)

Figure 12.17

In Figure 12.15c, the suspension point is lowered, the chest sinks in, the upper back is curved, and the legs weaken.

In Figure 12.15d, the force of keeping the body upright is even less than in (c), which causes the entire upper body to go down; the legs are even less strong.

Imagine the body of a marionette and how it would react to the attached string pulling it up or releasing it. The puppet would slowly collapse and sink down if the pull was less than the actual weight of the puppet.

Forces and body tension

While drawing the initial thumbnails it is helpful for the overall feeling of the body to include the main forces the body is exposed to and how they affect its shape. This will lead to the overall tension that the body is experiencing in its entirety. There are various internal and external forces, and aspects that affect the body tension or the lack of it:

- Overall weight of the character
- Weight distribution: how the body shape is affected by the physical attributes of the body type, muscle and fat distribution—top heavy or bottom heavy?
- Gravity and other external forces
- Strength of the character in the upper back and front, and legs
- The body's reaction and tilt of hips and legs to internal and external forces
- The character's personality and willpower to actually stay upright (do they want to or not?)

This last point about the character carrying their own weight is crucial as it not only defines the characters' weight distribution but also their shape and its eventual type. Figure 12.16a through c clearly show how a similar body significantly changes in its overall shape when the character

carries its weight in a different fashion, either being stronger than gravity and also pushing the chest forward (a), having the same force as gravity and keeping the body just about upright (b) or succumbing to gravity and allowing the body to slump (c). In 12.16c it nearly feels like the character is being pushed from an outside force as the chest is pushed inwards, whereas in (a) the energy and force seem to come from within the character pushing out. Every body type has a different way of dealing with the weight it carries. Just because someone is muscular and athletic doesn't mean they push out their chest in the same way. Figure 12.17a shows that the strength of the athlete can also be in the back, and the front is rather straight. Figure 12.17b and f deals with the same weight in the midsection in a different way. By changing the chest from being slightly curved outward in (b) to being curved inward in (c), the forces that push the weight out are very different. In (b) the force pushes upward against gravity, showing strength and solidity; in (c) the weight succumbs to gravity and sags, making the character feel much weaker. Where (b)'s belly feels solid, (c)'s belly is softer.

Body shape and spine

The distribution of weight, the tension in the body, and a strong shape language provide most of the character's foundation. To just draw a shape and exaggerate it is not enough to be convincing when it comes to characters that are based on realistic physicality, which most characters are. The shape needs to be supported by a skeleton and particularly the spine and hips are of major importance. The tilt of the hips has an impact on the bend of the spine, and the positioning of legs and knees. For the body shape to really work, the underlying anatomical structure of the skeleton is providing the necessary reason for the movement of the shape and its five aspects, and the needed reasons

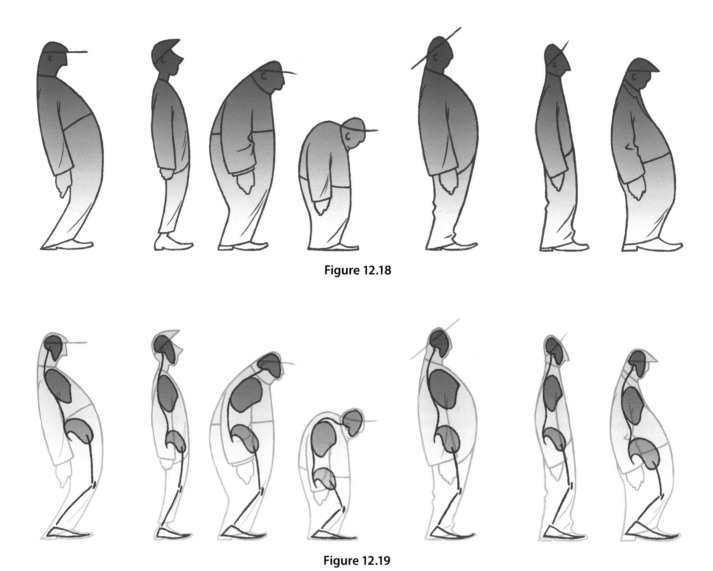

Figure 12.18

Figure 12.19

for where tension and compression is located within this shape. Keeping the character and their personality in mind while drawing weight, skeleton, muscles, fat, and tissue, and interpreting them as simple shapes is key. The need to not consider the details, but to articulate that specific character statement in the most simple way allows to exaggerate and push it into a very strong posture and character. Some points must not be ignored during this process of understanding the effect the bend of the spine has on the character's standing position:

- Always see the body as a whole and do not divide it into sections of upper body, legs, and arms.
- The head is connected to the spine.
- The spine defines the curvature of the upper and lower body.
- The hip tilt determines the position of the knees and legs.

The hip tilt

Tilting the hips forward or backward affects not just the pelvis region but the entire body's standing position. The connection of hips and femur affects the tilt of the legs, and the entire lower body. The connection of hips and spine affects the tilt of the entire upper body with rib cage, shoulders, and head position. In Figure 12.18, the characters all carry their weight in a different fashion and each character's hip position affects the distribution of the weight, which has to be balanced out by either pushing the weight of the upper body forward or backward. The basic stance thus depends on the position of hips and knees. A simple explanation of what happens when the hips tilt is given in Figure 12.19, which shows the effects the hip tilt has on spine and knees, and how the resulting forces change the entire system. What Figure 12.19 demonstrates needs to be imagined and felt when drawing the character.

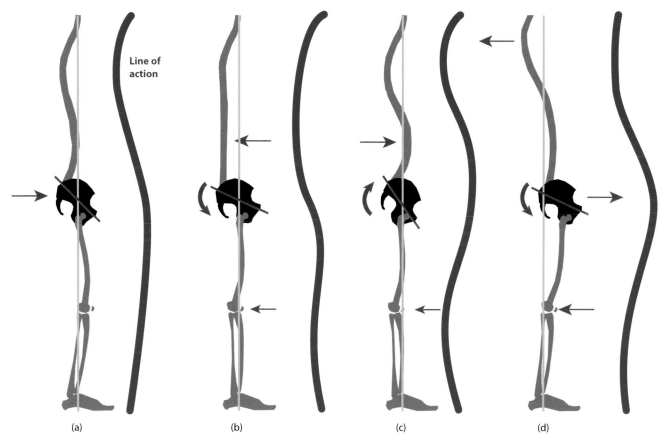

Line of
action

(a)　　　　(b)　　　　(c)　　　　(d)

Figure 12.20

A detailed explanation of what forces act upon hips, spine, and legs is shown in Figure 12.20a through d, and how the line of action is affected by those forces. Figure 12.20a shows the normal standing position with the hips slightly tilted. The spine that is attached solid to the hipbone is therefore just marginally bent inward. The knees are in a comfortable position with some tension in the legs. In Figure 12.20b, the hip's coccyx (tailbone) is tilted downward, pushing the pubic bone (crotch area) upward. The lumbar spine is pushed out, which straightens the spine in the lower back. The knees are slightly hyperextended and pushed back. Figure 12.20c has the hip being rotated down in the front, lowering the pubic bone and pushing the spine inward, creating a hollow back. The knees are also pushed back. The standing position (d) has the entire hip structure pushed forward and slightly tilted in the back, which causes the upper body to push back in order to balance the body and prevent it from falling forward. The knees are hyperextended. These different standing positions practiced on one's own body makes the relationship between pelvis, spine, and legs a clear and much easier to comprehend concept and one can actually feel the tension that is created in the knees and the lower spine. Practice this on your body, as it is an extremely important aspect!

Shape with a purpose

The difficulty in talking about shapes is that, aside from the just-mentioned impact of force on the shape, it is mostly about "feeling" the shape and how the shape responds to you while you draw it. This is obviously a personal experience that is difficult to communicate or explain. The only way of really understanding the feel of a shape is by drawing a lot and grasping shape from an emotional perspective. By drawing "a lot" I mean A LOT! Because there are so many aspects to consider when drawing, only year-long practice results in the habit where one just draws without keeping all the rules in mind, but they are happening subconsciously. It takes a lot of pencil mileage to reach the point where the drawing responds and tells *you* what to do. It's a communication between the artist and the drawing that starts when one concentrates solely on the work and nothing interrupts the workflow. The artist is at one with the drawing (sounds a bit corny, I know ...). Once you get into the rhythm of just drawing and actually being inside the drawing, the interaction between paper (or screen) and artist develops and the drawing does itself with the artist's hand involved; the hand is guided by the mind and its boundless imagination. Without practicing every day for hours the mind–hand connection probably won't happen (if you are not one of those lucky ones that just sits down and understands the concept of shape language immediately). When it comes to character design the basis for this dialog to happen is *purpose*. Before drawing you should ask yourself what the character is actually about and consider what direction would be a fit. However, do not obsess about these points as you still want the creative flow to take you into other directions and away from the typical cliché. Once these questions are answered the drawing process should be one of "emotional evaluation": judging the lines, shapes, and forms over and over and adjusting them to the need of the character and the feel of its personality. A big mistake is to want to draw a certain way and wanting to have a specific result by following an existing solid idea and style, without being open to surprises that can happen on the page by chance. The drawing process should always be one of flowing creativity that is not constantly stopped by rational thoughts. Just let the drawing develop itself, let the character evolve and take shape. It will show itself and demand what it needs. For this to happen the shapes of the character have to be not just drawn with one line, but sculpted. This means you start with the shape and follow its dimension on the page repeatedly. You feel its tension and weight, its distribution and expression, and connect all of those elements with the character's personality and body type. What you also need to keep in the back of your mind is:

- Character's background and personality
- Line of action
- Tension and compression
- Spine movement
- Tension in the belly and chest
- Tension in the legs and arms
- Form in relationship to shape
- Direction of the pose
- Hip and shoulder movement
- Aesthetics
- Tension in the distribution of the shapes
- Emotional expression
- Pose
- Pivot point and weight distribution
- Style
- Avoidance of repetition
- All the aspects of design
- And on top of it all, to be unique in your design

All these aspects of course take quite a while to be ingrained into your mind during the drawing process—they are not going to be present from the beginning, but they will all assist you in developing the right shape for the character. All the points mentioned can be improved upon on a second round of refinement, and a third, fourth, fifth ... the continuous refinement of the drawing will clearly show in the final design.

Drawing means having a vague goal in mind while you draw. Otherwise it is just random scribbling. Keeping all the aspects of weight, tension and compression, pose, expression, story etc. in mind while drawing (or adjusting them later on in the various refinement stages) is a huge task and they take time to just happen subconsciously, without interfering with one's creativity. But drawing without considering the actual purpose of that specific drawing seems pointless in character design. A shape that does not have the purpose of being created for a specific character makes no sense. Therefore just sitting down and drawing shapes is pointless other than practicing line flow and the understanding of tension. Creating shapes for a character with a personality teaches you shapes by actually applying them to a personality and only then the dialog between you and the drawing starts.

However, there is like always the aspect of practicing ones trade and enjoying the drawing process itself. Letting characters just evolve in front of your eyes is fun and entertaining, while it teaches and develops skills.

Sculpting the shape

This paragraph is about how to draw in general for our purposes in character design. There are many students that draw characters with only one line, never refining their characters by adjusting the shapes and lines and thus improving them, getting rid of imbalances and crooked shapes. They never built the character up from its basis but already work on the final without understanding the foundational structure of the character. They look at the final character designs of well-practiced artists and see the final line drawing that is based on years of experience, training, and a deep understanding of shape language. These drawings are usually the result of a work process that included many thumbnails and rough sketches. When shape language is understood and happens subconsciously, the method of quick sketches without the continuous refinement is of course working perfectly fine. This is because the development of the shape itself already happened in the mind of the artist and squashing and stretching the shapes is not necessarily something that has to be developed (this depends on the artist and their work method of course). But in order to grasp shape language and learn its complexity, the sculpting of the shape is a necessity. When drawing a shape, the feeling of the shape needs to guide the drawing and one way of learning this is to sculpt the shape. The left shape in Figure 12.21a is repeatedly improved upon and all the faults and mistakes that make the shape crooked are reduced, which leaves a shape that has strength and solidity. It is neither clean nor beautiful to look at, but that is not the point of this stage. The point is feeling the shape! The shapes that are drawn only with one line on the right (Figure 12.21b) can have

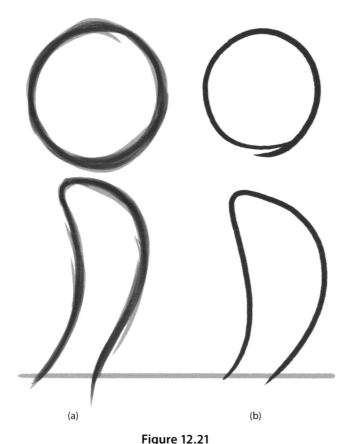

(a)   (b)

Figure 12.21

three-dimensional form, and how this form sits within the dimensionality of the character. The best example I can give for this is to draw a circle. If you just draw a circle with one line the outcome will most probably be crooked and not a proper circle. Sculpting the circle results in a much better outcome as you, by repeating the shape over and over, eliminate all the bumps in the outline and get it right. Small mistakes in the shapes, inconsistencies in their volume or size relationship to each other, add up and result in crooked and odd-looking characters.

Of course crooked characters can be a valid style decision, but that is an artistic choice, not due to a lack of ability or knowledge!

Feeling the shape

"Feeling the shape" can only be understood when actually experienced during the drawing process and it can only happen when practiced with the utmost focus on the very drawing. Feeling the shape means that at some point of the drawing process there is an emotional exchange between you, the draftsman, and the character that you draw, or the assemblage of shapes that make the character. The shape tells you what it wants you to do, how it has to be altered to feel right. The draftsman feels the shape and responds to its needs. This only works when one concentrates on the drawing and allows that conversation to take place without any other thoughts distracting this emotional state. First there has to be focus on the drawing. The draftsman has to not just draw but be in the drawing, be the character, feel the character with its traits and looks, its weight and pose, its surface, and the tactile feel of its clothing. What is crucial is that the draftsman does not predominantly think about the looks, but how the characters' looks and personality feel. Those feelings then are translated into the shapes on paper. It is a very meditative experience where the draftsman does not think about drawing a specific character, but becomes what is drawn. There is a major difference between the two. The one that thinks about what is being drawn is conscious about the page and the act of drawing whereas the one that feels what is drawn is themselves acting as the character on the page and feeling its physicality, weight, and personality. One can see the conscious approach in characters where the result was already planned out before it happened. This often leads to a character with just surface and no content. One wants to create a unique character that explores unknown and uncharted fields, so that the outcome is fresh and different, something that happened on the page as a result of this creative conversation between drawing and draftsman and not already in one's mind beforehand. The focus on feeling the shapes doesn't necessarily always give you characters that are great and unique, and not feeling the shapes doesn't always give you bad results. But practicing feeling the shape

solidity, but they lack the felt emotion of the shape and its inner forces and strength. This is needed to understand that particular shape, and communicate with it while drawing it. In order to understand shape language, the left approach is highly recommended. Drawing shape is not just a technical task but also an emotional one if one wants to step into the relationship between shape and the creative mind. One feels the lower shape in (a) pushing its chest and how that push causes a tension in its spine. This feeling causes the shape to want to be exaggerated and pushed because the artist feels that push in their own body.

While your pencil is going over the character, adjust the shapes to get them precise in their dimensions and quality. Don't just repeat the lines over and over, but see the shape behind the lines you want to find. This is like a projection of the very shape your mind projects onto the paper and you have to sculpt it out with the pencil. Your mind is able to quickly switch between that projection and the actual drawing. Concentrate on the drawing and sculpt the shape into exactly what you want it to be, and what it needs to be. Iron out any bumps or uneven lines that describe the shape; feel the relationships between the shapes in the entire character and how they contribute to its personality. See the shape in its two-dimensionality and also in its possible is making you aware of how to bring yourself with your emotions, your very own personality, and imagination into the drawing and digging deeper into the possibilities of the character. It means to allow the moment that you are alone with the drawing to count and be important, as this is the moment where you create a character out of nothing but your imagination.

Pushing the shapes

Animation is a medium of exaggeration, which is what makes animation so unique as it can exaggerate any part of the image. Character, backgrounds, sound, movement—there is nothing in the animated film that cannot be pushed to the extreme. It can either be pushed like a Tex Avery cartoon into the comedic and lunatic extreme, or like in Peter Jackson's *King Kong* into hyperrealism. The advantage of this medium is to make any point of the visual storytelling stronger, by pushing its components into unrealistic, surreal terrain or any other artistic direction. Films mostly live by the strength of their characters and how the character's personality is explored and presented. In order to get the personality as strong as possible in animation, it *has* to be pushed and the essence of the personality has to be distilled and then exaggerated. For the visual aspect of the character, shapes play a significant role in this as they contain the main points of the personality in a very simple yet concise way. Pushing the shapes means pushing the content and if done sensibly, and with thought and a good eye for balance, this can strengthen the character immensely—not just in the interpretation of his personality through shape, but also its uniqueness in design.

Pushing the character is not just about pushing one shape, but all parts have to be adjusted as they are a complex and subtle interplay of lines, shapes, and forms. Changing one shape or element requires everything else to be adjusted in order to not disrupt the balance of the character.

At a certain point when the exaggeration has been pushed too far, the character starts to fall apart. Be aware of this and let the drawings sit for a while; do something else and then come back to judge the design with a fresh eye, and you will see if there was enough or too much exaggeration.

Shape and storytelling

The body shape of the character should tell his story and should represent the character's personality in the best possible visual, and should be a distillate of the character. The following three characters were designed for Sprite Animation Studios for a version of *The Journey to the West*, the incredibly famous and spectacular tale of monkey king Sun Wukong and his friends in search of Buddhist scriptures

and their journey from China to India (Figures 12.22 and 12.23). This Chinese literary masterpiece, most likely written by Wu Cheng'en (ca. 1500–1582) in the Ming dynasty, is a well of ideas and surreal happenings and a *tour de force* of fantasy. The three characters (there are five in the actual story) have all unique personalities and show these throughout the story continuously. The task for the design was to create characters that are based on the original story yet have a slightly different take on them compared to what has been done in the past (especially Shanghai Animation Film Studio's very famous extravagant feature length film directed by Wan Laiming *Havok in Heaven* or *Uproar in Heaven* from 1965). As Sun Wukong, the monkey king, is a character that is very well known throughout Asia and has been depicted in hundreds of ways, the direction was to create a new look for him that was more contemporary. What I started out with was finding a simple shape that represents what the essence of each character is (Figure 12.22). Those shapes needed to be simple and very different from each other to have a character lineup that shows variation, and allows each character to stand his own ground visually.

Monkey king Sun Wukong

Sun Wukong is based on a Chinese Golden Monkey and is a very strong and agile character. Being the mightiest character by far in the story (and the entire universe) and exceeding everyone in physical strength and wit, he is rather mischievous. His shape is based on the masculine V shaped male back, to have a rather simple starting position. Despite his strength he is a smaller sized character, which I thought makes his mighty powers even more magical and unique. An angular shape seems more fit for strength and power than a round shape. Sun Wukong is by far the most famous character in Chinese fantastic literature and a very beloved one. To make him a little bit cuddly I thought would heighten his attractiveness and charm.

Pig monster Zhu Bajie

Zhu Bajie is a character that loves to eat. He is obsessed with food and everything that satisfies his physical needs. He is not actually a pig, but a monster that looks like a pig. Because of his gluttony, I chose a round shape that would fit his personality best. A round shape seems full, so full that it could burst. It's the shape with the most volume in it. I imagined him with lots of food, so much food that he is actually sitting in it. This would be his ultimate dream: to be surrounded by food continuously. Therefore I chose his lower body to represent the food in the shape of a rice bowl with the typical pattern found on actual bowls. The sign for food on the front makes it just so much more blatant. Zhu Bajie's pose is not heavy, but he seems to be light on his small feet. Exaggeration pushes his happy and gluttonous personality traits to an extreme.

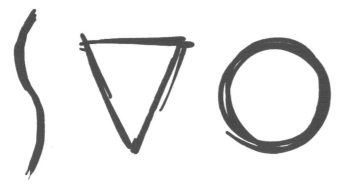

Figure 12.22

Figure 12.23

Sprite Animation Studios: *Journey to the West* (2007); character-development.

River god, Sha Wujing[3]

Sha Wujing's shape is based on a long and winding river. He lived on the bottom of a river and was an evil spirit until forced by the gods to join the group on their journey. Wujing's entire body has a connection to water, river, water creatures, or plants. His body is lean and curvy to suggest the flowing path of a river. The green on his eyes and beard derives from algae, the skin and forearms from water turtles, the bluish purple from the cold water. He is grumpy and slightly arrogant. He loves to play the guitar and

---

[3] This is the Japanese visual version of the character Sha Wujing that contains the look of a Kappa, a Japanese mythological river monster/spirit.

thinks he is talented in doing so, but in reality he is completely incapable. His entire pose has an extreme contrapposto to make the S-curve of the lean body more dominant and underline the river reference.

In all three characters I tried to incorporate as many aspects of their personality as possible, yet not overwhelm the audience with too much information that would be more confusing than helpful. Details like Sun Wukong's big hands represent strength, or Sha Wujing's hands with the webbing between the fingers make him look literally handicapped for playing the guitar. Those details do not have to be overly dominant, but they underline their personality in a subtle way.

Drawing and shapes

The major advantage of having shapes play such an important role in the drawing process is that it makes it so much easier to draw the character. You draw shapes first to create the character's foundation instead of paying attention to the three-dimensionality or details. The shapes help you to lay down the basis. By squashing and stretching them, with the overall flow of the pose in mind, you achieve a character that is not falling apart and being compiled of various elements and by adding its details. The character needs to maintain its underlying structure and shapes help to do exactly that.

Figures 12.24 and 12.25 shows how the character of the little monster in Figure 12.26 was developed by starting out with a simple foundation. First, the character needs to be fully understood in its basic body shapes and forms (a). The details of the character are insignificant for the first step and can be completely omitted. It is only important to draw the foundation and find solutions for the following points as shown in Figures 12.24 and 12.25:

- Action/emotion and its clarity
- Simplicity
- Line of action
- Tension and forces
- Squash and stretch
- Direction
- Consistency of volumes
- Silhouette
- Three-dimensionality

The chosen action can either be planned beforehand or developed by drawing a random interpretation of the shape (squashed and stretched with maintained volume) and then an action can appear through imagination, which is a very helpful tool to come up with more creative poses. Once all of these above-mentioned elements are working in the basic body shape, the finishing of the character is more or less just decoration and additions. All the details of course need to accentuate the foundation with its line of action, direction, etc. It needs to be

(a)   (b)   (a)   (b)

Figure 12.24   **Figure 12.25**

Figure 12.26

clear that the refining step is not going to cover up the direction established for the foundation.

This can obviously be expressed in various ways: to turn the character into a fully three-dimensional character, to keep it graphic, or find a way in-between where some parts are three-dimensional and others are flat. Every decision in this process is important insofar as it enhances the action and the personality of the character. There cannot be one line or feature that is not in relation to the basic action and emotion.

Figure 12.27

Tomm Moore: *The Secret of Kells* (2009); character-design by Barry Reynolds.

Case study: Character design and strong shapes in Cartoon Saloon's *The Secret of Kells* (2009)

The fictionalized story of the feature *The Secret of Kells* deals with the struggle of the monks in the Abbey of Kells to secure their monastery from marauding Vikings in eighth century Ireland. The abbot's nephew Brandon witnesses in the abbey the creation of *The Book of Kells*, created by Brother Aidan. He becomes Aidan's apprentice and in the end finishes the masterpiece himself. For the source of its design *The Secret of Kells* uses the famous Irish national treasure, *The Book of Kells*, the greatest example of insular illumination among which it is by far the most detailed and intricately illustrated. It is on public display at Trinity College's main library hall in Dublin. The painted characters in the book have a distinct design that follows the old tradition of Celtic and Anglo-Saxon art. Everything is line, abstraction, and simplification. The line is never calm, it bends and slithers over the parchment, always on the move. It creates patterns and shapes, continuously invents new decorative elements and keeps the eye busy, always offering a new visual treat. Those decorative elements are not merely there to fill the page, they are intricate characters, animals, plants, or even more complex geometric shapes. The floral patterns are moving on the page, growing and winding from one field to the next. Some pages have strictly geometric patterns which are so complex and intricate, it is difficult to grasp that someone over 1,000 years ago painted them with nothing else but simple drafting and painting tools. Translating *The Book of Kells* into a style that can be animated requires first of all to study the design rules of the book and then applying them to hand-drawn animation.

The responsibility in a production like this is that you want the design of *The Book of Kells* to be represented somehow truthfully by the film and also translated into a modern style aesthetic. This is a national treasure and therefore has not only art-historical value, but also a lot of national pride connected to it. The design therefore should be sensible and respectful, though it is design for entertaining feature animation, which comes with certain rules and regulations. Those are plenty as the audience wants to see a film that isn't a lecture in art history but a light and entertaining film for the whole family (Western feature animation is still mainly a family-oriented business, like it or not).

Some of the design elements from *The Book of Kells* are obvious as the paintings are graphic and flat in their characters and spatial treatment, which is also the main direction the film is taking. The characters and animals are often stylized toward abstract patterns and forms, that intertwine in complex Celtic knots and weaving, keeping a two-dimensional plane. The character animation therefore has to be as flat as possible, not to destroy with three-dimensionality in the movement the flatness of character and background. As for the environment in the film the flat page-like space constantly exposes its chosen limitation by keeping "modern" perspective completely out of the image. There is never any feel of the space fully opening up through line perspective into the third dimension, but always only through color, overlap, size relationship, and other compositional means.

The design of the film therefore:

- *Cannot be too abstract*

    If the design is too abstract and strictly following *The Book of Kells* it is very difficult to get convincing emotions into characters and scenes to keep the audience's attention for the length of a feature film of 75 minutes. Abstract is good for short subjects, but difficult to follow in features. The design of *The Book of Kells* is very stylized in parts and these elements can be used to enrich the design with decoration and textures. Or, they can used for more surreal scenes or dream sequences in the movie that have a short span, but are not a fit for the entire film. Realistic and convincing emotions are rather difficult to convey in extremely stylized characters, which the characters of the film are not.

- *Cannot be too simple*

    This concerns the target audience. The age group for family-oriented feature animation is usually from 3 years up, or not restricted. It is already difficult to get boys and girls over the age of 10 to watch animation, so the design helps to appeal to them if it has some complexity to it and does not resemble toddler qualities too much. This is important because the film wants to attract as wide an audience range as possible and the more sophisticated the design in terms of complexity the wider the range can be (though more aspects have to be considered: story complexity, overall content, or if the film is specifically targeted to boys or girls, or any specific-interest group).

- *Needs to be able to show emotions*

    The characters in their design have to be able to express any kind of emotion if embodied performance is the goal.

If the design is beautiful and unique, but very difficult to animate and express comprehensible emotions with, it is ultimately useless. The audience will look at the characters for an hour and a half and they have to believe what those characters are experiencing and feeling on screen is actually happening. The emotion has to be read quickly and without any doubt; there cannot be any vagueness for the sake of artistic expression.

- *Needs to be distinctive and unique*

    This is where it becomes rather tricky: what is unique is a very stretchable field. What is unique for one is plain and boring for another. A middle ground has to be found that pleases most of the audience. If the design is planned through a huge committee that decides on everything it is very easily washed down to the most common and plain look. There has to be an edge to the design and something that is unusual and striking. There are so many features in animation being released every year that the one film you are working on should be easily recognizable and not have too much in common with the next film around the corner. The film design has to look new and contemporary, better still, open the door design-wise and let people peek into a very new design direction. That would be the ultimate goal, although the look still has to be familiar enough for the audience to feel comfortable.

- *Has to have characters that have appeal*

    The appeal of the characters is obviously for the purpose of the audience being able to relate to the characters easily. This heightens the salability of the project. With characters that are immediately appealing it is much easier to sell the film than if the main characters are less likable. Of course this is of huge

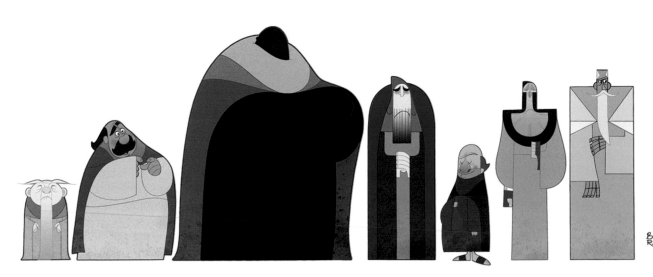

Figure 12.28

Tomm Moore: *The Secret of Kells* (2009); character-design by Barry Reynolds.

importance as the millions that the film gobbled up during its production should be coming back in in the form of movie tickets or any other form of revenue. To just think artistically is, for feature animation, not always the best way to go. It is hugely expensive and the money has to come from somewhere. The production is usually kept afloat with money from investors and studios. This is a responsibility that should be taken seriously. The more appealing the characters are, the better the chances to have a successful film. The exception of course makes the rule in this case.

- *Needs to be easily recognizable*

If three studios are working on a film with ants, you better make sure that they look very different from each other. In the first couple of years of CG feature animation there was a logical progression in the complexity of characters. There is a reason why the first feature film in CG *Toy Story* had toys as the main characters and not superheroes, as toys are much easier to animate—their structure is mostly rigid and stiff. This allowed an animation style that was on par with the technology at the time. The second step was insects, still rather rigid with their chitin exoskeletons. After that came fish, and then humans slowly started to be more and more convincing. The point is that there were two ant movies being released and the audience was slightly surprised about not only Pixar's *Bugs Life* but also PDI/Dreamwork's *Ants* both dealing with the adventures of insects. Both films looked very different and that was a necessary decision. The one film that gets released first of course has the upper hand as the second one will always be the second one and the audience will say: "Well, I have seen that before!" This can seriously damage the success of the film. Therefore, design a look that helps to sell the film and is easily distinguishable from all the other features out there with a similar topic.

- *Has to have a design that is feasible to be produced*

If the design is stunning but it can't be translated into animation because it is too complicated to animate, then how will the film be made? You need to look at the abilities of your crew and what they are able to achieve in the time they are given. This of course is not a decision that the designer has to make, but the director and the producers; but it is good to know about the film's means and take them into consideration. If I only have access to artists that cannot produce high-end feature animation then it is advisable to simplify the design in its complexity and make it easier for the animators. The ability has to fit the style, and vice versa.

- *Has to fit Into the available budget*

This is the most difficult aspect to understand for the nonproducer as the budget is seldom a concern to the artist. There is a difference between a film that costs $150 million and $5 million and that difference is always

Figure 12.29
Folio 292r, Book of Kells (9th century) (Courtesy of Wikimedia Commons)

visible on screen (at least it should be visible if you want to see the money you spent on the screen). There are of course films that look spectacular and were produced with a fraction of the budget of other films. (Don Bluth's *The Secret of Nimh* (1982) is one of those extraordinary examples and could only be produced in this unique quality because of the determination and hard work of many people, and a smart budget move to produce some of the films artwork at people's homes, saving in rent.) Usually it is advisable to have a vague idea of what is possible with the given budget, and what would be extravagant.

Now back to the design of *The Secret of Kells*.

What are the main design points of *The Book of Kells* in Dublin?

Overall:

- Circles, rectangles, parallels, horizontals, and verticals lead the design.
- There is very strong line work and bold compositions, filled with miniscule details.

- Curves and organic lines are juxtaposing straight and geometric lines.
- Color is nonrepresentational and flat, with very few gradients for emphasis.
- All filling components are boasting with miniscule decoration.
- Characters:
- Geometry and shape rule over anatomy.
- Geometry can rule over fluent poses.
- Emphasis in the face often lies in the eyebrows and nose (sometimes as one piece consisting of a flowing organic line).
- Characters can be very "rubbery" in their limbs, lacking a solid skeleton.
- The complex line work of fandangles is often finished with animal heads.
- Fabric and clothing have a flow to them that is still rather geometric.
- Clothing is often covered in a complex pattern.
- Strong geometric shape is more important than an easily comprehensible silhouette.
- There are two types of characters: round, and geometric, which shows in the treatment of the hands.
- Whenever possible eliminate complexities that suggest perspective in pose, clothing, or objects.
- The nose is either shown from the front or from the side in the frontal face in order to flatten the character.
- Objects have two sides: front and side view, or front and bottom view.

Not all of the aspects mentioned would make it into the character design as some are just not very practical for the translation from the book into a film. The extraordinary visual in *The Book of Kells* derives from the complexity of the images filled with the most intricate pattern. This is the key point of *The Book of Kells*: its Celtic, floral, anthropomorphic, and geometric designs. However, trying to use this in a feature film in the character design of a 2D movie would completely overwhelm the senses. What is good for a painting isn't necessarily good for a moving image. It would be so difficult to read that the audience would not be able to keep their attention on the story for too long. Additionally, it would be way too expensive trying to have that rather time-consuming look of pattern in every shot of characters and backgrounds. As the final film is a 2D movie, the characters themselves cannot have any complex pattern in their design or if so, then just a sparse amount as an addition, but not as the fundament of the design. Imagine having to redraw every pattern 12 times for every second. Simplicity is often the main concern in character design for 2D characters, so simple pattern is fine, complex pattern should be avoided if the budged isn't gigantic. It can sometimes be achieved with effects to display the pattern in the clothing and this should

be investigated if the style works and the pattern doesn't drag too much attention away from the expressions and poses. Otherwise, keep it simple!

Shape language:

The characters in *The Book of Kells* are all based on very defined and heavily outlined shapes that are clearly cut out by organic flowing lines. In its simplest form, that is what the shapes in the character design of the film are representing: organic flowing lines that contain clean, geometric, basic shapes. There are mostly variations of the pillar shape of a monk. The characters have a wide variety, that doesn't seem to be too strict and cohesive, but fits the design of the book, which is also not "out of one brush," but produced by various artists, which shows in the variety of styles within its pages. For example, the book's famous Chi-Rho page, Folio 34r, is very different in style and complexity to, for example, Folio 292r (Figure 12.29) with an image of John. So, the various hands that produced *The Book of Kells* are visible.

There is a beautiful idea in the character design of the film's character Abbot Cellach (lineup image, Figure 12.27): when he is depicted as a middle-aged man his neck is long, being the continuation of the rim of his open robe. In the old character, his beard is now replacing the shape of his neck: the exact same shape, but different content. The character's initial silhouette is therefore mostly kept intact, his shape is just "aged" by pushing the held-up head down. Additionally, by just lowering the saturation of Cellach's habit and skin color in his older version, the character ages dramatically, a simple yet very effective artistic decision.

Also, there is a clear relationship between Brandon and Brother Aidan: both have big ears and wear sandals, have both the same habit shape, just in a different color. Some of the side or background characters (lineup, Figure 12.28, the two monks on the right) have body shapes that are really pushing the stylization to an extreme and give us just two flat boards; but they still maintain a strong character that is able to be animated in the embodied animation style.

Animals and shape

When drawing animals the most important aspect is to grasp the shape of that specific animal first. Every animal has its unique body shape that is only valid for that one animal. Pushing it too far causes the animal to look like a different type and a rabbit can easily look like a cat or vice versa if the ears and legs are too exaggerated. How far the shape can be pushed depends on the style of course; the more cartoony the style, the more extreme the character can be.

Nevertheless, there are many characters that pretend to be something they are actually not: Jimini Cricket in Disney's

(a)   (b)   (e)   (f)   (g)

(c)   (d)

Figure 12.30

Pinocchio is definitely not looking like a cricket; we know he is one because his name says so. We would never guess what he is if his name wouldn't be Cricket. Also Ren and Stimpy from John Kricfalusi's show on Nickelodeon *Ren & Stimpy* (1991–1995) are a bit difficult to recognize as a chihuahua and a cat, but the show's design is so over the top that this is actually a positive point. It is only sometimes, when Stimpy does very cat-related things that remind us of him being one.

When starting out designing an animal, one needs to look at many pictures and film clips to get a feeling for the shape language of that specific animal. Like humans, animals are all different; no cat looks exactly like the next one. So a shape needs to be found that represents the entirety of that specific breed. The range of a llama's realistic shape for instance can depend on its hair being short (Figure 12.30a) or long (b). If the neck and legs are too short (c) it starts to look like a sheep or maybe even a poodle (d). It is the combination of all the physical attributes that pinpoint the viewer toward a specific animal. Once this distilled-down shape is understood it can be squashed, stretched, and exaggerated. This is the part that is really fun, but also the part where things can go wrong if pushed too far. Then the animal starts to look like a different species. In the drawings (e), (f) and (g), all with their silhouette displayed underneath: which one still has

the "llama-ness" in it and which one does not? It feels like (f) has, because of the short legs and the long neck suggesting a good resemblance. So this would be one option to explore further. Drawing (e) starts to look a little bit like a camel with the bent neck, so this direction is interesting, but one needs to be aware. Drawing (g)'s head is too much poodle-like, so that doesn't work at all. All the physical attributes in relation create the habitus of that specific animal. Those attributes that are unique to that animal have to be pinpointed and exaggerated. It is difficult to just judge the shape alone and often details help to define the animal further and with it, the character.

In the case of the llama that would be the length of the neck, the relationship between neck, body size, and length of the legs. Additionally, the interesting shapes of the hair, the various positions of the ears that are possible, the often bulgy eyes, the split hoofs … all those help to create a unique type of llama.

In Sony's production of *Storks* (2016) the stork's design was pushed to such an extreme that they started to resemble seagulls rather than storks. Their beak and head shapes began to lose their typical slender shapes in body and beak, and started to resemble a different type of bird. This can easily happen if squash and stretch in shapes, and exaggeration in the entire character design, is pushed too far.

Rhythm, shapes, and poses in Richard Williams' character of Zigzag in *The Thief and the Cobbler*

Richard Williams is most famous to the general public for his character animation of the title sequence of *The Return of the Pink Panther* (1975) and for being the animation director for Robert Zemeckis' feature *Who Framed Roger Rabbit* (1988), for which he won an Academy Award as animation director.

There is one feature film of his however that I can say is one of the few spectacles in animation that is worth studying over and over, the traditionally animated *The Thief and the Cobbler*. Being the film with the second-longest production period in film history[4] and unfortunately being unfinished, it boasts of breathtaking animation, effects, characters, and imagery that was deemed impossible until Richard Williams proved everyone wrong. The story is about a young cobbler who is destined to save the Golden City. It was prophesied that the city will fall if the three golden balls on the highest minaret in the city are stolen, and an unnamed thief steals them. The scale of this film is beyond anything that one can enjoy in any other hand-drawn animated feature so far. The main point of the quality of the film is its creativity in every shot and its unique style. Williams always pushes the images and characters further and further and is inventive on every level. He creates an epic scale that is very difficult to achieve in traditional animation. *The Thief and the Cobbler* can easily compete with David Lean's epics of the 1960s in grandeur and scope. Williams does not sacrifice the length of each shot and scene to just get the story point across. He plays with the scene, extends it, and enjoys the very moment and the character itself. He does what not many animators do: gives a scene time to develop an advantage that supports that very character and the story. In some shots and scenes however he falls too much in love with the technique of complicated animation that only serves the purpose of showing-what-can-be-done instead of driving the story further.

What we have is animation at its very best and an opulence that is unique. The film is not easy to watch unfortunately, but despite some shortcomings must be studied by any enthusiast of animation to learn and appreciate what this field is actually capable of. Richard Williams did not shy away from any complexity; on the contrary, he seems to have sought out what has been said to be most difficult or impossible in animation, just to prove that it isn't and that he can do it. No one can deny that he succeeded.

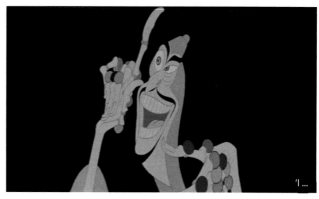

Figure 12.31

Figure 12.32

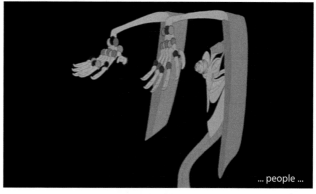

Figure 12.33

Figure 12.34

---

4 The longest feature film in production is now Yuriy Norshteyn's film *The Overcoat*, which he has worked on since 1981.

The character animation is in some characters a pleasure to watch as Williams gives most characters a strong and very unique personality that is an exaggerated animated one, not a realistic one, and celebrates the strengths of the graphic art form animation, always staying away from the cliché. The character animation is specifically designed for each character to not just add movement to the characters, but to give them a unique personality seldom seen to that extent in animation. Each character has a specific walk, and for example, Zigzag, the Grand Visier of the Golden City, has extraordinarily long shoes that are extending every time he takes a step and he is proudly striding when he comes into the city in a very pompous fashion. The character also has 12 fingers with more joints and two rings on each finger! Williams wants us to be visually blown away and he definitely achieves his goal by having a ten-minute destructive extravaganza at the end of the feature with a gigantic war machine being destroyed. The only reason why we don't get annoyed by the endless explosions and the collapsing in this scene is our following the impossible journey of the thief through the mess of the explosions. Williams gives us one idea after the other, never repeating himself, always being utterly creative. The film is a never-ending source of inspiration and proof of how many visual options there are in animation.

The card-game shot

This rather long shot of Richard Williams' animation from a scene with Zigzag meeting Mighty One-Eye, is one of the most complex pieces of character animation there is. The Grand Visier Zigzag meets Mighty One-Eye, the chief of the monsters called "one-eyes" who will try to take over the Golden City. The shot shows Zigzag's rather theatrical presentation of himself. It is one of Richard Williams' most famous animated shots and its magnificent timing, variety of poses, and graphic qualities are not very often seen in animation. The amount of detail and quality makes this card trick scene difficult to fathom. The character animation is smooth and moves in perfection, and every keyframe pose is a pleasure to look at and study. Even graphically the line quality is of utter beauty, because it does not want to be realistic, but wants to celebrate the possibilities of animation, which is exaggeration, shape, and timing. Richard Williams gives us a scene that is pure animation in its most complex and perfect form. The character animation is very cartoony and uses squash and stretch, and exaggeration to a delightful extreme. The design is kept in a graphic two-dimensional style, though animated with three-dimensional aspects. The character is very shape-oriented rather than form-oriented, though the dimensionality of the character is still exceptional. The smoothness of the character's movements is due to the animation being shot on ones, which means there are 24 frames drawn and painted in one second of animation, compared to 12 frames in a regular 2D animated feature film. This nearly doubles the workload and the costs; nevertheless, the animation is obviously much smoother.

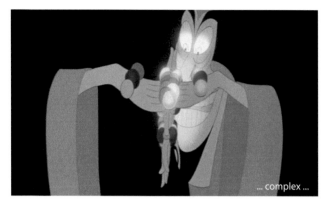

... complex ...

Figure 12.35

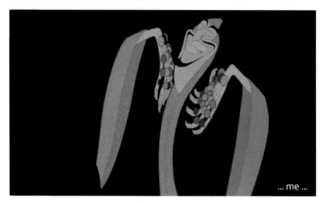

... me ...

Figure 12.36

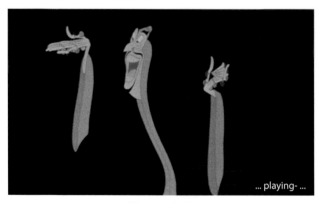

... playing- ...

Figure 12.37

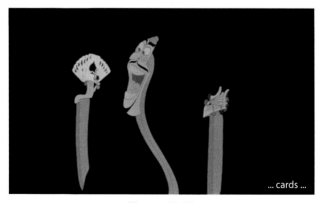

... cards ...

Figure 12.38

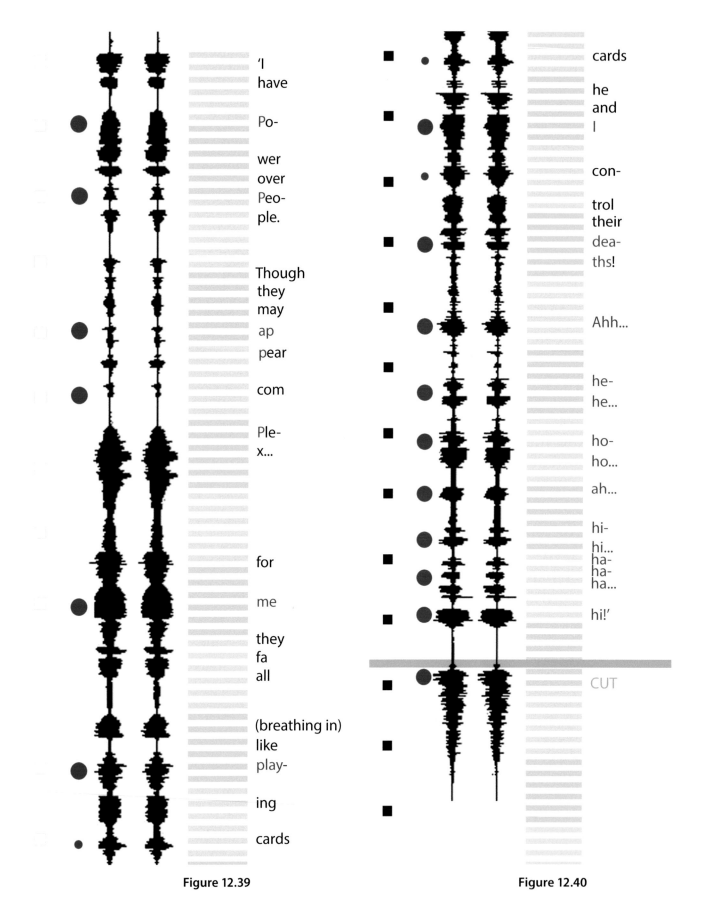

Figure 12.39

Figure 12.40

Figure 12.41

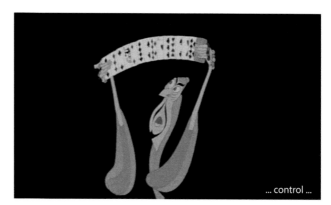

Figure 12.42

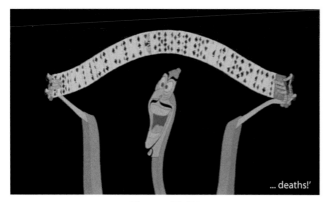

Figure 12.43

Figure 12.44

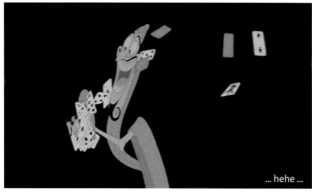

Figure 12.45

Figure 12.46

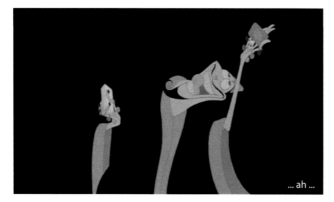

Figure 12.47

Figure 12.48

Figure 12.49

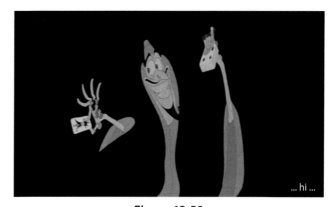

Figure 12.50

An animated shot with dialog always works best if the dialog has an imbedded rhythm to it. This not only makes the sentence flow but also gives the animator points of rhythmical beats that can be used to emphasize poses and the content of certain words. The character of Zigzag is vocalized by Vincent Price in such an exaggerated manner that it is a pleasure to listen to as it shows this pompous and arrogant weirdo in all its odd glory. Zigzag's dialog in the card-playing scene is as follows (emphasis on certain sounds are in red): *"I have power over people. Though they may appear complex ... for me they fall like playing-cards and I control their deaths! Ahh ... hehe ... hoho ... ah ... hihi ... hahaha ... hi!"* The accents hit a certain measure that is after "for me" sped up until the end (see the visualized soundtrack in Figures 12.39 and 12.40). The speeding up of the rhythm fits the struggle Zigzag has with the playing-cards trying to catch them very well, which is becoming more and more difficult.

Visual emphasis on certain accents

The scene starts with the word "I" and Zigzag raises the index finger of his six-fingered hand—the more complex the better for Richard Williams. He gives us a character with six fingers, each finger has two rings, which adds 12 rings to animate plus another three at the wrist: that makes overall 24 rings with six additional gems on the wrists! To visualize the word "I," Williams uses the index finger to symbolize a line as the letter "i" and opens Zigzag's own eye, creating a visual pun. The entire facial expression is designed toward the finger and the eye, which is close to the raised finger. The raised eyebrow and the mouth shape contribute to the face opening toward the left.

The word "power" gets a very strong snap because of his eye popping open, his hat snapping back due to the raised eyebrow that pushes it backward. This pose flows smoothly into the next word "people" in the facial expressions. His right eye that just opened widely now pops out even more in a hypnotic stare while his hands suddenly snap back at the word "people."

"Appear" gets another emphasis in the head moving toward the camera and the eyebrows being raised.

"Complex" is accompanied by a light effect in his eyes while he interlocks his finger in a complex manner, giving the word "complex" a visual representation. Here, the light serves as the visual accentuation.

Zigzag's unquestionable self-confidence and self-love finds a representation in the pose for the word "me" that is filled with glee and pride. Everything in the pose moves upward and underlines his schmuck grin—everything reeks of bragging.

The next weight is given to the word "playing" that Williams accents with a flick of the hand to produce the game of cards. Zigzag's eyes are closed all the way through "fall like ..." and open at "playing" to stay open until the word "cards." That gives those two words the highlight they need. Additionally his head makes a little jerk at the word "playing" and an anticipation of closing his eyes at the end of "cards" to lead into his little giggle "he" afterward that is accompanied by his wide-opened eyes.

When Zigzag says "control" his whole body goes down, his voice is suddenly deeper and the cards create a significant shape above him that frames his head and accentuates that very pose.

"Deaths" has again a strong accent in the vocalization and the visualization with an affective jerk of the head.

The following part of him catching the cards is just a visual feast of strange expressions and very funny poses that sometimes don't even look like Zigzag anymore because they are pushed to such extremes. Nevertheless, it works perfectly because of the speed of the animation and that the audience feels the flow rather than exactly sees every pose. Williams rounds the shot up with a little "gimmick" at the end when Zigzag raises his brows three times toward Mighty One-Eye as he just exposed himself cheating (a card slipped out of his sleeve). This cheeky eyebrow movement follows the established rhythm and gives the shot a nice and comfortable ending, and also a visual bridge to the next shot as Zigzag connects with Mighty One-Eye, who he is looking at. We cut and see One-Eye being ... well, One-Eye: grumpy and doubtful.

Rhythm and flow in the pose

What is so extraordinary in William's animation for Zigzag is the line quality of the character. Its flow is so seamless and always succumbs to the focal point of the pose, and assists the direction of the frame. The character of Zigzag is not a three-dimensional form that moves with a rigid skeleton underneath. Zigzag has a skeleton in his forearms and that is about it. Everything else is able to succumb to the rules of aesthetics and design. This sequence of Zigzag playing with the cards is a *tour de force* of animated lines with an exceptional, graceful fluidity.

Poses

The following dissection of the key moments of Richard Williams' animation of Zigzag is just scratching the surface. It mentions the key ingredients of the poses but doesn't go into the details of each line; it deals with the broad idea of the shapes, directions, and vectors of the poses.

Red shapes in the screen-shots 12.51–12.91: direction of the main shapes of Zigzag.

White Lines: Directions, Vectors, Connections, and Overall Flow of the Pose.

1. Concave upper body shape, arms and hands on the same level are creating a movement forward. The left eye bigger than the right opens up the image to the left. The flow goes from the eyes into the hands and upward (Figures 12.51 and 12.52).

2. A convex pose opens up to the left. The bigger left eye and the raising eyebrow pushes the viewer's eye toward screen left. The left hand (his right) is positioned just underneath the left eye, allowing Zigzag's view to be unblocked. Left thumb's vector flows into the nose, as right thumb's vector also flows into the nose, both vectors finally leading into the eyes (Figures 12.53 and 12.54).

3. There is a very strongly stretched concave pose where hands are above the head, creating a line just above the eyes, not blocking the view. The strong line of action is repeated in the sleeves and the hands, and it gives the whole pose a very gentle flow. The trio of sleeves and lapel juxtaposes the trio of hands and head (Figures 12.55 and 12.56).

4. The gentle flow of the pose before is broken by the right hand spreading the fingers and breaking the smooth flow of the energy in pose three. Zigzag's viewing direction is made obvious by the left thumb's vector leading the direction. The right-spread hand points down into the face, the two

Figure 12.51

Figure 12.52

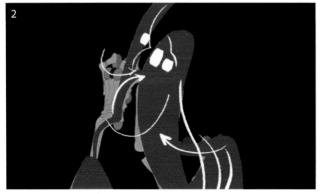

Figure 12.53

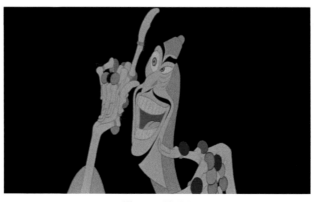

Figure 12.54

sleeves being on the same height, push the view forward to the left (Figures 12.57 and 12.58).

5. The strong concave bend continues and is now intensified by the bend of the fingers that push the whole pose forward to the left. The left eye is bulging out, the right one is closed. The right eye and brow are flowing into the nose, which points to the left. The left hand is blocking the view, but very much strengthens the flow to the left. The sleeves balance the downward movement of the hands by counteracting their direction: hands go from right to left down, sleeves go from right to left up (Figures 12.59 and 12.60).

6. The left eye bulges out even more and additionally has a hypnotic swirl to it. Still the pose is concave, the hands still point strictly forward and even the thumbs, in the awkward position they are, point toward the front (design is more important than anatomy!). The flow is obvious in the nose ridge that moves into his goatee which itself undeviatingly aims to the left. The lower parts of the sleeves, left hand, and lower arms create a continuing vector directed left (Figures 12.61 and 12.62).

7. The hands form a bowl with the head in the center. Eyes are both open and focusing on the space between the hands.

Figure 12.55

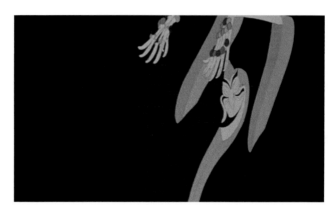

Figure 12.56

Figure 12.57

Figure 12.58

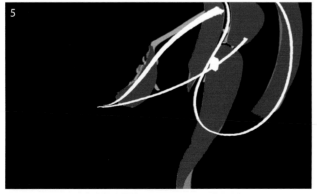

Figure 12.59

Figure 12.60

The right thumb with its bend draws attention to the eyes. A connecting curve can easily be drawn between both thumbs and the eyes (Figures 12.63 and 12.64).

8. The sleeves create a negative space with the hands in its center. The magic glow that streams out from behind the hands (much like in the paintings of George de la Tour) makes this moment exceptionally important. The bend in the fingers goes downward allowing the eyes to be seen and also repeating the grin of the mouth. Both sleeves form a vignette around the character. The fingers that are pointing down are positioned next to the head, to allow the facial expression to be read (Figures 12.65 and 12.66).

9. This is a very strong concave pose with a strong line of action expressing boasting pride. Both hands flow with the yellow trim of the coat. The yellow sleeves bulge out and again create a frame for the character, inscribing it into an oval shape. The hands also repeat the shape of the mouth, repeating his smug grin (Figures 12.67 and 12.68).

10. Here, a convex forward bent pose in which the left hand is on the level of his eyes, creating a continuous vector and also supporting the viewing direction. The sleeves rise from the right to the left and therefore form a shape that pushes the view upward to the left hand (Figures 12.69 and 12.70).

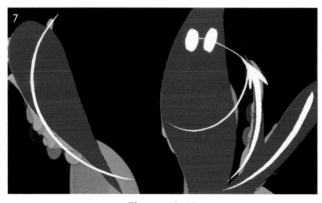

Figure 12.61

Figure 12.62

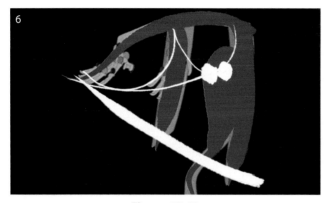

Figure 12.63

Figure 12.64

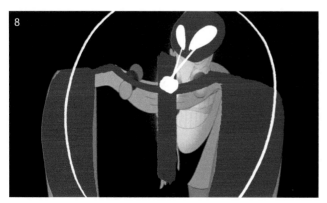

Figure 12.65

Figure 12.66

11. Convex pose: hands are on the same level (the joint of the left wrist seems broken), mouth shape, opening toward the left, leads into the cards. See how the right hand is in line with the mouth and cards. The head being closer to the cards than to the right hand also moves the eye toward the left (Figures 12.71 and 12.72).

12. The sleeves flow into the elongated face and the curve of the cards happens underneath the face so as not to obstruct the expression. Right and left hands are crossing each other and are placed next to the head for the same reason of keeping the expression free from overlap (Figures 12.73 and 12.74).

13. The row of cards are forming a frame for the face with hands, arms, and sleeves. The shape of the sleeves taper toward the elbows and their bend additionally flows smoothly into the forearms, both generating a visual thrust to the game of cards. The fingers are pointing inward and strongly accentuate the flow of the cards. Again, Williams sacrifices anatomy for composition (Figures 12.75 and 12.76).

14. In this frame, the vignetting of the face is even stronger. Williams takes the idea of the earlier pose and pushes it to the extreme to give the audience more variation. The overall composition follows a simple, yet effective and beautifully unique shape (Figures 12.77 and 12.78).

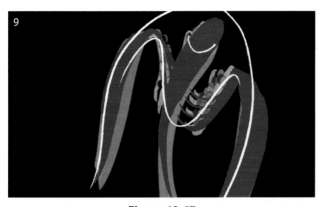

Figure 12.67

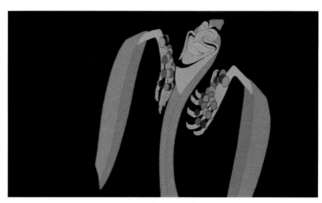

Figure 12.68

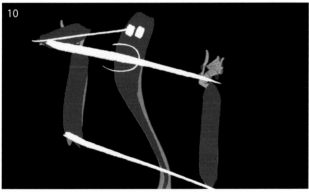

Figure 12.69

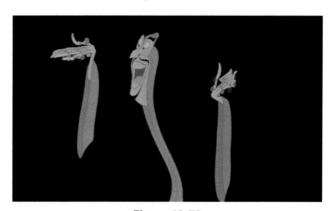

Figure 12.70

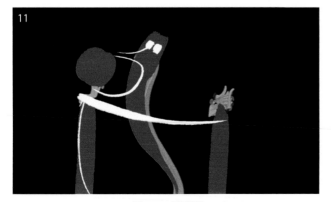

Figure 12.71

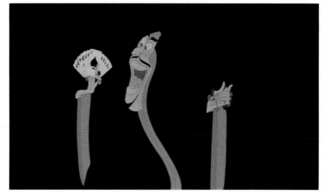

Figure 12.72

15. In this chaos we still can see clearly the facial expression that is kept free of obstructing flying cards. The rather odd position of the right hand works perfectly fine in the animation. This is where Williams' inventiveness comes in: he is breaking joints and creating odd poses that work perfectly fine in the animation, making the animation more interesting and giving it that "snap" that it needs. The entire composition is following one smooth curve (Figures 12.79 and 12.80).

16. Here is a convex pose with a slightly concave head and facial expression, where the center of attention is the game of cards in Zigzag's hands. His eyes and the long

grin point toward that focal point. The flow of the face continues in the yellow trim of his coat. Once elongated, the right sleeve's curve also ends up in the focal point (Figures 12.81 and 12.82).

17. This rather funny-looking expression with the strangely curved head has two focal points: the card on the right and the one on the left. The eyes are staring to the left, whereas the nose and face is pointing to the right. What a brilliant idea to solve the problem of two focal points! (Figures 12.83 and 12.84)

18. William's inventiveness is just never ending. He doesn't shy away from the most extreme ideas in order to make his

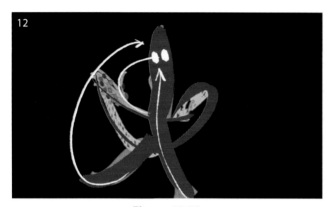

Figure 12.73

Figure 12.74

Figure 12.75

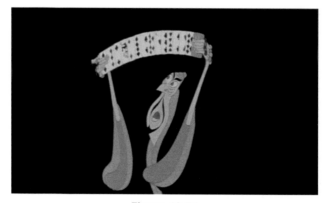

Figure 12.76

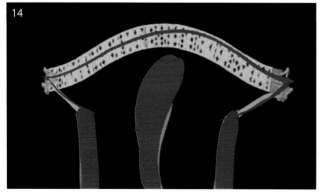

Figure 12.77

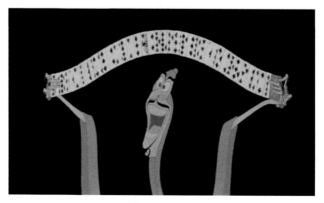

Figure 12.78

visual point. Focal point here is the green card. The right sleeve and the odd head tilt are leading into the green card; left hand connected with the angle of the tilted head strengthens the flow toward the green card. The lower part of the left sleeve's curve connected to the upper part of the right sleeve (continuous vector) underlines the position of the head (Figures 12.85 and 12.86).

19. Richard Williams uses the whole frame and lets the character move left and right, up and down, never allowing the audience to be bored by either the poses or the composition. He gives us one variation after another

and therefore keeps the audience interested with ever-changing visuals at all times. The concave pose with both hands follows the tilt of the head. The one raised finger has enough visual energy to support the viewing direction of Zigzag. The left sleeve is pointing forward to the eyes, with the tip of the finger on its path. The shape of the nose keeps the important left eye visible, opening up the pose to the left (Figures 12.87 and 12.88).

20. The shape of the whole pose is a bloated triangle with the head as the top. Hands are again next to the face keeping the expression visible and the silhouette clear. Having the

Figure 12.79

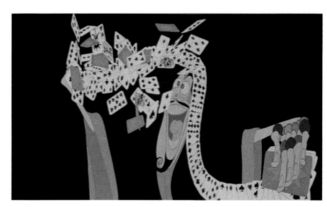

Figure 12.80

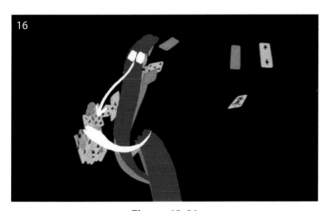

Figure 12.81

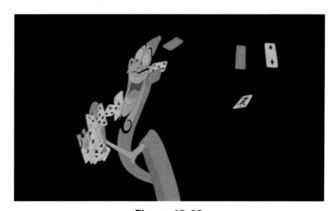

Figure 12.82

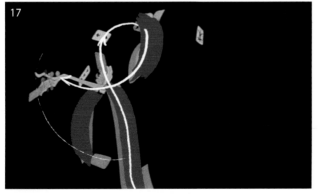

Figure 12.83

Figure 12.84

right sleeve long and the left sleeve short (hidden behind the coat) gives us an upward drift that is supported by the forearms' tilted upward position. The upward pointing left fingers serve as vectors toward the eyes. There is a very effective staggering effect in terms of shapes and distances happening in the hands, and the positioning of the game of cards that lead into the eyes. The shape of the card and the left hand (additionally the position of the left wrist), the shape of right fingers, and the shape of the eyes are three similar shapes that have a curved movement leading to the eyes (Figures 12.89 and 12.90).

21. A concave pose with a concave right arm and sleeve, both parallel each other. Both upper parts of the yellow sleeves are on one line that also includes the lower part of the face, which leads to a good compositional arrangement. The game of cards and the fingers in the right hand are flowing toward the focal point. The single card in his right hand and the stack of cards in the left hand are in line with the eyes, pointing toward to the focal point that is accentuated by the flaring fingers. Right arm, head, and left hand form a triangle (Figures 12.91 and 12.92).

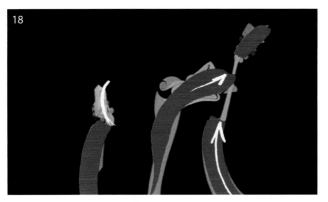

Figure 12.85

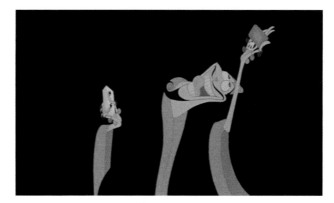

Figure 12.86

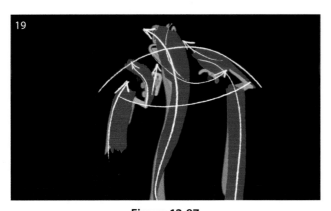

Figure 12.87

Figure 12.88

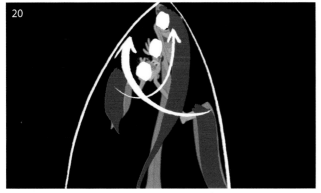

Figure 12.89

Figure 12.90

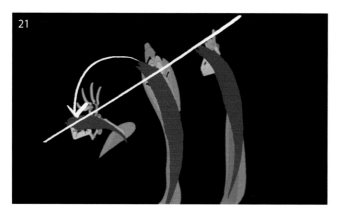

Figure 12.91

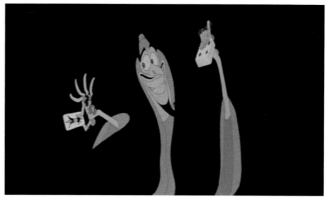

Figure 12.92

Let us recapture the main points that make Williams' animation so successful:

- Variation: avoid repetition in the poses.
- Poses are all designed to perfection to serve one purpose only: focal point.
- Every new pose has one simple line of action that most of the lines follow or accentuate.
- The dimensionality of the characters' parts changes from dimensional to graphic depending on the compositional needs.
- Composition always rules over anatomical accuracy.
- Joints can be broken in order to support the composition.
- Each single element within the pose is connected to other elements within the pose, creating a complex system of flowing vectors.

- There is a strong relationship between dialog and pose.
- The graphic quality of the arrangements of shapes is crucial for the pose and composition.

The sheer scale of inventiveness of this shot is stunning and shows what animation can become in the hands of a master animator and how the complexity that hand-drawn animation already has can be pushed to a level that is nothing short of spectacular!

More on *The Thief and the Cobbler*:

Schreck K. (2012). *Persistence of vision*, Documentary, 83 min.

CHAPTER 13

Form

Where shape is dominating the two-dimensional plane, form is dominating the three-dimensional space. Form gives the character substance, makes them more graspable, and places them in a reality that is closer to our own than the two-dimensional plane. Stop-motion and puppet animation has a substance to it that is as much related to the form and dimensionality of the characters, as it is to light and shadow, and texture. Its visuals are closer to reality than a drawing. Form is either created by light and shadow, which is the most obvious sculptor of form, or by lines that suggest dimensionality and render form, even on a two-dimensional plane. Light and shadow make it seemingly much easier for form to be understood, but that can be an illusion. Figure 13.1a through e shows how form can be suggested incorrectly, but still giving the illusion of a three-dimensional space. An object can suggest a highly refined form and still not be "correct." We are often seeing form if there is a semirealistic treatment of light and shadow that seemingly renders the object correctly. When it comes to drawing, there is a very smooth transition from shape to form, which can be used as a graphic advantage in designing not only the characters but also the character animation.

In Figure 13.2a through c, there are three different treatments of one character. From very flat (a), to seemingly dimensional (b) and finally three-dimensional (c). Form is not an issue in the first two versions, as shape dominates. Version (a) has full flatness and there is barely any suggestion of dimensionality. Even the nose is not in the middle of the face, but on the side to let the character be even more connected to the flat plane.

This version allows for some design decisions that are of interest:

- The flatness of the facial features allows full visibility of both eyes, which helps to read the emotion. Especially the nose does not obstruct the eyes. We have two very important views: side view and front view.
- Perspective is avoided in all parts, allowing the character to fit into a flat and graphic environment.
- The flatness allows for a graphically driven style.
- Parts of the character can be detached and still the character is convincing as the flatness increases the stylization of the character.

An example of this style is the UPA animation *Fudget's Budget* by Robert Cannon (1954) or Bruno Bozetti's shorts and features with *Signore Rossi* (1960–1978). Rossi however also mixes elements of all three examples (a), (b), and (c).

Version (b) has suggested form, but there is no accurate construction of the underlying structure. The character in its core elements only follows the shape, not the form. The nose is in the middle of the face, which suggests an accurate architecture of the face, but it is not correctly constructed.

Version (c) is a fully constructed character, with a slight connection to the flatness of the plane; not everything is perfectly dimensional. But obviously the character is stepping out of the plane into a dimensional space. This can be pushed further and further until the character is in every element precisely following the character's form, which would end up in a character that is mimicking the form-driven aesthetic of computer animation or puppet animation.

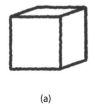 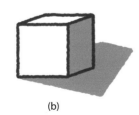  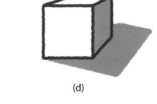 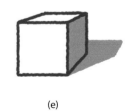

(a)	(b)	(c)	(d)	(e)

Figure 13.1

This cube has parallel perspective, which makes it look flat and tied to the two-dimensional plane. It struggles to leave it.

The same cube with a wrongly constructed shadow lifts the cube from its plane and creates a false impression of form and perspective.

A cube constructed with two-point perspective has clearly more form than cube A as it shows width, height, and depth correctly.

With a falsely constructed shadow the cube still has strong form and depth. The shadow really accentuates the ground plane.

The correctly constructed shadow adds form and perspective, but it does not open up the space more than in (d).

DOI: 10.1201/b22147-13

(a) (b) (c)

Figure 13.2

All three versions still have in their silhouette a similar shape. However, the more complex the body shape, like example (c), the more the three-dimensionality will affect the silhouette and it might be more difficult to get a clear graphic silhouette. For example, the hat in (a) is clearer because it is simpler. The nose is also being seen in (a) in its accurate dimensions without perspective, but not in (b) or (c). Two-dimensional character's silhouettes like (a) can be forced to be the same from pose to pose on purpose. What is important with form-driven characters is to allow the dimensionality of the form to dominate the character but not let the shape of the silhouette in its simplicity disappear. The shape of the silhouette is still important as it often defines the character and distinguishes them from all the others.

Hand-drawn animation that focuses very strongly on form is Richard Williams' animation for the character Roger Rabbit where accurate form can actually be felt and seen in the character's

underlying structure, especially in his arms and elbows. In the beginning of the feature *Who Framed Roger Rabbit,* when Roger for instance talks about taking care of Baby Herman, the dimensionality of the skeleton of the character is clearly felt underneath the final character. Williams actually starts out with a skeleton and then dresses the character with the final version. This can be seen in the animation of Zig-Zag in *The Thief and the Cobbler,* when the Grand Visier walks up the spiral staircase in the tower; Williams' animation is still very rough and unfinished, so the skeleton is obviously drawn first to give the character as much dimensionality as possible and then the actual character is added. Williams animates a form version first, with its geometric complexity in perspective. The next round adds the character on top of the skeleton with its graphic qualities and design. The end result still contains the complexity of accurate perspectives, but also has the pleasant graphic qualities to it. The anatomical structure underneath with the complex dimensionality is a stark contrast to the extremely shape-driven animation of, for example, the section of George Gershwin's *Rhapsody in Blue* in Disney's *Fantasia 2000* (2000), directed by animator Eric Goldberg, who is also the animator on the Genie in Disney's *Aladdin* (1992). The feel of form is strongly present in Williams' animation and much reduced in Eric Goldberg's, creating two different styles that approach character animation from very different fundamental structures. Goldberg's animation celebrates the line and the shape, not so much the form in its solidity.

Technical characters

Without a good understanding of form, characters like robots or technical accessories can't be drawn properly if accurate three-dimensionality is the goal. Starting out with simple thumbnail drawings provides the direction of the characters' shapes and helps collect simple ideas (Figure 13.3a). Once the direction is

established the shapes need to be translated into forms, which can be a bit tricky and just takes time and pencil mileage by refining the drawing again and again, and constantly bringing more form into the character and correcting it (b and c). This can be a long process and takes patience and can't be done quickly (by most draftsmen ... there are the few that can draw machinery, robots, spaceships, and such in a split second and it will still be much better than the general draftsman can accomplish). What is important with form? Practice and simplification! Simplification of the complex form into straightforward, manageable pieces and then refining it little by little is the key to getting it "right" and not becoming lost in details. Look at the thumbnail drawing and figure out what the actual simplified form of the character is and get the dimensionality of that right first, then do the next step of refining it. When the fundament of the character, its shapes and forms, are not accurate, the decoration on top isn't going to end up in the right place either. So take your time getting the foundation right and then put in the details.

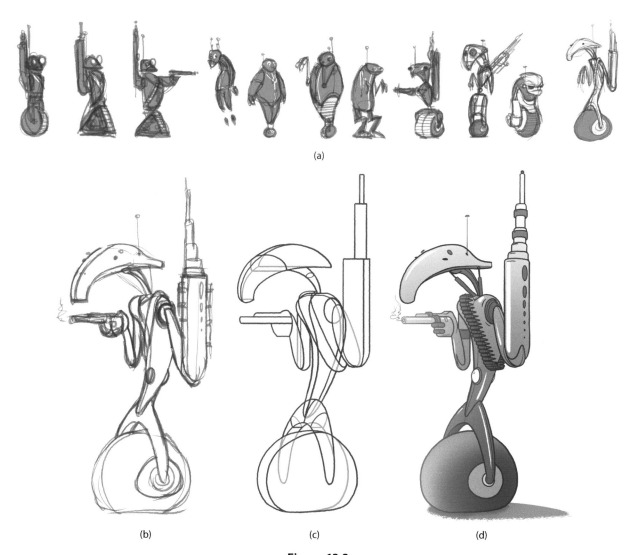

(a)

(b)   (c)   (d)

Figure 13.3

Always define the dimensionality (Figure 13.4)

Perspective will be killed by front and side views. Those two views do usually lack perspective and will always look flat. So avoid them and add elements to the design that support dimensionality. Especially elements that accentuate the bilateral symmetry of the character on the back, front or face (nose, belly button, crotch, chest/sternum, spine, and butt crack which all can be also accentuated/interpreted in the dressed character by designs on the clothing with zippers, pockets, line of buttons, colors, shapes, prints, folds, etc.). The perspectival foreshortening of those elements will greatly accentuate the form. Even if it is just a small and insignificant line, it will help to see the character in its space-occupying form.

More on how to draw robots:

Thompson K. (2006). *50 Robots to Draw and Paint*. London: Barron's Educational Series.

This shape has no obvious direction which way it is facing. We can determine that it is probably facing to the right with the tension being right, the compression left. But there is no proof that we are right.

This shape has only a dot which gives us a hint of how the shape/form is sitting in space. In a character this could be the belly button, a button, or a decoration on the clothing.

This version with a line defining the form's back side (or front side) gives us precise information of the form's positioning in space. In the actual design this line could be the spine on the back, or decoration on the clothing.

Figure 13.4

CHAPTER 14

Line of Action

Line of action: Single character

Line of action: this imaginary single line describes in animation the main movement and direction of the body's action. It is the result of the observation of body physiques and its thorough understanding, combined with an artistic impact that serves the purpose of the pose. There is a line of action to be found in every body that is either at rest or in motion. It follows the direction that drives the body's action and is most often the main reading direction of the pose. Paying attention to this line helps the animator immensely to comprehend and design a pose. Where the line of action determines the main forces and direction of the pose, every secondary movement in the composition of the pose should as much as possible support the line of action, otherwise the pose can look cluttered, disorganized, and easily loses its believability and aesthetic appeal. Every pose should always seek balance and simplicity, which includes the flow in the limbs, and also the movement and curvature of the mentioned line of action. Usually the line of action follows the curvature of the spine and the direction of the head; however, this needs to be judged on every single pose.

Because the line of action is not an actual physical line, but rather an imaginary line based on the judgment by the viewer, there is no rule for what exactly this line would look like or where exactly it flows. It can flow along the chest, or along the spine, where ever the viewer "feels" the tension

and movement in the character's body. The line of action is however separate from vectors in the character. These are two different ideas. The line of action determines forces, where the vectors *can* determine forces, but are more concerned with the compositional arrangement and the direction toward the focal point. The illustration shows a boy holding two balloons (see Figures 14.1 through 14.3). The line of action is the tension in his body and the flow from head to toes. In Figure 14.2, the line of action is either running along the front or on the back of the body. It describes the overall movement of the whole body and then additionally the secondary movement of the arms holding the balloons. This secondary movement is sometimes included in the line of action, sometimes it is not; this depends on the pose. It can also be simple or more complex; however, it always deals with the physical forces in the body. One can also find a line of action in limbs for instance: every arm has its own line that determines the overall flow of its various elements. However, those secondary lines would always succumb to the main line of action. The aesthetic forces or vectors in the pose are shown in Figure 14.3 and many of the lines are actually the same as the line of action; however, their purpose is different. Vectors lead the eye from one significant point in the pose to the next, guiding through the character's action and emotion. This is an aesthetic and artistic decision to improve the readability of the character. Line of action and vectors are heavily entangled and can never really be seen separately, as they affect and influence each other.

Figure 14.1	**Figure 14.2**	**Figure 14.3**

DOI: 10.1201/b22147-14

Line of action and artistic content

In the sculpture of *The Dying Gaul*, a Roman marble copy of a Hellenistic bronze statue from approximately 220 BC, we see a naked Gallic soldier reclining exhausted, due to a lethal wound he received to his right side (Figures 14.4 and 14.5). Objects of war are surrounding him: a sword, a shield, and a Celtic horn, and the soldier is depicted by the Romans as a wild, barbaric enemy. His messy hair, stiffened by chalk water, makes him look very different from sculptures that show Greek or Roman citizens. He is also shown naked, the preferred fighting style of the Gauls. The hairstyle and mustache are in the typical Gallic fashion, as is the thick torc that proves his higher status. He holds his forward-leaning upper body erect with his right hand that, yet once strong, slowly bends due to exhaustion caused by the lethal

Figure 14.4

The *Dying Gaul* (~ 220 BC) (Courtesy of Wikimedia Commons).

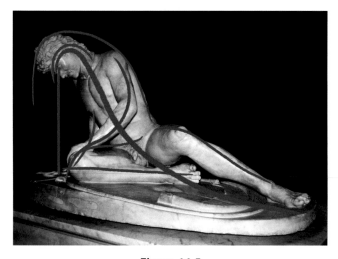

Figure 14.5

wound. His upper body weight mainly rests on this right arm and right side of the pelvis. This allows the weight of the stretched left leg to balance out the weight shift that is caused by the upper body leaning toward his right and lifts the left side of the pelvis slightly off the ground. As the whole sculpture is opening up toward his right arm, the reading direction of course is toward his right (or in the image the left).[1] The line of action in this case would be the line that is created by the left leg, through the upper body into the head, which is tilted down toward the insignias of war, that symbolize his pride as a soldier and the cause of his own death. The line of action forces the audience's eye through the whole sculpture and guides them visually through the Gaul's body to end up in the center of his emotions: the face. The tilted down head then leads the eye toward those insignias of war, which are the story's fundament as they are the reason for his demise. The vectors in the pose are either following the direction of the line of action, or they point toward the face or insignias on the ground. His left arm, the angled leg, the flow of the right side of the body into the hairline straight down to the weapons all accentuate the general composition of the pose. As well as the technical side of the pose, which deals with forces, anatomy, and weight, there is the artistic side that deals with vectors and directions in relationship with the story point and aesthetics. Both need to work together and not against each other!

Animation and line of action

In animated characters the line of action is to be pushed in every key drawing for maximum effect. Animation is about exaggeration and the line of action provides us with a great tool to do exactly that.

In the next couple of frames from Chuck Jones' *Duck Amuck* (Figures 14.6 through 14.8) Daffy's line of action, added in red in the image, is always very clear and gives the character determination and strength. There is no hesitation in the line, no softness in the pose, only tension. The pose is pushed to its limits, which in animation is so important and a big part of the expressiveness of the character (if the animation style allows it). Observe how all Daffy's limbs and even his hat and plume follow the main line of action and guide the eye into the direction of the action.

Line of action: Multiple characters

In a group of characters, each character of course has their own line of action. In order to avoid the group looking messy or cluttered, all lines of action have to follow some kind of structure or composition as the whole group obviously follows one story point, has one theme or one direction. All characters' lines of actions therefore should always support each other and play off each other, depending on the story. They can go toward

---

[1] Image right or image left are the actual right or left sides of an image. Character's right or character's left are, if the character is facing us, the left or right side of the image.

Figure 14.6
Warner Brother's *Duck Amuck* (1953)

Figure 14.7
Warner Brother's *Duck Amuck* (1953)

Figure 14.8
Warner Brother's *Duck Amuck* (1953)

each other, against each other, or flow in the same direction. The famous Roman/Greek sculpture of *Laocoön* (Figures 14.9 through 14.14) and his sons was created by three sculptors from the islands of Rhodes, Hagesandros, Athanadoros, and Polydoros. The *Laocoön* group has already been described and mentioned by Plinius as a major and significant piece of art in the first century BC. The marble copy that has come to us is based on the original Hellenistic sculpture from the first century BC. It is a strictly frontal sculpture as it is composed with the front view in mind, which is its preferred viewing position.

The dynamism of this group of the priest Laocoön and his two sons fighting sea serpents is convincing in it depicting the struggle for survival and the horror of the situation with its luring death. Laokoön was a Trojan priest that served the god Poseidon, though being disobedient by marrying and having sons, was killed by divine intervention by the bite of two serpents. The seemingly busy composition of the group has at closer inspection a complex system of vectors and directions that express the impression of struggle, desperation, and intense movement. The seemingly busy composition itself therefore reflects the story and interprets it in its own abstract fashion through vectors, arranged lines, and juxtaposing elements. This already vibrant composition is significantly intensified to the extreme by the bodies' exposed muscles and utmost struggle through their strong impressive physicality. Presenting the man and his sons naked just makes them appear the more vulnerable and exposes their flesh to the bites of the serpents. What in this ostensibly uncontrolled mess would be the lines of action of the three characters? As mentioned before, the line of action is the main movement and direction of the characters' actions. In this case, having three characters, every character has its own composition and its own line of action though all of them are related to each other. Laokoön, being the center of this sculpture and the most dominant character, is in his line of action the one that dominates the other two. His twisted body that fights the snakes—one of them is just about to bite him in his left side—reflects all the agony of the coming end. His face is expressing all the pain of the bite and its inescapable death. The wild hair and desperate expression, the open mouth that seems to scream, and his wide-open eyes in combination with his physical strength, presence, and body size make him the obvious center of the composition and attention. His line of action goes along his left leg, abdominal muscles, and chest, and curves upward into his face (Figure 14.10). Laokoön's line of action connects with his sons' movements relating the characters to each other compositionally and thus emotionally (Figure 14.11). Both sons' lines of action have a similar bend as their father's and thus create a strong correlation between the three. Though the body of the son on the right bends away from the father, he looks back at him and closes the emotional connection between the two. The son on the left is bending toward Laokoön's chest and his head is continuing the bend of his younger upper body. All three characters' lines of action relate to each other, group the characters together in their

Figure 14.9

Figure 14.10

Laokoön (~ first century BC) (Courtesy of Wikimedia Commons).

struggle, and emphasize the focal point: Laokoön's head which in its expression reflects the unavoidable lethal outcome. The gap between the father and the son on the right allows for the serpents bite to be very dominant and visible.

Another aspect that makes this sculpture interesting is the dealing with weight and weightlessness.[2] The sculpture being obviously carved of stone, defies all gravity as the characters seem weightless and light. Each of the three is balancing on their toes and are only on the ground with one foot. Laokoön is touching the ground with his left foot; his right foot carries less weight. This leads to the feeling of the characters not really resting on the ground but being very light in this frontal composition; they move because of their struggle upward. This compositional decision to visually lift the group from the here and now into another realm, which in this case is death, is supporting the dynamism and the intense movement of the group.

The complexity in the Laokoön composition

The sculpture of Laokoön is of course more complex in its composition than just being concerned about the lines of action. As mentioned before, the viewing position of this sculpture is mainly frontal. The group itself is not complete, as some limbs and parts are missing, so the final examination can only be an approximate one and an interpretation. In a complex group like this there is a chaos in

the composition that follows a method. Chaos is precisely what the story tells us, which is the intense struggle in an "action sequence," the struggle for life itself. A sculpture is one moment in time, merely one glimpse of an action, nevertheless the most important moment. It is more or less a keyframe of one sequence that tells the whole story in one frame.[3]

Just showing the chaos of the moment would be very difficult to grasp by the viewer, so the artist has to find a way of composing the group that on the one hand shows chaos, but on the other hand controls each part of the composition and creates a pleasant and organized piece of art. The artist needs to make connections between the various parts to organize the whole. This gives the sculpture a structure that the audience doesn't necessarily have to understand immediately, but feel in being able to read the content easily. Organization is the basis of composition and pose.

Figures 14.12 through 14.14 show various ideas the artists might have thought about when creating the composition of the group and determining which parts of the characters they wanted to relate to each other. First, the group is framed by vertical elements like the drapery of the boys left and right, and the boys' poses. The temple structure Laokoön is leaning on frames the bottom of the group. Determining the top of the group is difficult as parts of the sculpture are missing.

---

[2] The history of the art of antique sculpture III Hellenistic sculpture. Darmstadt: Verlag Philip von Zabern, p. 328.

[3] A sculpture can also be composed by grouping several moments of a longer action together into one moment and therefore revealing the full story with various aspects of the same story.

Figure 14.11

Laokoön (~ first century BC) (Courtesy of Wikimedia Commons).

Figure 14.12

Figure 14.13

Laokoön (~ first century BC) (Courtesy of Wikimedia Commons).

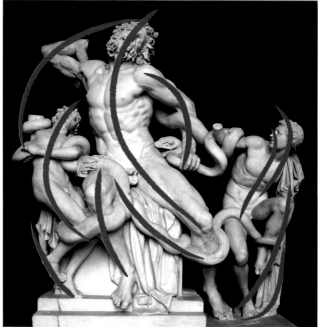

Figure 14.14

The group is also inscribed into a circle (Figure 14.12) and certain parts of the sculpture are following its outline. The circle's center is the head of the serpent that is just about to bite Laokoön in the side. The centrifugal lines that point toward the serpent's head underline some significant parts of the sculpture. Either arms or legs, the tilt of a head, the position of a foot, or the tilt of hips point seemingly unseen toward the head of the snake. "Seemingly unseen" means it is still felt by the viewer. The composition's centrifugal power leads strongly toward the bite and connects all three characters with the snake, and therefore binds the group together.

Laokoön's left leg supports his line of action and pushes the viewer's eye straight toward his upper right arm (Figure 14.13). The dominant diagonal of this line that ends in the right son's knee and foot is balanced by two other diagonals that follow the serpent's body and the arms of father and son. Both sides of the group composition have a dominance in curvature (Figure 14.14) which separates them to give space to the serpent biting Laokoön, but also accentuates the sculpture's overall round compositional elements. The longer one observes the complicated composition and structures all the parts, the more one realizes what composition in the pose can actually do and what power it has. There is a mathematical logic imbedded in this piece that is aside from its technical brilliance an artistic *tour de force*.[4] All of the complexity of the sculpture's directions and vectors have the line of action as the most fundamental compositional element. They all follow the line of action's main direction.

Case study: Relationships between the lines of action with multiple characters in three shots of Disney's *Pinocchio* (1940)[5]

In a group composition in animation, compared to a still image, we have to additionally consider the aspect of time and the constant change of the lines of action and their poses throughout the shot. Each frame is a moment in a continuous flow of the characters' actions and reactions to each other. I'd like to address this relationship between the characters in three shots from Disney's *Pinocchio* (1940). In the first shot, Honest John, Kitty, and Pinocchio meet on the street and are just about to leave for Pleasure Island (time-code 00:55:28). Honest John says and sings in this shot: `Come! The coach departs at midnight! *Hi diddle dee dee, it's pleasure Ilse for me. Where every day is a holiday, and kids have nothing to do but play.*' Very clearly the lines of action of each character relate to each other.

In the very beginning of this shot, Honest John and Kitty envelop Pinocchio, who is just standing between them and his line of action clearly says "inactive." The two villains create a negative space around the puppet that leads in a circular motion toward his wooden head, the focal point in the group. Throughout the shot, Honest John is leading the action and Kitty and Pinocchio are following in their poses and lines of action his dominating lead.

The relationship between the characters' poses and their flow of movement, makes it very easy to read the poses as action and reaction, and to see the three as a compositional group rather than a group of three different characters. There are no elements in their poses that break the compositional rhythm of the group and thus would potentially point one character out as a singular entity. All lines (lines of action and clean-up lines), limbs, glances, facial expressions, are aesthetically and compositionally flowing into each other and following John's lead. The three characters are always responding to each other through action and reaction, creating a comfortable group dynamic. The forces that are interacting with each other (action-reaction) form a network of various movements throughout the group, yet the lines of action never fight with one another but always flow gracefully and create a group dynamic and composition that has one direction and purpose. Each line of action either acts or reacts, which makes it overall a very controlled group movement where only one character is the focus at a time, with the viewer's eyes mostly shifting between Honest John and Pinocchio.

Pinocchio is the inactive character and serves as the connecting element between the two in the entire shot. In the beginning he is just standing there, while the villains around him act and move. Especially Honest John is going into extreme poses, dragging the attention, and his lines of action serve on the one hand as a lead of the movement, but also as vectors leading to the puppet. When John, for instance, reaches out for Pinocchio's hand to drag him down the street, the arms are forming as a secondary line of action a continuous vector that point toward Pinocchio. He is the smallest character in this scene and thus must be strengthened compositionally to be clearly seen and pointed out as the focal point (Honest John is the leading character in the shot, though Pinocchio with his reactions is at times the focal point). This is achieved on the one hand through his brighter colors, and on the other hand by the positioning of the two villains on either side. During John's song of "Hi-Diddle-Dee-Dee," one can clearly see how John and Kitty's lines of action relate to each other, swerving back and forth, and Pinocchio's line of action follows through. If the characters would not act or react to each other's dynamic poses and lines of action, the connecting group aspect, important for the understanding

---

4   Of course, my interpretation of the composition does not claim to be the only one. Everyone can see different compositional elements that seem more important for them.

5   Due to the fact that the Disney Company did not release the copyrights for images of the feature *Pinocchio* to be used in this educational section, which would have tremendously helped the understanding of the discussed poses, it is necessary for the reader to check and compare images from the movie via the provided time-codes alongside the text to fully grasp the characters' lines of action.

of the shot, would be significantly weakened. One can also witness John building up an anticipation for his grand exit off the stage before parading with the other two down the street. His exaggerated bulging line of action serves as a build-up of force and anticipation in order to lead into the swerving exit, where the rest of the group then joins in.

There is a beautiful rhythm and tension in this shot that is difficult to top. The interplay between the characters is perfect and always pushes Pinocchio into the center of attention. Therefore, going the extra mile of posing the characters with each other carefully not only connects them physically but also emotionally through action-reaction.

The character's position within the frame also changes throughout the shot, them taking advantage of the entire stage, which adds the needed variation to not have the shot feel rigid and artificial compositionally. With Kitty being on the left and then swooping to the right while coming closer to the audience, is a very nice move as it not only changes perspective and adds significant depth to the group, but also anticipates the move toward the right and into the distance. The camera move toward the right enhances the action of the characters in just the right moment.

The next shot (time-code 01:05:05) has Lampwick turning into a donkey while Pinocchio is watching. Lampwich screams: "Help! Help! Somebody help! I've been framed! Help! Please, you gotta help me! Oh, be a pal!" Where there was a connection between the characters in the earlier scene with Honest John and Kitty, this scene has the lines of action between Pinocchio and Lampwick often opposing each other, or Pinocchio following Lampwick's movements literally as a follow-through. Lampwick leaves to the left, Pinocchio's direction changes toward the left

following him; Lampwick comes toward Pinocchio which makes him bend away from Lampwick in horror, though following him again when he leaves the frame to the right. Then Lampwick comes in again toward Pinocchio, who bends away from him being literally pushed against the wall. Action and reaction, the forces of Lampwick's transition and Pinocchio's reaction act similar to waves that push and pull depending on the internal struggle of the characters either toward each other or away. One can clearly see the limbs of the characters being always composed in a way of supporting each other's pose and leading toward the characters' focal points or directions. In the shot with Lampwick, Pinocchio is following Lampwick's lead, whereas in this next shot Ghepetto is following.

The third shot (time-code 01:19:10) has Pinocchio talking to Ghepetto about starting a fire to make Monstro the Whale sneeze. In this shot Pinocchio says: "A raft? That's it! We'll take the raft and when the whale opens its mouth…." During this speech Pinocchio is leading the action, and Gheppetto is following with his reaction. The old man acts like a follow-through to Pinocchio's movements and their lines of action constantly relate to each other and act in unison, never on their own. Even Cleo in her movements is following the timing, rhythm, and directions of Pinocchio's lead.

Group composition cannot be addressed without considering the action of the main character and how the group then follows their "lead" in their reactions to his or her actions. They cannot act independently from each other. If they do, they don't feel connected but separated, which then would not create unity but distance (which would of course be a possibility if the story and its emotions ask for it).

CHAPTER 15

Anatomy

There are literally thousands of tutorials out there that explain how to draw the human body, which for the starting artist is a daunting task. In order to be able to draw a body, one needs to study the body and grasp its complexity in a simplified form. However, there is no shortcut to this other than really studying the different elements. The more realistic the character needs to be, the more one has to study anatomy in detail, but too much detail prevents one from staying away from just representing the human form and actually interpreting and exaggerating it (if not realism is the goal).

To make things a bit easier is to understand, a few points first that apply to the muscles in general and to their purpose. These points are important even if the character is very cartoony and lacks realistic anatomical architecture for the most part.

There are four elements in the movement:

1. The muscle itself
2. Tendons that attach the muscle to the bone
3. The bone itself
4. Joints

The muscle itself

First we need to understand what actually happens when a muscle moves. There are three parts involved in the movement: the muscle that contracts, the connection of the muscle to the bones, and the joint. This seems rather obvious but it is often not fully understood which muscle is responsible for what movement.

A muscle, which is a bundle of fibers, can only do one job but it does that job very well: to contract. When it contracts it pulls both ends toward each other, which is the only active movement the muscle can accomplish (Figure 15.1). During contraction, it also slightly bulges and hardens. For instance, the biceps on their lower part are inserted into the radius and their upper part originates in the coracoid process, a hook-like bone that extrudes from the shoulder blade. Contracting the biceps pulls up the radius, and with it the forearm (Figure 15.2a). It can only pull up the forearm, because the other end, which is attached to the shoulder blade, is more stable in that instance (the shoulder blade being stabilized by surrounding tissue, muscles, and bones). So the only way the muscle can pull is by lifting the forearm. This causes the triceps on the opposite side of the upper arm to be stretched: action causes reaction. When the triceps contract, the biceps are pulled and stretched (Figure 15.2b). There is the *agonist*, which causes a movement

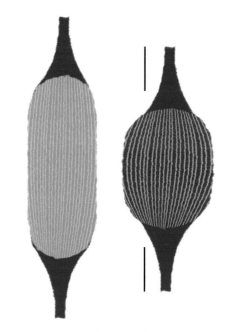

Figure 15.1

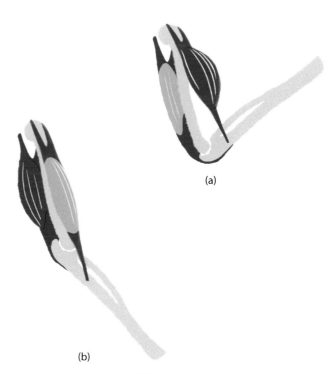

(a)

(b)

Figure 15.2

DOI: 10.1201/b22147-15

(biceps contracting) and the *antagonist*, which releases the joint again into its initial position (biceps are being stretched). Without opposing muscles, agonist and antagonist, the body would not be able to move as every muscle needs other muscles to stretch it again and pull it into its neutral state. However, a muscle can be agonist and antagonist, depending on the movement involved. Most muscles come in pairs (biceps–triceps, quadriceps–hamstrings), but there are muscles that work on their own and do not need an antagonist. The deltoid, or shoulder muscle for instance, is responsible for lifting the arm up (Figure 15.3). It is connected to the clavicle, or collarbone, and to the scapula or shoulder blade in its origin and then inserts in its lower part into the upper arm bone. Contracting it lifts the arm as the shortening of the muscle lifts the humerus. Gravity then lowers the arm if the muscle relaxes again. The weight of the arm itself does the job of bringing the muscle into its initial position.

A muscle only then makes full sense in its function when the connection points on the bones are taken into consideration. Otherwise the muscle is just sitting there without an attachment, and the four points of muscle–tendon–bone–joint are not considered.

Tendons and Sinews

Tendons (which are sinews) are bands of fibrous tissue that connect the muscle to the bone. Tendons can have two functions: to transmit energy from the muscle to the bone, and some tendons serve as springs and store energy to then release it (the tendons at the calves for instance). Tendons can therefore be elastic or not, depending on their function.

Ligaments are similar to tendons—strong bands of fibers that connect bone to bone. They are responsible for stabilizing joints. Ligaments also can limit the range of the joint movement to prevent injury.

Bones

Bones are the solid structures of the skeleton where the muscles are attached via tendons. Every bone has several points and areas where tendons are attached to a rough surface. For example, Figure 15.4 shows the humerus bone and its attachment points in blue, in the front view. Every blue patch on the bone signifies a tendon/muscle group being fastened.

Joints

Joints are points where two bones meet. They are supported by bands and ligaments that tightly wrap the joints for more stability. Especially the shoulder and knees are covered in ligaments. The ends of bones are covered in cartilage to allow smooth movement. Two bone ends meet, for instance in the knee, and there is cartilage on cartilage which, by constantly being lubricated, allows very precise motion.

Structure underneath

Even though many animated characters are seemingly simple in their anatomy and often don't seem to have a solid skeleton or obvious musculature underneath their malleable bodies, one needs to imagine the physical substance the character consists of in order to be able to draw the characters correctly. At the beginning of animation's development the artists evolved in their expertise and drawing abilities from short film to short film, and discovered what animation is capable of and how it can be used as a creative tool. Watching the most famous and successful characters of early animation,

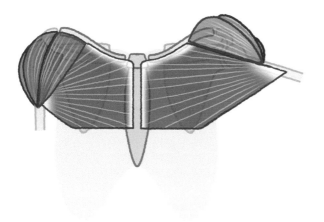

Figure 15.3

Figure 15.4

Figure 15.5

Figure 15.6

Koko The Clown dances to Cab Calloway's song St. James Infirmary
Blues in Betty Boop's short *Snow White*, 1933.

Figure 15.7

Figure 15.8

Betty Boop in *The Old Man of the Mountain*, 1933, in which
Betty Boop is also paired up in a duet with Cab Calloway.

the superstar of the 1920s Felix the Cat, we can see how the
animation style changed over the years. In 1919 Felix is still
comparatively stiff in his movements, the joints of arms and
legs feel wooden. Three years later the movement has a much
wider range and is more fluid. The more organic the motion
of the character became, the more alive he felt. This led to an
animation style that is referred to as "rubber-hose" animation
which was mostly used in the 1920s and early 1930s. The
characters seem to lack a solid structure and skeleton below
their cartoony surface and therefore appear rubbery in
their poses and movement (Figures 15.5–15.8). The joints of
elbows and knees especially are nonexistent and the bend
in the leg happens in the full length of the leg instead of just
the joints. In many shorts this is a style that works perfectly
fine for very cartoony animation of that time (Figures 15.7
and 15.8). In Betty Boop's short, for example, *The Old Man of
the Mountain* from 1933, the old man is, whenever he is not
rotoscoped and dancing (which is based on Cab Calloway's
moves), animated in that very same rubber-hose style which
works beautifully and convincingly with his cartoony design.
One year later we have Disney's famous short *The Goddess
of Spring* in which the Disney artists tried to portray human
motion in order to prepare for their feature *Snow White and
the Seven Dwarfs*. The animation of the goddess is rather
dismal and boneless and she has an awkward motion that
makes her appear like a floating corpse on strings. This
feeling of lifelessness is enhanced by her more realistic
design compared to Betty Boop's for instance. The rubber-
hose animation doesn't fit a realistic character and the artists
had to learn the important connection between the level of
design, the detail to anatomy, and the character animation
style and how all go hand in hand to create a believable
character. The style of motion cannot be separated from
the design. More realistic design requires more realistic and
observed motion, which requires a solid understanding of
anatomy and motion. The more realistic the characters are,
the more we expect the structure underneath, its skeleton
and muscles, to be realistic too; otherwise the character
lacks persuasive power. From one feature and short film to
the next, the Disney artists taught themselves the complex
knowledge needed to animate believable realistic characters
that are based on anatomy rather than pure imagination. The
pinnacle of this was the preparation for *Bambi* (1942) which, in
its complexity of the study of animal anatomy, was the most
advanced and required lessons for the animators to be able
to not only draw, but also understand the anatomy of a deer.
Without the solid knowledge of what happens below the skin
one is not able to create drawings of characters that are based
on realism and convincing in their physicality. One of the
most complex 2D characters in terms of his muscle structure
and anatomical accuracy was Disney's Tarzan, who has full
anatomy that cannot really be simplified, but only stylized.
He needs to be rooted in solid anatomical knowledge for the
result to gain the acceptance of the audience.

In your design or character animation the knowledge of the underlying structure doesn't mean that you need to be realistic; it means to understand the character's anatomy, the body's expansion in space, which still can be interpreted in rather simple visuals. Nevertheless, with the knowledge of skeleton and muscle structure, weight, and physics, the movement and poses will be more convincing and movement itself makes more sense. However, too much use of anatomy can also ruin a character that needs to be simple or has a specific design that rejects realism. Then, the understanding of the anatomy has to support but never dominate.

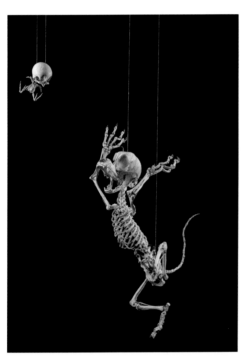

Figure 15.9

Hyungkoo Lee, a Korean artist from Seoul, takes cartoon characters and presents them in a scientific manner. He just shows their skeletons and proves to us that those characters, that we assumed being just color and paint, are actually real. Above is a skeletal version of Warner Brothers' Sylvester and Tweety.

More on anatomy and figure-drawing:

Hampton M. (2013). *Figure Drawing, Design and Invention*. Published by Michael Hampton.

Bammes G. (2011). *Complete Guide to Life Drawing*. Tunbridge Wells, UK: Search Press.

Bammes G. (2009). *Die Gestalt des Menschen: Lehr- und Handbuch der Künstleranatomie*. Freiburg: Christophorus Verlag.

Bammes G. (2010). *Menschen Zeichnen, Grundlagen zum Aktzeichnen*. Freiburg: Christophorus Verlag.

Hands

Artistic possibilities of hands

Hands are of course aside from the face the most significant tools we have for communication, to emphasize emotions and additionally give thoughts and words significance. The complexity of the hand, its expressiveness, and relation to language is not to be underestimated. Hands grab, touch, hold, stroke, poke, built, point, push, pull, tuck, turn, and perform so many other tasks (Figure 15.10). Most of all, hands talk and tell stories in images and sculptures, in illustration, and even more in animation. Hands have their own complex poses that are able to support any emotion and are key components of a well-balanced pose. Hands function also as vectors, especially as index vectors that carry much visual energy. Hands attract the eye and are being used as connectors between characters to release or withhold energy in or from the pose. They are extremely important as artistic tools! They are the complex endpoints of the body where the energy gets released into the environment. Michelangelo's painting in the Sistine Chapel *The Creation of Adam* (around 1512) (Figure 15.11) is a stunning example of how hands are the culmination of an exchange of energy between two characters. God is pointing at Adam and their two index fingers nearly touch. It is the moment just before God releases his spark of life and the tension between is at its highest. The two bodies of God and Adam have the same reclined angle and both poses are composed to face each other. Adam's vectors flow toward the right (line of action, head tilt, arm, right hand, and knee) and God's vectors to the left, creating that intense focal point right between them. But it is not just their bodies and poses that count, but also the volumes and shapes surrounding them. Adam is surrounded by a simplified landscape (directional force to the right) and God by a bloated red cloth, which is filled with angels, who all have a group direction

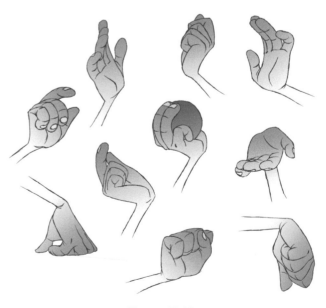

Figure 15.10

Figure 15.11

Michelangelo Buonarroti: *The Creation of Adam* (~ 1512) (Courtesy of Wikimedia Commons).

to the left. Both those shapes contribute to the accumulated energy that is then creating this intense void just between the two fingers. It is the hands and their poses that create grace and the very moment of the creation of humanity. We anticipate the spark of life to be released exactly because they are not touching yet. It is the anticipation that creates this tension. In the case of Adam and God the visual energy within their bodies is released.

But the energy that is released from the hands can also be withheld from leaving the body. The obvious example is Auguste Rodin's (1840–1917) famous statue of *The Thinker* (Figure 15.12), where the hands are pointing back toward the man's own body, keeping the energy within (Figure 15.13). The nude man has a clear purpose and represents intellect and poetry, and thus the hand position interprets the idea of self-reflection and thoughts in general. Rodin's sculpture is referring back to Michaelangelo's characters that also emanate intellect, physical, and mental strength and bridges the Renaissance with Rodin's time. Rodin wanted his sculpture to be connected to Michelangelo's pieces, which in turn are connected to *The Laokoon* and other Greek and Roman sculptures. *The Thinker* visualizes Dante Alighieri[1] (1265–1321), the creator of *The Divine Comedy (1308–1320)*. The sculpture was part of a commissioned door that Rodin worked on from 1880 throughout his life. The door with its myriads of characters depicts Dante's *Inferno*, the first of the three parts of *The Divine Comedy*.

The sculpture does not allow the audience to fully connect with the man, as he is completely with himself. His legs are not spread very widely, his back is bent, head lowered, and arms close to the body. He is concentrating on his innermost thoughts and does not connect with his surrounding at all; is all closed off and compact, is introspective and introverted rather than extroverted like Michelangelo's Adam and God.

How strong the effect of releasing the body's energy into the surroundings is shown in Figure 15.18: despite the small size of the hand, the flaring fingers do attract attention and one can literally feel the energy release.

Michelangelo had a very keen eye for showing the subtleties in hand gestures and interpreting complex emotions through hands. They feel relaxed, yet have still an obvious strength and tension to them. The fingers are never all parallel to each other, but contain a playfulness and three-dimensionality that is striking. This creates movement and avoids the danger of the fingers becoming just elongations of the arm; they are sculptural elements in their own right. Michelangelo's hands have grace in their gestures and seem to support the wisdom and thoughtfulness of the characters. *David*'s (1501–1504) hands, for instance (Figure 15.14), that hold the stone are bent toward his body accentuating and repeating the movement of the body's right outline and smoothly flow into the thigh. David's other hand that holds the sling which is hanging over his shoulder has a bend in the wrist. This bend creates a compositional movement back into the face, linking the sling with his determination in the expression (Figure 15.15). One of Michelangelo's other famous sculptures is *Moses* (1513–1515), housed in the church of San Pietro in Vincoli, Rome (Figure 15.16). His right hand, which is on top of the still blank tablets, is twirling the locks of his beard which adds play and thoughtfulness to his impressively

---

[1] It "might" represent Alighieri; there is a discussion about who it actually is. Dante is never mentioned in the text as being naked.

Figure 15.12

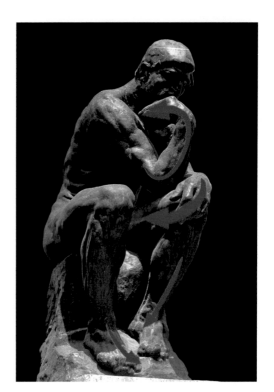

Figure 15.13

Auguste Rodin: *The Thinker* (between 1880 and 1902) (Courtesy of Wikimedia Commons).

Figure 15.14

Figure 15.15

Michelangelo: *David* (1501–1504) (Courtesy of Wikimedia Commons).

Figure 15.16

Figure 15.17

Michelangelo: *Moses* (1513–1515) (Courtesy of Wikimedia Commons).

Figure 15.18

strong physique. He is in the moment of "seeing" God and receiving the commandments a second time. But there is also a compositional reason for why the hand gesture is chosen. The playfulness of Moses' right hand drags attention to the plates and by pulling the long locks of the beard, despite him turning his head to the right, the locks create a vector to the left, pointing at the plates (Figure 15.17). All the gestures have meaning and carry not only the story but also the character's struggles, thoughts, and complex emotions. A gesture is never just the anatomy of a hand, but always a carrier of great responsibility for conveying the story point emotionally or interpreting it artistically. Just look again into the complexity of Richard Williams' animation of Zigzag and how the hands contribute to the composition and pose (see Chapter 12).

Drawing hands

Getting accustomed to how to draw hands is a complex task by itself and takes some practice. Then to be able to interpret the hand with a design sensibility that tells a story is yet another matter. Everything in the pose including the hands should have some story and content to describe the character's personality and emotion. A character only shows a unique personality when the pose describes that. A beautifully designed character with an empty pose swallows the content of the design. Therefore, use the hands for the pose thoughtfully and with purpose.

First we need to look at the anatomy of hands. There are three groups of bones (Figure 15.19). The first group comprises the fingers, which consist of the distal, middle, and proximal phalanges; those all have joints that move. The thumb only has two phalanges whereas the other fingers have three each. The second group comprises the metacarpals that form half of the palm, which can only bend one way (when you touch your pinky with the thumb the palm will bend). The third group is the eight carpal bones, which are the lower part of the palm and are part of the wrist.

There are some points that really help to get hands correct, shown in Figure 15.20a through f. The finger joints follow in length

concentric arcs (Figure 15.20a and b), with the middle finger being the longest one. It is much easier to keep those curves in mind when drawing the fingers and arranging the joints. The length of the thumb that joins the arc of the finger's first phalanx is the same in both positions of fingers closed (a) or fingers spread (b).

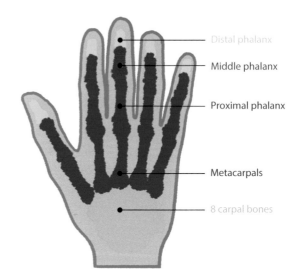

Figure 15.19

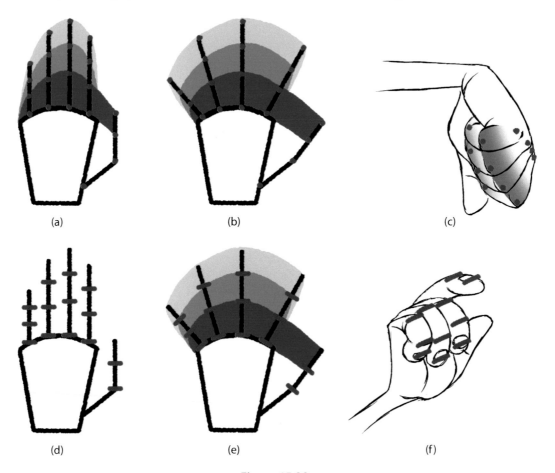

(a)   (b)   (c)

(d)   (e)   (f)

Figure 15.20

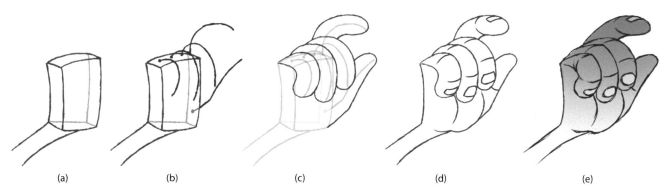

(a)   (b)   (c)   (d)   (e)

Figure 15.21

That makes the thumb shorter in length, making it reach only to the index finger's half proximal phalanx. All the spread fingers also follow those arcs (b). Even in a closed hand the arcs dominate (c). The joints of the phalanges are all parallel to each other in the closed hand (d) and in the spread hand parallel within one finger, but again follow the arcs in their angle (e). When drawing the hand, always check if all the joints are parallel to each other otherwise the fingers will easily look broken (f). This is a simplified version of the actual hand, in which there is some flexibility in each finger being able to also twist slightly.

Always see the main elements that the hand consists of in perspective (Figure 15.22). The palm of the hand, for example, can be reduced to a simple geometric shape that makes it much easier to draw in perspective and then add the complexities of fingers and joints. A simple building up of elements makes the hand manageable (Figure 15.21a through e). This is an example of how to refine the hand based on a quick sketch and then adding details correctly. Only a thorough understanding of form in space and perspective will give a good result.

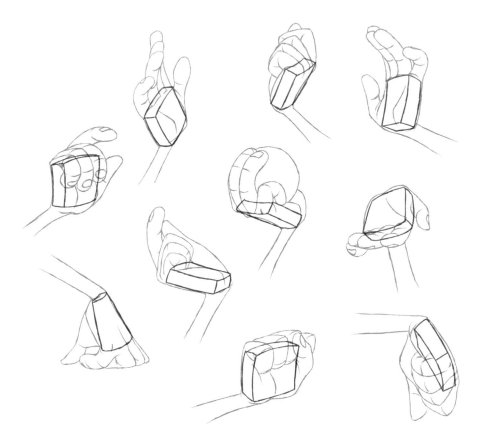

Figure 15.22

Forearms

The complexity of the muscles and how they connect to the bones makes this part rather complicated, as the whole forearm system twists with muscles *and* bones. Dissecting the whole system will make it a bit clearer.

First, the bone structure (Figure 15.23a through c) shows us the three bones involved: **humerus**, **radius (thumb side),** and **ulna (pinky side)**. The radius and ulna sit next to each other when the thumb is in the front view pointing away from the body (c). When the hand is turned inward the radius crosses the ulna (a). The attached muscles can be seen like rubber bands attached to the humerus in their upper part and to the wrist in the lower part. When turning the hand, those also get turned (Figure 15.24a through c). Figure 15.25 shows what functions the various groups of muscles have in the forearm.

In Figure 15.26, we see more clearly how the attachment points of the muscles rotate with the wrist. The brachioradialis, being attached to

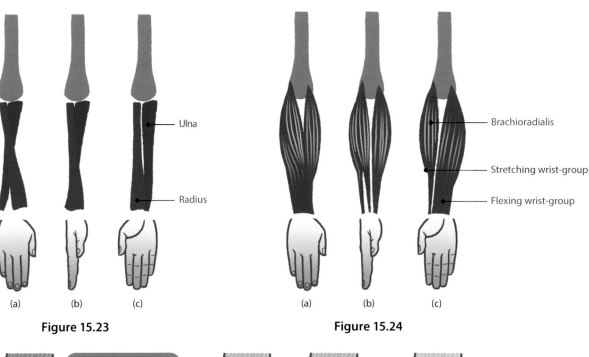

Ulna

Radius

(a) (b) (c)

Figure 15.23

Brachioradialis

Stretching wrist-group

Flexing wrist-group

(a) (b) (c)

Figure 15.24

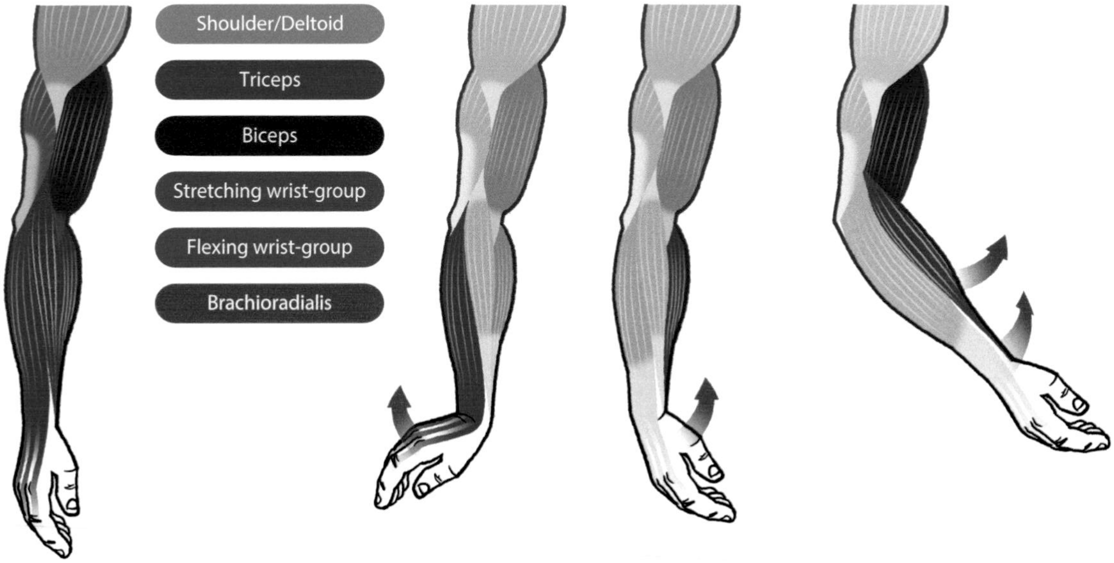

Shoulder/Deltoid

Triceps

Biceps

Stretching wrist-group

Flexing wrist-group

Brachioradialis

Figure 15.25

A simplified arm gives us six muscle groups.

The stretching wrist group lifts the hand.

The flexing wrist group pulls the hand in and closes the fingers.

The brachioradialis is responsible for flexing the forearm at the elbow, and rotates it.

where the thumb originates, rotates in one clear point. The other two muscles, stretching wrist group and flexing wrist group, are running either on the back of the hand or the palm, and are responsible for opening the hand or closing it (also shown in Figure 15.25).

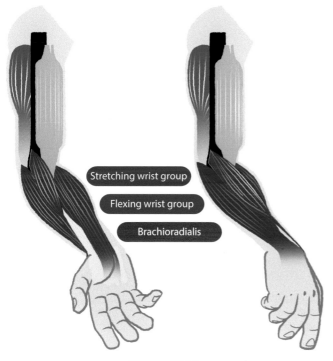

Figure 15.26

Brachioradialis

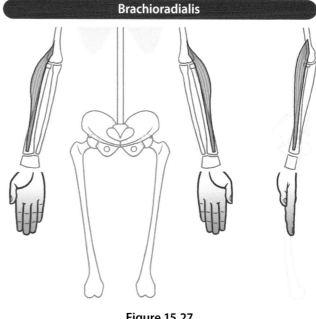

Figure 15.27

Attached: The upper end is attached at the lower side of the outer humerus; the lower end is attached to the lower end of the radius, the side of the thumb.

Function: It assists the raising of the forearm and also turns the hand/forearm inwards, toward the body.

Flexing wrist-group

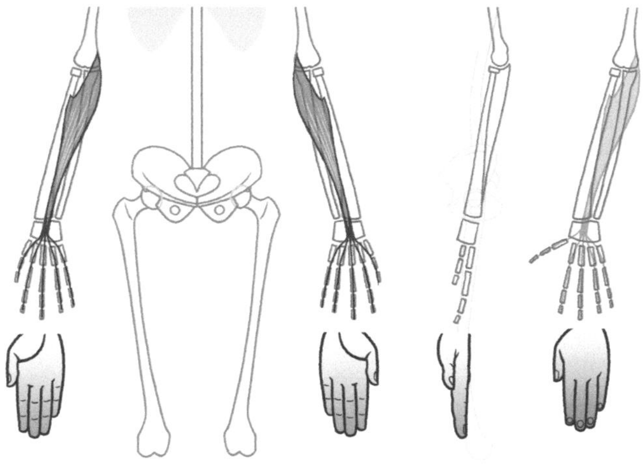

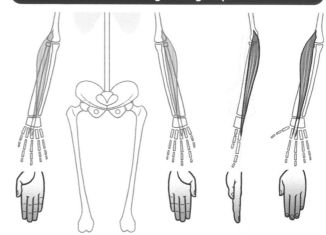

Figure 15.28

Flexing wrist group (inner forearm): group of six muscles

Attached: The origin is on the inside of the lower humerus.

Function:
• Flexing and adduction of the wrist
• Flexor of the fingers
• Pronation of the forearm

Stretching wrist-group

Figure 15.29

Stretching wrist group: a group of nine muscles located at the back of the forearm

Attached: These are attached to the lower outer side of the humerus, then to the phalanges and metacarpals of the hand

Function:
• Flexion of the hand
• Abduction of the fingers, opening of the hand

Biceps

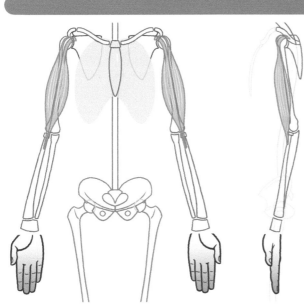

Figure 15.30

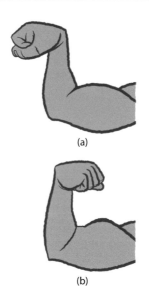

(a)

(b)

Figure 15.31

Attached: Connections are at the shoulder blade's coracoid process on the upper end of the muscle, the lower end is at the upper radius.

Function: Raises forearm, also involved in turning the forearm (supination of the forearm). Agonist of the upper arm, with the triceps as the antagonist

The wrist showing toward the body has the biceps at its shortest.

The fist position has an impact on how the biceps shows: fist turned outwards relaxes the biceps (a), fist pointing inwards flexes the biceps (b).

Triceps

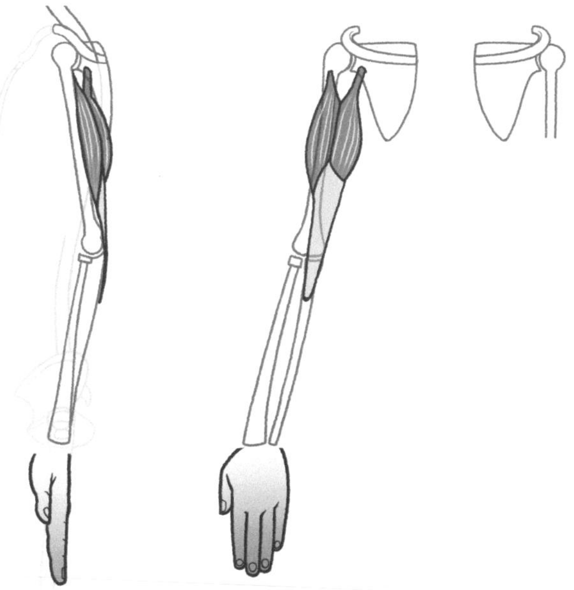

Figure 15.32

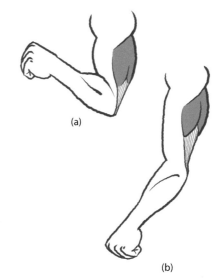

(a)

(b)

Figure 15.33

Attached: The two heads at the upper end are attached to the humerus and shoulder blade, the lower end goes over the elbow and is then attached to the upper part of the ulna.

Function: Elbow extension, moving the forearm backward.

The triceps is the antagonist of the biceps (a), so it lowers the forearm (b).

Muscles of the entire arm

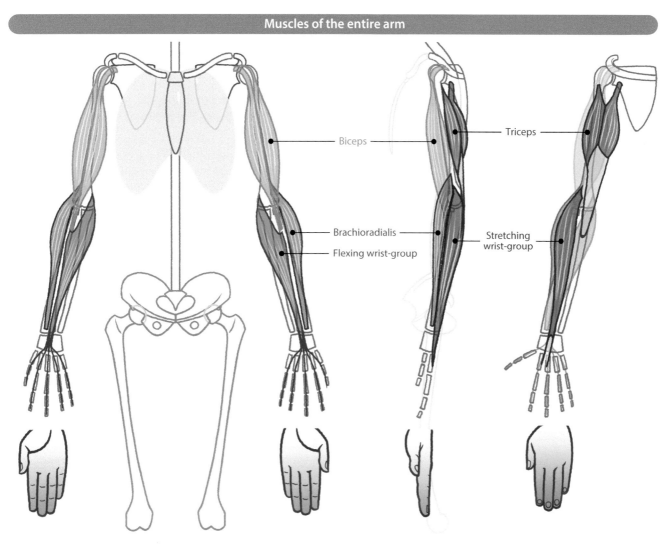

Biceps

Triceps

Brachioradialis

Stretching wrist-group

Flexing wrist-group

Figure 15.34

Architecture of the skull

The head in Figure 15.35 is drawn without any form in mind, but only shapes. The dimensionality is flat and incorrect, but fully convincing. This style of shape-oriented drawing is very popular for character design as it is quick and efficient. However, the knowledge and skills to take this character and

turn the head in space as a three-dimensional form needs to be mastered if the character designer wants to be able to draw any character for any animation technique in any perspective. A style decision does not replace the skills for the job. Only the one that practices the geometry of the skull can master the perspective turns in space. Again this is only fully understandable with practice and study of form and shape!

Unfortunately there is not really an easy way of drawing the head, or any other part of the body, accurately in perspective without constructing its various forms. However, there are some simple tips and aids that allow better results when constructing the head semianatomically correct. The most common way of constructing the head is using a simple oval that serves as the main form for the face. However, this method gives one the container for the face, but disregards the complexity of the jawline and the protruding back of the cranial cavity, which often results in awkward-looking flat heads. Therefore, starting with the cranial cavity as an oval (Figure 15.36) and then constructing the facial mask on top of it plus adding the two lines of the jawline simplifies the architecture to its most basic forms and gives a semirealistic skull with a good basis. Adding the spine just between the ears will also give you a good balance of the skull. Do not disregard the jawline because it is rather difficult to grasp in its dimensionality. Always have the full three-dimensional architecture of the skull in your sketches as a basis for the head, despite the jaw being complex. If the jaw is however seen as two simple planes that are set on an angle toward each other (Figure 15.37), it is much easier to construct. All the red lines in the two plates need to be parallel to each other and to the chin, mouth, nose, eyes, and eyebrows in their most basic construction. Once all of these elements are parallel to each other, the entire architecture has a solid foundation that one then can built on and apply the various facial features. Figure 15.37 gives two variants either without a vanishing point, or with one-point perspective.

Figure 15.35

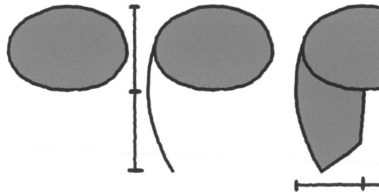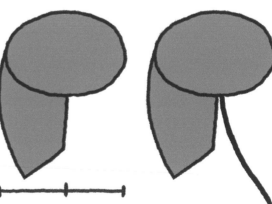

Figure 15.36

Once the skull is constructed, the details of the face can be added in perspective. The nose is just a simple triangle (Figure 15.38) that protrudes from the facial plane forward. Draw a triangle onto the facial mask and then determine the length of the tip of the nose, and construct the form of the nose. The same method is used to construct the eyes (Figure 15.39). However, the eyes are set inside of the skull,

not on top like the nose. Their arrangement needs to be also parallel to the horizontals in the facial mask. As long as the architectural arrangement of the elements is accurate, like the elements being parallel to the facial horizontals, the foundation is set. Every other element of the skull and face can be constructed the same way as the nose or eyes (Figure 15.40b). It is the initial foundation and ability of drawing the complex forms and geometries in perspective that is the stepping stone.

The next step of the dimensionality in the head is the correct placement of the neck (Figure 15.40a). The spine connects to the skull between the ears and balances the head evenly. This position is crucial in making the skull sit correctly on the neck. From then on, the facial mask can be refined and additional forms will add to the personality of the character (Figure 15.40b). All the forms that the skull and face are compiled of can be squashed and stretched, and then the real fun of character design starts where the characters are stepping away from being generic and starting to represent personalities.

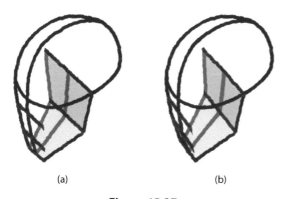

(a)   (b)

Figure 15.37

(a) parallel perspective and (b) one-point perspective.

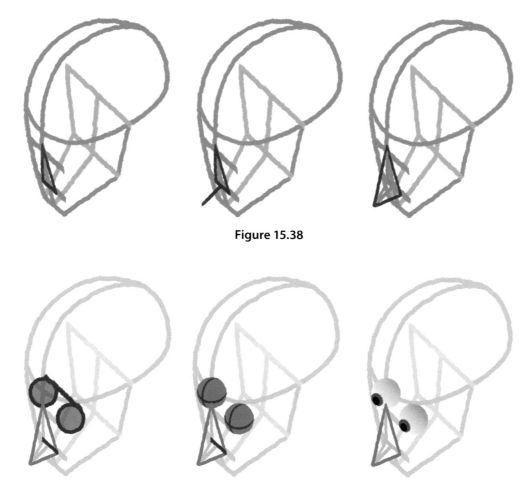

Figure 15.38

Figure 15.39

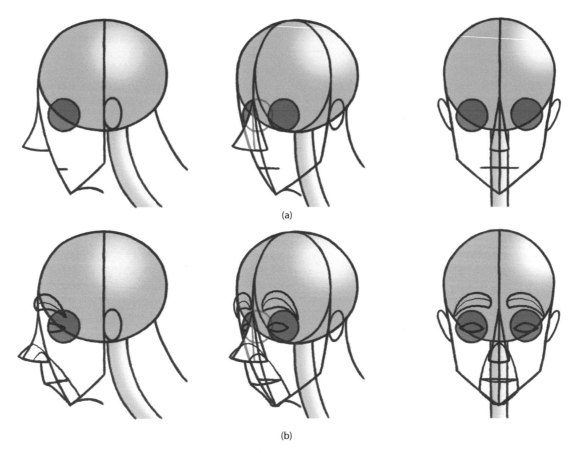

(a)

(b)

Figure 15.40

Hair

There is never just one way of drawing hair but many possibilities that are all valid if they interpret the hair in an interesting way and make it "feel" like it is hair, and has a unique texture and consistency to it.

The lines need to portray how the hair feels. Is it dry, wet, moist, oily, straight, curly, coarse, soft, hard or bristly, shiny, or matt? The examples in Figure 15.41 do not really mimic hair, but rather express a possible feel of the hair. One is semiaccurate, one is organic, one organized, the other messy, one is soft, the other feels hard. It is also important where the hair on the body grows. Is it on the forearms or the face, the head or the legs, the chest or armpits, on a human, a deer or a sloth, an elephant, or a baby? Each one's hair looks very different!

For instance, look at the side view of hair (Figure 15.42a through e): the first one is hard and organized, feels inorganic and rigid whereas further toward the right the hair feels softer and disheveled, which makes it appear more organic and alive. The fascinating challenge is to find a representation of hair that is unique and expresses in the best of cases the uniqueness of the character, and has a style that is not just a representation but also an artistic interpretation of "hair."

There is always a range from an inorganic to organic look when drawing hair and each have their purpose. The more organic the hair is supposed to be, the more variation should be within the line (in terms of thickness, direction, length, and curvature). The more clean-cut and rigid the hair is supposed to be, the more arranged it should appear, have a clear order, and sameness in line and thickness.

The main points that need to be covered when drawing hairstyles:

- Where is the hair growing out of the skull and which direction does it spread (Figure 15.43a)? The growing patterns are slightly different in every person.
- How do the strands of hair as a whole flow toward one or several directions ((b) and (c))?
- Is there is a difference between the direction of the hair on top of the head compared to its sides? Are the hair whorls clockwise or counterclockwise?
- What is the texture of the hair? Is it dry, wet, moist, oily, straight, curly, coarse, soft, hard or bristly, shiny or matt, clean or dirty?
- Where does the hair split and create different forms (e.g., left and right of the split on the skull)?

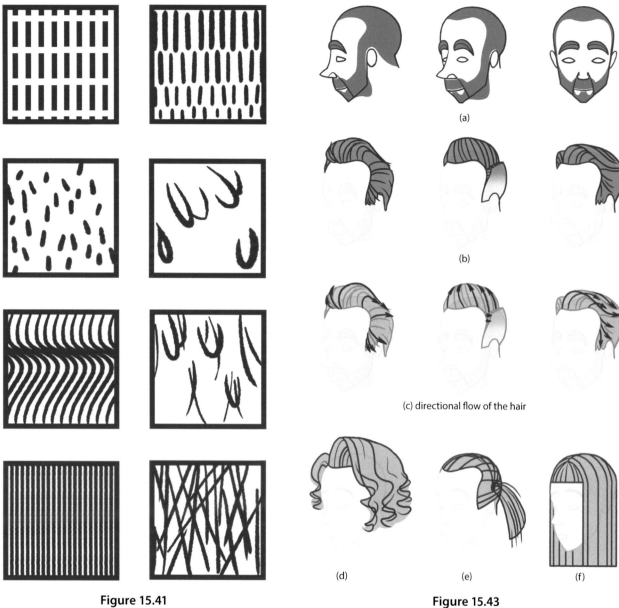

Figure 15.41

Figure 15.43

(a)

(b)

(c) directional flow of the hair

(d)   (e)   (f)

a   b   c   d   e

Figure 15.42

- How can the complexity of the hair be made into a simple statement that still reads and expresses the style without mentioning each detail?
- In example (d) (Figure 15.43) the hairstyle is rather complex, not because of the shape but because of the locks. Drawing all the locks in animation is a bit of an effort, so simplification is key. However, the fullness of the hair needs to be maintained, just in a reduced fashion.
- Example (e): Braids have a point where the hair is bundled into the braid and all the hair goes toward that point. The strands need to be seen in perspective, striving toward the root of the braid.
- Example (f): Straight hair still has a root on the skull and falls along the skull down. Make sure that the front part of the hair is also having shape and logic to it.

- How fluffed up is the hair and how thickly is it covering the skull? How dense is the hair?
- What are the main forms that contribute to the hairstyle? Never see the hair as single strands, but as one or more forms.
- How can the essence of that hairstyle be exaggerated for the design?

The shoulder girdle

Without a proper understanding of the shoulder girdle and its ability to move, it is very difficult to get the feeling of the upper body right and thus the weight and believability of the character. The hip and shoulder relationship will be discussed in the section "Contrapposto" with its countermovement of hips versus shoulders, one of the most important aspects when it comes to the pose. Compared to the hip bone, which is a solid bone that has no movement in itself, the shoulders have a wide range of movement that can be a bit difficult to grasp because so many elements are involved.

The shoulder girdle consists of three different bones (Figures 15.44 and 15.45): sternum (breastbone), clavicle (collar bone), and scapula (shoulder blades). The construct of the girdle is connected to the chest cavity which in turn is connected to the spine, which is linked to the hips. This chain of attachments causes the hip–shoulder connection and is responsible for the entire chain reaction in the body. Because of this secondary connection via the sternum to the spine, the shoulders react to the movement of the chest cavity. There are three moving joints in this construction, which are the groupings of the sternum–clavicle: the sternoclavicular joint, the clavicle–shoulder blade: acromioclavicular joint, and shoulder blade–humerus: the glenohumeral joint. Those joints are supported by ligaments to stabilize the construct. The shoulder blade itself is connected via the acromion process with the clavicle. The acromion is a protruding horn that grows out of the actual blade. Underneath the acromion process is the connection between shoulder blade and humerus (Figure 15.48), the glenohumeral joint. It is a ball and socket joint, where the upper end of the humerus has a ball that fits into the socket of the shoulder blade. The glenohumeral joint has the widest range of motion of all joints in the human body (up to 180°), which also makes it rather weak and is prone to injury as its strength depends on the protection of muscles, tendons, and ligaments that encapsulate it tightly.

The shoulder blades rest on the upper back, imbedded into the back muscles. It is "swimming" on the back and can move in all directions, up and down, left and right, forward and backward. When the shoulders move, the entire construct of the shoulder girdle also moves. But it can only move as far as the connection of clavicle and sternum allows, the sternum is therefore the center around which the shoulder can rotate. Figure 15.49 shows what movements are possible. It is its wide range of movement that makes the shoulder such an exceptional joint.

Back view

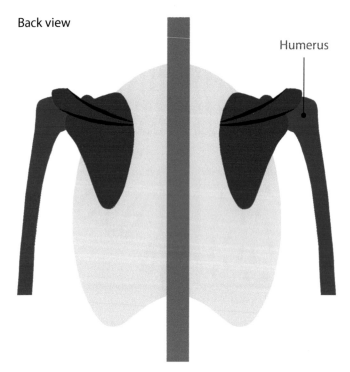

Humerus

Figure 15.44

Front view

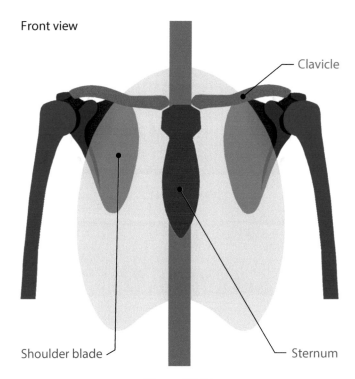

Clavicle

Shoulder blade

Sternum

Figure 15.45

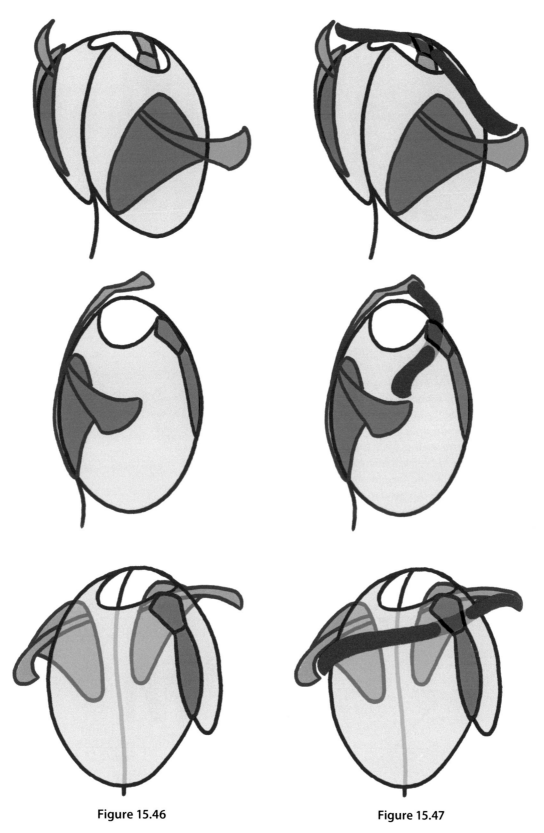

Figure 15.46

Figure 15.47

The shoulder blades are sitting on the back like two curved plates that are then connected via the acromion, the bony process (the elongation that protrudes from the blade) with the clavicle. The clavicle is curved and bulges towards the sternum. It looks like an old-fashioned bow. The actual realistic clavicle (and shoulder blade) however is more complex in its three-dimensionality, which is for the purpose of cartoony design not too important.

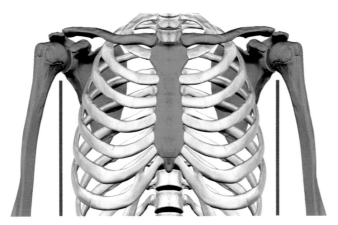

Figure 15.48

Humerus/scapula joint or glenohumeral joint (Courtesy of Wikimedia Commons).

Simplifying the system

Because there is so much information in the shoulder girdle the need for simplifying the structure is apparent. We will see in Chapter 18 that contrapposto is the juxtaposed tilt of the hips and shoulders in order to achieve a comfortable standing position. However, because of the immense flexibility of the shoulder girdle, the shoulders can move additionally to the contrapposto, can even go against it if needed. What helped me to understand the movement of the shoulder girdle in relationship to the arms and their movement is by seeing it as a flexible plate which can bend in any direction depending on the position of the arms (Figures 15.50 and 15.51). The entire system clearly only has one stable point that does not move: the joint at the sternum. Everything else around it can move forward, backward, up, and down. It is only the sternum that keeps the entire system in place. Rather than thinking about the whole complexity, just reduce it to its most basic concept and then, if needed, add the details afterward.

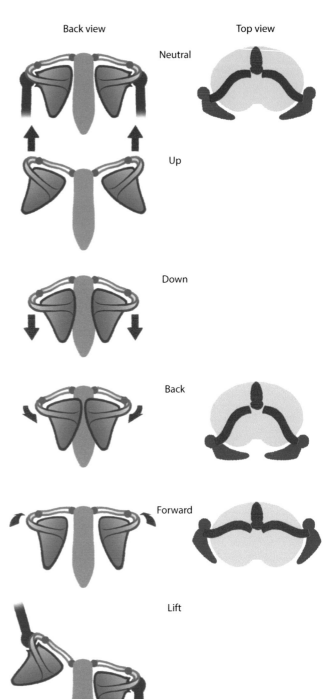

Back view   Top view

Neutral

Up

Down

Back

Forward

Lift

Figure 15.49

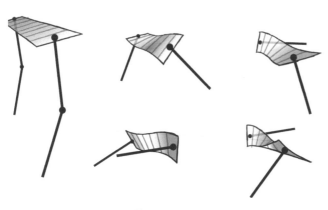

Figure 15.50

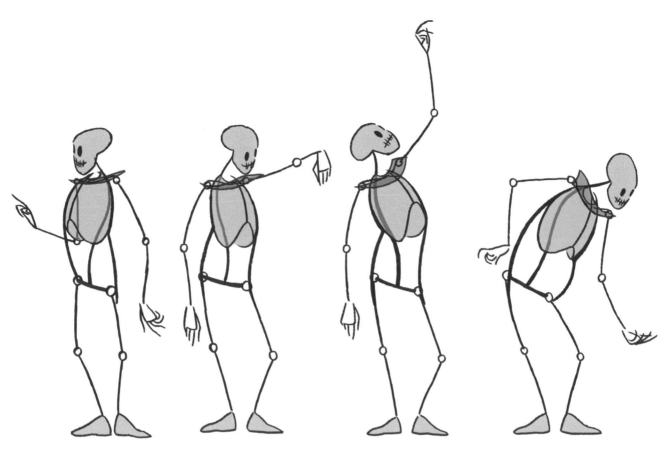

Figure 15.51

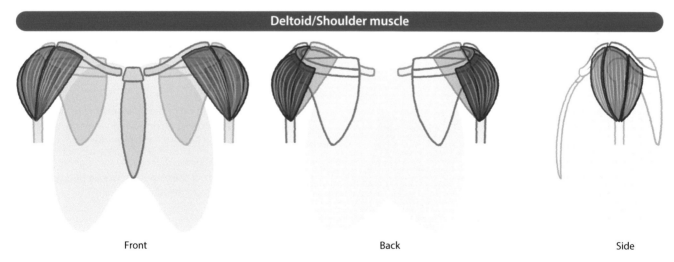

Deltoid/Shoulder muscle

Front   Back   Side

Figure 15.52

Deltoid (shoulder muscle): group of three muscles

Attachment: The upper humerus on the lower end of the heads and the origins of the muscles are attached to the clavicle, the acromion (the process on the shoulder blade), and the spine of the shoulder blade.

Function: Raising the arm

The deltoid is the antagonist of the chest muscle (pectoralis major) and the latissimus dorsi, the lower back muscle, whose function is to pull the arm toward the body.

Pectoralis major/Chest muscle

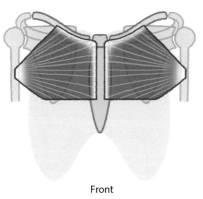
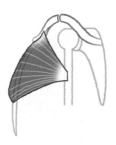
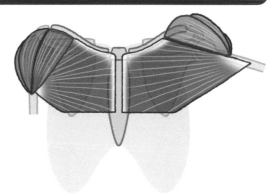

Front   Side

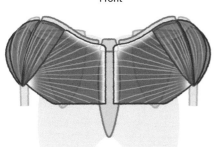

Attachment: The origin is the border of the clavicle and the sternum, and it ends in the upper part of the humerus.

Function: Adducts and rotates the humerus

Figure 15.53

Sternocleidomastoid

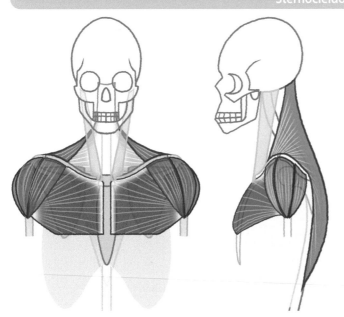

Attachment: Its origin is at the upper part of the sternum and it is inserted onto the skull behind the ear.

Function: Rotation of the head and flexion of the neck. The muscles can function on their own and then lower the head toward one side only.

The sternocleidomastoid muscle is the antagonist of the upper part of the trapezius, whose function is to lift and also tilt the head.

Figure 15.54

Abdominal muscles

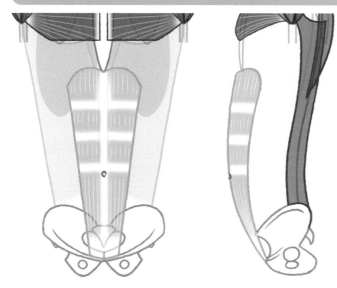

Figure 15.55

Abdominal muscles: a pair of muscles

Attachment: The origin is at the crest of the pubis, which is the middle part of the front of the pelvic bone. The pair of muscles then run up toward the rib cage and are inserted around the fifth, sixth, and seventh ribs and sternum.

Function:
- Flexion of the lumbar spine (section between the rib cage and the pelvic bone)
- Assists in breathing

There are more sheets of muscles and tissue that cover the entire lower body.

Trapezoid

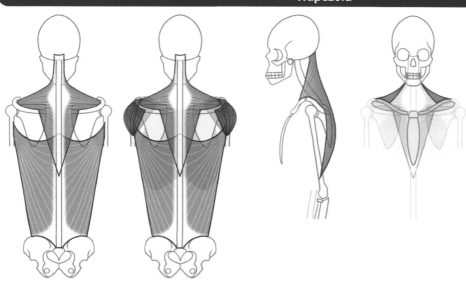

Figure 15.56

Attachment: Its origin is along the spine and the fibers then run outward toward the spine of the scapula, the acromion process, and the clavicle.

Function: The muscle is divided into three parts each of which is responsible for a different movement (Figure 15.57).

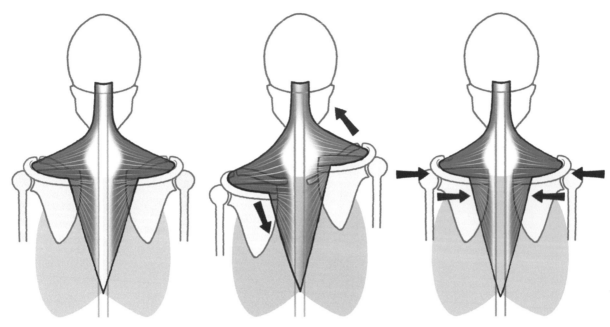

Figure 15.57

1. The upper part raises and also slightly twists the head. It is also responsible for supporting the weight of the arms. Shrugging and also when carrying a weight this muscle keeps the arms from being dragged down. The upper part elevates the scapula.
2. The middle part is responsible for keeping the arms steady and also for pulling the shoulder blades toward each other.
3. The lower part is depressing (pulling down) the scapula.
4. Together the three parts can move the scapula in various directions.

Levator scapulae muscle

Rhomboid minor muscle

Rhomboid major muscle

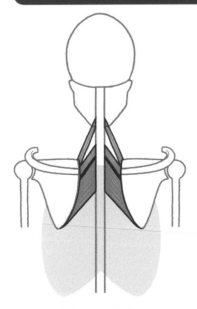

The three muscles of levator scapulae muscle, rhomboid minor muscle, and rhomboid major muscle connect the shoulder blade to the thoracic wall and also lift, rotate, and retract the shoulder blade.

Attachment: The origin of all three muscles is along the spine and their insertions are stacked above each other alongside the border of the scapula.

Function:
• Levator scapulae muscle: lifting the scapula
• Rhomboid minor and major muscle: retraction of the scapula toward the spine and rotation of the scapula

Figure 15.58

Latissimus Dorsi

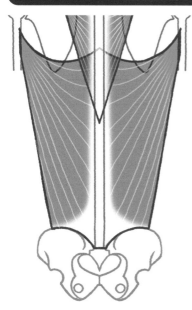

Figure 15.59

Attachment: Upper bowl of the back of the hip bone (the iliac crest), the spine, and the inside of the upper humerus.

Function: Pulling the arms (and with it the shoulders) down and back. Also assists the spine's hyperextension.

Supraspinatus muscle
Infraspinatus muscle
Teres minor
Teres major

Supraspinatus muscle:
Insertion: head of the humerus
Origin: upper corner of the scapula
Function: Abduction of the arm, assisting the Deltoid

Infraspinatus muscle:
Insertion: outer rim of the scapula
Origin: middle head of the humerus
Function: External rotation of the humerus and stabilization of the shoulder-joint

Teres minor:
Insertion: lower rim of the scapula
Origin: lower head of the humerus
Fuction: Rotation of the humerus

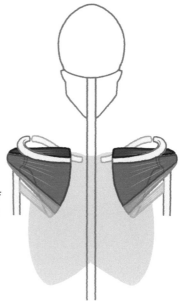

Figure 15.60

Teres major:
Insertion: end of the scapula
Origin: inner side of the humerus
Function: Rotation and adduction of the humerus

Serratus anterior

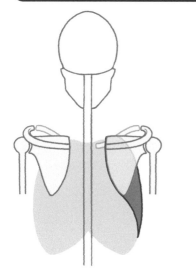 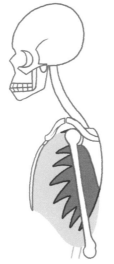 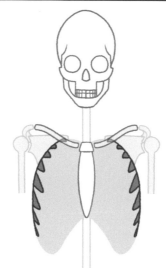

Origin: side of upper 8 or 9 ribs
Insertion: underside of the outer rim of the scapula
Function: pulling the scapula forward

Figure 15.61

Gracilis muscle

Hip adductors

Gluteal muscles

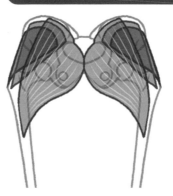

Figure 15.63

Gluteal muscles: A group of three muscles.

Attachment: The muscles originate at the ilium and sacrum of the hip bone (the two upper wings of the backside of the hip bone) and insert into the upper femur.

Function: Extension and abduction and rotation of the hip joint. It pulls back the entire leg and helps with the movement of the hips.

Hip adductors: A group of five muscles

Attachment: Inside the femur all along its length, then at the inside of the tibia (gracilis muscle purple), and the ischium and pubis of the hip bone (the two wings underneath the hip bowl).

Function: Adduction of the femur and flexion, and rotation of the hips.

Figure 15.62

Quadriceps Femoris

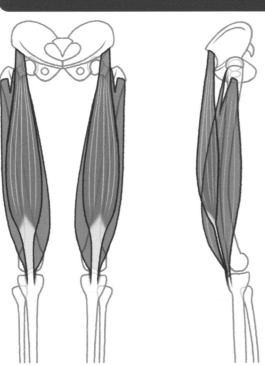

Quadriceps femoris: A group of four muscles.

Attachment: The rectus femoris muscle (purple) origins to the side of the hip bone and inserts into the tendon of the quadriceps muscles (blue). This tendon runs underneath the kneecap and then attaches to the head of the tibia. The other muscles of the group originate on the upper part of the femur.

Function:
- extension of the knee joint
- the rectus femoris (purple) is also assisting the tilt of the pelvis and is the antagonist of the hamstrings.

Figure 15.64

Sartorius

Tensor fasciae latae

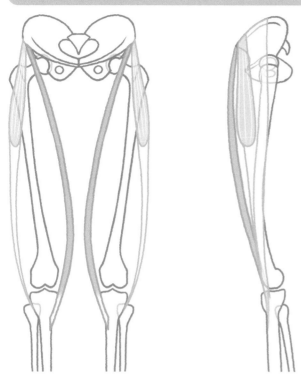

Sartorius muscle:
Attachment: Originates at the outer spine of the pelvis bone and runs all the way down to the upper part of the inside of the tibia.

Function:
- Flexion of the knee
- Rotation of the leg (looking at the sole of the foot)
- Tilt of the pelvis forward

Tensor fasciae latae:
Attachment: Originates at the outer spine of the pelvis bone and runs all the way down to the upper part of the outside of the tibia.

Function:
- Lifting the leg sideways
- Rotating the leg while lifting

Both muscles are very obviously seen and are important in the shape of the upper leg.

Figure 15.65

Hamstrings

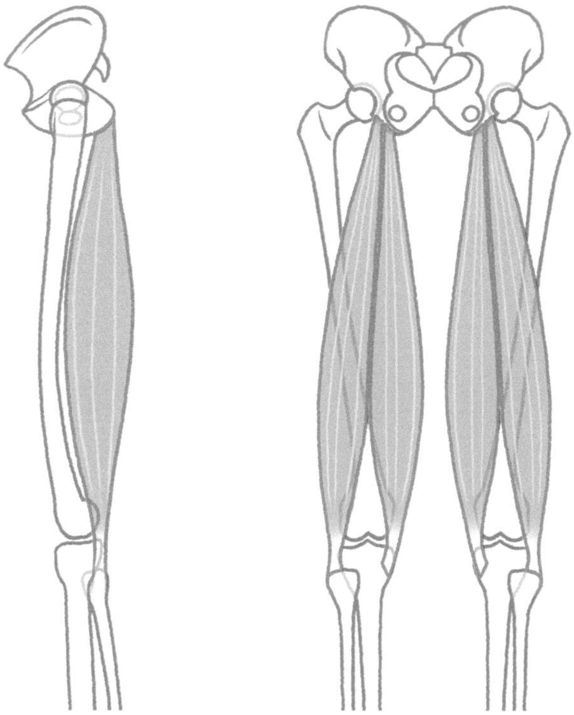

Hamstrings: A group of four muscles

Attachment: The muscles originate at the lower wing of the hip bone and insert into the heads of the tibia and fibula.

Function: Lifting the lower leg.

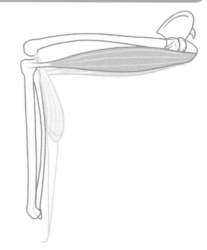

Figure 15.67

Because the hamstrings attach left and right of the tibia and fibula, the two calf muscles are running in-between. When bending the knee this causes the hamstring tendons to clearly show in the bend of the knee, causing the significant tension of the tendon to be seen underneath the skin.

Figure 15.66

Gastronemicus/ Calve muscles

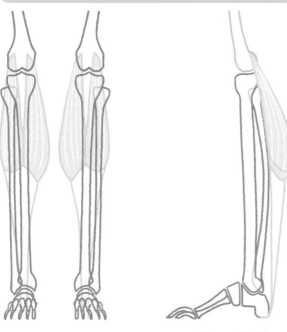

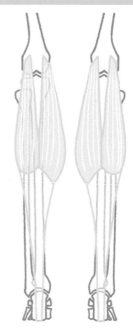

Calf muscles (gastrocnemius): one muscle with two heads (plus one smaller muscle underneath)

Attachment: This originates on the lower part of the femur bone and inserts all the way down at the heel bone (Achilles tendon).

Function:
- Pulling down of the foot
- Active while running and jumping, not so much walking
- Flexing of the leg at the knee

Figure 15.68

Tibialis Anterior and Peroneus Longus

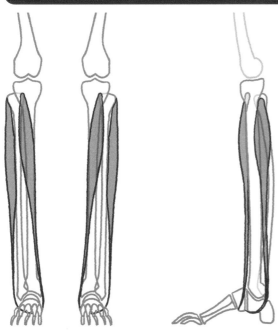

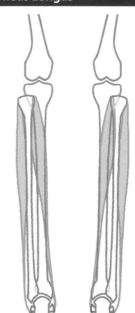

Tibialis anterior and peroneus longus: visible on the side of the calves and the shin.

Attachment:

- The Tibialis Anterior's insertion is on the outer head of the tibia and its lower end on the base of the first metatarsal.
- The Peroneus Longus inserts into the outer head of the fibula and then runs all the way to the fifth metatarsal bone in the foot.

Function:

- Tilting the foot inward (looking at the sole of the foot)
- Lifting the foot upward. The tibialis anterior is the antagonist of the calves.

Figure 15.69

Muscles of the sole

Figure 15.70

Muscles of the sole: A group of three muscles

Attachment: Originates at the heel and inserts into the phalanges of the toes

Function: Flexion of the toes

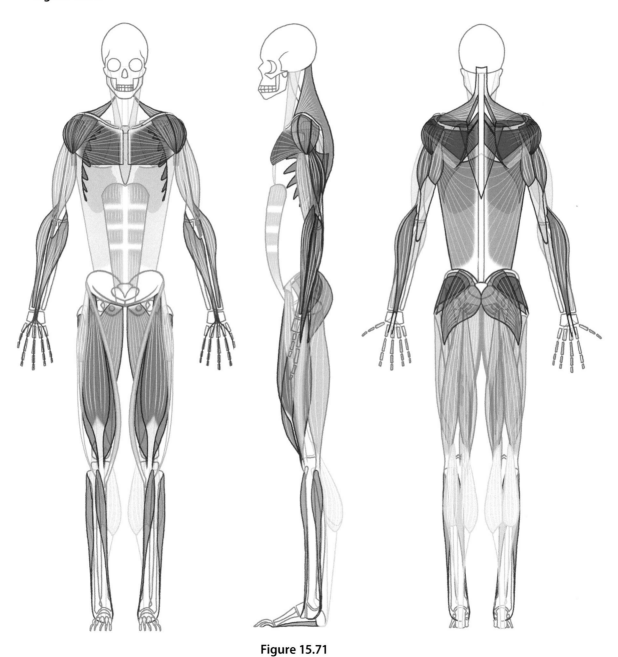

Figure 15.71

All significant muscles together.

Feet and shoes

The construction of the foot is very similar to the construction of the shoes as it follows a similar basic shape. But there are a couple of points that need to be covered for the foot itself to look convincing. The sole is the basis of the entire shape of foot and shoe. This shape can obviously vary and be wide or thin, long or short; nevertheless, its shape is the foundation of the foot's basic form. The foot carries the body weight in the sole in the purple section, which is mostly heel, balls, and toes, seen in Figure 15.72a; the blue section in the same illustration is part of the sole that does not have contact with the ground. The arrangement of the bones in the foot (Figure 15.72b) is, like the bones in the hand, very even and geometrical, and can be arranged in arcs that make it easier to draw (however, the length of the toes can vary in individuals). The toes have the same number of phalanges as the fingers (Figure 15.72c). Like the thumb, the big toe lacks a middle phalanx. The toe's movement only goes back to the joint between proximal phalanx and metatarsals; the metatarsals are fused with the tarsal bones, only allowing a shift through weight,

not full joint movement (Figure 15.72d, which shows in the red dots the joints in the foot).

The construction of the foot starts again with a simple shape (Figure 15.73a). What shape is preferred is obviously up to the style of the character and the preferences of the artist. The next step is to add form to the shape with the outline of the sole in mind (Figure 15.73b). The sole is crucial in getting the foot's form correct! Adding the most simple form keeps the overall foot uncluttered and logical. Just drawing the entire sole and with it the foot flat on the ground disregards its most significant aspect: the arc (Figure 15.74). The tension in the arc is needed to give the foot elasticity and flexibility. There are two arcs in the foot that give it its specific look (Figure 15.75): the transverse arc (purple), which goes across the back of the foot, and the longitudinal arc (red), which goes from the heel to the proximal phalanx. These two arcs provide the foot with a shock absorbing function for running, walking, or jumping. The arc consists of the heel and

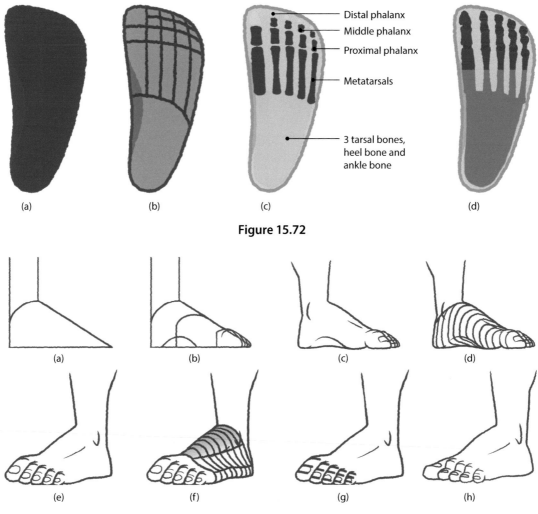

Figure 15.72

Figure 15.73

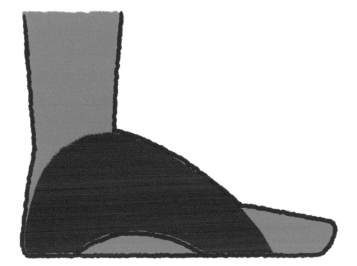

Figure 15.74

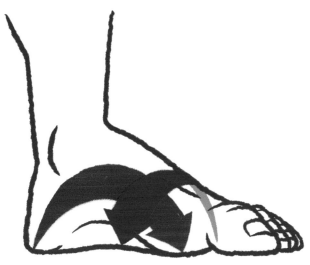

Figure 15.75

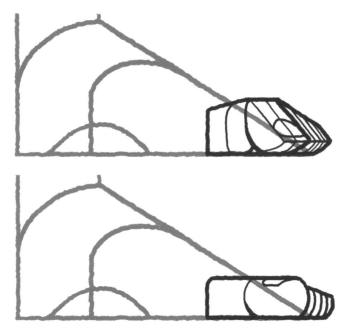

Figure 15.76

ankle bone in connection with three other bones, which shape an arc that makes the foot elastic when putting weight on it. The metatarsals are also included in this arc. It is not a completely rigid structure but one that allows a slight mobility and absorbs some of the shock forces caused by the body weight. The two arcs give the feet a specific form that can be seen in Figure 15.73d and (f). In (d), the curving of the sole on the side of the big toe shows the arc clearly; however, the outside of the foot is flat on the ground (Figure 15.73f).

The next step is drawing the toes in a simplified form (Figure 15.76). The type of form added will obviously determine the toes and

their positioning. Those details again depend on one's artistic interpretation (Figure 15.73g or h). It is crucial to keep the geometry consistent among the toes to prevent them looking broken. The horizontals in the toes all need to be parallel for the toes to show their relationship to each other (Figure 15.73g), very same as in the fingers.

Shoes

Shoes are designed with the same foundation as the feet. The main and simplified shape of the shoe is determined (Figure 15.77a) with the height of the sole and then refined toward form (Figure 15.77b), and finally details are added. This time the shoelaces need to be strictly parallel to each other in order to not break the perspective. The shoe in Figure 15.77c however looks rather new and rigid.

To give the shoe a more organic and also used look the sole has to be bent upward slightly in the front section of the foot (Figure 15.78a). Constant bending of this section while walking slowly lets the sole bend upwards. Many new shoes also have a slight upward bent in the sole already. Adding the bend gives the shoe not only more of an organic feel, but also more personality.

Drawing the shoe in perspective follows the very same procedure only the form is being constructed in perspective. Depending on the type of perspective (one-, two- or three-point) the shoe is constructed from its foundation: the sole (Figure 15.78b). The sole determines the basic form of the shoe!

A woman's shoe is constructed the same way (Figure 15.79). You can start with the overall shape of the shoe and then refine it by determining the sole and then working your way up.

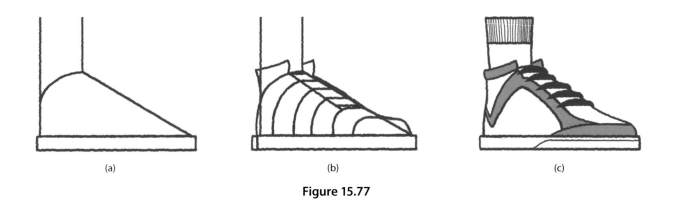

(a)   (b)   (c)

Figure 15.77

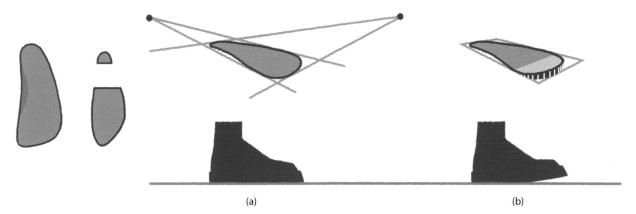

(a)   (b)

Figure 15.78

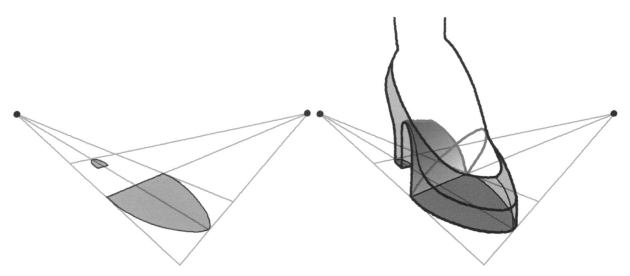

Figure 15.79

Skeletal comparison between different species

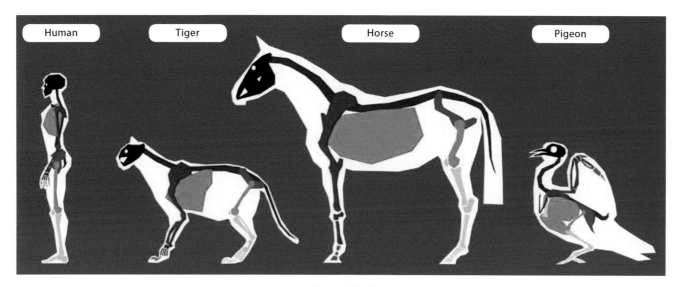

Figure 15.80

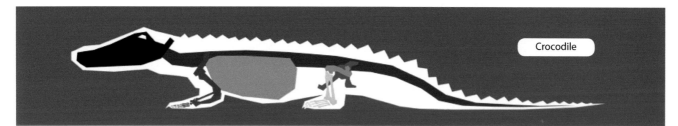

Figure 15.81

Human, tiger, horse, crocodile, and pigeons, despite being from three different species, have surprisingly similarly built skeletons (Figures 15.80 and 15.81). Nevertheless, the length, shape, and angle of the bones are different depending on their use and the habits of the specific animal in their habitat. Those differences are significant as they determine the look, movement, and ability of the animal. There are also some bones that are fused together in some animals, for example:

- The coracoid and scapula/shoulder blade are fused in humans into one bone.
- Horses and other hoofed animals have their metacarpals and metatarsals fused into one bone.

Having the same kind of, or similar, bones does not necessarily allow the same movement! Every animal has specifics in their build that are responsible for their very own movement and habits. The comparison between the skeletons just helps to understand the overall foundation of each animal.

Teeth

Carnivore: Sharp and long teeth that are more for ripping and cutting meat. The teeth are designed for tearing into the meat

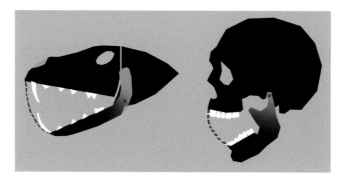

Figure 15.82

and each bite is chewed much less than the food of a herbivore. The acids in the stomach are breaking the meat down rather than the teeth. The motion of the jaw is more vertical (up and down) rather than a grinding, horizontal motion. The molars for grinding are less important than the teeth for cutting. The bites of a carnivore are bigger, the mouth opening is larger in order to have a more solid bite while holding the prey but also the bite itself is much stronger that those of herbivores. The joint in the jaw bone in carnivores is at the height of the molars; in herbivores and humans it is above the molars (Figure 15.82).

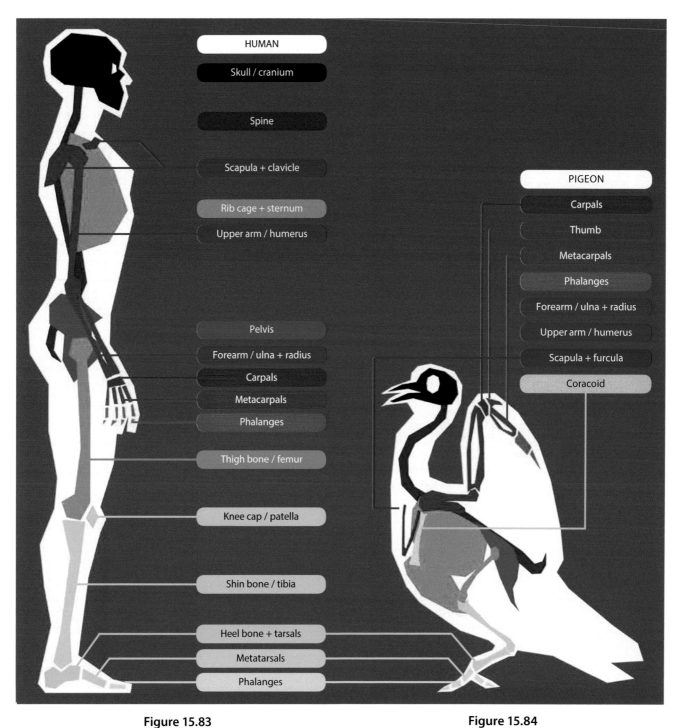

HUMAN

Skull / cranium

Spine

Scapula + clavicle

Rib cage + sternum

Upper arm / humerus

Pelvis

Forearm / ulna + radius

Carpals

Metacarpals

Phalanges

Thigh bone / femur

Knee cap / patella

Shin bone / tibia

Heel bone + tarsals

Metatarsals

Phalanges

PIGEON

Carpals

Thumb

Metacarpals

Phalanges

Forearm / ulna + radius

Upper arm / humerus

Scapula + furcula

Coracoid

Figure 15.83

Figure 15.84

There is a resemblance between the bones of human and bird that once understood helps tremendously in drawing birds with their seemingly complex wing structure and leg anatomy. Juxtaposing both skeletons makes the similarities very clear.

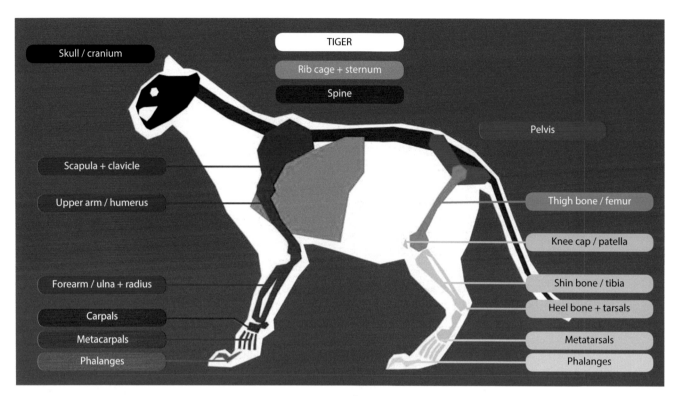

Figure 15.85

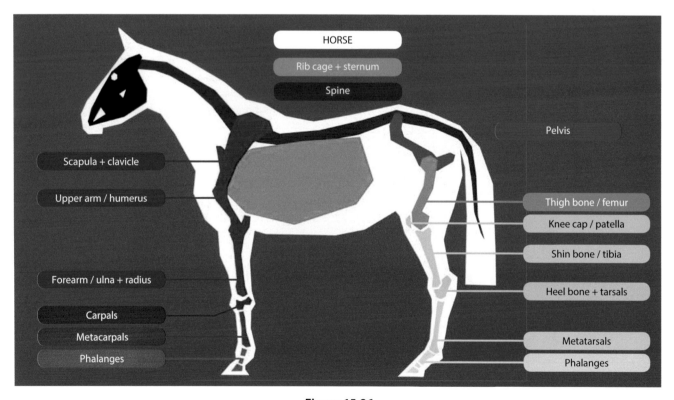

Figure 15.86

Juxtaposing the skeletons of a tiger and a horse, clarifies which parts of the skeletons are similar and which parts vary significantly. The overall arrangement is the same, what differs are the shapes of the bones and, in the case of the horse, many bones in the leg are fused together.

Herbivore: Teeth are more for grinding and cutting grass and leafs, so the molars have a wider surface. The jaw is able to perform a wide horizontal and vertical motion that makes the grinding of the food possible and more efficient. Sharp teeth are less important and the mouth opening is usually smaller (grass usually doesn't run away!).

Differences between Carnivores-Herbivores-Omnivores-Frugivores

Carnivores (Cats, Hyena, and Dog)
Very flexible spine and limbs that can twist, larger mouth with big, sharp canines, eyes on the front of the skull for binocular vision, joint of the jaw is on the same height as the molars; jaw movement only up and down.

Herbivores (Horse, Cow, and Giraffe)
Rigid spine and limbs that cannot twist; smaller mouth with spade-like teeth and molars, eyes on the side of the skull for panoramic vision, joint of the jaw is above the molars; wide range of motion in the jaw (up/down/back and forth).

Omnivore (Raccoon, Bear, and Humans)
Very flexible spine and limbs that can twist; large-mouth opening, big, sharp canines, eyes on the front of the skull; jaw movement only up and down; joint of the jaw is on the same height as the molars.

Frugivore (Orangutan, Owl Monkey, and Fruit Bats)
Flexible spine and limbs that can twist; smaller mouth, canines for defense, eyes on the front of the skull.

Forearms

The ulna and radius are two separate bones in humans that allow the twisting of the forearm. In some other animals the ulna and radius are fused into one (for instance, horses). The radius is the main weight-bearing bone of the forearm which makes the ulna in animals that cannot twist their forearm expandable. Some animals have the ulna and radius modified, depending on their motion habits (flippers for instance).

Clavicle

The clavicle or collar bone: Not every animal has clavicles as it depends on their movement and if they actually need one, so in some it is dominant, in some rudimentary, in others it is nonexistent. Animals that are adapted to running do not need a clavicle, like horses or cows, animals that are climbing like monkeys have one. Cats have a free floating clavicle, which allows them to squeeze through small spaces. A human, because the clavicle is attached to the sternum, does not have that ability. The clavicle allows muscles to be attached that help climbing, grabbing, or twisting of the arm/front leg, which cats and humans can do but horses cannot. A bird's furcula, or wishbone, is a fusion of the two clavicles and there to strengthen the thoracic skeleton for flight (although flightless birds like the penguin also have it).

Hoofs and feet (Figure 15.87)

- The hoof of an Equus (horse, donkey, zebra) has developed into single phalanges and one metacarpal, which is then surrounded by soft tissue and a nail.
- The cloven-hoofed animal has the metacarpals fused into one whose end splits into two. There are two toes, which the camel, for example, walks on (with nails in the front), but the goat, sheep, or ox have also cloven hoofs, but are walking on their nails.

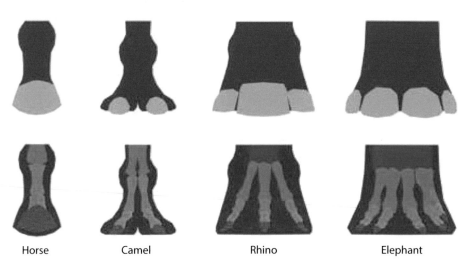

| Horse | Camel | Rhino | Elephant |

Figure 15.87

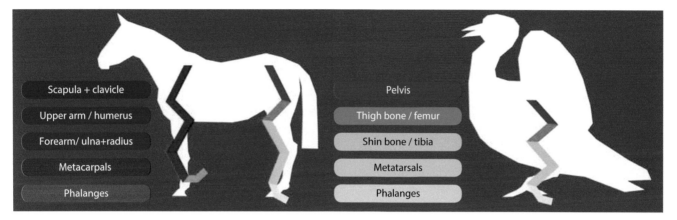

Figure 15.88

- The rhinoceros has three metacarpals and three-digit phalanges, with three toe nails.
- Elephants walk on their stretched finger bones with four or five metacarpals, which are covered by soft tissue, creating one big pillar-like foot (three to five toenails depending on the genera of either Asian of African elephant).

Animal legs

Figure 15.88 shows the bend of each joint in a horse's hind legs and a pigeon's legs, which are actually the same. Front and hind legs work like springs in which the first three joints are alternating and finally the phalanges curl the hoof or toes in. In the horse, front and hind legs are mirrored in their first three joints, so scapula and pelvis, humerus and femur, ulna and shin bone are mirrored in their position. Knee and elbow in most animals are just underneath the belly in height.

It is of tremendous help to feel the movement of an animal in one's own body, to imagine what happens in the body of another species when they move. Animators act out the animal's movement to get a better understanding of their anatomy and it does wonders for the imagination and understanding if one uses one's own arms to figure out the wing of a bird for instance, or the movement of a four-legged animal.

Eyes

The position of eyes in the skull: Most carnivores have their eyes in the front of the face which allows them a peripheral vision, like eagles, snakes, wolves, but also humans. Peripheral vision refers to the width of the visual field and how much can be seen left and right, up and down. But not every skull that has the eyes forward-facing is a carnivore: fruit bats and many primates also have binocular vision but are frugivores, herbivores, or omnivores. Some predators don't have their eyes on the front of the face, like robins, tree shrews, or mongooses. But then there are also herbivores that have their eyes forward-facing,

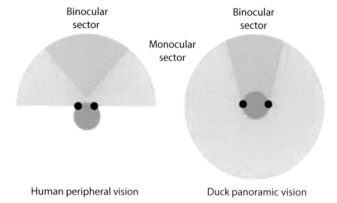

Figure 15.89

like pandas or koalas, both strictly herbivorous. The opposite of peripheral vision is panoramic vision, which allows most herbivores to see up to 360°. Horses, cows, or gazelles have panoramic vision which allows approaching predators from every angle to be seen (their eyes being on the side of the skull). Peripheral vision, because of the two eyes in the front of the skull, allows accurate depth perception, so predators can allocate their prey's distance more accurately (however, all of this is always much more complicated, as some predators like mongoose, tree shrews and robins don't). Birds of prey also have forward-facing eyes to enable binocular vision, like the bald eagle or hawks. Ducks have panoramic vision, like many other birds that are preyed on (Figure 15.89). Then there is binocular and monocular vision. Binocular vision is the field where the eye is able to see three-dimensionally and has depth perception. This is the area where the two eyes' visuals overlap and dimensionality is possible due to the slightly different image each eye receives. Therefore a panoramic view has to be mostly monocular, lacking depth perception, because of the lack of overlap in the right and left eye's visual field (Figure 15.89), whereas peripheral vision has a wider binocular field of vision. The further the eyes are on the side of the skull the more panoramic the view, and the less depth perception and dimensionality is seen.

Ears

The ears are positioned differently on the skull depending on their use and the species. In some animals the ears are huge, like the desert fox or the fennec fox, and in other animals the ears can't be seen at all. But there is still an ear canal that allows hearing. Crocodiles, for example, have a slit just behind their eyes that closes shut when they go underwater. The position of the ear hole in the skull is behind the jaw joint, but the actual ear is positioned differently on the side or near the top of the skull, depending on the animal. The ear canal, once exiting the skull in humans, just runs horizontally out of the skull, and places the ears on the side. The same is true for goats, cows, or sheep. Cats have ears that are further up on the skull; however, their ear canal runs vertically from the ear down and then horizontally into the skull (Figure 15.90). What makes it more complex is that many animals can move their ears and direct them toward where the sound is coming from. This allows them highly directional listening. The shape of the ears is obviously significant in defining the animal's silhouette.

Constructing the animal skull

The skull of a wolf simplified: the overall shape is an oval with a rather small cranium, but large snout and nose (Figure 15.91). Peripheral vision has the eyes located further to the front of the skull. It makes the drawing of the skull much easier if started with a simple oval shape that is refined to show form and volume, and is then equipped with the details and the joint of the jaw. The three-dimensionality of the jaw is crucial insofar as the jaw has to be imagined in its width and trapezoid shape, thus the width in the front is shorter than in the back of the jaw. The joint of the jaw is located slightly lower than the eyes and further back. The joint (red dot) of the jaw is set much lower in carnivores compared to herbivores or humans, where the jaw joint is higher up.

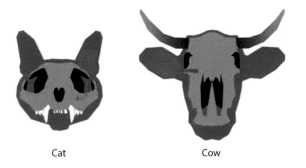

Cat   Cow

Figure 15.90

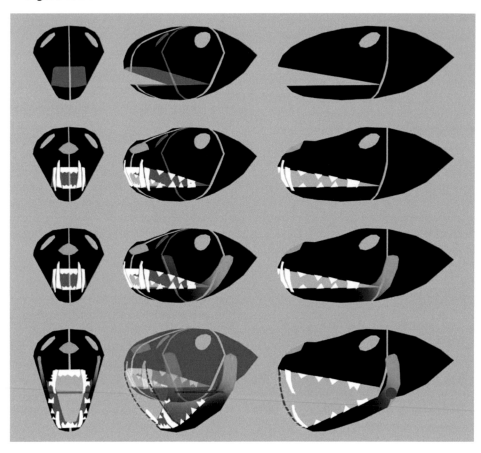

Figure 15.91

Simplified development of a wolf's skull

Animal fur and coat

Some animals' coats are so thick and long that the actual anatomy of the animal is hidden. The task is to give the animal the thick coat, but still let the anatomy be visible to an extent.

How to represent fur

There is not one way of representing fur of course but endless ways, depending on style, creativity, and experience. Any visualization is acceptable if it serves the purpose of expressing the texture, feel, and look of the fur (and even that can be stretched, for example, to make a connection between the fluffy fur of a white little bunny and a marshmallow—the fur can be a form rather than "hair"). It doesn't have to follow the cliché of "how to draw fur" at all. The more creative and different the more interesting it is, without dragging too much attention to itself.

In Figure 15.92, the fur feels soft, because the end of the fur is rounded, whereas in Figure 15.93 the fur feels slightly more

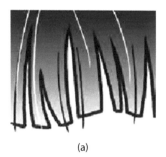
(a)

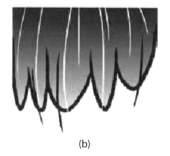
(b)

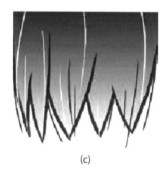
(c)

(d)

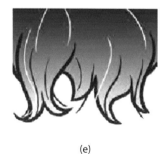
(e)

Figure 15.95

Figure 15.92 **Figure 15.93**

Figure 15.94

Figure 15.96

Figure 15.97

coarse, moist, or oily because the ends are pointy. The question is, which style fits which personality and what does the character need to express the role they play in the story? What "feel" does the character need to express through their hair? If the character however needs to be simplified because the style of detail in the hair is way too complex, then the task is to reduce the line work but still keep the same idea of that feeling in the character (which is difficult, because you cannot really get the same feel by reducing line work). Reducing all the details will obviously flatten the character and take away some of the form (Figure 15.94).

Figure 15.95 proposes options of the same theme: a typical and rather common interpretation of hair. However in those five drawings, each one has a different feel to it. They could express for instance groomed, fluffy, moist, oily, curly.

A completely different line work for hair is in Figure 15.96 where the flatness of the characters is also in the hair, only suggested by simple lines that accentuate the flow within the body. But because the characters are rather odd and cartoony, not following actual anatomy, it would not fit if the hair would be realistic. It interprets hair, but does not realistically represent it. Figures 15.97 and 15.98 give you another idea of how to represent hair by not copying it but "feeling" it.

What is important to consider when drawing hair:

- What is the overall form of the body underneath and how does the hair alter it?
- Too much fur texture is too busy and drags attention.
- Too little fur texture and it lacks the feel of fur and becomes empty space.
- It needs to express the feel of the fur (soft, dry, moist, hard, oily ...)
- What is its thickness and density, curliness, length, and texture?
- If an organic feel is the goal, then variation is the key. Avoid sameness in every line.
- Make sure the flow of the hair follows the overall composition in the pose and accentuates it.
- Understand the natural growing direction of the hair and where there are natural hair whorls that could be integrated into the design.

Figure 15.98

Figure 15.99

Birds and wings

For birds, like with any other animal the main body shape is what counts first. But because there are nearly 10,000 bird species the shapes and varieties are immense, which does not mean you can't invent new ones. Nevertheless, the lineup of different randomly picked body shapes in Figure 15.99 for exploration shows that most of the birds remind of the shape of a heron, a crane, duck, sandpiper … only the really weird ones don't evoke a specific bird, probably only because we aren't very familiar with their shapes.

Coat of feathers

What is sometimes rather difficult to comprehend is that what we see of a bird is not its actual body, but the feathers that cover the body. What we consider being spectacular and graceful creatures, like herons, are lean in their shapes because of their complex arrangement of feathers. Look at a chicken and look at a feathered chicken and it's a whole different story. Therefore, in order to draw birds properly one needs to know how the anatomy looks underneath and how the feathers cover up the body, giving it a very different shape, adding features

like the tail and obviously the wings and also giving the body much volume (Figures 15.100–15.102).

The problem with the beak

The beak has two different parts: the boney parts called upper and lower mandible are the core elements of the beak (Figure 15.103). Usually only the lower mandible can move up and down, very similar to the human jaw. The mandibles are covered by a horny sheath that shapes the beak and can vary significantly in size, shape, color, and function depending on the eating, grooming, and living habits of the bird. Each bird has a very specific kind of beak that is highly adjusted to its habitat and eating habits. Because of the beak's solid structure it cannot move other than up and down. In animation however, this can be expanded by giving the beak itself movement and thus

Bammes G. (2013). *Complete Guide to Drawing Animals*. Tunbridge Wells, UK: Search Press.
For bird anatomy, see Webster C. (2012). *Animation Analysis for Animators*. Waltham MA: Focal Press, pp.119–156.

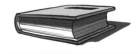

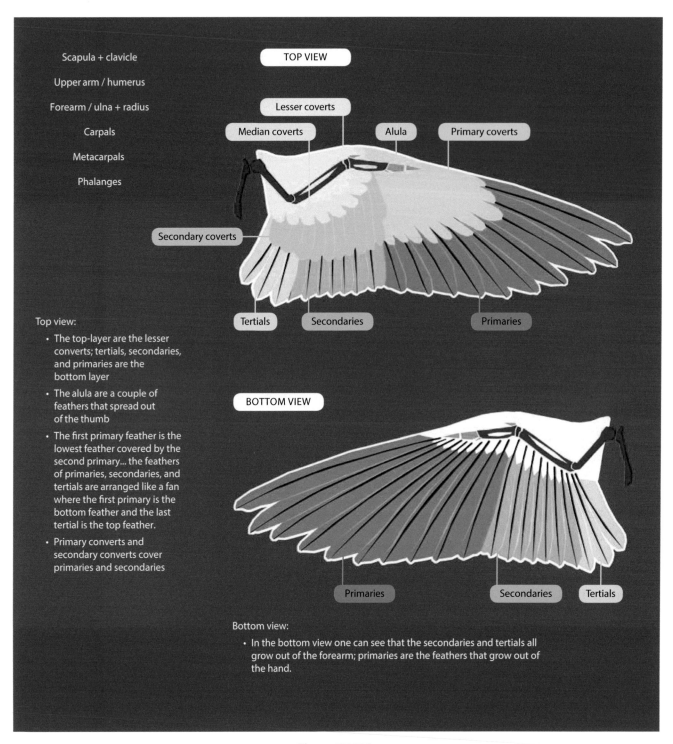

Scapula + clavicle

Upper arm / humerus

Forearm / ulna + radius

Carpals

Metacarpals

Phalanges

TOP VIEW

Lesser coverts

Median coverts

Alula

Primary coverts

Secondary coverts

Tertials

Secondaries

Primaries

Top view:

- The top-layer are the lesser converts; tertials, secondaries, and primaries are the bottom layer
- The alula are a couple of feathers that spread out of the thumb
- The first primary feather is the lowest feather covered by the second primary... the feathers of primaries, secondaries, and tertials are arranged like a fan where the first primary is the bottom feather and the last tertial is the top feather.
- Primary converts and secondary converts cover primaries and secondaries

BOTTOM VIEW

Primaries

Secondaries

Tertials

Bottom view:

- In the bottom view one can see that the secondaries and tertials all grow out of the forearm; primaries are the feathers that grow out of the hand.

Figure 15.100

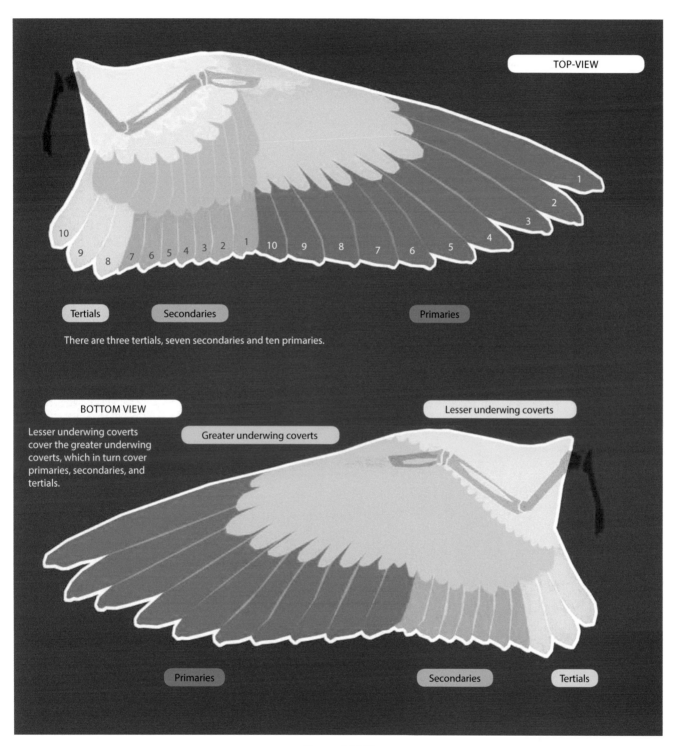

TOP-VIEW

Tertials   Secondaries   Primaries

There are three tertials, seven secondaries and ten primaries.

BOTTOM VIEW

Lesser underwing coverts cover the greater underwing coverts, which in turn cover primaries, secondaries, and tertials.

Greater underwing coverts   Lesser underwing coverts

Primaries   Secondaries   Tertials

Figure 15.101

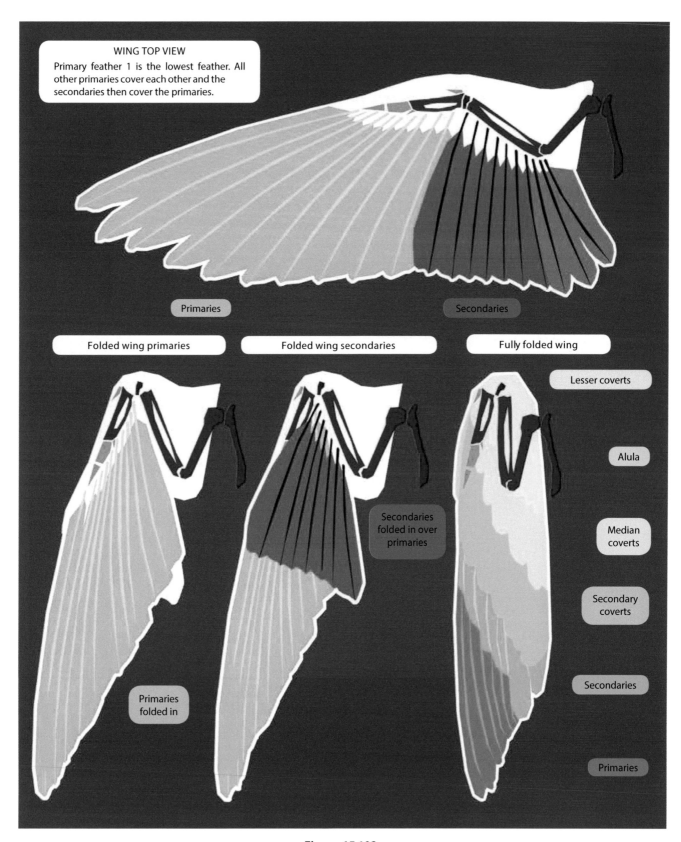

Figure 15.102

increasing the bird's expressiveness. For example, Wilburt in Disney's *The Rescuers Down Under* (1990) has a beak that keeps its shape but varies the corners of the beak and thus creates emotions. This gives the illusion of it being solid, yet still expressing enough emotions to be understandable. What is significant in the beak is finding the balance between showing that the beak is a solid piece of horn and bone, but also showing expressions (Figure 15.104). If the beak is only solid, there is no expression possible. Birds are actually not capable of facial expressions. If the beak is having too much movement in itself, then the beak looks rubbery and more meaty than solid. Many beaks in animation therefore keep the beak's outer shape solid, but play with the expressions through the corners of the beak. To find beak shapes that are pleasant and are readable in their emotions takes pencil mileage and a sensibility for design.

Fish

Most fish have very similar building blocks that vary greatly in their shapes and sizes. In some fish, it is rather easy to distinguish one fish's silhouette from another (Figure 15.106). There is an

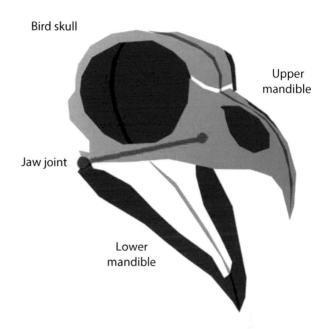

Bird skull

Upper mandible

Jaw joint

Lower mandible

Figure 15.103

Figure 15.104

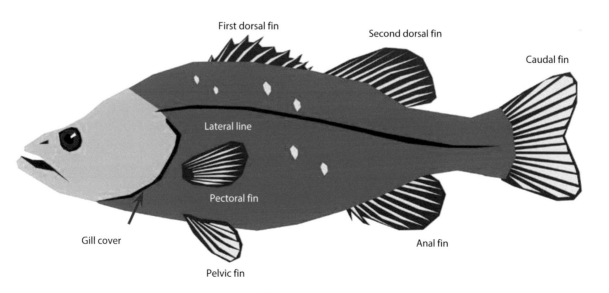

First dorsal fin

Second dorsal fin

Caudal fin

Lateral line

Pectoral fin

Gill cover

Anal fin

Pelvic fin

Figure 15.105

Figure 15.106

Figure 15.107

endless array of shapes not only in body shape but in fin shapes, position of eyes, size of head, the position and type of the mouth etc., and all support the silhouette. Additionally, there are different body and marking patterns, and different colors and skin textures, which makes it very easy to come up with various possibilities for new designs (Figure 15.107).

Fish have a caudal fin that is vertical whereas sea mammals have a tail fin that is horizontal (whales, dolphins, orcas, even otters, beavers, or sea lions have all horizontal tails or hind flippers).

More on bird and fish anatomy:

For bird and fish anatomy, see Webster C. (2012). *Animation Analysis for Animators.* Waltham MA: Focal Press, pp. 156–176.

CHAPTER 16

Weight

A character that is rooted in realism, or even in a cartoony world, is only then believable when they are convincing in their physical presence and their body is consciously and subconsciously responding to external and internal forces, in short: showing the character's weight and thus assisting with the illusion of life. There are various types of weight that affect the pose. One is the weight of the body itself, the other is the weight of objects/props the body is dealing with. Every body has a specific weight that you have to consider and feel when you draw its poses, as the weight of the body affects its parts and vice versa. A very skinny character does not need to carry around much weight; therefore, the poses could be showing the weight as clearly being light. This all deals with the actual physical weight that just follows physical laws. There is however also the weight that the character experiences or how they "feel." Is the character feeling light or not? The dancing hippopotami in Disney's *Fantasia* (1941) are most obviously heavy, but they do not look heavy in their dance, as they are ballerinas that feel light as a feather. So there is one more perspective that needs to be considered when it comes to weight: the felt weight. Additionally, there is the emotional weight the character go through. Someone that is happy feels much lighter than someone that is weighed down by emotional problems. Weight has many shades!

There are many ways of showing weight in the drawing:

- Body tension
- Squash and stretch
- Correct pivot point (correct distribution of body-mass)
- Contrapposto
- Weight and tissue
- Weight and objects
- Forces
- Emotion
- Personality
- Connection to the ground

Body tension

Forces act on the body and the body reacts by adjusting itself. The three lines in Figure 16.1 clearly show how to visualize a variety of forces in a simple line: compression on the left, no force in the middle, and tension on the right. We can feel how the left line is pushed down and the right one stretched. Forces act on them and make them feel active instead of passive, like the middle one. When applied to the line of action, the question is how much tension is in the body, either from internal or external forces. Figure 16.2 shows how much the amount of force affects the tension in the line and at what point the tension is the strongest

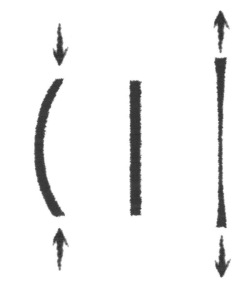

Figure 16.1

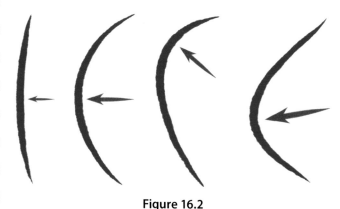

Figure 16.2

DOI: 10.1201/b22147-16

Figure 16.3

Body tension

Weight of fabric
(and hair, body-
parts, muscles,
fat...)

Ground connection

Figure 16.4

within the line (this is the force that Mike Mattesi in his book series *Forces* (2006) calls the "applied force"). There is always one point where the line feels like being pushed by the force. The same idea is in the line of action that determines how much tension is in the body and where that tension lies. Figures 16.3 and 16.4 show the body tension in the line of action, but also the tension in the arm and hand that hold the ball. The ball isn't very heavy, so the arm is easily held up, the tension however, especially in the hand, is still strong as it supports the idea of willfully "presenting" the ball.

Squash and stretch

Squash and stretch show the reaction of the body to external and internal forces; for example, a big belly will sag and stretch because of its own weight. Squash and stretch happens at all times to the body. Soft tissue that sags or leans against something, fingers grabbing an object, the body sitting, and the buttocks being pushed to the side when sitting—every action causes some sort of reaction: squash and stretch. We can see in Figure 16.5 how the amount of pressure obviously affects the amount of squash and stretch involved. It can be tissue against a surface, or tissue against tissue.

Figure 16.5

Correct pivot point (also see Chapter 20)

The correct pivot point makes it clear that the body is balanced and correctly reacts to gravity. Forces are balanced and the body is in a comfortable resting state.

Contrapposto (also see Chapter 19)

Contrapposto shows the internal reaction of the body to the distribution of its own weight. Without contrapposto, the body will look out of balance and incorrect.

Weight and tissue

Tissue itself has weight and always reacts to gravity and pressure. If the weight of the tissue is not considered, the body will have a weightless and weak feel to it. Figure 16.6 shows that the tissue around the lifted bone sags down slightly and gets pushed left and right due to its own weight. How much it sags depends on the strength and solidity of the muscle and tissue. A trained muscle is usually more dense and solid than an untrained muscle and thus sags less. The opposite happens when the limb is pressed upon or rests on a surface. The tissue gets pressed away from the contact point and bone. It is pushed upward, colliding with the sagging tissue. The softer the tissue, the more it gets spread out around the contact point: fat gets pushed more easily than muscle does. But it is not just the soft tissue that gets squashed and stretched because of its own weight, it is also the skeleton that shifts and bends, moves, and "falls into place" due to forces acting on it (Figure 16.7). The body reacts to everything that happens to it: action → reaction and the skeleton is no exception just because it consists of solid bones. They still need to adjust—not bend, but adjust.

When raising the arm for instance (Figure 16.8), gravity pulls the muscle and tissue of the triceps down because the muscle is inactive. The opposite side, the deltoid, is active, pulling the arm up. This tension between the two muscles has to be felt by the artist when drawing the character and should also be visible in the final drawing (if believability is the goal). Only by feeling the body's actions and knowing which muscle is performing the movement and which is passive can the weight be experienced, and then visualized convincingly. There needs to be a solid understanding of which part of the body is responsible for the action in order to exaggerate it and make clearer what is happening. A very simple way of doing this is by just performing the action with one's own body and figuring out which muscle is active and which passive. Your own body is a good tool to use!

Weight and objects

The character that holds an object, no matter how light or heavy, will be affected by the object's weight in the pose. The heavier the object is, the more the body has to adjust to its weight.

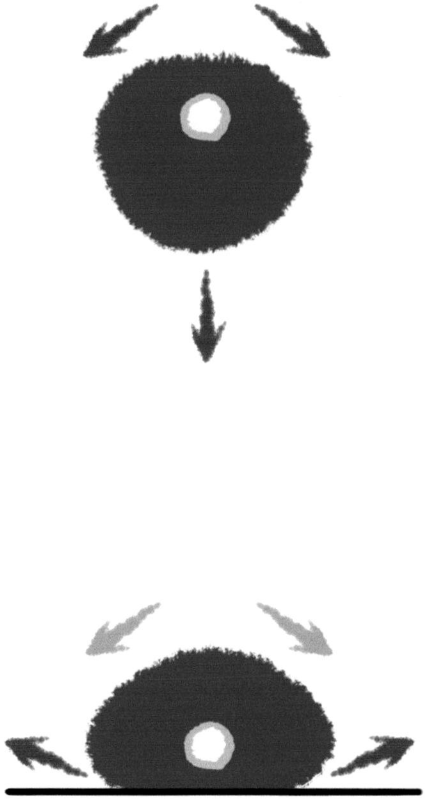

Figure 16.6

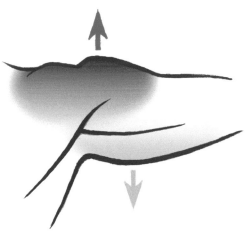

Figure 16.8

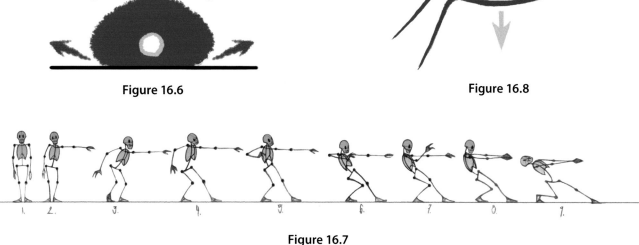

Figure 16.7

Muscles and skeleton will need to show the effort to hold those objects and the body needs to adjust its pivot point in order to balance itself. The tension needs to be visible in every part of the body, because the body is a complex system where everything is affected as it is not consisting of single pieces that are unrelated to each other. The character that holds up a football (Figure 16.3) shows tension in the fingers, in the arm, and the entire body. Holding up the ball puts pressure not only on the fingers but also on the shoulders that need to hold up ball and arm, then additional pressure on the entire body to push forward the chest and the arm, which causes the spine to bend; the feet need tension because they have to carry and balance the entire body. If the object is soft and heavy, it will have its own squash and stretch, and thus visualize its own weight.

Weight of fabric is also extremely important to follow realistic physics. The fabric needs to have folds that make sense and that flow naturally over the body. Fabric without this visual weight will give the feeling of a character being underwater.

Forces

A body that is either resting or in motion is exposed to various forces which affect the body, and with it the pose. Understanding and using those forces in your drawings can add another level of realism, exaggeration, and believability to the character.

The three forces that act on a body are

- Change in speed
- Change in direction
- Gravity

Figure 16.9

Change in speed

We can feel the forces acting on the body when we are for example sitting in an airplane that is speeding up the runway in order to take off. The soft and hard tissues in the body are exposed to unusual forces that press us into the seat and accelerate our bodies to a final speed of hundreds of miles per hour. The forces accelerate the seat and us sitting in it. The only visual clue for what happens with the body if we are inside the airplane other than seeing the landscape outside zip by is us feeling the body getting pressed into the seat and there being some deformation in the body's soft tissue. The contact point between body and moving source (moving source in this case is the plane, then the seat) is where the force of movement enters and pushes the whole body forward. A chain reaction causes every part to be exposed to the force one by one, each part affecting the next. The force would, for example, start in the airplane, then go into the seat, then into the body. This chain reaction is what in animation is called *overlapping action*. It is the offset movement of the different joints following each other the further away they get from the source of the force.

In animation, change of speed is very often exaggerated with not only the overlapping action but also squash and stretch and an exaggerated line of action. Soft parts heavily drag behind the accelerating character or keep going once the body stops. The interpretation of those forces is what makes animation such a great tool for exaggeration and visualization of otherwise unseen forces.

Change in direction

A fast car going into a curve pushes our bodies out of the curve and we have to hold onto something to not topple. Our bodies still want to go into the direction the car was going before, as we still have the same speed and direction as the car had moments ago. But once the car is changing direction under us, as we are still connected to the car, it forces us to also change direction. As in the change of speed, the change of direction also has overlapping action and a follow-through in the character.

Change in direction in animation is used, for example, when the character quickly turns their head and the soft tissue is following the lead of the skull in an arc.

Gravity

Gravity obviously drags the objects down and has an effect on the body as a whole. Aside from the mentioned sagging of soft tissue, it is also visible in the bend of the spine, the position of the head/neck, and the hardening of active muscles.

Questions that need to be asked for understanding the relationship between character and gravity:

- Is the body strong enough to withstand the gravitational force?
- Are muscles and skin solid enough to not sag or is gravity pulling the character's features closer to the ground? How does this relate to the character's personality?

- Are the facial muscles/features strong enough to withstand gravity?
- What weight does the fabric have and how does that show in the folds and overall flow of the clothing? Does the weight of the character and their behavior represent the character's personality?
- What is the weight of the hair, wig, or hat, and how does it affect the head position? Is the character proudly and confidently carrying the additional weight or is it too heavy?
- How do pose, gravity, and personality or current emotional state go hand in hand? If the character for example is depressed, then the effects of gravity could be exaggerated to show that the world itself is much more difficult to bear for the character in this moment.

Forces and flow

Forces can be shown in the character not only in their broad form of change of speed or direction but also in a subtle way in the *flow* of the pose.[1] Every character should have a direction in their movement, a goal the movement goes toward, where the character's action is facing. Without this direction, the pose would be literally pointless because the character's attention leads nowhere. Even a character that is only resting and directing their forces back into themselves, like *The Thinker* by Auguste Rodin, still has a direction, which *is* inward. So every pose has to have a focal point where the forces and the energy of the pose lead to. Even abstract sculpture often has movement in itself that expresses these forces.

The whole body is one living organism, one being that cannot be looked upon as consisting of different pieces that act separately but one organism whose elements act in unison to perform one action. In our language, we break the arm into an upper arm and a lower arm which is separated by the elbow joint. We name the parts and thus separate them from each other. However, they are part of the entire body, not only connected through muscles and tissue, but they ARE the body. This is an important aspect in order to understand the concept of flow. If the character's action is to push toward one direction, all of the body's parts are assisting that push and a flow happens into that direction that every body part partakes in. Without that flow, the forces are not properly transferred from one body part to the next, but are interrupted. The painting of the little boy with the balloons (Figure 16.10) shows the flow of the forces in the pose in a red line. There is movement throughout the character which transfers forces from one body part into the next. The tension in the belly is released into his

Figure 16.10

left leg and toward the yellow balloon. Also, there is a flow going from the back of the head along the jawline, into the shield of the cap and toward the red balloon. The forces are kept within the pose and do not leave the body. It is a closed system in which you keep as much of the force in the pose as needed. An example for a pose where the forces are leaving the body is a knight raising his sword toward the enemy in a strong and forward pose. All the forces of the body flow into the sword and toward the enemy.

The flow consists of two different forces: the actual physical forces of the character (weight, strength, directional forces) and the aesthetic force or vectors, which is the flow that gives the character an aesthetic appearance, helping to compose the various parts of the character into one.

When designing the pose consider your story first and find through thumbnails that mainly deal next to shapes with the composition of the character. Vectors, directions, and the overall flow of the lines within the character are part of that composition. Once the thumbnails work and give you the wanted flow, but also have room for design elements, start with your final character drawing. Flow can come from any body part, objects, attire, or even light and shadow. Always keep the flow in mind at any stage of the design as the various vectors that are created only strengthen the story and readability (well hopefully they do).

---

[1] Mike Mattesi uses directional forces and applied forces to explain his theory in his book *Forces* (2006), which is an excellent educational book that points out forces in the model and how to express them visually in the drawing.

Movement and counter movement

The body can react to the forces it is exposed to in three different ways:

1. Succumbing to the force
2. Creating a counterforce that has the same value as the one acting on the body
3. Creating a counterforce that is bigger than the acting force

As mentioned earlier, every force has an effect on the body, the skeleton and the muscles, the tendons, and finally the pose itself. A force acts on a body, the body reacts: movement requires a countermovement in order to create balance. This struggle between the two forces has to be visible in the final pose in order to be believable and convincing. Think of the difference between an arm that is just reaching forward and one that is pulled forward by an outer force. You can clearly see in the pose what happens to the arm, because the rest of the body has to react to the arm being pulled (Figure 16.7). With the force pulling the arm, there are again various options: first, the arm being weaker than the force; second, the strength of the arm equaling the force; and finally, the arm being stronger than the force. Every single option can be clearly shown in the pose as such. Imagine and feel in your body what the force would do to your muscles and bones and how you would resist that pull. Stand in front of the mirror and act the situation out. Figure out what happens to the body in every stage of the pull. Feel in your muscles what the force does to the whole body, what the action is, and which parts of your body are responsible for the reaction. It is never just one part that reacts but the whole body, as everything is connected and therefore affected. The reaction is again a chain reaction going from one body segment to another.

Emotion

A tired character's pose is clearly showing that the body weight is too much to carry at that point as the character is exhausted. That can also be shown if the character is sad or depressed, and emotionally drained: the current state prevents the character to stand straight and strong, the weight "on his shoulders" is too heavy to be invisible. The emotions therefore affect the pose and in reverse the weight of the character (Figure 16.11).

Personality

Personality ties in with the emotions the character has. One that is physically strong, but is lazy and bored, will show in the pose that their physical strength is covered up by a lazy personality. A character that is heavyset and seemingly weak can have a very upbeat personality and thus carries themselves strongly, and can be light on their feet. The personality has an impact on

Figure 16.11

the character's actions and poses, which in turn affect the felt weight of the character or even the actual weight (Figure 16.9). It is animation and make-believe, so exaggeration knows no boundaries.

Connection to the ground plane

A connection to the ground roots the characters into their environment and makes it believable for them actually being there, that they are part of it. They are affected by the light and shadow of the space, and in turn they also affect the space with their own shadow and weight. This however strongly depends on the style and purpose of the piece created. The man in Figure 16.12 has only a rudimentary connection to the ground as most of the information is omitted and he still has weight (the tension in his elbows, for instance, or the pushed-up shoulders). Reducing the information or stylizing and abstracting it allows more freedom. The eye does fill in the blanks, which is often the allure of drawings—to leave out information and let the viewer be part of the process of exploring the image. The drawing in Figure 16.13 has a strong and dark shadow and stylized folds on the ground plane which does make the reclining woman heavier than the model in Figure 16.13. The connection to the ground plane can increase the weight of the character gradually by the use of shadows, for instance. How it increases the weight is shown in Figure 16.14a through f, where the character is more and more locked into the space the more information is provided, and finally in (f) the character does feel the heaviest (the weight however is also increased because of the shadow itself being darker

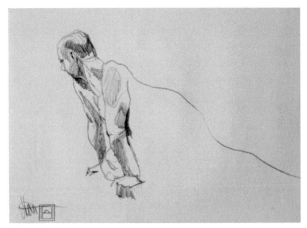

Figure 16.12

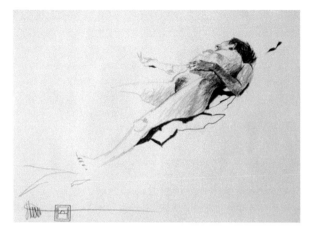

Figure 16.13

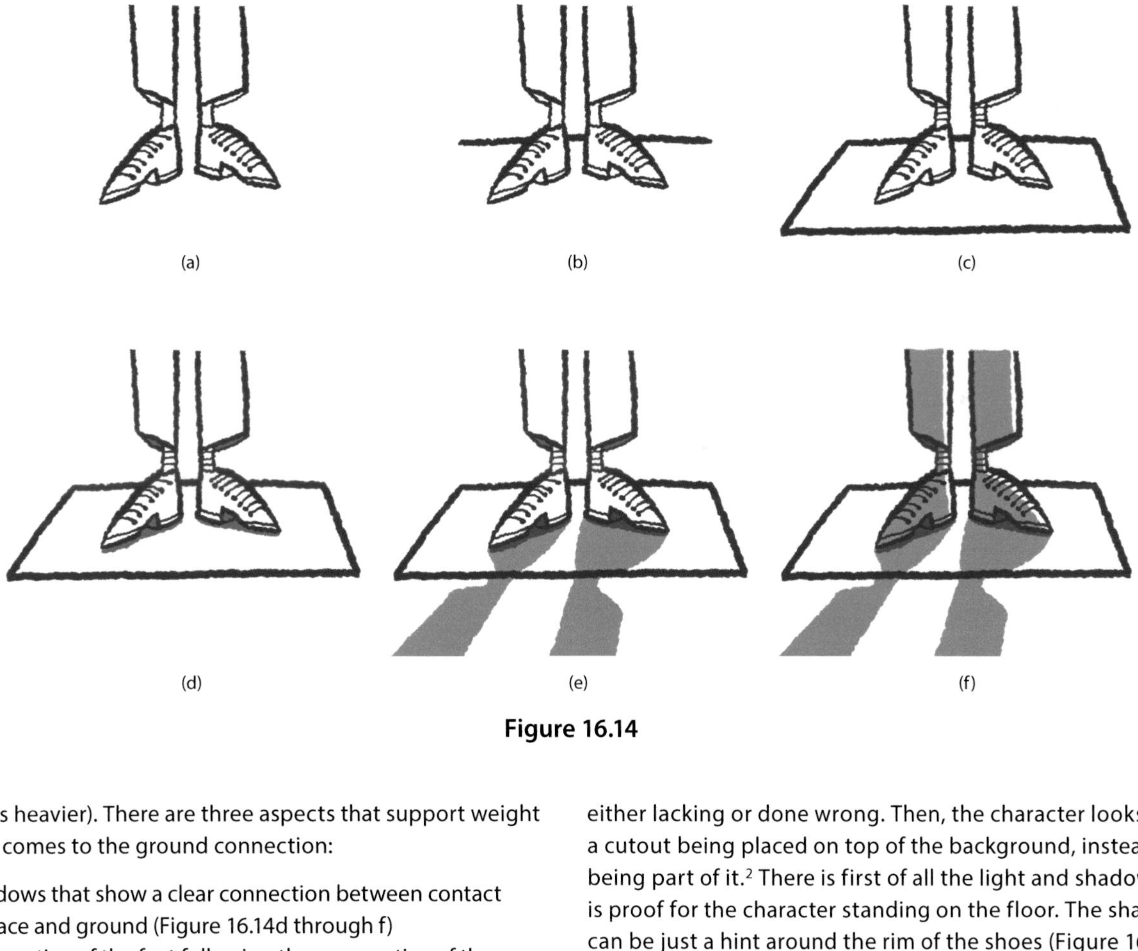

(a)   (b)   (c)

(d)   (e)   (f)

Figure 16.14

and thus heavier). There are three aspects that support weight when it comes to the ground connection:

- Shadows that show a clear connection between contact surface and ground (Figure 16.14d through f)
- Perspective of the feet following the perspective of the ground plane (Figure 16.14c through f)
- Yielding of the ground material (Figure 16.15)

Shadows

It can happen easily that the character does not feel being part of the background because this ground connection is

either lacking or done wrong. Then, the character looks like a cutout being placed on top of the background, instead of being part of it.[2] There is first of all the light and shadow that is proof for the character standing on the floor. The shadow can be just a hint around the rim of the shoes (Figure 16.14d) or go much further and have a cast shadow like in (f). The shadow expresses not just the connection but can also

---

[2] In this case however, there is the option of the cutout feeling being actually the style decision for the show: South Park, for instance, has no ground connection at all, but this being the style of the show, the style of cutout animation, it is not trying to cover up what it is, but accentuates it.

emphasize the ground's horizontality or tilt. In Figure 16.16, you can see how the left character seems to float on top of the rock, not being part of the same level because the shadow that connects is missing. The right side has that connection and the character's feet immediately connect with the ground, and thus show weight. The right character seems heavier because of the connection and makes them an actual, physically convincing part of the world.

Perspective

As long as every element in and around the character follows the same perspective principles, the character will be part of their environment. The more complex a character is in terms of form, the more significant are small changes in the perspective, which affect the character's positioning within the space. In Figure 16.17a, the shadow of the character has a different perspective than the horizon line (the horizon line is too high if the ground would be totally flat), whereas in (b) they both match. A character with less perspective, like the business guy in Figure 16.18 can even walk on a ground plane that is tilted vertically and still looks like he is walking on the plane.

Yielding

The ground can react to that weight by giving in: for example a carpet that is yielding slightly because of the character's weight. This can be mimicked with overlap like in Figure 16.15.

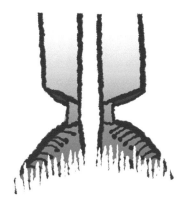

Figure 16.15

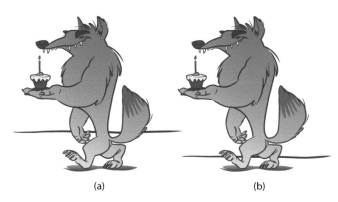

(a)   (b)

Figure 16.17

Figure 16.16

Figure 16.18

Figure 16.19

Emmanuel Fremiet: *Pan and the Bear Cubs* (1867) (Courtesy of Wikimedia Commons).

Figure 16.20

Further options of bringing the character into the environment:

- Style of background and character need to match (however, this can be overruled, for instance, in Cartoon Network's show *The Amazing World of Gumball* where an array of completely stylistically different characters are placed within Gumball's world).
- Colors of the character follow the same rules of the background.
- Overlap with objects, other characters, architecture helps to place the character into the background.
- Interaction between character and environment: the character reacts to something within their vicinity.
- The textures used in the character are following the logic of the space in terms of perspective, granularity, and how much the texture draws the attention. If the texture is illogical then the character falls out of the background.

Example for the use of the ground in composition

Figure 16.19 shows how the ground plane can be used as a compositional element that itself reacts to the needs of the interaction between Pan and bear cubs. In the sculpture of Emmanuel Fremiet (1824–1910) *Pan and the Bear Cubs* (1867) (in the photo only one of the bear cubs can be seen, the other one is hiding behind the front one), the pose of Pan is following the movement of the ground upward. Its curvature points toward the bear cubs. Pan's elbows raise the upper body and also accentuate the downwards movement of the ground plane, strengthening the focal point. A very effective composition and pose that has lightheartedness and plays with the three compositional elements of bears, Pan, and nature. There is a clear interaction between the three elements as one reacts to the others.

Doing the opposite

There is however also the possibility of not following the suggestions in this chapter and outright avoiding them for a certain style. The character in Figure 16.20 has no shadow, has no realistic aspects at all, and is completely flat. There is only a rigid line of action and no weight of any kind in the character—even the glasses are floating above the nose. Yet, the character still works and does not look like they are floating away or are wrong and flawed. They are still rooted on the ground, that is only suggested by the line behind them. The more reduced, flat, or stylized a character is, the more freedom one obviously has to play creatively with all the aspects of weight.

More on action analysis and forces in animation:

Mattesi M. (2006). *Force: Dynamic Life Drawing for Animators*. Burlington, MA: Focal Press.

Webster C. (2012). *Action Analysis for Animators*. Burlington, MA: Focal Press.

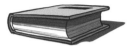

Tension and Compression

Where there is movement there are forces at work, and those forces need to be visualized and also exaggerated to make them clear in the drawings and designs. Via tension and compression we can show those forces in the drawing. An action will always cause a reaction, meaning a force will always be in relationship with a counterforce. A force that is acting on an object or body will cause a counterforce that is either smaller, equal, or bigger, meaning the body will have to either resist the force or succumb to it. The square in Figure 17.1a is in a resting state with no movement, as no forces act upon it. As soon as there is a force stretching one side of the rectangle, the opposite side will react by being pushed down, as seen in Figure 17.1b. There is no action without reaction! The changing outline and shape of the body depend on the consistency and velocity of the material; the volume will always stay the same. The left side of (b) therefore shows tension and the right side compression. Both forces are exaggerated and therefore made visible. If we take this concept and apply it to the upper body, we get Figure 17.2a and b. The chest cavity is a semirigid box that consists of bones and cartilage that can slightly move and shift. The belly underneath however is all soft tissue that can bulge and stretch when exposed to tension and compression. When the chest cavity is tilting in either direction, the stomach is exposed to forces, either pulling the abdominal muscles on the left (Figure 17.3a) or compressing them (Figure 17.3b). The chest cavity's lower part pushes into the muscles and tissue and they in turn get pushed out (simply spoken and simpler illustrated in Figure 17.2b). The more tissue there is, the more there is to be pushed out and folds appear. When the abdominal muscles get compressed because of the upper body leaning forward (Figure 17.3b), the muscles of the lower back and around the spine get stretched. Tension, therefore, always leads to compression on the opposite side of the body and vice versa. We have seen the same concept in the opposing muscles where the biceps that contracts will stretch the triceps.

Every living being undergoes some deformation during movement. Even in a resting position, the body is still exposed to gravity and other forces that act upon it. Animation, being an art form that likes and lives by exaggeration, uses squash and stretch to an extreme where it can become one of the main aspects that drive the character animation

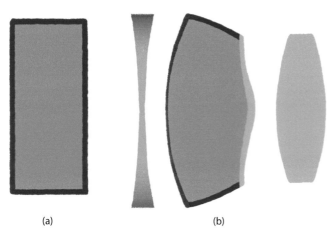

(a)   (b)

Figure 17.1

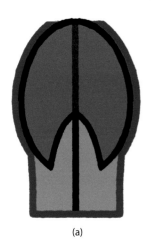

(a)   (b)

Figure 17.2

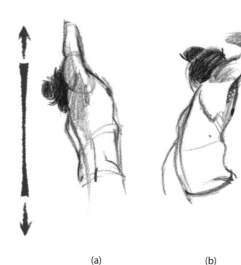

(a)   (b)

Figure 17.3

DOI: 10.1201/b22147-17

Figure 17.4

Richard Williams' *The Thief and the Cobbler* (1964–92); Zigzag's blue finger bends to an extreme creating a very strong silhouette and showing in its exaggeration the tension

Figure 17.5

in the index finger, thumb, and arm. The exaggeration goes along with the whole composition in the frame.

styles (*Ren & Stimpy*, for example). A convincing pose that uses realism as its base needs to have tension and compression in it, even a sleeping character on a bed. A cartoony character however also has realism as its foundation as can be seen in Figures 17.4 and 17.5 in which the tension of Zigzags index finger is affecting the compression of the cobbler's pose's composition. Our body mostly consists of soft tissue that shifts when pressed on or moved. The muscles of an arm shift when we lean onto a wall. The skin and the muscles of our fingers shift when we grab an object. Our feet flatten slightly when we are standing—there is no rigid part in our body that does not shift or react to an outer force or its own body weight. Even our skeleton has ways of balancing out the forces it is exposed to and keep itself in an equilibrium. As there are two forces that always act with each other, force and counterforce, in a resting position both should equal each other out. If one is greater than the other, the body reacts to the greater stress and either needs to shift to keep the balance or needs to succumb to the greater force and deform or fall over. The more pressure and force, the more deformation there is. When the forces of gravity or any other force that acts on the body is not taken into consideration, the character looks weak and lacks the necessary strength and tension.[1] In Figure 17.6, the character leans on his hand and there is tension and compression in every part of the body. The weight of the head that rests in his right hand is shown in the shift of the facial skin. The push in the left shoulder points out the weight of the body and its struggle to stay upright. Forces are obviously fighting with each other, and when visualized correctly, they make the body feel more organic and alive.

---

[1] If you don't yet understand the effect of those forces onto the pose that you want to draw, stand in front of a mirror and act the pose out. Feel the muscles and the tension, understand the interplay of shoulders and hips, and use your body as a tool.

Figure 17.6

The relationship between the forces and the line of action is obvious in Figure 17.7. *Tension* in the body is visualized in the red line and its opposing force *compression* in the turquoise line. One can see that the tension does not just flow on the front of the body and compression on the back, but the tension goes from the upper front to the lower back and is juxtaposed by its opposing force. Exaggeration then helps to make those forces more visible.

Hence, poses that show tension and compression create dynamism in a character and underline the existence of forces struggling with each other to keep the body in balance or in its stable position. In character poses, we can see through tension and compression that there is weight and counterweight in the body and that there are gravity and other forces pushing and pulling. Figure 17.8a through c shows the strong relationship between the position of hips and shoulders, and their effect on the tension and compression in the body. When drawing, one needs to feel the tension in the body; otherwise, the forces that are not felt by the artist are not able to be exaggerated and thus produce a significantly weaker pose.

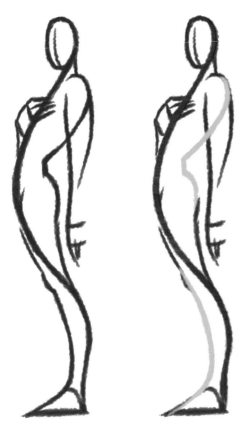

Figure 17.7

More on action analysis and forces in animation:

Mattesi M. (2006). *Force: Dynamic Life Drawing for Animators.* Burlington, MA: Focal Press.

Webster C. (2012). *Action Analysis for Animators.* Burlington, MA: Focal Press.

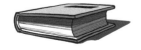

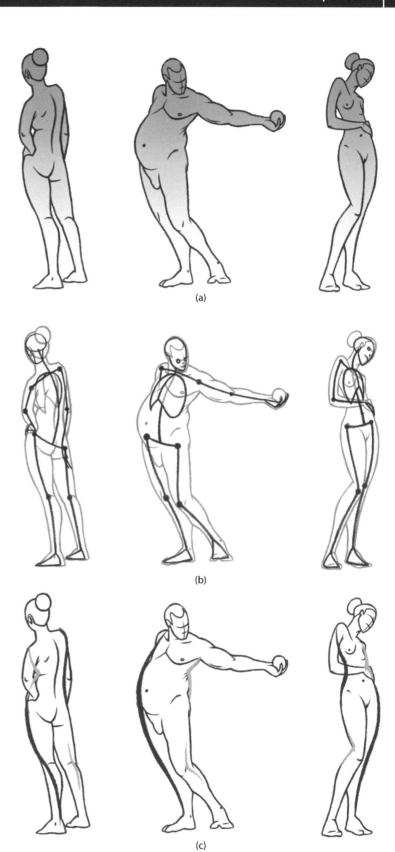

(a)

(b)

(c)

Figure 17.8

CHAPTER 18

Contrapposto

Contrapposto

The weight of the body can be carried by either both legs or one leg. Whenever the weight shifts from one leg to the other, the whole body reacts to that change; the system of hips, spine, and shoulders responds. The weight that was carried evenly by both legs but is now carried by only one causes the whole upper body to shift and move to counterbalance the change in the weight distribution. This countereffect of hips and shoulders caused by the shift of the body weight is referred to as *contrapposto,* an Italian term meaning "counterpose."

I use as an example an image of ancient Greek sculptor Polycleitos' famous sculpture of the *Doryphoros,* the Spear Bearer, a statue that was another step toward understanding the physics behind and the artistic use of contrapposto. The original bronze sculpture (around 440 BC) is lost but survived as a Roman marble copy (Figure 18.1). The long, now missing spear was carried by the athlete in his left hand and was resting on his left shoulder.

Studying the pose of Polycleitos' athlete, we can see how the hips tilt toward his left caused by the weight that pushes from the body above. Imagine the hips being like a bowl that holds the weight of the intestines and entire upper body in a standing position. The legs hold that bowl up. If one leg is lowered, which happens when one knee is bent, that side of the bowl is tilting down. Both sides of the hips have to carry the same amount of weight, and they pass it on to the knees and feet. If one leg reduces its ability to carry that weight by bending the knee or replacing the foot, the weight of the upper body pushes down that side of the hips, causing them to tilt. The other leg has to bear the additional weight. The bent leg, carrying no or little weight, is now free to be more leisurely positioned. The leg that carries the weight is called the engaged leg, and the one that is leisurely placed is called the free leg.

What happens to the upper body now if the hips are tilted? The spine, being attached to the hips, bends toward the lowered side, stretching the left side of the upper body, which you can see in the tension of the muscles and the skin. The athlete's right side of the upper body is then of course squashed. Further up, the spine is connected to the shoulders through the ribcage and connective tissue. The bend of the spine causes the ribcage and with it the shoulders to counterbalance the tilt of the hips (Figure 18.2). If the ribcage/shoulder-system would not tilt, the

Figure 18.1   **Figure 18.2**

Polycleitos: *Doryphoros* (~ 440 BC) (Courtesy of Wikimedia Commons).

body would be out of balance, since the pivot point would shift toward the downward tilted side of the hips, which would cause the body to fall.[1]

Artistic use

Contrapposto allows more dynamism in a figure compared to an even distribution of the weight on both legs, as you can see in all Egyptian sculptures, for example, the sculpture of *Menkaure* from 2548–2530 BC (Figure 18.3). Egyptian sculptures always have a very stiff pose because of the lack of any hip or shoulder movement. This does give the characters in Egyptian art a distinct style and strength. Even the head never tilts, never looks left or right. The focus of pharaoh Menkaure and

---

[1] You can try that with your own body: stand upright and slowly shift the weight from both legs to just one and concentrate on what the shoulders are doing. When you now move your shoulders into the direction of the weightless leg, slowly your body starts to fall over, because it loses balance.

DOI: 10.1201/b22147-18

Figure 18.3

Menkaure (2548–2530 BC) (Courtesy of Wikimedia Commons).

Figure 18.4   **Figure 18.5**

Polycleitos: *Doryphoros* (~ 440 BC) (Courtesy of Wikimedia Commons).

goddesses Hathor and Bat lies straight ahead, causing the characters to seemingly look into the future and the past, being divine characters, not mere human beings. The stiffness also underlines in the case of Menkaure the determination of the pharaoh, his strength, and his ability to lead the country. He steps with one foot slightly forward suggesting movement, not stagnation. The strictness in the pose and the reduction in movement are not necessarily a lack of ability, but an artistic choice and strength because it provides clarity and stylized simplicity.

The next major developmental step in sculpture happened in Greece in the already mentioned work of Polycleitos in the fourth century BC, who introduced a more naturalistic depiction of the human body in his work. Where Egyptian sculptures have strong horizontals and verticals, and a geometric composition, sculptures with contrapposto, because of the bent spine, have an S-curve that often defines the pose. That S-curve's movement can be heightened with arms and legs, thus creating a more organic and curvy composition (Figure 18.4). Polycleitos creates in *Doryphoros* a movement upward toward the head by lifting the athlete's left arm up. That upward shift helps to push the head toward his right. A vector is created starting at the right hand, through the crotch, up the outer abdominals into the left forearm, left hand, along the shoulders, into the eyes (Figure 18.5, blue). The raised left forearm and the tilted-up hand pushes the viewer's eye up toward the face. Therefore, the movement of the spine that reflects in the abdominals and the sternum, lead the eye into the face. Furthermore, we see that an opposite vector being created by the knees, right hand and stretched arm, his right shoulder, to finally end in the face (Figure 18.5, red). The two separate vectors lead into the face that allows us to relate with the athlete on a more personal level. The shift of weight and the placing of the athlete's free right leg behind the standing leg create a forward thrust that pushes the figure slightly toward us, because a step in our direction is expected. This adds movement and again life. Compared to the Egyptian sculpture, where the leg is placed forward too, the expectation of movement is by far not as strong as in the *Doryphoros*. The contrapposto in the pose exaggerates the liveliness and believability of the statue and heightens its action into a more realistic space, but the realism reduces the stylization of the body (one element is gained, whereas another one is lost). Additionally, contrapposto allows a play with the emotional impact of the character. Now that the pose is giving us more stronger possibilities with movement and directions (not necessarily better!), we don't just have a singular moment in time but we have a moment with something going to happen, which completely changes the storyline of the sculpture. Mykerinos and his wife are moving forward, too, as you can see in the legs that stride out. But they are still firmly rooted to the ground; there is just little movement expected and that expresses stability and unshakable strength. With the

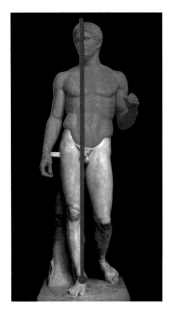

Figure 18.6   **Figure 18.7**

Polycleitos: *Doryphoros* (~ 440 BC) (Courtesy of Wikimedia Commons).

Figure 18.8   **Figure 18.9**

Alkamenes: *Ares Borghese* (~ 420 BC) (Courtesy of Wikimedia Commons).

contrapposto in the *Doryphoros* on the other hand the more lifelike body can now, because of its ability to express more physical emotion, more intensely take part in the obvious storytelling, imitate reality, yet lose a more abstract undertone.

Contrapposto and pivot point

The contrapposto is inextricably connected with the pivot point and both need to work in unison if a convincing weight distribution is the goal. What has been successfully solved by Polycleitos in his *Doryphoros* is the hip–shoulder relationship; however, the weight is not yet convincingly distributed as the upper body is leaning too much toward the free leg. The weight needs to be over the leg that is carrying it (see Figures 18.6 and 18.7). This is more convincingly achieved by Alkamenes' *Ares Borghese* around 420 BC (Figure 18.8). The upper body is actually shifted toward the weight-bearing leg. This can be seen as the pivot point, which is underneath the engaged foot if it solely carries the weight. In Figure 18.9, the red area approximates the amount of volume the engaged leg carries and the blue area approximates the amount the free leg carries. Alkamenes' sculpture has the engaged foot carrying more weight, which causes the athlete to be in balance, whereas Polycleitos' sculpture has the athlete off balance, which would cause him to actually fall over if he was in a standing position (Figures 18.6 and 18.7) (he does seem to be taking a step toward us, which still would make him to fall over). What Alkamenes did is he shifted the hips and with that the entire upper body toward the weight-bearing side.

Twinning

In the composition of the pose, we have to pay attention to each part of the body and how it affects the whole to get the most convincing and natural pose, or a pose that embodies the artistic/aesthetic idea behind the story point. Part of a convincing and natural, organic pose is variation. Variation can make a pose visually more interesting and organic than offering a repetition. When both arms or legs do the same movement at the same time, in animation it is called *twinning*, which in a moving character tends to make poses rigid and lifeless; we most often want the characters to express the opposite and be full of movement and life. As we are bilaterally symmetrical in our build, there are only some body parts that have to be considered to avoid sameness on either side: arms and legs, and their positioning in relationship to each other. A pose that works in an early Greek sculpture like the *Kroisos Kouros* from around 540–515 BC (Figure 18.10), being very symmetrical and mostly still aside from the stride forward, does not always work in animation. The *Kroisos Kouros* was used as a grave marker for a soldier called Kroisos. In the context of death and memorial, a pose like this seems very much appropriate. It expresses calmness and quiet, peace and reflection. The symmetric positioning of the arms doesn't seem to be a problem at all, quite the contrary: it enhances the very idea of death with grace and silence, and is part of a particular style of the time. Compared with the *Doriphoros*, the *Kroisos Kouros* seems to have less life and is less organic because it has both arms straight at the side of the body, which feeds

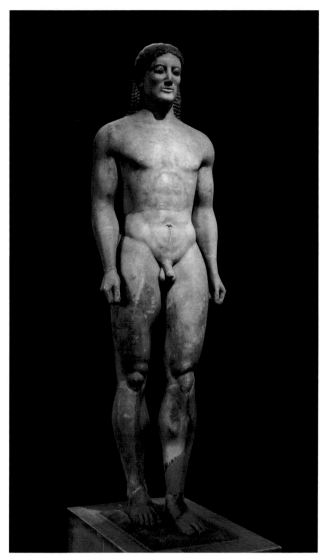

Figure 18.10

Kroisos Kouros; Greek (530 BC) (Courtesy of Wikimedia Commons).

this case, therefore, is a positive aspect of the sculpture as it supports the meaning.

Though if we take the same approach for any moving animated character, the symmetrical movement of the limbs, especially when talking and using the arms to gesticulate, can hinder the goal of making the character move in a natural and interesting way. Traditional sculpture of the Kroisos type and time frame lacks strong sense of motion, although it can suggest and mimic movement, despite being still. Contrary animation lives off movement, which is the very foundation of animation; therefore, stiffness and restraint in the form of twinning can hinder this "illusion of life" if the animation style is realistic.[2]

Therefore, avoid letting the arms or legs do the same movement at the same time, either in the character design poses or in the character animation if organic and lifelike poses are the goal. Giving each arm its own interpretation of the action can make the pose more interesting, plus it can also add more information to the story. Don't limit yourself to the same idea on both sides.

In the characters on the right and left (Figures 18.11 and 18.12), you can see on one side the arms and legs having the same position (Figure 18.11) and in the next image they vary (Figure 18.12). Both seem fine and describe a specific moment, and also personality. The image with the twinned limbs underlines the character's conservatism. They feel much more restrained in their movements, and more closed to the outside. The character seems slightly more introverted. The other image (Figure 18.12) is more loose and active, and has more movement, and the character seems less restrained. There is slightly more upward thrift in the pose, because of the additional movement being created by the left leg and left hand. There is a hint of movement there where the two hands seem like two different phases of the motion, like two keyframes in animation.

There are many examples of characters in animation falling into the trap of twinning, where twinning is giving the pose a negative touch, but there are some examples where twinning is actually used to its full advantage and it describes the character's personality further. In Disney's *The Hunchback of Notre Dame* (1996), the judge Claude Frollo is often twinning his arms and hands when gesticulating in order to enhance his personality's strictness and irreversible morals. In this case, the twinning makes the character actually gain in believability because it supports the character's rigid personality.

the idea of death and makes the young man appear like he is between life and death, being on his path away from life, but also being stoic accepting the fate. But a piece of art cannot and must never just be seen from one perspective, which is in this case comparing the two in their level of realism. This obviously leaves out many other levels of information that a sculpture has: historical context, content and storytelling, historical development of a style, representation of an idea, etc. The *Kroisos Kouros* is older than the *Doryphoros* and was a step toward more realism in Greek sculpture. But it was also an artistic high point in its own time and right. Twinning in

---

2 There are many examples though where the character animation style is rigid and stiff, and that is the artistic choice and appeal of the character.

Figure 18.11

Figure 18.12

CHAPTER 19

Movement and Twist

Twist: Single character

The body is an extremely flexible structure and provides the artist with a limitless array of poses from completely still to dynamic, each with their very own storytelling ability. Where a quiet pose might portray self-reflection, movement portrays agility and life. The full range of the body's flexibility gives the character the spirit that we aspire to in character design and animation, because animation means after all: *The state of being full of life or vigour; liveliness.*[1] The question is how to show movement and distinguish between still and moving, and making those different states visually clear. There is many a sculpture with poses that exactly show that state of movement. There is a moment in the development of sculpture where the still and constrained sculpture breaks free of its vertical confinement and learns to portray complex actions, mimicking life more realistically and with more vitality. One important element that brought more realism to sculpture was—as described in Chapter 18, "Contrapposto"—the contrapposto or hip-and-shoulder movement, highlighting the counter action of the shoulders and hips. Additionally, the horizontal rotation of hips and torso, the "twist," pushes the animacy and dynamic movement of the character to yet another level. Both contrapposto and twist provide the artist with two very strong elements to increase believability in the actual movement and its foundation in realism. The twist shows a high degree of tension and compression in the muscles, and also pushes the underlying structure of the anatomy into the foreground as the action itself makes muscles squash and stretch. In art, the twist in the body became more and more popular from the Renaissance on when precise anatomical studies and the realistic depiction of the human body were reintroduced into art, having been rejected since the Roman interpretation or copy of Greek art in Europe. Especially the archeological finding of the Roman *Belvedere Torso* (Figure 19.1) in the early fifteenth century had a significant influence on the development of European sculpture and was one of the major pieces of art that shaped and influenced the artists of the Renaissance. The torso is probably a Roman marble copy of a Greek original from the early second century BC. It was highly respected by Michelangelo Buonarroti (1475–1564) at the time of its discovery and used as an inspiration for various characters in his ceiling in the Sistine Chapel. This obviously heightened the fame of

the fragmentary body; the bulging musculature of the man, whose only remaining part of the body is the torso with upper legs. Because of the missing limbs and head, the viewer focuses mainly on the movement in the upper body and the balance in the legs, and thus, the twist and physicality of the man make this the sculpture's main point. It exhibits the movement and action

Figure 19.1

Belvedere Torso (2nd century BC) (Courtesy of Wikimedia Commons)..

---

[1] http://www.oxforddictionaries.com/definition/english/animation (retrieved March 19, 2016).

Figure 19.2

Figure 19.3

Gian Lorenzo Bernini: *David* (1623–1624) (Courtesy of Wikimedia Commons).

of an extremely muscular body; however, it also shows silence and contemplation. The resting body slightly twists in the upper torso toward the body's left. The position of the legs accentuates the movement and composition by lowering the right knee, thus opening the pose toward the right. The re-creation of life with its elements of anatomy, weight, and movement is impressively intertwined with an artistic sensibility and urge for storytelling. Renaissance artists were stunned by the torso's depiction of movement, strength, and pure vigor, and it affected the opening of sculpture into space. The sculptors imagination was not limited anymore by the vertical standing pose, but allowed their characters to freely move and express action with a space-consuming composition. The twist in the body does not just intensify the dynamic physicality of the body and its actions. It also heightens the emotional impact of the story and action, thereby adding to the character's inner life and emotional state. In the sculpture of Gian Lorenzo Bernini's *David* (1623–1624) (Figures 19.2 and 19.3), we see the young man just about to throw the lethal stone that will kill his enemy Goliath. David's body is arched and will use its tension like a spring to soon release the lethal stone. The whole body twists up from the feet on all the way up to the shoulders. The head though surprisingly reverses the twist and looks in the direction the stone is going to be thrown. The muscle tension of this action is made highly visible by the naked physique. He is just lightly dressed in a dynamic floating cloth that underlines the movement of the twist through

the folds. There is action everywhere in the body, and the arched line of action reminds of a full drawn bow with the stone in the center where the arrow would be placed. The twist in the body is also accentuating the three-dimensionality of the pose and the composition leads the eye through the various important elements of the story through the body into the face. The cloth around David's waist guides the eye toward the stone and the little bag's strap that he carries around his chest, then into the face with its utmost determination and concentration. The twist adds so much life to the sculpture that it actually distances itself from the fact that it is made of stone. The sculpture looks like it is just about to literally move and throw the lethal weapon.

What happens in a twist

To draw the twist, it helps to break the body into separate parts that are offset in relationship to each other and then drawn in perspective. Those parts are head, shoulders and chest, hips, and knees (Figure 19.4). Especially the chest and hip section can be drawn easier if imagined as a rubber box with tilted segments that twist (Figure 19.4c). Be reminded that the legs can only twist in the hip joint and the ankle joint, and the knee can only bend; however, it can also shift left and right.

At the beginning of the twist, the head turns, and then, the chest follows. The body can turn quite a bit without the hips being affected. However, if the upper body keeps turning, the

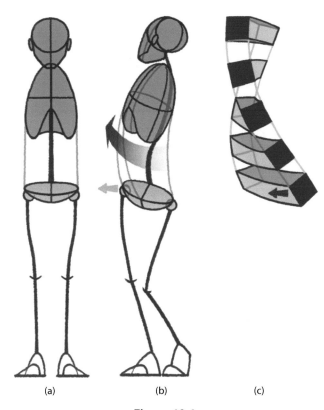

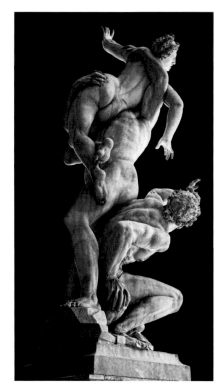

hips will have to follow as the tension in the tissue on both flanks will drag the side of the hips forward (position Figure 19.4b). This causes the knee to bend and also be pushed ahead.

The hips can turn as long as the foot that is on the other side of the twist direction starts to lift off the ground due to the knee bending more. At this point, the body weight shifts slowly toward the engaged leg. The weight shift during the twisting action from both feet (Figure 19.4a) to one foot (Figure 19.4b) also shifts the pivot point toward the twist, which means that the hips have to move slightly in the direction of the twist for the body to stay balanced.

When the character is sitting, the twist of the upper body also causes a shift in weight, which would have to be compensated by either the position of the legs or the shift of the upper body. One can feel the slight movement in the hips and the reaction of the legs due to the twist in the chest and head. In order to twist further, one side of the hips would have to lift off the seat.

Twist: Multiple characters

To intertwine several twisting characters and develop a group composition that is still clearly understood is spectacularly solved, despite its complexity, in Giovanni Bolognas' group sculpture *The Rape of the Sabine Women* (1574–1582) (Figures 19.5 and 19.6). The sculpture's title is not the story that

(a)   (b)   (c)

Figure 19.4

Figure 19.5

Giovanni Bolognas: *The Rape of the Sabine Women* (1574–1582) (Courtesy of Wikimedia Commons).

Figure 19.6

Figure 19.7   **Figure 19.8**   **Figure 19.9**

Giovanni Bolognas: *The Rape of the Sabine Women* (1574–1582) (Courtesy of Wikimedia Commons).

Bologna intended. He wanted to express with the sculpture his technical and virtuoso ability in carving a group out of one piece of marble. The title and story were added after the completion. We see a young man carrying away a young struggling woman, which an older man is trying to prevent him from doing, crouching on the ground between the legs of the younger man. Bologna created a screwing movement upward toward the woman, crying for help. Every character has its own twist and the next character takes over the very same direction in their twist, creating a strong movement that climbs up in steps from character to character. The way Bologna positions his three characters is perfectly following this upward twist, with arms and legs, shoulder movement, and head tilt complementing the upward screwing movement. The complexity in this group composition is nothing short of stunning. Each character is perfectly balanced and supports the next one in their movement. In Figure 19.7 we see the main flow in the group sculpture, the movement from the old man upward to the young man and the young one to the woman. Directions are taken over within each of the characters, movement is enhanced, and the eye follows the flow from one character to the next. The overall S-curve in the composition ultimately forces the eye toward its

peak and into the helpless expression of the woman. Figure 19.8 shows in turquoise the young man's own action lines and how they relate to the woman he carries away. The woman's curved body flows out of the line of action of the young man's and continues his motion, as much as her lower right arm accentuates the tilted position of the young man's twisted shoulder. The same can be seen in the old man's movement and his relationship to the young man and the woman. The complexity of a group composition is to have the entire direction of the group being accentuated by every element and still have the story clearly understood. The old man's hand, for example, that he holds in front of his face channels his view toward the woman and also prevents him from looking at the young man. Story and composition are the elements that constantly have to reinforce each other. Figure 19.9 suggests various compositional lines that correlate with each other.

The twist in this sculpture creates the dynamism of the ensemble and is also responsible for the eye being dragged upward. The stagnant silence of a Gothic sculpture is surely replaced by realism and energy in this late Renaissance, Mannerist masterpiece.

CHAPTER 20

Pivot Point

In order for the body to be in balance, the weight has to be equally distributed around the pivot point. The position of the pivot point is important insofar as it helps the draftsman to determine if the balance of the character is accurate or not. In a drawing, the pivot can be approximated by dividing the volume of the character in half, and the resulting axis, that falls as a perpendicular onto the ground plane, creates the pivot point (example Figures 20.1 through 20.4). As long as the pivot point in a standing character is within the area where the main weight is connected to the ground (feet), the character is still balanced. Once the pivot point is outside the area where the main weight is resting, the character is off balance, ergo: if one side of the body is heavier than the other, the body loses balance and either keels over or needs to be adjusted.

In a pose where both feet carry the weight equally in a standing position, the pivot point is right between the two feet. Shifting the weight from one foot onto the other, the pivot also shifts toward the foot that carries the weight. Shifting the weight further leads to the pivot point traveling outside the ground connection and thus the body starts to fall over. The relationship between contrapposto and pivot point can be seen in Figure 20.5. The hips will shift left or right depending on which leg carries most of the weight.

The standing character 1 (Figure 20.1) that is leaning forward has the pivot point still under the left foot (see Figure 20.2). The right leg reaching back only carries its own weight. The further the character leans forward, the further the pivot point shifts forward.

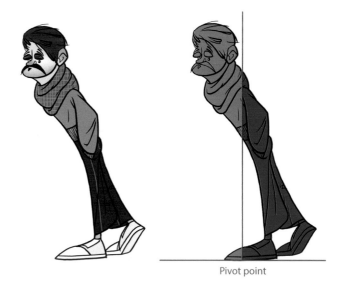

Pivot point

Figure 20.1   **Figure 20.2**

Figure 20.3

Pivot point

Figure 20.4

DOI: 10.1201/b22147-20

Figure 20.5

Both sides of the hips carry the same amount of weight. The hips are horizontal and parallel to the shoulders.

The hips are tilting and shifting towards the right IF the weight of the upper body rests on ONE foot. The pivot point is underneath the engaged leg.

The hips are shifting less to the right if both legs carry the weight. The pivot point is between both feet. Technically there is no "free leg" as both legs engage in the support.

Once it leaves the contact area of the left shoe, the character loses balance. One can easily feel this in one's own feet when standing in a balanced position and first feeling the weight on the entire foot; leaning backward shifts the weight toward the heel and leaning forward toward the toes. At some point, the toes are firmly pressing down to prevent the body from toppling forward. If character 1 however leans further forward and at the same time stretches his free leg further back, then the balance can be still maintained.

A standing body has a fixed pivot point, a body in motion a moving one (a standing character that only moves its upper body, still has a moving pivot-point). In the walking character 2 in Figures 20.3 and 20.4, the pivot point is now between the two feet. In an animated character, this point would travel with the character moving forward. In the walking figure, the main weight is on the leg that is stretched backward. Technically, the character is off balance when appearing to go forward. But in this case, this is the point: to *suggest* a movement forward. The leg that reaches out does not carry any weight as of yet. The pivot point however is between the two feet. The character is obviously unbalanced, but is just about to touch the ground with the right leg. Because the pivot point is between the two feet, however, only one foot touches the ground; it allows the walking body to fall forward and get the motion going. There is only balance of the weight in the contact and the passing position of the walk cycle.

The pivot point in animation

In animation, it depends on the animation style and the scene whether the pivot point is of importance or not. When Wile E. Coyote is standing on the edge of a cliff and leaning dangerously into the abyss, the breaking of the laws of physics and the lack of a proper pivot point are the whole joke of the shot. Only when he himself realizes his lack of balance, he falls. But this is the exception to the rule and is an artistic choice. In *Triplettes of Belleville*, the waiter in the restaurant is walking in an extreme fashion that defies all rules of gravity or flexibility of the spine (Figure 20.6). Nevertheless, his design and the character animation work perfectly together without the proper distribution of weight. They actually define him as the ultimate waiter. He is so eager to please that everything in his movement is bending to the extreme for the customer in order to serve. Exaggeration is a cornerstone in animation!

If not disregarded on purpose, the pivot point must always be considered in every key pose. The audience would not necessarily see that the character is out of balance, but they will definitely feel it and know that something is not right. Just because they don't see the single frame or drawing, but 12 or 24 of them in a second, doesn't mean they don't feel it being right or wrong.

The pivot point of a hand-drawn character only has to be checked in that one key drawing. Determining the pivot point for a 3D character is very similar to a free-standing sculpture: the character has to be balanced out in every view. If the character's balance looks correct from one angle, that does not necessarily guarantee that it is balanced from all the other points of view. It is important to constantly turn the 3D character around and check its balance.

Figure 20.6

The Triplets of Belleville (2003); dir. Sylvain Chomet.

CHAPTER 21

Balance and Tension

Balance and tension are two opposing aspects that always need to be considered in relationship to each other, never on their own, and it is crucial to keep them in mind at all times during the development of the character. Balance describes the even distribution of elements within the character, whereas tension is the uneven distribution of these elements, which are or can be:

1. The parts that divide the realistic or stylized human body into sections:
   - *Body ratio*: At what points do the head lengths divide the body into different segments?

- In the realistic body, the crotch is halfway down, dividing upper and lower body.
- Hips, knees, and feet, elbows and hands are significant compositional points.
- *Head and face:* Consider the length of the head and the overall composition and distribution of the elements in the face like chin, mouth, nose, eyes, brows, hairline, and ears.

2. The elements that are attached or specific to that very character: clothing, apparel like backpack or satchel, glasses, hairstyle.

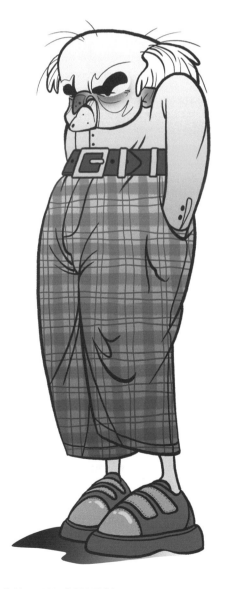

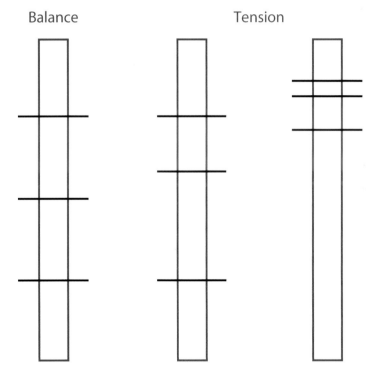

The distribution of three different elements (e.g., hips, knees, and chest) in the character is too even to be really interesting. The same distances between the elements also do not lead toward the face as all three lines have the same distance from each other. This even distribution can be found in the realistic human body, therefore can relate to realism.

Shifting only one of the elements within the character slightly already creates some tension and makes the distribution more interesting. It would be odd of course to just shift the hips up and not adjust the knees. But one can push the belt line up and thus fake a higher hip position.

Once the elements are really pushed to an extreme, the tension is highly dominant in the design. In this example, everything pushes the attention toward the upper part of the character. Those pushed elements do not necessarily have to be hips and knees as suggested in the examples before, but can be any parts that call attention to themselves.

This is a very effective way of pulling the viewer's eyes upward.

DOI: 10.1201/b22147-21

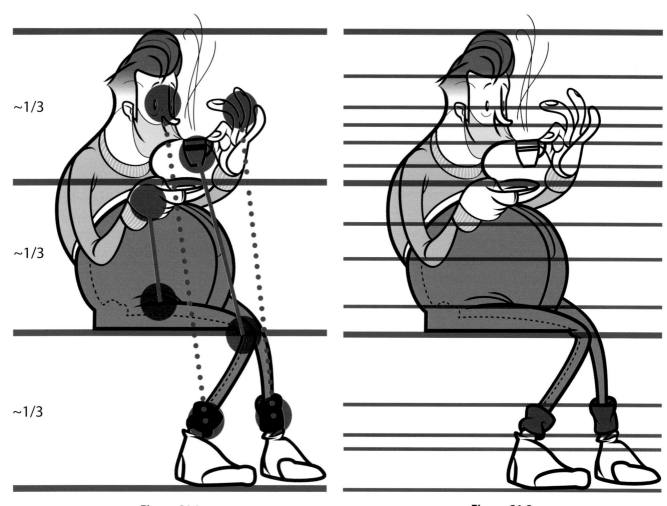

~1/3

~1/3

~1/3

Figure 21.1   **Figure 21.2**

Too much balance is plain, too much tension can make the character look awkward and odd. Nevertheless, what does not work in one character might be very appropriate in another character. There is no rule that one can follow, but only a sensitivity can help the artist in what point the design is "right," and when does it start to fail. Because the balance and tension relate to all of the elements in the character, which obviously are plenty, it is impossible to discuss all the various choices. Each change affects the whole, and therefore, every adjustment might need another adjustment. All these also depend on the style of the film and how balance and tension are represented in the overall design. A cartoony design allows much more playfulness in the extremes of balance and tension within the character than a realistic design provides. Usually the more cartoony and stylized the design is, the more tension can be pushed. However, the characters in the final character lineup should go along one level of tension to keep things somehow cohesive and the characters look like inhabiting one world. However, even in the lineup, there needs to be tension as sameness would create too much balance.

It is always an advantage to have some structure in the character, a structure that helps to not only organize the character but also to give it a compositional idea by arranging the above-mentioned elements. To explain this, the example shows how balance and tension are applied in a sitting character (Figures 21.1 and 21.2). The overall illustration has a ratio of 3 (Figure 21.1). What elements are included in this ratio is every artist's own decision; mine was top of the head, right hand, knees, and feet. The composition of the head, for example, can be balanced or juxtaposed by the composition of the feet, that is, for example, one important element on the head (eyes) are in the same mirrored position as an important element in the feet (the socks). What element is juxtaposed with what develops through the drawing process. The subdivision of each third also has its own structure (Figure 21.2). The blue lines show balance and the red ones, tension. Eyes, nose, mouth, and lower beard shadow on the neck have the same distance from each other, which is then juxtaposed by less balance in the forehead: brows, lower hairline, and a thicker line in the middle of the hairstyle. Again which elements one needs to use for this composition is personal preference.

Elements also relate to each other in terms of accentuating important areas. The middle and ring finger, for instance, point toward eyes or brows, leading back toward the face. His right hand holding the saucer is positioned to lead toward the hand holding the cup, accentuating the movement up, however also taking over the flow and curve of the lower jawline (from the ear down), creating a circular movement that constantly goes toward the cup.

The upper part of the character is much busier in the amount of lines used, but also in the action, which overall attracts the eye.

To what degree all the elements refer in position and shape to each other depends on the degree of the stylization and the compositional sensitivity of the artist. Obviously, this "game" of composition can be pushed to the extreme.

The two elements of balance and tension play off each other and need to be very carefully arranged for a well-designed outcome. There are some tips that can help to arrange the elements:

- *Avoid repetition*: Keep it organic (if that is the design goal). In Figure 21.3a, the first three lines on the left are parallel and have the same thickness. They feel very accurate and geometric, and rather technical and inorganic, thus have balance. The second set (b) in the middle has the lines with a different distance from each other creating tension, which makes them slightly more organic. Example (c) has the lines with differences in distance, thickness, and position. In this case, more tension can make it more organic. This is one of the very important rules in character design:

> **If the character is supposed to be organic, avoid the repetition of same distances.**

As you can see in Figures 21.3 and 21.4, this applies not only to the overall body, but especially to the small details throughout the design. The upper example in Figure 21.4 has the folds at the same distance, which makes them look inorganic; the lower one has them at a different distance, which makes them look more organic and natural. This needs to be considered in every single line that is drawn! Always avoid the same distances. However, it can of course be a style

decision to have the sameness be part of the style, like the example of the Greek vase painter Epiktetos' (~ 520–490 BC) Palaestra scene (Figure 21.5) on a pottery plate. The folds of the fabric are parallel on purpose and even, to enhance the rather geometric style of the piece.

- Avoid anything that drags the attention away from the focal area (usually the face).

In Figures 21.6 and 21.8, the focal point is represented by a red dot, and the assisting elements (hands and eyes) are shown with a blue dot. The example on the left however has two more dots in the striped socks that are very busy in their design. The stripes constantly drag the eyes downward and away from the upper part of the character. In Figure 21.7, the socks are much more neutral and the focal area is less disturbed.

- *Simplicity is always key*: Do not overload the character with too much tension in many of the details as that also takes away the attention from what is important: the focal area.

- Everything should be treated with the same level of stylization. It can be an interesting concept to have the same tension from the distribution of the elements in the body appear again in the head and face to give the character an additional conceptual design element.

- Create a design that leads toward the head, not away from it. All the visually important elements should be arranged in a way that enhances the face and leads toward the expression (if that is the focal point).

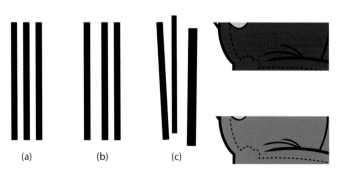

(a)   (b)   (c)

Figure 21.3   **Figure 21.4**

Figure 21.5

Epiktetos: Palaestra scene (~ 520–490 BC) (Courtesy of Wikimedia Commons).

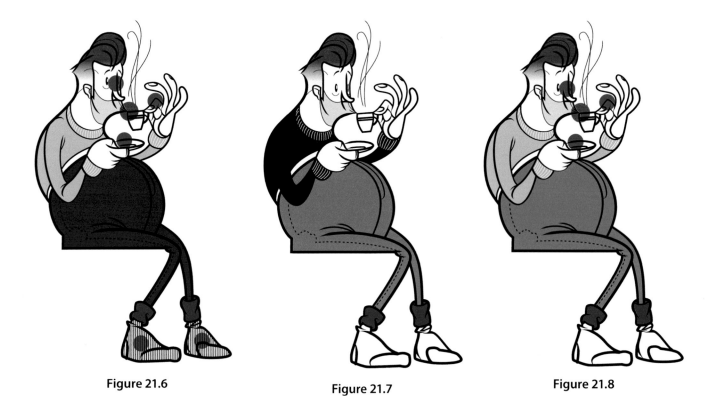

Figure 21.6

Figure 21.7

Figure 21.8

- Also create balance and tension in the contrast of the character's tone/color. In Figure 21.6, the pants are very dark and make the character feel heavier. The darker pants also create tension between the various shades within the character. Pushing the contrast between white and dark upward (Figure 21.7) to the shirt also pulls the eyes up and places the focus more on the facial area, rather than the lower part of the body. In Figure 21.8, the contrast of the pants is much less, making the overall contrast of the character more balanced.

Balance and tension in the face

The same distances of the facial elements have the tendency to create a rather plain face with too much balance (Figure 21.9a). Shifting the elements up and down gives the face tension (Figure 21.9b).

The eyes are placed right between the hairline, nose, and beard shadow which makes the face look very even (Figure 21.10). This version also takes away the focus from the tea as the eyes are further away from the cup. The focus is rather in front of the character contemplating, not on the tea.

Pushing the eyes down toward the nose creates tension, making the face more interesting (Figure 21.11).

Here the eyes are closer to the tea, pushing the elements that are important toward each other. There is much more flow in mouth, nose, and eyes. The focus is on the tea, however because of the

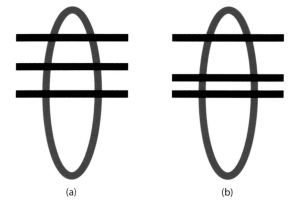

(a)   (b)

Figure 21.9

Figure 21.10

Figure 21.11

style of the button eyes, it can also be in front of the character. Characters with eyes, like these need additional care in the pose, so that it reads well where they actually are looking. The character's left hand is preventing the glance from going into the distance and keeps the eyes on the tea.

> **Difference between character design and illustration in regard to balance and tension:** In character design, balance and tension need to be incorporated into the *neutral* character pose because the character is posed later on, whereas in illustration both need to be considered in the *posed* figure.

The facial ratio can also be repeated in other features of the character or in the overall distribution of significant elements within the design. In Figure 21.12, the ratio in the face is very extreme having mouth, nose, and eyes pushed into a small section of the face. This extreme can be repeated in the overall body ratio and in various elements like the rolled up sleeves, the chest pockets, hands, and crotch that are all pushed into one horizontal segment to create areas of condensed information versus areas of emptiness (lower face, hat, lower part of the shirt). Also, the long and skinny nose's shape can be repeated in the hat or the shoes.

Figure 21.12

CHAPTER 22

Silhouette

The silhouette of a character is among the very first information we perceive, and it tells us the basics of that character in a split second. In Figure 22.1 and 22.2, the silhouette and the simple side view of a character provide you with a very basic suggestion of their personality (or rather what you interpret it to be—personality is obviously much more complex than that). Posture, body type, age, clothing, weight, pose, and maybe even occupation through specifically shaped head gear or clothing can be seen in a well-defined silhouette. A clear silhouette is one of the tools to improve the readability of the character and make the pose obvious in its action. Simplicity, being the main point that drives readability, in turn helps the silhouette. Too many details that break up the silhouette in its clarity, or make it difficult to read the initial message it contains, and the silhouette starts to lose its overall body, if lesser shapes are starting to dominate. Lesser shapes are folds, objects, attachments, strains

of hair that break off the main hairstyle or anything that is subordinate to the main body shape, which should always be the visual leader of the silhouette. In this hierarchy of shapes, first the body shape has to dominate the silhouette and then secondary or lesser shapes accentuate—this is important, otherwise the silhouette will fall apart. Figure 22.3a through (f) shows how the main oval shape is being more and more diluted by lesser shapes and in version (f) the oval is unrecognizable. There is a point where the rectangles dominate the initial shape. Some rectangles make the oval more interesting; too many break it apart and the silhouette disappears.

The optimal achievement in terms of the silhouette is to create a character whose silhouette becomes iconic. *Indiana Jones* (a) and *Lara Croft* (b) in Figure 22.4 are easily recognizable as such and we immediately recognize the characters in their silhouette.

Figure 22.1

Figure 22.2

DOI: 10.1201/b22147-22

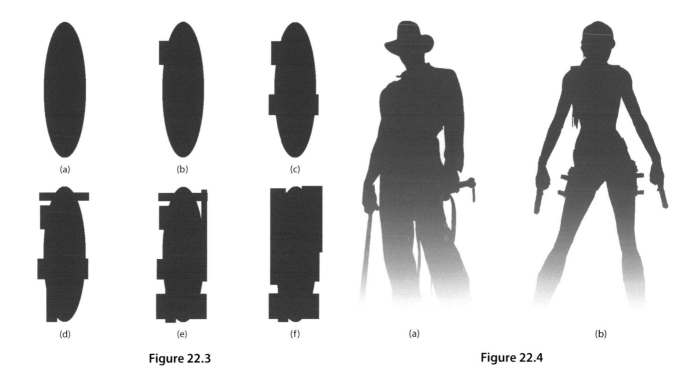

(a) (b) (c)

(d) (e) (f)

Figure 22.3

(a) (b)

Figure 22.4

Clothing in that regard is an important aspect of what drives the silhouette: without the well-known shape of Indiana Jones' hat it would be difficult to recognize him. We can see in fashion and haute couture the focus on silhouette by the fabric creating interesting shapes and forms to exaggerate and enhance certain parts of the body and create unique silhouettes. Making the silhouette an important design element leads to the character being easier to be distinguished from the other characters as they carry around their very own visual icon.

Silhouette in animation

In the characters of Lotte Reiniger's *Prinz Achmed* (1926), the most famous silhouette film in animation and the first (surviving) feature length animated film, we clearly see that the silhouette of the characters is not always simple and easy. It is rather complex and some of the characters don't read very well among the architecture and nature, as everything that is black blends together into one block. But because the film has a very lyrical and slow pace, this is not affecting the viewing. The character's movements help them to be read and Reiniger gives the audience enough time to observe the image and understand its complexity. Whenever the performing characters are partly covered up by an object in front or behind them, the movement of the characters reveals them and they never get lost in the frame for more than seconds. In her design and style, Reiniger only uses silhouettes to show the characters; circumstantially, the only aspects that she has to her disposal are therefore shape, pose, clothing, body type, and body ratio. If she had made the characters simple and also kept the silhouette simple with uninterrupted outlines, she would have given away a very

important aspect of her design. Simplicity in this style could make the image look plain. Adding many details allows the image to appear cinematic in scale as long as the main shapes of the characters aren't hidden by other characters or architecture. She also focuses on the two-dimensional plane, using only shape, not form, to define the characters. This takes away one complexity that three-dimensional characters can struggle with: the aesthetics of the character from every perspective. Their silhouette must read from every angle, not just from one, and by twisting and turning the forms of the three-dimensional character the silhouette changes. The two-dimensional characters' silhouettes in *Prinz Achmed* are kept very much the same.

Here again is where the difference between illustration and visual development artwork for film comes in: the moving image comes with different complexities that cannot be determined from the drawing or painting alone. It cannot easily be determined how the various silhouettes look in a three-dimensional character without building it in CG as a model. Then we can actually conclude if the silhouette and the forms work with the planned movement, or if they need to be adjusted.

In the famous series *La Linea* from the 1970s by Osvaldo Cavandoli, we have a character that consists only of an outline. Signore Linea is a very outspoken and passionate man in his personality. His outline however is simple and only compiled of the fundamentals. Cavandoli designed Signore Linea by showing the mere basics of the character which is his silhouette in a white outline, on monochromatic backgrounds. The series consists of a couple of minutes long episodes where the character is experiencing situations that are challenging his patience.

He is always in communication with his creator's hand that draws anything he demands or adjusts the line Signore Linea is walking and "living" on for his amusement. The character himself talks in Italian gibberish and is extremely emotional. Cavandoli created an image with the most basic ingredients: line, color, and movement. Because of this reduction he uses the line in its aesthetic cleanliness. His outline is very precise, yet not equally thick in its flow, but changes in thickness and tension, thus provides an interesting and "designed" style far away from being technical or boring. Because Cavandoli discharges all other visual information but the silhouette, he pays much attention to the readability of his key poses and the acting of the character. The interesting part in his character animation is that the character itself is depicted not like Reiniger's puppets, that are completely two-dimensional, but Signore Linea is semi three-dimensional. Despite that added difficulty, there is never any doubt about the movement or the clarity of the pose; most of the time he is only shown without a negative space between his legs, which makes the pose even more graphic, however that never influences the clarity of the poses negatively but makes the character more blocky and rooted on the ground line which he is derived from.

Silhouette in 2D or 3D animation

Silhouette has a different significance in two-dimensional versus three-dimensional character design, and character animation. In two dimensions, the shapes that the character consists of don't necessarily have to change when the character is moving. For example, in cutout animation like *South Park*, the shapes rarely change, and therefore, the silhouette stays nearly the same.

2D hand-drawn animation or digital 2D animation can either be very flat and graphic, and use the silhouette as an important part in the design (*Power-Puff Girls, Dexter's Laboratory, My Gym Partner's A Monkey, Fairly Odd Parents* and especially *Forster's Home for Imaginary Friends*), or go to the opposite end of the spectrum and mimic a look that is similar to 3D animation (some of Richard William's work in *Cobbler and the Thief*). Hand-drawn animation allows cheating in the rendition of the character's dimensionality. One can "fake" the three-dimensional appearance of a character so that it looks dimensional, but actually it is not. An example here is *The Secret of Kells* (2009) where quite often in the character animation one can discover "cheats" where the transition from one significant silhouette to another is quick and sudden, not smoothed out by in-betweens. This gives the characters a silhouette that is always clear and designed.

In a three-dimensional character, the silhouette is less controllable as the character turns in space, and the turning of the forms with additional overlaps can affect the shape of the silhouette and make it less iconic. The designer needs to make sure that the silhouette of the character can be maintained from various angles, not just from one. An excellent example for the strong silhouette of a 3D character being part of the design is Sony Pictures Animation's character of Dracula from *Hotel Transylvania* (2012). The extreme shapes of the character's cape are creating an endless row of exciting and inventive silhouettes that read very well and give the character a unique design element. It also flattens out the character slightly and makes him more graphic, which is not shared by all the other characters unfortunately.

Case study: Silhouette, rhythm, and character animation in Disney's *The Lion King* (1994) character Scar[1]

To fully understand the text about the complexity of this discussed shot, one needs to watch the shot over and over again and study it; otherwise, the following points will not be grasped.

The discussed shot of *The Lion King* (1997) introduces the antagonist Scar to the audience, and we see him catching a little mouse for lunch and contemplating about the fairness of life (the shot starts at time-code 00:04:40). His villainous character is refreshingly evil as he is sophisticated and exudes an air of arrogance and elitist boredom, which is caused by the fact that he will never be king, as Scar is the second-born next to his older brother Mufasa, the reigning and rightful king.

The character Scar was animated by Andreas Deja, one of the top animators of the hand drawn features at the Disney Studios, creating the character animation of memorable characters like, for instance, Hercules, Lilo, Gaston, Jaffar, and Scar.

This case study explores Scar's pose and silhouette, the character animation, and the relationship with the rhythm of the monologue.

Scar's monologue in this shot is: "Life's not fair, is it? You see, I, well I shall never be king, ha! And you shall never see the light of another day hmhm anew." Certain words are emphasized for impact and/or rhythm to give the entire sentence a pleasant flow. The animation follows that flow and in turn also emphasizes those rhythmic accents with movement. The perfect relationship between the two creates this pleasantly exaggerated piece of high-end character animation.

The shot starts with the mouse coming out of a cave and running toward the screen (time-code 00:04:40). Scar's paw slams down

---

[1] Due to the fact that the Disney Company did not release the copyrights for images of the feature *The Lion King* to be used in this educational section, which would have tremendously helped the understanding of the discussed compositions and poses, it is necessary for the reader to check and compare images from the movie via the provided time-codes alongside the text to fully grasp the intended compositions.

and catches the mouse. This is the first beat in the rhythm of the scene (study the visualization of the rhythm in Figures 22.5 and 22.6, in which the red dots signify rhythmically significant points in the dialogue or action). The second and third beat are the mouse's squeaks, the fourth one is Scar's contemplation about life. His main expressions and poses change for the words "life," "not," "fair" and "is it." Before he speaks the first word "life," his lower jaw moves twice up and down, following the rhythm of the music and introducing the pace of the whole shot. The double bounce of his lower jaw is the anticipation of his first

word "life," this being accompanied by a blink and a strong eyebrow movement. This first pose opens up the mouth toward the mouse and also the nose points toward the mouse creating a negative space the mouse is inscribed in.

The line from his pupils through the nose and nostrils points directly to the mouse, his victim. Then, he starts to twist and tilt his head and another eyebrow movement comes with the words "is it?" His whole facial expression is drooping, showing his bored and "miserable" existence. Through drooping, the movement

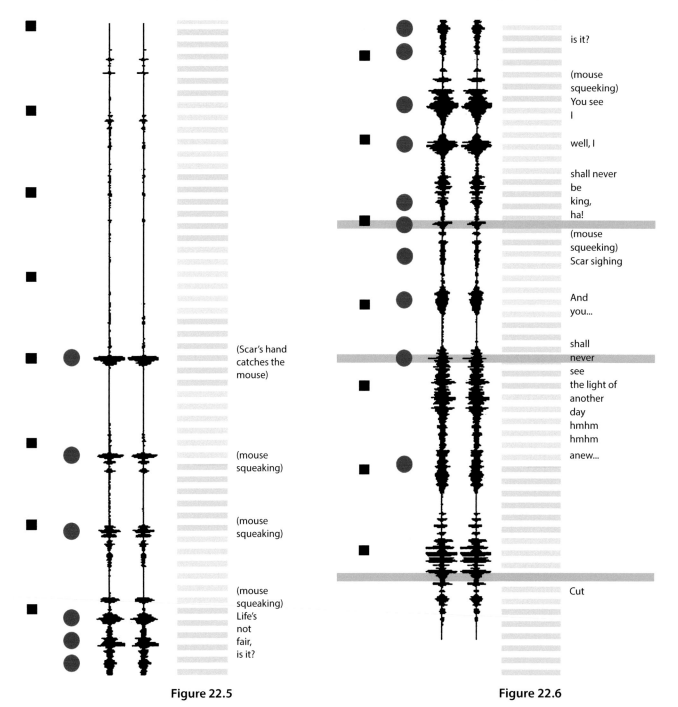

Figure 22.5   Figure 22.6

and direction of each expression goes toward the mouse, closing the circle around the mouse with his left paw curving to the left, and head and facials are curving to the right.

The next part of the speech "You see, I ..." is spoken in a rising volume ending with "I" as the loudest part. This is visualized in Scar's slowly opening eyes and the twisting head toward screen left that stops right at the word "I," giving the moment an accent.

The next part "well I" has two beats to it. The first beat is "well" while the head moves down a bit and the eyes are closing; the eyebrows go down. The second beat is "I" when the head is up again and rests in position while the lower jaw now moves upward. It feels like the eyebrows and skull lead the action and the jaw is following.

The phrase "shall never be king" has four beats that are dramatized by Scar's head moving back and forth in the rhythm of the beats to come to rest in the position of "king." Through his left paw he makes a movement right at that moment of "king" and the mouse gets released from him holding the tail. The mouse starts to walk on the paw and crawls around his toes. When Scar sighs his "Ha," it cuts to a closeup of the mouse crawling on the paw. The three-dimensionality of the movement of the paw and the mouse running over it is astounding!

The word "you" is another accent that Scar drags out and gives it its own melody. The animation of the hand reflects that accent in a twist and a dominant presentation of the mouse on the toe. The melody of the word "you" is visualized in an elegant twist of the paw and ends with a little skip of the mouse onto Scar's bent paw.

At the word "shall," the mouse jumps forward off his toe toward camera right and is caught by Scar at the word "never." At the end of the word, it cuts back to Scar in a close shot, and we see him twisting his head back toward the mouse stopping at the word "day" with a self-righteous smirk on his face, again presenting the mouse in a vignette.

The whole next part "hmhmhmhm ... anew" has a beautiful flow to it in movement and expression. It starts with an anticipation of his right shoulder rising slightly for the head to go down and twist to the left. The head then lowers and twists slightly right and left. From this down position, the eyebrows lead the action. At the "a" of "anew," his head twists upward, his ears droop, and his eyebrows rise, while the jaw drops. This gives the whole expression a lot of tension that is released by the jaw moving up and ending in the puckered lips for the letter "u" to express the sound of "new." This whole movement is perfect squash and stretch combined with meticulous timing, beautiful shapes, and follow through, all visualized with a simple silhouette. Flowing stylized lifelike animation in perfection!

CHAPTER 23

Perspective and Dimensionality

Various aspects can be used to create real perspective and dimensionality, or to suggest dimensionality in the character. There is on the one hand the obvious constructed perspective with one, two, or three vanishing points that create a real sense of form; on the other hand, there are also aspects that create perspective in a more subtle way, but are by no means less important!

Those aspects are:
- Overlap
- Foreshortening
- Character turn
- Color and contrast
- Gradient
- Light and shadow
- Size
- Organic feel (in the case of the given example)
- Zero-, one-, two-, and three-point perspective

Figure 23.1

The character is seen from the front, taking away any suggestion of form. The only perspective here is overlap in hands, tie, horns, and feet. The body is kept flat with just overlapping shapes. Shoes and hands are just seen from a simple side view. The entire character is symmetrical, underlining the flatness.

This character has a much more organic look to it due to the lack of symmetry. The forms are suggested by refining them with details, but are not yet fully in the round. Shoes and hands are turned a bit to see more form; a tuft of hair in perspective and the glasses that overlap the eye also give more depth to the character. Many elements in the character's dimensionality are unclear, like the facial architecture, that cannot be determined by a front view alone.

The quarter turn explains the roundness of the character and we fully understand its forms and their spatial expansion. The facial architecture is clear and we can see the flatness of the nose and the relationship of mouth and nose clearly, which in the two views before could not be determined.

Color adds a fake feel of substance and gives us the impression that the character is more real than it actually is. The gradients especially enhance the dimensionality.

Light and shadow, even just a simple suggestion like in this version, renders the character three-dimensional and gives it an additional feeling of weight and substance. The perspective can be strengthened by color perspective, size perspective, and contrast.

DOI: 10.1201/b22147-23

Example 23.1 demonstrates how a very flat character can gain form and perspective by adding one mentioned aspect after another, ending up with a three-dimensional character. The next step for even more perspective is shown in example 23.2 where the character is explored in a one-, two- or three-point perspective. The character can technically go through all three types of perspectives in one show depending on the needs of the specific shots.

In the case of Tomm Moore's *The Song of the Sea* (2014), the design strives for flatness and the lack of strong perspectives in terms of one-, two-, and three-point construction are used as the main design elements. Floors are tilted vertically and objects are either seen from top or side/front view. The characters have to fit stylistically and also move around in this world that lacks vanishing points. Therefore, they cannot have realistic shadows and cannot have a fully three-dimensional animation or form-defining

elements; instead, they need to underline shape and the flatness of the cinematic screen. The character's front, side, and back views by nature strengthen the flatness of the character; the three-quarter views are not fully three-dimensional, yet due to their deliberate lack of correct forms, they underline the flatness of the frame. To develop a style that plays with perspective and dimensionality, one needs to dissect the image that the style of the film is going to be based on and create a list of rules that must not be broken in any character if one strives for consistency in style and a unique design. The following example discusses the use of dimensionality in the character Dexter in *Dexter's Laboratory*.

Not every character needs to be three-dimensional; some play with the flatness of the design and use it as the strength of a show. Genndy Tartakovsky's *Dexter's Laboratory*, for example (Figure 23.3), is a hybrid of shape-oriented elements and form-defining parts. The drawing of Dexter (a) shows him in an overall

Zero-point perspective

One- or two-point perspective

Three-point perspective

Nothing in the character is seen in perspective; instead, everything is strictly from a horizontal view.

One- or two-point perspective show if the horizon line is in hip-height, the feet from a down view, and the head from an up view. However, it could also be only an up view or a down view. The character does not taper toward a third vanishing point.

The three-point perspective up or down view that is tapering toward a third vanishing point allows the character to be shown in realistic perspective and its diminishing size away from the viewer's point of view.

Figure 23.2

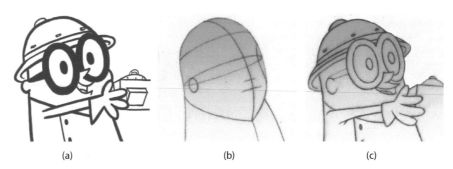

(a)   (b)   (c)

Figure 23.3

graphic and flat style that is all UPA design from the 1950s, though some parts in the character suggest a three-dimensional form. The hat for example isn't completely flat and neither is the face, nevertheless the arm doesn't reach out of the two-dimensional plane. If Dexter would be rendered more three-dimensionally "accurate" and redrawn with the imbedded forms being followed (b), he would end up looking very different (c). This version of Dexter has more volume to it, which makes him appear more correct and "real." However, the downside is that he doesn't look like Dexter anymore. One of the design rules that the TV show has established is missing in (c) and ends up changing the character significantly.

The creative use of perspective and dimensionality can obviously be pushed either way into more realistic or more cartoony design, more flat, or more three-dimensional. Or, like in Ben Bocquelet's show *The Amazing World of Gumball*, completely ignored and the characters occupy the entire range of dimensionality from completely flat to fully CG three-dimensional.

Figure 23.4

Example

In Figure 23.4, the characters are dimensional and everything follows form and dimensionality. The face of the boy is located in its correct position dimensionally, and the diving goggles accentuate the accurate twist of the head. All other elements, like pattern on the chest, the lead belt, the position of the feet with flippers also support a three-dimensional world.

Figure 23.5 has some of the elements that support the z-axis be reduced and follow the x- and y-axes. The result is a character that is more flat and graphic. This type of character is shape-oriented. The face is shifted toward the left to go against the form, as are the goggles. This flattens out the dimensionality of the face. The pattern on the chest is also shifted, the belt is accentuating the horizontal and vertical, the x- and y-axes. The feet are vertical and horizontal rather than tilted in an angle. The lobster is only shown from the side in its body; his eyes are shifted and do not show any overlap. The stones on the ground are round, rather than oval. The details are slightly reduced to let the shape dominate, but this is not necessarily reducing the dimensionality.

Figure 23.6 is pushing all the points that have been changed in illustration Figure 23.5 which flattens the image even further. The ground plane is only a line and has no depth at all. Many of the tilted or curved lines are now either horizontal or vertical, or straightened out (e.g., the lead belt is just a geometric block, and

Figure 23.5

the fingers are horizontal and vertical). The shapes are simplified and more geometrical. The face is in the middle of the three-quarter head, but the jawline is seen slightly from the front. The result is a character that clearly lives on a two-dimensional plane and has no dimensionality to it. What is important in this exercise is that the characters stay the same! The perspective is changed but the personality is not.

Case study: Dimensionality in Blue Sky's *The Peanuts Movie* (2015)

Blue Sky's feature *The Peanuts* (2015) interpreted Charles Schulz's famous comic strip for the CG screen, turning drawn characters that are utterly flat and never fully defined as dimensional

characters in Schulz's comic, into three-dimensional CG characters (however, there were always toys and puppets that suggested the Peanuts' dimensionality). The style of Blue Sky's

Figure 23.6

feature also follows Bill Hernandez' famous TV show that gave the Peanuts their unique movement and voices, which the feature strongly relies on, plus the famous music by jazz-pianist Vince Guaraldi without which the feature would have not had the reminiscing emotion that the film is going for, and that those knowing the Peanuts expected. (The voices of Woodstock and Snoopy are actually spoken by Bill Hernandez himself.) The animated characters as much as their comic versions are rudimentary in their three-dimensionality, only following a horizontal zero-point perspective, which makes them flat. They always appeared in the same visual style throughout their entire publication, only changing slightly in the first couple of years. Blue Sky translated their flatness into the computer graphic look with a limited range of photorealistic textures, yet still kept the idea of flatness in their design that contains Schulz's original idea. The overall compositions are very simple, as they are in the comic strip—only horizontal views, scarcely a tilted view. The characters are most often in a central position or evenly balanced left or right. All of this is successfully translated in the film. However, the design language that the characters are created with is not fully followed in the backgrounds. They are rendered three-dimensionally and in perspective instead of inventing a style that accurately reflects the same rules the characters have. Objects are, however, often shown in three-quarters, from a perfect front view that doesn't allow a down view or an up view onto the furniture for example. That goes perfectly hand in hand with the comic strip. Nevertheless, the environment these objects are in is a three-dimensional environment with a three-point perspective, putting the flat(ish) characters into a world that is defined by perspective.

Much of the character animation and its dimensionality is successfully achieved and one can see the complexity in the movement and the flatness of the forms. The character animation

stays truthful to the TV show, and it is sometimes awkward, yet always has a unique and creative use of movement. There are some movements being translated directly from the TV show into the movie (especially the dance moves at the dance competition). Those are little treats for those that grew up with the show.

The characters are beautifully converted from their comic-page flatness into the 3D world, but there are elements in the design that do not speak the same language as others. What doesn't work is the complexity of their hair, which is rendered in single strings of hair instead of just a form. The complex hair textures juxtapose the simplicity of other parts of the characters. Simplifying the hair by just allowing form to dominate and texture to be barely visible would have been the appropriate design decision that follows the main direction of the film. The character's simplicity in style, form, skin texture, and design contrasts with the details in the hair and also some clothing textures; this constantly points out the character's artificiality instead of underlining their simplicity in every other aspect of the design. The choice of giving the characters photorealistic curls and hair is a very awkward one indeed as the textures of the hair makes the characters look unfortunately cheap and like a photo collage instead of a feature film from 2015.

Perspective and movement

We have a character that is constructed without any perspective at all in Figure 23.7. His perspective is just mimicked and faked, but not based on any constructed perspective. The character is also in an environment that lacks vanishing points and thus is fully two-dimensional and flat. As a still image this works and there is no clash between character and background, because both follow the same or similar perspective. The problems start when the character needs to move and be animated within its space. Movement itself in its full range can only exist in a three-dimensional space. When a character walks from the back door toward the camera, the third dimension is required. The same is true for the character just moving their arm in a semicircle toward the camera. A flat character could only wave their arm up and down on the x- and y-axes, but not back and forth on the z-axis, because in a flat background the z-axis does not exist

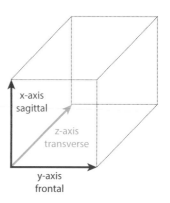

and perspective is just mimicked but not constructed. However, the space in Figure 23.7 is flat and has no vanishing points or dimension that opens up the space into the needed third dimension.

Movement can exist on a two-dimensional plane or a three-dimensional space, but it often looks odd when a three-dimensionally designed character moves freely three-dimensionally and the background is flat or vice versa. Logically, the character in Figure 23.7 would not be able to use the third dimension for any of their movements as they are not constructed three-dimensionally with forms, but only consists of overlapping shapes (the character could however easily be redrawn in a fully three-dimensional fashion). Any turn of a three-dimensional character, which is the traditional approach of hand-drawn animation from the late 1920s to the early 1950s, runs into an aesthetic clash with a flat background at some point.

If the character in Figure 23.7 started to move and for instance turned their head, this movement would not be following the space's flatness, as a full turn only works if the head is based on a form; only forms can accurately turn in a three-dimensional space, but not a two-dimensional one (the turn would work if it is imitated without actually being constructed). For instance, one option of turning the head without introducing vanishing points would be just flipping the head as in Figure 23.8. Then there is no form involved and the character is still flat. Or as in Figure 23.9a through (e) where only elements of the facial mask are shifted on the plane (nose, eyes, and mouth are not changing at all as a group) and then the head is flipped horizontally (Figure 23.9d) and the shift of the facial mask is then continued in (e). That simulates a head turn convincingly enough without the third dimension being involved. This is part of what is called *limited animation*: letting parts of the character move while others stay still. What we did is separate the elements the character consists of and place them on different levels to mimic perspective.

Figure 23.7   Figure 23.8

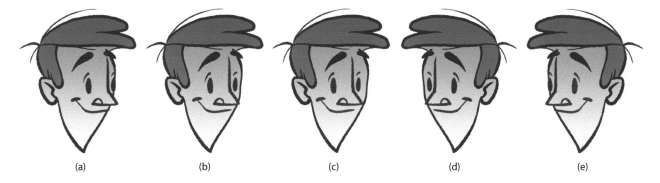

(a)   (b)   (c)   (d)   (e)

Figure 23.9

Zero point
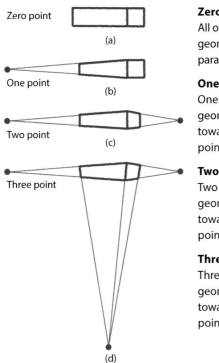
(a)

One point
(b)

Two point
(c)

Three point

(d)

Figure 23.10

Zero point:
All of the lines in the geometry are either parallel or perpendicular.

One point:
One set of lines of the geometry are tapering toward one vanishing point.

Two point:
Two sets of lines of the geometry are tapering toward two vanishing points.

Three point:
Three sets of lines of the geometry are tapering toward three vanishing points.

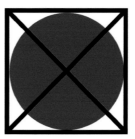

Figure 23.11

We need to now look at the four different perspective methods and see how they affect the design and the movement of the character (Figure 23.10).

Let us see how a regular shape behaves on a two-dimensional plane simulating perspective. First, there is a size relationship where a shape looks bigger when it is closer and smaller when it is far away (Figure 23.12a). This is obviously one interpretation that the size difference is due to the distance between the two rather than to one just being bigger than the other. The second option is overlapping shapes which are proof of them not just being different in size, but having a different distances from the viewer (b). The simplest and most effective way of creating perspective is with overlapping shapes! In example (c), a stacking of shapes leads to foreshortening as there is clearly one shape in front of the other, but there is no real depth yet as the shapes are all the same size. Additionally, adding diminishing size in (d) contributes to the impression of perspective with depth, and the shape furthest back feels to be much further than in example (d). These four examples all simulate perspective on a two-dimensional plane but do not create "real" perspective with vanishing points.

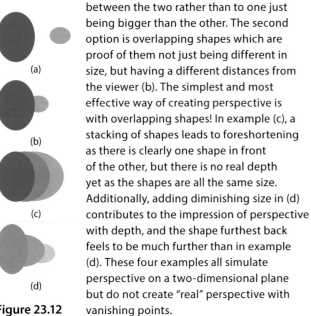

(a)

(b)

(c)

(d)

Figure 23.12

The two shapes of circle and square in Figure 23.11 add exactly that: depth which is caused by introducing vanishing points. The shapes are angled toward or away from the observer and will therefore change their initial shape once tilted. The tilted circle looks like an oval and the square like a trapezoid shape. Perspective with vanishing points gives the illusion of shapes changing their angle and with it, their shape. The change in shape gives enough of the illusion of perspective to be convincing to the eye. This nevertheless would not work with the head turn of the character in Figure 23.7 as the background has no constructed perspective and also no vanishing points, so having the character constructed with vanishing points would cause a clash. We would have to fall back to the technique of examples Figure 23.12a through (d), which is exactly what we did in Figures 23.9a through (e).

The question is to what level can the various methods of perspective be used as a creative tool for the design and the movement of flat, or mostly flat, characters and have them moving logically in the given space?

We need to mimic the z-axis, and foreshortening can help. Foreshortening in characters means that the eye sees the body or body parts not from a side view, but parts of the body are coming or are angled toward the viewer, seemingly being shorter, longer, bigger, or smaller than they actually are. The four different types of perspectives are going to be discussed in their ability to express foreshortening, as every perspective deals with it in a different visual way that affects the design and the character animation.

As seen in Figure 23.9a through e the character can be divided into levels (head, facial features, and body are separated and placed on three different levels to mimic the turn). Logically then, any part of the body can be placed on a different level and then animated with perspective as a goal. Shapes that are stacked on top of each other to mimic foreshortening, and perspective gives however only slices of the full information of a character in space. Depending on the style and design, it can be enough to suggest a dimensional character, but it does clearly not give one a character that is fully three-dimensional as we are still only dealing with shapes, not full forms. Full form is only possible with a three-point constructed perspective. It depends on the style of the animated show if shapes alone, shapes and forms, or just forms are used to create the effect of perspective and foreshortening.

Let's see how zero point and the three vanishing points affect the design of the character and its ability to move within the given space.

Zero-point perspective

The character in Figures 23.14 and 23.15 only lives on the flat and two-dimensional plane of the paper and there is no foreshortening of any kind—there is no form, just shape. The only perspective is created through overlapping shapes (and the hint of color gradient which suggests dimensionality). Even the moving character will not leave the plane, only shift arms and legs like cutout animation.

Figure 23.14   **Figure 23.15**

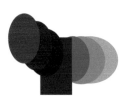

Figure 23.13

The only direction of any part of the body would be up and down on the x- and y-planes, offsetting the shapes on the vertical plane (Figure 23.13). Very much like cutouts, the shapes can be moved on the desktop, but cannot be moved toward the viewers or away from them. However, the facial features, for instance, can be shifted on the vertical plane-up and down, left or right, to give the illusion of a slight head turn even though there is no actual perspective involved. Additionally, the head can also be rotated clockwise or counterclockwise (Figure 23.15). Together that can bring into the animation the illusion of a slice of dimensionality that is actually not there (like the head turn in example Figure 23.9a through e).

In the actual character animation, the solid shapes move on top of each other and the limbs only move on the x–y plane. A character walking toward the camera would only have the option to shift the shapes of the legs up and down, or along the x- or y-axis, but not the z-axis (Figure 23.16).

Because there is no depth of the z-axis, the overlapping shapes that suggest the foreshortening are not changing in size, as seen in example Figure 23.17. However, this needs to be discussed anew for every show or feature.

Example: South Park is for the most part flat; there are some suggestions of foreshortening, but they are achieved mostly by simply overlapping shapes.   **Figure 23.17**

Figure 23.16

Figure 23.18   **Figure 23.19**

character animation, the character could not fully turn around. If the character needs to be turned it can only do that via the technique suggested in Figure 23.9a through e. One-point perspective keeps the character therefore mostly flat, but shapes or forms that are overlapping can diminish in size (Figure 23.17). The rabbit would be able to tilt its head left and right (clockwise or counterclockwise), but still cannot turn it in perspective. Nonetheless everything that comes forward or goes backward can be changed in size due to the opening of the z-axis. As in the zero-perspective example, in one-point perspective the characters' facial features can also be shifted on the x- and y-planes (Figures 23.18 and 23.19). The size change of the ears going back due to the illusion of the perspective can be achieved because they are on the z-axis. The feet, that due to walking come forward or reach backward, can also diminish or enlarge in size. All this however can only be done with overlapping shapes, not the actual form.

One-point perspective

One-point perspective already allows simple foreshortening with a change in size of the different elements due to the one vanishing point. In zero-point perspective, there is no form; with one vanishing point, we have form. However, the form cannot be freely constructed and does not yet have the full range of a three-dimensional space. The front panel of the form is always parallel to the x- and y-planes but it still cannot tilt (Figure 23.20 and 23.21).

The character can only be seen from one side and only the z-axis is in perspective, not the x- or y-axis. In the actual

Two-point perspective

The character can be seen from any side in perspective. Figure 23.23 shows that the forms can freely rotate and turn. Two-point perspective opens the space toward the x-, y-, and z-axes, which gives us the full three-dimensionality of the character. They can now not only rotate but also turn (Figure 23.22). The character however does not taper toward up or down, which means it does not include real foreshortening in its full range as the shapes overlapping each other downward/upward are not yet diminishing in size but still have the same length (Figure 23.24).

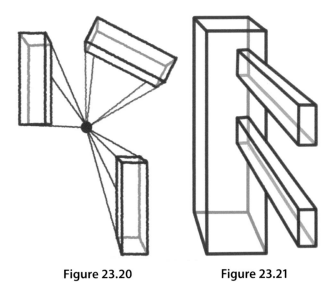

Figure 23.20   **Figure 23.21**

Figure 23.22

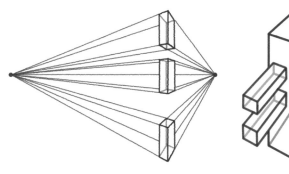

Figure 23.23   **Figure 23.24**

Three-point perspective

Three-point perspective adds the tapering toward the third vanishing point, and the character is fully three-dimensional (see Figures 23.25 and 23.26). They can move freely in any direction (Figure 23.27), plus the forms change in size in all three directions: left/right, up/down, and back to front.

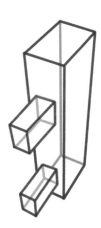

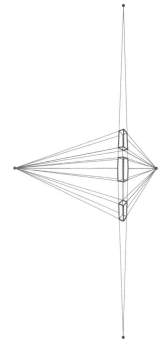

Figure 23.25   **Figure 23.26**   **Figure 23.27**

CHAPTER 24

Foreshortening

To create true foreshortening, the full form in perspective is unavoidable, and there is no shortcut in mimicking depth. Seeing every single element of the body in perspective requires a visual thought process that is very accurate and precise in the space-occupying form of the character. Drawing this requires a certain amount of expertise and practice of form (Figure 24.1). The simplified wireframe projection onto the forms (Figure 24.2) helps to render them in their perspective correctly. Having this kind of image in your head and projecting it onto the character will make it much easier to draw the overlapping forms, which can be separated into several segments for further simplification. In the example, the separation would be the fingers on the level closest to the viewer, then hand and thumb, forearm, upper arm, and shirt/shoulder being the furthest away from the viewer and therefore placed on the lowest level. Separating those elements makes it easier to level the body, which can help planning out the possible movement we have been talking about in Chapter 24, "Perspective and Dimensionality."

Figure 24.1

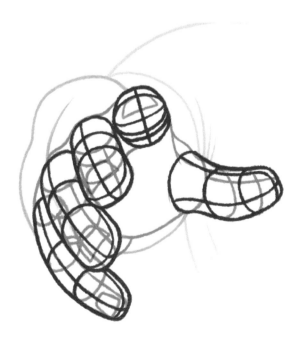

Figure 24.2

Figure 24.3

DOI: 10.1201/b22147-24

Foreshortening can be enhanced through the line quality and thickness (Figure 24.3), the different textures of the staggered segments, light and shadow, or the contrast between foreground and background. In the examples of Figures 24.3 and 24.4, it doesn't matter if the foreground is dark or light for the effect of foreshortening to be strengthened.

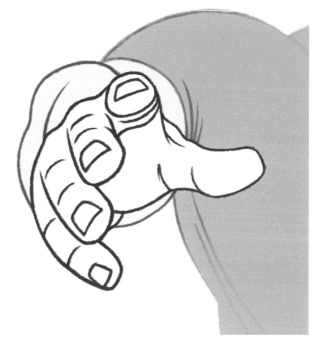

Figure 24.4

CHAPTER 25

Tangents

Tangents happen when parts of the body inadvertently touch other parts or other elements/characters around them and therefore destroy perspective. The point where those two elements touch suggests in a two-dimensional plane that they are actually physically connecting; however, in a three-dimensional space, they might not, because one might be further back than the other.

Tangents must be avoided at all cost as they flatten the character and image, can create awkward unwanted effects, and also reduce the readability. In Figure 25.1, there are two tangents that are very much destroying the full effect of not just the dimensionality but also the content. One tangent is the thumb that touches the cap (Figure 25.2). This suggests that the thumb is on the same level as the cap. However it could actually be much closer to the viewer. The tangent also changes the story: When the thumb touches the cap, it could be interpreted as the thumb pushing the cap up, instead of the boy giving us a "thumbs-up" gesture (Figure 25.3). The second tangent is the continuous line in the socks, which pushes the sock of the left leg forward to the same level as the one from the right leg and thus completely destroys the perspective created in the shoes. By lowering one sock (Figure 25.3), the perspective is reestablished.

Figure 25.1

Figure 25.2

Figure 25.3

DOI: 10.1201/b22147-25

CHAPTER 26

Light and Shadow

"Who knows what evil lurks in the hearts of men. The Shadow knows." This is the beginning of the famous radio show aired in the 1930s with the character *The Shadow*, who is protecting the innocent and punishing the guilty, fighting evil as a never-to-be-seen vigilante crime-fighter. The Shadow's true identity is unknown, his persona is shrouded in mystery and the term *The Shadow* perfectly embodies what kind of character he is—hidden, secret, mysterious, dark, and secretive. The sentence "Who knows what evil lurks in the hearts of men …" could be interpreted as one needs to have been, or be, in the shadows to truly understand the secrets hidden in the hearts of men. A person existing in the shadows can grasp the true depths of evil. *The Shadow* was the inspiration for Batman, the superhero par excellence associated with the secrecy of shadows and the dark. Shadows are always hiding something, they cover and prevent the full truth to be revealed. Nevertheless, exactly *because* shadows obscure, they also expose that there is something hiding or that someone is hiding something from the viewer. This is an artistic advantage we can use in designing a character with the use of shadows and light. If there is no shadow, there is seemingly no place to conceal information. This can be used practically, artistically, and metaphorically. Light and shadow is never just the illumination of the character and background by the light source, but always reflects, comments, or questions the character's emotions and thus can complement the story point.

Traditional character design is usually more concerned with shapes and personality than refining the character with complex light and shadows. Simple form-defining shadows that don't have much storytelling impact are preferred to theatrical lighting, which can give too much information and allows an interpretation that is often avoided for the sake of clarity and simplicity. Character design strives for clarity in shapes and personality, whereas final character presentation pieces can be more refined with intense and obviously story-driven lighting situations. The question that should be asked when approaching light and shadow in the character design is if it accompanies and amplifies the intended personality or not. If it does not, then it should be eliminated.

Obviously, shadows follow the form and movement of the body and describe its surface in space. Being too concerned about the accuracy of shadows, however, can make the outcome look rigid and lack an element of artistry. When designing the distribution of light and shadow, it only needs to look right; it does not have to be 100% accurate (if it isn't a photorealistic or hyperrealistic rendering of course). Artistic decisions are as important as the following of technical and anatomical requirements! Don't make only realistic choices, make artistic ones as light and shadow have a highly metaphorical impact. They are extremely powerful agents for the character's personality and story. Study the examples in Figure 26.1a through h of the same neutral face being lit from different angles and how the emotion or the situation the character is in changes. The neutral face in Figure 26.1a is seemingly more concerned in Figure 26.1b and determined in face Figure 26.1d. The shadows are not fully accurate, but accentuate a mood by covering the facial features or highlighting them like in the example where the eyes are lit. This opens up myriads of possibilities of reinterpreting or intensifying the character's personality. In relationship with the story point, there are literally endless options. Everything in design goes back to

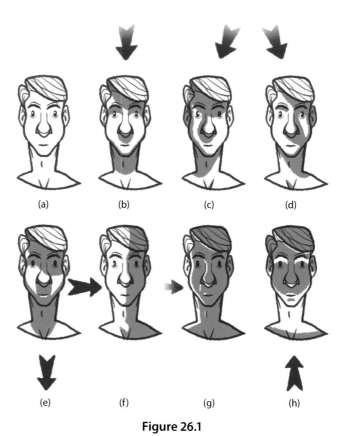

Figure 26.1

DOI: 10.1201/b22147-26

the story; without it, there is nothing but an empty visual. That is especially true for light and shadow as it visualizes the emotions of the character in that very moment of the story and additionally influences the emotions of the viewer.

Aspects and types of shadows

- *Direction:* Where the light is actually coming from determines the direction of the shadow.
- *Contrast:* There needs to be contrast between light and shadow for them to clearly separate.

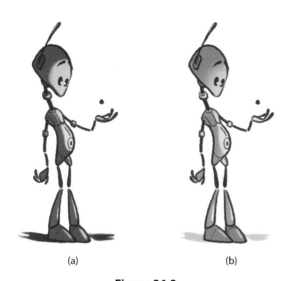

(a)   (b)

Figure 26.2

- *Fast falloff (Figure 26.2a):* Spotlights, which have highly directional beam, produce fast falloff. There is a high contrast between the shadow side and the light side.
- *Slow falloff (Figure 26.2b):* Diffused light creates little contrast between the illuminated side and the shadow side.
- *Connected shadow (Figure 26.3a):* The shadow is connected to the character that casts it. The perspective of the shadow determines the position of the light source and also defines the surface of the terrain.
- *Disconnected shadow (Figure 26.3b):* The shadow is not connected to the character that casts it.
- *Cast shadow (Figure 26.3c):* A shadow that falls onto the character. This type of shadow places the character in an architectural setting or a scenario (jail with bars, house, forest...)

Types of light

Basic lights

- *Key light (Figures 26.4a and 26.5a):* The main and predominant light (not necessarily the brightest). Light that gives shape, form, and definition (usually from the front, but there is also side-key, side-back key ...).
- *Fill light (Figures 26.4b and 26.5b):* The fill light balances out the key light and softens the light and shadow areas to let them appear less harsh.
- *Backlight:* This is any light that comes from behind the subject or slightly back-above (which is then called *hair light*).

(a)   (b)   (c)

Figure 26.3

(a) Key light	(b) Fill light
(c) Kickers and rim	(d) Eye light

Figure 26.4

Soft light that is diffused

(a) Key light	(b) Fill light
(c) Kickers and rim	(d) Eye light

Figure 26.5

Harder light that creates harsh shadows

- *Kickers and rims (Figures 26.4c and 26.5c):* These give a sharp outline around the subject that defines its silhouette (rim light) or skims along the side of the subject, which is then referred to as kicker or three-quarter backlight.
- *Eye light (Figures 26.4d and 26.5d):* This is to point light into the protruding eye sockets to take out heavy shadows and also lighten up the eyes.

High key light

Bright and generally nonspecific. It has a high overall light level, slow or no falloff, and usually a light background.

Low key light

Low overall light level with highly selective lighting. The lighting has fast falloff with dense shadows and dark background.

Strengths of light and shadow in characters

- Strengthen the story point
- Accentuate directions and focal points
- Create a mood
- Explain the space

- Enhance emotions
- Enhance the character's personality
- Mark the leading character
- Comment on present, past, and future happenings
- Define form

Strengthen the story point

Questions that need to be answered before designing the distribution of light:

- What is the character's personality and how can light and shadow help to enhance it? How can the personality traits of greed, confidence, benevolence, etc., be visualized through light and shadow?
- What is the character's emotional state either in the entire movie or in this specific moment? How could light and shadow be a metaphor for this?
- What is the character's objective in this very moment? What does the character seek and how can this be interpreted by the present light situation? Is it a positive goal they are looking toward, then the example 26.6b might be a good choice, or is it a negative goal that is in the long run not beneficial for the character's development? Then, example 26.6a might be the direction to go in. This can be independent of the facial expression as the shadow can forebode what is going to happen unknowingly to the character. There is also the possibility of doing the exact

opposite if the character is looking toward a dark future, but in the end they will prevail. The character can look into the shadows, but there is an intense reflection in their eyes that gives hope. Do I want the audience to know that the future is dark, or do I want to keep the suspense?

- What is the relationship of the main character with the surrounding characters? How can that be accentuated with light and shadow? Light and shadow can be used as a vector to connect two characters, or a character and an object.

- Is the intended light situation and with it the weather situation reflecting the character's emotional and psychological state, and also does the weather represent the story point visually and emotionally in its mood?

Accentuate directions and focal points

The light and shadow situation needs to go with the flow of the entire pose and not against it, and has to accentuate the focal point. This is part of the compositional needs of the pose. But it also has to follow the overall direction the story point requires realistically and/or metaphorically. A balance needs to be found where both needs are met.

Figure 26.7a through c:
(a): The character is looking backward and the shadow covers their front; the light is coming from the behind. Light and shadow not only illuminate, but also carry information. The character is looking over their shoulder in melancholy, and one interpretation could be that they seem to also look into the past, but the future is dark and gloomy. The focus needs to be on the face and its expression. The shadow therefore should not cover up the expression if possible. Nevertheless, the rest of the body can be used to play with light and shadow.

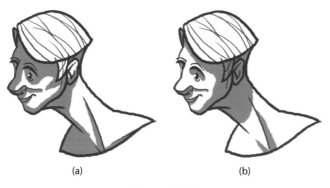

(a)   (b)

Figure 26.6

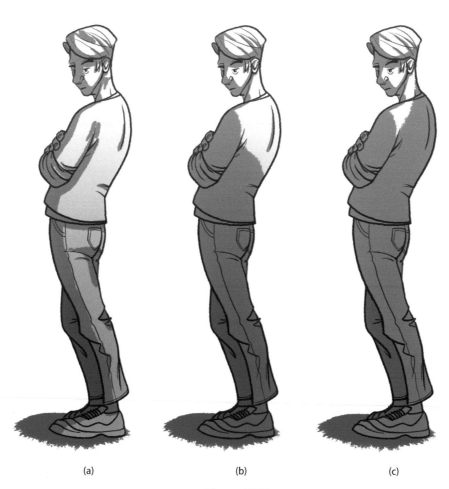

(a)   (b)   (c)

Figure 26.7

Figure 26.8

Because the focus should be in the face, the light can intensify from the feet upward and have the strongest light in the face. This simple gradient in the shadow will push the eye of the viewer upward.

(b) and (c): To keep the attention of the viewer in the face and torso of the character, the shadow can just cover the lower part (b). However, the two lighting options in (b) and (c) give us two different story points. In (b), the shadow only covers parts of the back, leading with its curve and angle toward the face. The eyes of the character are free to look behind and see the "light at the end of the tunnel," and there is no shadow that interrupts the character's glance. In (c), this option is gone and the shadow also comes from behind. Consequently, version (c) has the least hope of the three.

To keep the directional flow, the shadows in front of the eyes or other important elements of the pose can be opened up.

(a)

(b)

Figure 26.9

In Figure 26.9a, the shadow is cut short in front of the eye in order to open the direction the character is looking in (to the left). If the shadow in pose (26.6b) would cover the whole eye like in Figure 26.9b, the important flow toward the left would be broken and the eye–object connection the character is focusing on is interrupted. This of course does not need to be realistic, but needs to be effective in telling the story!

Create a mood

The mood is the emotional expression of the environment and how it reacts to or reflects the character's psychological state. Accordingly, light and shadow must never be seen as just the illumination of the scenery and its resulting physical effects, but have to always be recognized with their metaphorical implications they have on the character and the story. The mood of the environment reacts or acts in unison or contrary to the character along the story point to comment or reflect on the character's situation. This relationship usually has the character's emotion as the fundamental element. The environment usually caters to the character, seldom the other way around as the character is the focus.

Explain the space

Light and shadow does not only define the character itself but with a cast shadow that falls onto the character can explain where the character is located and define the off-screen space. Figure 26.8 has the character clearly sitting under a tree. Only the shadows of the leaves explain the location. Light and shadow in this case clearly define the environment and create a mood despite the tree not being visible. The off-screen space has a tremendous influence in this case on the happenings within the frame, reducing the restrictions of the frame and opening up the space.

Enhance emotions

For increasing emotions (the characters and those of the audience) in a subtle way, colors and light and shadow are very helpful tools as they do not, like facial expressions and poses, immediately describe the emotion, but approach them from a rather abstract perspective and give us visual clues. This can lead to a subtle undertone that is more felt than immediately read. A rather blunt approach is, for example, in Figure 26.10a and b. The shadow covers the face of the sleeping guy in (a) and in (b) it leaves the face open and covers the rest of the body. The interpretation is very obvious in (b), as the shadows of the leaves seem like a blanket on the body of the sleeping guy, which makes him look safe and comfortable. In (a), the leaves' shadows cover his face which exposes his body, but he seems to be sleeping deeper.

Light and shadow can also show the character's momentary ability to grasp a situation. In Figure 26.11, the character's face is partly covered by a cast shadow to suggest that some of his senses might be reduced or eliminated and that he does not (yet) sense what he is supposed to in order to understand the situation he is facing. Covering body parts or objects related to the character with a shadow removes or reduces the direct connection between story and character/object.

Enhance the character's personality

This only works if the character's personality can be interpreted via light and shadow, which is not always possible. Placing a moody character always into a position where there are shadows or a character with a positive outlook on life where there is light helps to accentuate this aspect of the personality. It could be one of the staging rules of that specific character in the final film. Batman, for example, is usually shown in the shadows whenever possible and not in bright light.

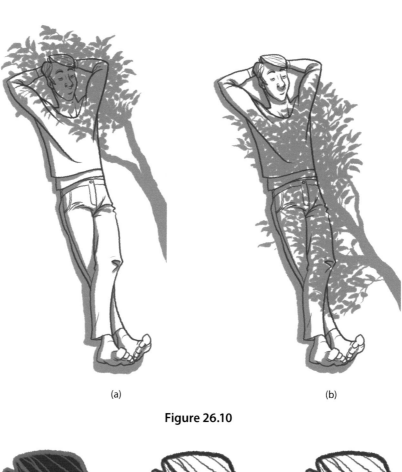

(a)   (b)

Figure 26.10

Figure 26.11

Mark the important character

In a group situation, light and shadow help to mark the important character that leads the story point. This can be done either with light or with shadow. The only important point is to have the light and shadow complement the story. Figure 26.12a and b offers two different versions of a group situation where

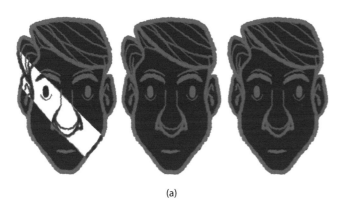

(a)

(b)

Figure 26.12

one of the characters is visually the significant one. Group (a) has the important character being pointed out by a shred of light, whereas in (b) the character that drags attention is the one that is partly covered by shadow. The importance is that either light or shadow accentuates the "otherness" of that specific character and therefore attracts the eye.

Comment on present, past, and future happenings

Light and shadow refine the happenings of that very moment of the story and illuminate what the character experiences in the present. But it likewise can comment on the past and the future of the character's journey. It can be foreboding or revoke happenings of the past. The metaphorical side of light and shadow allows us to add various levels of complexity to the character. Figure 26.13 shows how light can disapprove of the character's action.

Define form

Light and shadow are the very qualities that define form and give it its body. What usually counts is that the shadow renders the form believably not necessarily fully realistically, which doesn't mean that the thorough study of complex forms is unimportant.

What makes the believable design of the shadow on a character difficult is the character's surface, which is rather like an uneven terrain with mountains and valleys than a clear and simple geometric form. And the complex form of a character changes from one character to the next as every character's surface terrain is different. Additionally, the shadows change depending on the different positions of the light source. The final shadow is most often an approximate that gives an idea of the shadow plus an artistic interpretation, not necessarily a fully realistic light situation. Nevertheless, the understanding of the form and its accurate spatial extension is crucial and cannot be ignored.

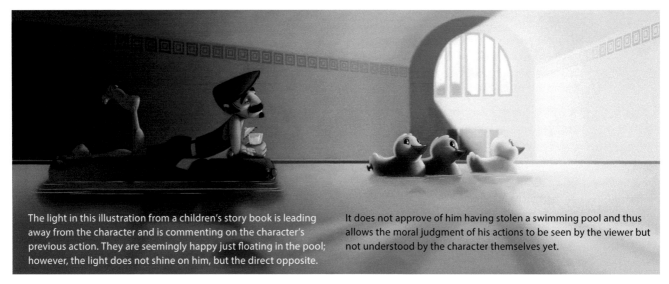

The light in this illustration from a children's story book is leading away from the character and is commenting on the character's previous action. They are seemingly happy just floating in the pool; however, the light does not shine on him, but the direct opposite. It does not approve of him having stolen a swimming pool and thus allows the moral judgment of his actions to be seen by the viewer but not understood by the character themselves yet.

Figure 26.13

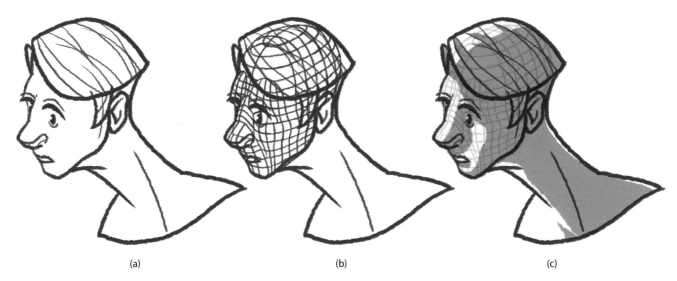

(a)   (b)   (c)

Figure 26.14

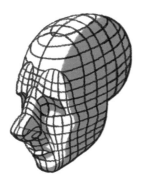

Figure 26.15

An excellent book on realistic shadows and rendering is Scott Robertson and Thomas Bertling's (2014) *How to Render, the Fundamentals of Light, Shadow and Reflectivity*. The book goes into extraordinary depths of the matter and explains how realistic light and shadow can be constructed.

There is also the more free approach of constructing shadows, which is less accurate but quicker and serves the purpose in character design. It is approximating the shadow and allowing it to be adjusted to the artistic needs of the story.

Painting or drawing a final character presentation piece nonetheless is in need of the shadows being accurately constructed with their form-defining qualities.

Figure 26.14a through c and Figure 26.15 show how form is crucial in developing a believable shadow. Without form and the knowledge of where the light hits the surface, the shadow will probably not convince. Be careful to not allow the fear of being "accurate" control the creative process. It is very easy to forget what the shadow needs to feel like and only focus on what is realistically correct. Light and shadows are tools and storytelling elements, not just aspects that render an image more realistically.

Direct and indirect illumination

Direct illumination lights objects and the environment from one light source: the light hits the object and lights it up. Indirect illumination does the same with one light source, though it adds the reflection of the bouncing light of other objects. This adds tremendously to the photorealistic effect of an image. Every lit object, either reflective or not, bounces light back into its environment, which then lights up other objects. The color properties of the lit object are affecting the colors of the object next to it. Indirect illumination is usually called "global illumination" in CG animation. The further the indirect illumination is pushed, the more the image is shifted toward hyperrealism.

Global illumination and reflected colors

It is not just the light that is reflected from objects onto other objects, but also the color of the object itself. As there are often countless objects in a room/environment the reflection becomes rather complex and has to be dealt with in each medium differently. In CG, global illumination is an effect that can be achieved. In a painted background global illumination has to be chosen sporadically in order to not overwhelm the eye with details or the painter with too much complexity. Defined reflections of specific objects can heighten the image's believability and add to its realism or its sense of design. The goal is not to depict the veridical but choose what is important and what can be omitted. This allows the artist to control the image and not be controlled by it.

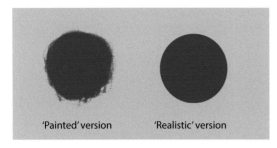

'Painted' version   'Realistic' version

Figure 26.16

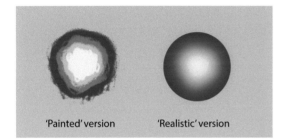

'Painted' version   'Realistic' version

Figure 26.17

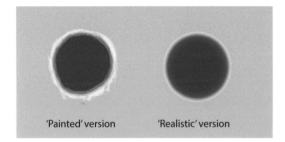

'Painted' version   'Realistic' version

Figure 26.18

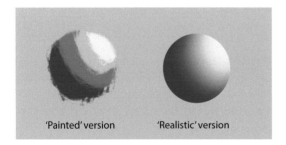

'Painted' version   'Realistic' version

Figure 26.19

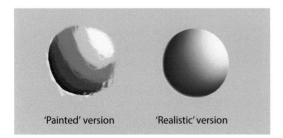

'Painted' version   'Realistic' version

Figure 26.20

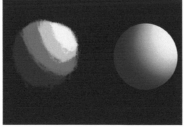

Figure 26.21

Figure 26.22

Light and form

There is no light defining the object (left painted, right airbrushed). Volume is nonexistent. One cannot say if the object is three-dimensional or not. Shape dominates the object, which has no connection to any surface (Figure 26.16).

The light hitting the object from the front gives it definition and form, though the circle on the left is due to the lack of gradient still a bit flat (this does not mean that a light situation painted with fewer brush strokes and rendered less accurately is less convincing). The light hitting the object from the front renders it still somehow flat. More perspective is achieved if the light hits from an angle (Figure 26.17).

The light hits the object from the back, and the area in the middle is dark, as the light is behind the object. This creates a rim light that accentuates the silhouette.

The silhouette is wider the further away the light source is. The closer the object is to the light source, the less rim light is there (Figure 26.18).

The light hits from top right, there is no reflective light in the dark area, and the object reads very well in its form and three-dimensionality (Figure 26.19).

Figure 26.20: There is some reflective light on the lower left, defining the form in the darker area. Light passes the object, hits a surface behind the object, gets reflected, and illuminates the back side of the object slightly. This is very helpful if the shadow area of the object is blending into the background (Figure 26.21). A reflective light then helps to separate the dark areas and give the object back its form (Figure 26.22).

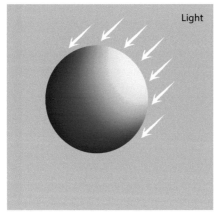

Figure 26.23

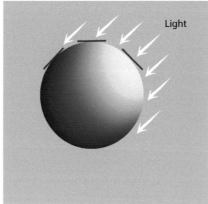

Figure 26.24

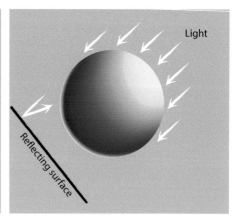

Figure 26.25

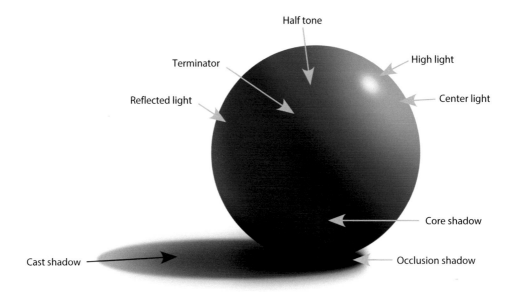

Figure 26.26

A short visual explanation of how light creates the gradient on the object. In Figure 26.23, light hits the object's curved surface in parallel lines. In Figure 26.24, the more perpendicular the light hits the surface, the more light illuminates that specific part of the object (as more rays of light are actually hitting the object).

Once the light is parallel to the surface, no light will hit the object and the rays will just pass the surface without affecting it. In Figure 26.25, light that passes the object and hits a reflective surface will bounce and illuminate the back of the object creating a subtle rim light.

More on light and shadow:

Robertson S, Bertling T. (2014). *How to Render: The Fundamentals of Light, Shadow and Reflectivity.* Culver City, CA: Design Studio Press.
Hogarth B. (1981). *Dynamic Light and Shade.* New York: Watson-Guptill Publications.

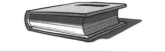

Vectors and Directions

certain strength. The tension affects the overall flow toward the focal point. It can easily guide or allow the eye to rest briefly on its path toward the visual goal.

For character design, vectors are of crucial importance in giving the poses an overall structure and improving the readability (Figure 27.1). Any part of the body or clothing can be used to enhance the general flow in the pose and to exactly plan out where the eye of the viewer should rest or where to move onto the next visual goal. Everything in the character's pose needs to follow one path, which is, like always, the interpretation of the portrayed story point.

Types of vectors

Index vectors:
Index vectors are lines that are clearly
going in one direction, defining with them not just a connection between two parts but also giving them a clear direction.

Graphic vectors:
Those vectors do not have a direction, but only suggest a path that can be
followed either left or right. That path is a line or shapes, colors, textures ... that the eye follows one by one.

Continuing vectors:
One vector follows another and creates a
chain of vectors that lead into one direction. Continuing vectors are the ones where the eye moves along a path, clearly going from one point to the next.

Converging vectors:
Two or more vectors go toward each other and create tension.

Diverging vectors:
Two or more vectors go away from each other. These vectors can, for example, show a strong aversion in the pose. If the character holds the glass of wine (Figure 27.2), but rejects it and looks the other way, the diverging vectors would accentuate this dislike.

Figure 27.1

A pose has one purpose—to express nonverbally through the character's body their emotional state and the story point. Both need to go into the same artistic direction and express the same intellectual thought. For the pose to be understood more easily, the various body parts, clothing, and also props need to work in unison to make the action and the thoughts unmistakably clear and create a path for the eye to be moving along, exploring the pose easily, step by step. The direction of a pose is simply where the character's focus goes toward and where all the vectors lead. Directions deal with the entire pose, whereas vectors are visual guides within that pose; they are forces imbedded into the character that guide the eye toward the center of attraction. This visual destination can either be located inside the frame or outside. Vectors are lines, clusters of lines, shapes, forms, colors, textures, etc., representing a force that leads to this visual goal, thus enabling an easy viewing experience. Those forces are defined by three agents: direction, magnitude, and tension.

- *Direction:* The direction of a vector is usually toward the focal point or various vectors will ultimately end up in the focal point.
- *Magnitude:* The strength and intensity of the vector's force.
- *Tension:* The vector itself can be simplified as a line and the tension within that line is what gives the vector a

DOI: 10.1201/b22147-27

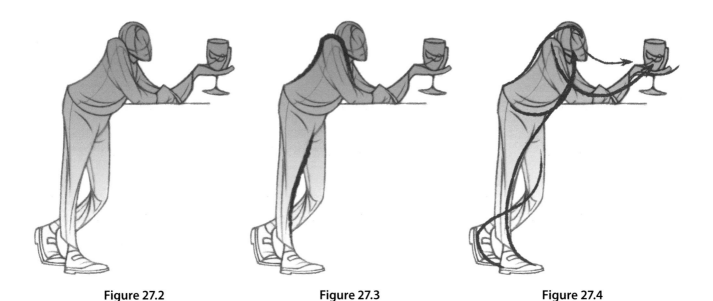

| Figure 27.2 | Figure 27.3 | Figure 27.4 |

Motion vector: The motion vector is suggesting movement, either by mimicking actual movement (speed lines, speed blur) or by having a character just walk or run. The movement is obviously only hinted at in a still image, not seen as actual motion.

The character in Figure 27.2 holds a glass of wine and looks at it. The pose itself is very subtle; however, it has very strong vectors to enhance the action. First, it needs to be understood where the character's tension is in the body and how the body carries its own weight in that very pose. The tension is in the engaged leg that flows upward into the face. Then, there is tension in the lower back flowing upward and down into the upper arm. This tension in leg and upper body affects the flow of the fabric and with it its folds (Figure 27.3). Those have to be also considered as possible and very often strong vectors for emphasizing the focal point which is the glass of wine. In Figure 27.4, the major vectors that guide the eye on its path through the pose are highlighted. They all travel through the face and from there flow toward the glass. The details of pose and fabric can also be designed with the vectors and the flow of the pose in mind. For example, the right leg's hemline is tilting downward to the right, which accentuates the flow of the pants clinging on the shin, going toward the shoe, and flowing into the ground also leading visually to the left shoe, connecting left and right. The hair of the man is falling to the left and not to the right of the face as it would interrupt the connection of eyes and glass. Additionally, the flow of the hair on the left of the face also goes along with the long curve of the upper body: everything connects!

Diverging and continuing vectors

Diverging vectors compete against each other and lead the eye in two different directions. The old man (Figure 27.5) holding up a sign has a pose direction toward the right, so the index and graphic vectors are facing right, but the strong index vector in

form of the sign with the arrow points toward the left. Which vector has more magnitude? The pose gives a rather strong statement and the mind cannot stop wondering what the sign to the left indicates. In the pose in Figure 27.6a and b, the character is holding a billiard cue and is looking onto the ground toward

Figure 27.5

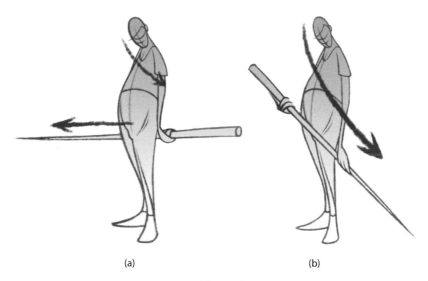

(a)   (b)

Figure 27.6

the right. In Figure 27.6a, the two vectors of cue and face are contradicting each other and flow into different directions, whereas in (b) the directions are both the same. Therefore, (b) is stronger in its overall index vector's magnitude than (a) and the direction is clearly going toward the right. All elements in the pose speak the same directional language. However, the question is: what is the story point? What emotion needs to be expressed? Only because the technical aspects of the pose in terms of its vectors are stronger in (b) doesn't necessarily make it the better pose. Pose (a) feels more rested as the character seems

to think about the next move without having the cue readily at hand. Pose (b) has the character more or less already lifting the cue to play the game and it also feels slightly more aggressive as the cue can easily be used to stab. Because story is always key, it depends, if you interpret the pose, what story the viewer puts into the pose. What happened in Figure 27.6a and b before this very moment and what will happen afterward? Every viewer will have a slightly different story to tell on what kind of character this is and what they are doing. Vectors can help to shape the story; they are not always just simply technical forces.

Even a simple little addition like the socks in Figure 27.7 being lower on the right than the left helps to create a graphic vector that leads smoothly up into the face going along significant points in the design. The socks being on the same level in Figure 27.8, however, lack this upward drift in the lower part of the pose, and thus, the graphic vector is slightly weaker in its magnitude. This is seemingly just a miniscule addition that has little impact on the overall character but there are obviously myriads of examples like this in one pose and together they improve the readability.

Figure 27.7   Figure 27.8

More on vectors and directions:

Zettl H. (2008). *Sight Sound Motion Applied Media Aesthetics.* Belmont, CA: Thomson Wadsworth.

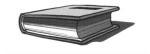

Facial Expressions

The study of facial expressions was always a topic for artists, interpreting in their work the emotions of the characters they portrayed. Emotions were simplified and reduced to one moment for the audience to understand the emotional state the characters were finding themselves in. One of the first examinations on expressions and emotions in art was executed by French Baroque painter Charles Le Brun (1619–1690) in his theoretical work, published posthumously as *Methode pour apprendre a dessiner les passions*. He categorized various emotional states in a simplified manner, creating a library of emotions artists could fall back on in their paintings in order to tell emotionally convincing stories (Figure 28.1). Le Brun's theoretical works had a significant impact on art theory throughout the next centuries. The simplified expressions he depicted in drawings and scientific illustrations greatly influenced artists and art theorists. Nevertheless, more scientific depth was needed once the psychological complexities of the characters on the canvases deepened. Charles Darwin took a deeper scientific approach in his book *The Expression of the Emotions in Man and Animals* (1872) in which he explored facial expressions not through an artistic eye in drawings like Le Brun but with photography and the comparison of expressions between humans. It was based on thorough scientific research and was one of the first widely published steps into the complex system of trying to understand human facial expressions. Recent scientific methods for studying the complexity of facial expressions has advanced in technology and methodology and therefore give a much deeper and accurate account of the type of emotion that results in a specific facial expression in not only the clearly visible muscles causing it but also micromuscle movement that is barely seen with the eye. Since Darwin there have been plenty of studies and approaches over the last 150 years from various scientific disciplines dealing with the topic of emotions and expressions, which shows the growing complexity of the topic itself. There is the already mentioned artistic and art theoretical treatise of Charles Le Brun, the evolutionary approach initiated by Charles Darwin, a psychophysiological one by William James, a neurological one by Walter Cannon, and the psychodynamic tradition by Sigmund Freud. Additionally, there is a cognitive perspective and the most recent neurobiological studies.[1] It is obviously a rather wide field.

Adding to the complexity is the fact that facial expressions are not always clear and obvious in their meaning as they sometimes do *not* show the true emotion felt at that very moment, but an emotion that covers up or tries to cover the one that is experienced. People hide important emotions to deliberately deceive the one they are communicating with. Emotions are extraordinarily complex systems of past happenings, present situations, and aspirations or goals. They are intertwined with beliefs and socialization, with culture and social standing. No two people react to the same situation equally and two people that experience the same emotion do not necessarily have the same facial expression. Neither does one in a similar situation at a different stage in their life react again in the same way. Then, there are people that are

Figure 28.1

Charles Le Brun (1619–1690): *Anger* (Courtesy of Wikimedia Commons).

---

[1] Plutchik R. (2001). The nature of emotions. *American Scientist*. 89(4) (July/August): 344–350.

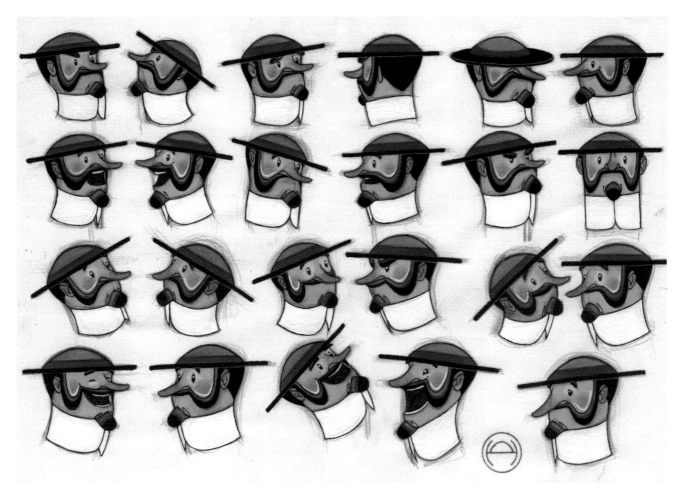

Figure 28.2

extroverted and thus show their emotions more clearly than people that are introverted and where emotions are not easily readable. What makes emotions even more complex is the fact that people do not always understand their own emotions and cannot clearly say if they are happy or sad, if a situation is relaxing or not. Emotions can also be fighting and contradicting each other at the very same moment. For instance, smiles do not just express the happiness of a person, but can have many other meanings like a greeting, embarrassment, agreement, or even disagreement. A smile might look different if someone wins a million dollars in their own living room by checking the winning numbers on their lottery ticket compared to someone that wins one million dollars on a TV show seen by millions of people. The surroundings and the situation always affect the emotions and with it the facial expressions, as the person in public deals not only with themselves but with the effect the social setting has on them, knowing they are being scrutinized. One might burst into tears when happy, whereas someone else might be stoic in their expression, not showing any sign of happiness in their face at all; it all goes back to the character's personality and their emotional baggage; present emotional state, wishes and aspirations; the entire social setting; and the

cultural background. It is a cacophony of emotions that fight for dominance. This somewhat difficult system of emotions is rather nicely interpreted in Pixar's feature *Inside Out* (2015) in which the emotional foundation is simplified into five core emotions of joy, anger, fear, sadness, and disgust represented by little characters living in baby girl Riley's mind. Sadness is portrayed in the first half of the film as a rather negative emotion that can be dangerous in her tendency toward apathy and depression and through it, slowing the brain system down. However, throughout Riley's development it becomes apparent that sadness is also having positive powers of, on the one hand, creating memories of nostalgia and, on the other hand, being the emotion that is assisting in the creation of empathy toward others. All emotions in the film develop throughout childhood from simple emotions as a toddler into systems where emotions work together to create subtle shades of ever-growing complexities later in Riley's life.

Approaches

There are two different scientific schools when it comes to facial expression studies: one that believes that facial

Figure 28.3

expressions are universal and not related to cultural influences (starting with Darwin's book and still subscribed to by psychologist Paul Ekman) and one that opines that facial expressions are not universal and that culture has an influence on how we naturally react in our faces (anthropologist Ray Birdwhistell). It is clear that every culture has its specifics in body language and the way people carry themselves. But are facial expressions learned or are they universal, meaning a general human trait detached from socialization or background?

Much of what we see in facial expressions in animation, film, or comics is a learned visual cliché rather than a scientifically accurate representation of the actual expression. Also, using feature films for learning about expressions and emotions is only giving one a section of the actual expression as acting is not realism, even if it is coming very close to realism it is still an artistic interpretation of reality. Therefore, the study of actors' emotional expressions in feature films can only

approximate to the complexity of real facial expressions, which are a small part of the entire emotional range the human face is capable of. Most of the expressed emotion is articulated through not only the face, but the whole body with shoulder position, arms and hands, legs, etc., it is by no means just the face that is responsible for articulating an emotional state.

Voluntary and involuntary facial expressions are the two different types that affect the reading and understanding of a person's emotional state. Voluntary facial expressions can be controlled, whereas involuntary ones cannot and happen subconsciously. Those include miniscule muscle movements in the face showing the "true" emotion. For example, the Duchenne smile (from Duchenne du Boulogne 1806–1875, a French neurologist) is a smile that involves mouth and eyes. There are wrinkles on the sides of the eyes that make the Duchenne smile a "true" smile. If someone has a fake smile that is not honestly felt by the sender, then the eyes are not as

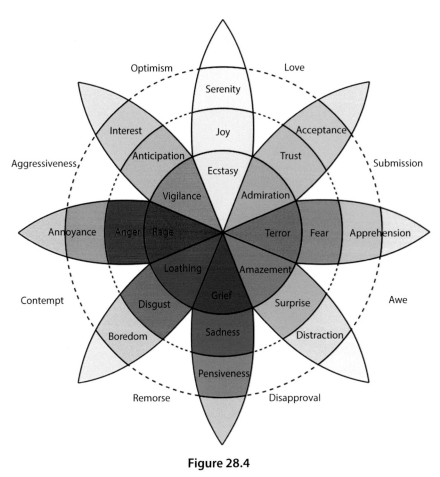

Figure 28.4

Pluchnik's Wheel of Emotions (Courtesy of Wikimedia Commons).

involved in the expression, but stay neutral, which causes the smile to be detected as fake by the receiver.

Facial expressions are obviously based on emotions and those go far beyond happy, sad, angry, jealous, fearful, or surprised. To visualize human emotions, psychologist Robert Plutchik's emotional wheel[2] suggests four bipolar emotional pairs that are arranged on a color wheel across from each other (Figure 28.4). The following eight emotions: are the basic or primary emotions rage, vigilance, ecstasy, admiration, terror, amazement, grief, and loathing. The emotions that oppose each other the most are like complimentary colors, set in the emotional wheel across from each other. Those eight can be mixed with other emotions. For example, joy and trust produce love. Sadness and disgust produce remorse. Emotions are not always perfectly clean cut, but are a mix of different feelings that might even contradict each other. To convey those rather delicate differences requires a sophisticated character that is emotionally able to not only feel those complex emotions but also reveal them in their pose, and

actions and reactions. A character that is animated via figurative acting doesn't have the nuanced emotional foundation in their personality to express subtlety in their emotions, whereas the character that is animated through embodied acting is more sophisticated in their personality and thus can show emotional complexity in their expressions. As a result, the depth of the emotion goes hand in hand with the degree to which the character's personality has been defined and the emotional range the character is able to experience. Simple characters for a very young audience should always only show simple emotions for the kids to understand what the emotions actually are. Emotional complexity in programs for a very young audience is inappropriate and cannot be understood. The more complex the story, the more sophisticated the emotional range can be.

Understanding of emotions

The very point of the visualized emotion in the character is for it to be easily understood. Emotions that cannot be read by the viewer are rather pointless and neither support the character's personality nor the story. It is not enough to just show the

---

2   There are obviously many other visualizations of emotions, but Plutchik's is a rather visually logical one.

emotion in the face, but the entire body has to underline in its pose what the character feels. The shoulders, for instance, are very important in supporting the face's actions. If tense or relaxed, pulled up, or hanging loosely, shoulders accentuate the face. Face and body can, however, contradict each other. For instance, in a person that shows affection while hugging someone, the face can articulate dislike. Nevertheless, the contrary facial representation of dislike is usually rather subtle. Emotions that are expressed totally over the top also often come across as fake and tend to not convince in realistic characters.

When it comes to animation, the aspect of time is added and emotions can develop instead of the drawing or illustration, where only the key emotion can be visualized to explain the story point. As humans usually don't go from one emotional state quickly into another but emotions come and go in waves and evolve, the time needs to be given in a feature, scene, or even shot for the character to develop believable emotions and not snippets of a quickly changing mental state here and there. We quickly detect people in day-to-day life situations that are not truthfully showing their emotions and we also can see if the emotions portrayed in an animated film are believable or not. Therefore, give the characters time to evolve, and allow them to grow!

A very interesting artist that dealt with the extremes of facial expressions is Franz Xaver Messerschmidt (1736–1783), a German–Austrian sculptor that dedicated the last years of his life to a very personal project called Charakterköpfe/Character heads (Figures 28.5 and 28.6). The heads show distorted faces that include a whole range of feelings or expressions that are not always clearly decipherable, but often leave the viewer confused; they do not relate to an easily understandable emotional state as Charles Le Brun had described, but seem to explore the emotional states of the face that are in-between or far beyond the core emotions and pushed the sane human mind into unknown territory. The pieces are utterly hypnotic and intoxicating in their strangeness. "If we can't read the mind through the face, we often think the mind itself must be damaged."[3] Messerschmidt's heads do exactly the opposite of what late Baroque sculpture tried to achieve in terms of clear storytelling, and he can be seen as a vanguard of modern art sensibility. His work that seemingly dives into the incomprehensibility of the human expression underlines the fascination we have with the face and its ability to also hide information. Animation could be the perfect medium in creating characters that do the opposite of being easily understood, but playing with the utter discomfort of the audience by acting unintelligibly. Characters like Cheese in *Forster's Home for Imaginary Friends* celebrate this insanity where the character's personality seems to live on another planet far away from the

Figure 28.5

Franz Xaver Messerschmidt Emotions X (Courtesy of Wikimedia Commons).

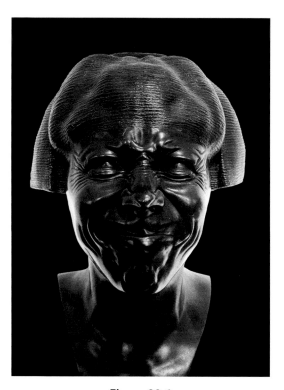

Figure 28.6

Franz Xaver Messerschmidt Emotions III (Courtesy of Wikimedia Commons).

---

[3] Yonan M. (2009). The man behind the mask. Looking at Franz Xaver Messerschmidt. *Eighteenth-Century Studies.* 42(3): 431–451.

sane grasp. Those characters make us very uneasy yet constantly trigger our interest and fascination exactly because we do not understand them.

Design of the facial expression

Facial expressions need to be designed and styled to give the character a personalized expression and also to use composition for the reading direction and aesthetics of the face. In this stage, don't just use the typical mouth shapes or facial expressions that are standard to show emotions. Be unique and use the character's specific facial attributes to design individuality and uniqueness. Every character should express emotions in their own particular way to further strengthen the personality. What is the point of designing a unique character when his expressions are bland and empty, and just show clichés of happy, sad, or angry? The human face has so many ways of visualizing the mental state; there is no other face in nature that comes even close to its capabilities and subtleties. Especially the eyes are a very important carrier of communication through which complex emotions can be transmitted. Though the face is the center for the emotion, the pose reflects the face's expression and interprets with the rest of the body what the psyche feels. Like a stage actor who uses their whole body to express the necessary emotion needed to be seen and understood by the audience member on the last seat, we can use the whole body of the character to express and clarify the emotion much further. We are not dealing with separate parts in a body, like face, hands, torso. They are not separate entities, but connected and complement each other to create the full pose. Subtleties in the face can be underlined through the hands and the shoulder movement, the turn of the face and a slight tilt of the head might strengthen the readability through a well-designed composition. There is an innumerable amount of possibilities that can be

played with to get the right expression. The body is an intricate system in which every part is connected to create a whole.

Facial design possibilities

For the expression to be understood, there is the technical side of facial expressions, very similar to the technical aspects of the body pose. Examples in Figure 28.7a through d show some of the possibilities for a relationship between the facial parts and how they interact with each other, and how the different lines of the face can be used as vectors guiding the eye of the viewer into the needed direction or as design elements to create balance. In example (a), the mouth and eyebrows tilt upward to the right, and the cap, therefore, is pointing toward the opposite side to balance the strong direction given by mouth and brows. Example (b) opens up the expression toward the left, and mouth and eyebrows create an oval movement which is open to the left. In examples (c) and (d), brows, mouth, and cap are going toward the same direction, and thus, the expression in its composition is rather plain, which goes well with the emotion in the character.

The construction of the facial vertical and horizontals

Like the pose itself can have various levels of technical and artistic complexity, the face can also either interpret emotions in an easily graspable or in a rather complex way where the interaction of the different facial parts become an aesthetic design challenge. There are two ways of approaching the facial arrangement: in the first example (Figure 28.8a), the entire head is not changing shape or exposed to squash and stretch, only the facial parts themselves move and shift (Figure 28.9a and d);

(a)	(b)	(c)	(d)

Figure 28.7

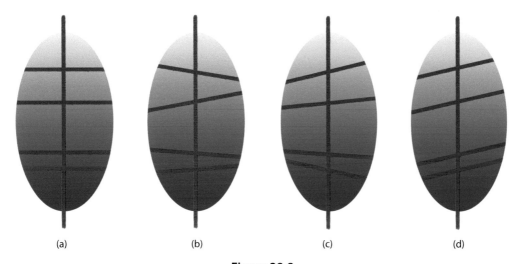

Figure 28.8

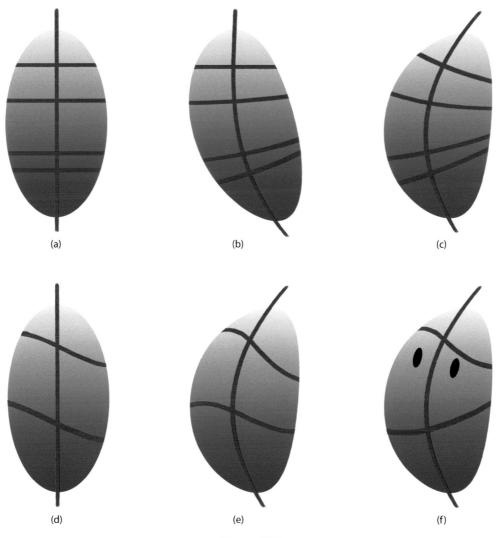

Figure 28.9

the second one affects the head's shape/form as a whole due to squash and stretch, which means that the facial movement affects the head shape (Figure 28.9b and c, e and f).

The face itself can be divided into several horizontal lines besides being bilateral symmetrical through its vertical middle line (Figure 28.8a). These horizontal lines represent mouth, nose, eyes, and eyebrows or anything else that is required. As we have seen so often before, an action always results in a reaction. One part of the face that moves has an effect on the rest of the face. A smile, for instance, pushes up the cheeks and puts slight pressure on the lower lids (Figure 28.10). Likewise, any other action in the face will have an effect on the rest of the expression. No part moves without making something else shift if ever so slightly. Animation deals with exaggeration, so the facial expressions can be pushed to the extreme, which in turn has a stronger reaction from the rest of the face.

There are various options that are important to consider when designing the facial expression and that is the relationship between the mentioned facial horizontals. They can be parallel (Figure 28.8a and d) or independent from each other (Figure 28.8b and c). Figure 28.8a seems rather plain, compositionally. There isn't any tension in the face because everything is even and geometric. Usually, this is visually uninspired. In Figure 28.8b, the upper and lower horizontal couples act against each other which makes the face already more interesting. However, this wouldn't really work in the lower part of the face as the nose is always reacting to the position of the mouth and thus always moves along the main shift of the mouth (Figure 28.10). The upper horizontal couple in (b) can work when the eyebrows are down and the cheeks push up the right eyebrow. In Figure 28.8c, all the horizontals taper more or less toward one point positioned outside of the face on the left, giving the entire face a clean arrangement, whereas in Figure 28.8b the overall feel is slightly disorganized. There is no rule how to use those horizontals as

it really depends on the emotion, personality, and the overall physical action in the face. Nevertheless, despite exaggeration and cartooniness, the design still has to follow somehow the physical laws of the face. In Figure 28.8d, all horizontals are parallel which also has the tendency to be too even, lacking tension.

Not only can we push the various individual parts in the face, but we can bend and thus squash and stretch the entire head depending on the animation style (Figure 28.9b and c); in Figure 28.9b only the lower half of the head is bending which could be the jaw but also the shape of the lower head; in Figure 28.9c, it's the entire head that is bending. When the face bends left or right, it is exposed to squash and stretch which in turn again affects the horizontals (Figure 28.9b and c). They can be seen as being attached perpendicular to the vertical central line. If that vertical line bends, the attached horizontals will move accordingly. Figures 28.8c and 28.9c though have one aspect in common: they open up the facial expression to one side. This can be used for the overall composition of the pose and improve the readability and the direction of the pose. One needs to feel the horizontals and verticals and their connection with each other. A facial expression that is ordered and clear, and that follows a compositional concept is easier to read compared to an arrangement that is busy and unclear.

To further refine the facial expression, the tilted horizontals can be bent and curved themselves in order to bring more movement into the face as Figure 28.9e and f demonstrates. In Figure 28.9d, the bend looks a bit plain, because of the verticals being parallel to each other, whereas in Figure 28.9e and f it shows dynamism and an interesting arrangement.

Opening up the facial expression

The composition of the facial expression and its direction toward the focal point or away from it can be supported by any of the features in the face and also hair, headgear, or clothing. They are all part of the compositional arrangement to push the eye of the viewer in the intended direction and thus make the strongest connection between character and focal point. The character in Figure 28.13 is looking over the shoulder toward something/someone. The red lines show which elements in the character's design are used to accentuate the direction toward the right. The lines open up the face toward the right as all the important lines create a flow toward the focal point. The viewer's eye is literally forced to the right. It is very difficult for the eye to actually go against it and scan the image toward the left as there are so many vectors whose magnitude prohibit it. Figures 28.11 and 28.12 show how the facial horizontals and verticals are squashed and stretched in a more abstract way in order to accentuate the intended direction.

Which element in the face is used for this combination of vector forces is up to the sensibility of the artist, and rules should not be established.

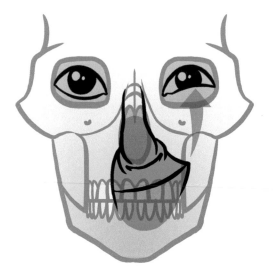

Figure 28.10

Playing with shapes and exploring expressions

Especially when it comes to facial expressions, it is not only great fun, but also of help to explore the character's expressions by not just repeating clichés but letting the character develop their own facial expression. Playing with shapes and allowing mistakes and chance assist the exploration (images 28.2 and 28.3), one will "find" expressions that one would not have thought of without the surprising happenings on the page. A playful approach brings one closer to the character and steers one (hopefully) away from the repetitious cliché.

Sometimes one needs to make conscious mistakes to see if the outcome still works or not. Only then can true learning occur!

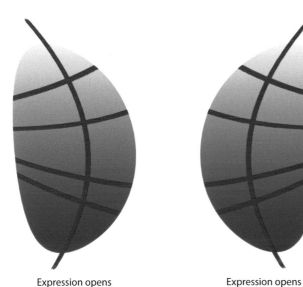

Expression opens up to the right	Expression opens up to the left
Figure 28.11	**Figure 28.12**

Expressions and shapes happen on the page and the emotion is attached throughout the drawing process. The shapes therefore determine the direction of the emotion, not the other way around. This is an exercise of shape that leads to emotion. It is exciting to draw shapes and trying to figure out which expression they could contain and then pushing them further.

Following examples of facial expressions that express the simple emotions of happy, jealous, angry, suspicious ... helps to get started with a kind of cliché (I mean this term now in a good way) on which you can build and expand. Just sticking with a cliché emotion however does not help to be creative and find a unique and personal expression for that one character. So, sit in front of a mirror and explore your own face and study what all the different features do and how they move and interact with each other. The basic cliché of an expression is a rather simple display of emoticon-like qualities that aren't very complex (Figure 28.14). The "symbols" for a variety of emotions are just that: symbols, they lack personality and artistry. Find expressions by exploring them, finding them, and stumbling across combinations of shapes that suggest a probably weird expression, but it might open up a new path or direction for the character. Avoid copying and stay away from repeating the same expression over and over. We have seen already too many angry Orks and overly aggressive bodybuilders with swords ...

Impact of the skull on facial expressions

When it comes to moving the facial elements, one needs to keep in mind what parts of the face are actually moving and what parts don't (nevertheless, the possibility of a very cartoony style does reduce the impact of the skull on the facial expression, but doesn't eliminate it). The skin shifts slightly on the skull, but some parts are able to move much more than others.

Figure 28.13

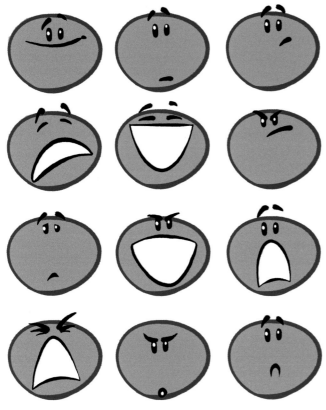

Figure 28.14

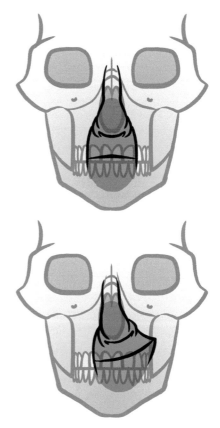

Figure 28.15

Figure 28.15 shows, for example, the mouth and its ability to shift in its entirety, but the nose can only shift in its lower part, not its upper bony ridge which is part of the skull. What one wants to move or squash and stretch is completely up to the artist, but it is important to keep in mind if semirealism/realism is the direction to then consider the skull's impact on the facial expression. The elements that do not move are (Figure 28.16):

* Bony ridge of the nose
* Eyeball sockets (the eyes themselves are not shifting in their position because they are solidly placed within the skull)
* Teeth (they obviously move with the jaw)
* Everything else in the facial mask does move a lot! However, in a cartoony style even the eyes can shift and the nose can do whatever is still convincing and aesthetically pleasing. A cartoony style more or less allows everything. It is however very helpful to know what is prone to movement and what is not.

Figure 28.16

The tilt also provides further movement and direction, and can add subtlety to the emotion and the overall reading direction of the head and pose (Figure 28.17).

Facial expression and tilt

The tilt of the head creates additional three-dimensionality for the architecture of the skull. With a tilt it is much easier to understand the skull as an object with a complex form instead of a flat, two-dimensional piece as it appears in a front or side view.

Mouth

What makes the mouth tricky to draw is the tendency to want to be anatomically accurate from the beginning, instead of playing with shapes and letting creativity take over rather than realism.

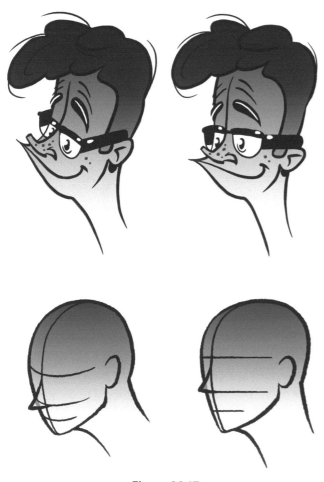

Figure 28.17

If one does not see the mouth as a complex structure with the complex opening and the row of teeth (especially in perspective) that have dimensionality and depth but as a simple two-dimensional shape, it is much easier to draw and design the shape as the basis for the mouth (Figure 28.19). The flatness of the two-dimensional shape makes the exploration much easier and the complexity of depth and perspective can be added after the mouth's shape is found. Often, the mouth's opening direction is already suggested by the overall pose and flow of the character's face and entire body. Explore its shape first and find a solution for it before you get into the perspective and refinement. Additionally, do play with the aesthetic and decorative possibilities and the variation in every single part of the mouth (Figure 28.18). It is exciting how much the mouth as a shape can be pushed, squashed, and stretched in order to find new and interesting ways to interpret the expression. What is often important is finding a pleasant shape that comes without symmetry to avoid an inorganic and rigid feel (if the inorganic feel is not the whole point of the design, of course). When refining the mouth, don't eliminate the organic flow of the initial shape; only add the perspective, don't change the

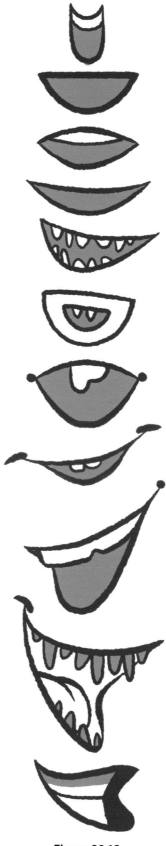

Figure 28.18

Figure 28.19

shape when refining. All additions need to be subordinate to the shape's importance.

The mouth's movement is heavily affecting all other parts of the facial mask as it pushes against the cheeks, the chin, and the nose: action again leads to reaction. The mouth's flexibility and ability to change its shape makes it one of the most flexible parts in the human body and animation most definitely has given it the exaggeration it so often deserves. The mouth is rather wide open to exploration of its shape and its graphic possibilities.

There are many animated films that deal with facial expressions in a different way than just going down the realistic or cartoony path, but develop a design that is unique without sacrificing the clarity of the expression. Richard Williams' film *The Cobbler and the Thief*'s main character Tack does not have a mouth, but only tilting nails that give the mimicked mouth shape very interesting emotions. Him being a cobbler, the nails make perfect sense, give you the shape that conveys his emotion, and, additionally, add uniqueness to the character in a way that hasn't been seen before.

Eyes

Like the mouth has endless options of being interpreted, the eyes also have graphic possibilities that are vast and can add to the personality of the character. Even the weirdest design often allows a good range of expressions and can make the character graphically more interesting (Figure 28.20). A character with button eyes is not necessarily emotionally less expressive than one with the typical Disney/Pixar eyes. The boy in the Brazilian animated feature *Boy and the*

World (2013) has only button eyes and nothing else in the entire face. It is just a round head with two black ovals and throughout the entire feature there is never one moment where the emotions are not clear and expressive. Eyes are the center of emotions; however, the pose, story, and overall mood in the film are also very important carriers of emotions and are all there to support the easy understandability of the expressiveness of the eyes.

Squash and stretch of eyes

Well-observed cartoony eyes aren't much different from realistic eyes only that they lack details and realistic shapes. If both squash and stretch are involved, in the cartoony design it is exaggeration that clarifies the emotion. To have more control over the shapes when drawing eyes there are various points one can pay attention to:

- Emotion
- Viewing direction
- Eyebrow position
- Cheek position
- Level of exaggeration

Because the eyes are predominantly the points of the character the viewer pays most attention to, care should be taken when the eyes are drawn and designed.

The eyes are in-between the brows and cheeks, both of which affect the shape of the eyes by putting either pressure on them or pulling the lids up and down depending on the emotion involved (Figure 28.21). The cheek is pushed up because of a smile, the lower lid is also pushed upward. If one sees the eyes as rubber balls attached to two plates that push or pull on the balls

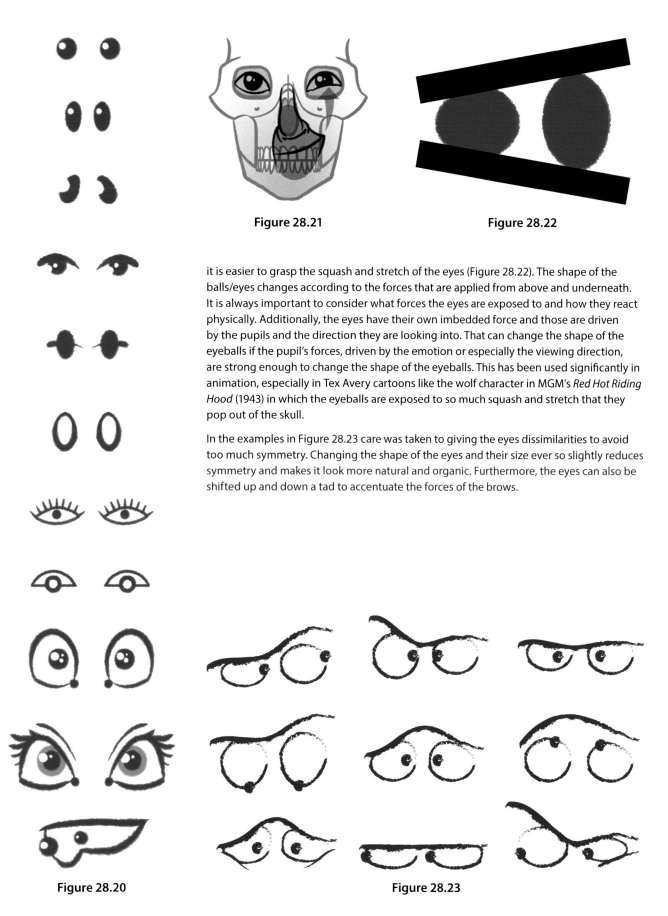

Figure 28.21

Figure 28.22

it is easier to grasp the squash and stretch of the eyes (Figure 28.22). The shape of the balls/eyes changes according to the forces that are applied from above and underneath. It is always important to consider what forces the eyes are exposed to and how they react physically. Additionally, the eyes have their own imbedded force and those are driven by the pupils and the direction they are looking into. That can change the shape of the eyeballs if the pupil's forces, driven by the emotion or especially the viewing direction, are strong enough to change the shape of the eyeballs. This has been used significantly in animation, especially in Tex Avery cartoons like the wolf character in MGM's *Red Hot Riding Hood* (1943) in which the eyeballs are exposed to so much squash and stretch that they pop out of the skull.

In the examples in Figure 28.23 care was taken to giving the eyes dissimilarities to avoid too much symmetry. Changing the shape of the eyes and their size ever so slightly reduces symmetry and makes it look more natural and organic. Furthermore, the eyes can also be shifted up and down a tad to accentuate the forces of the brows.

Figure 28.20

Figure 28.23

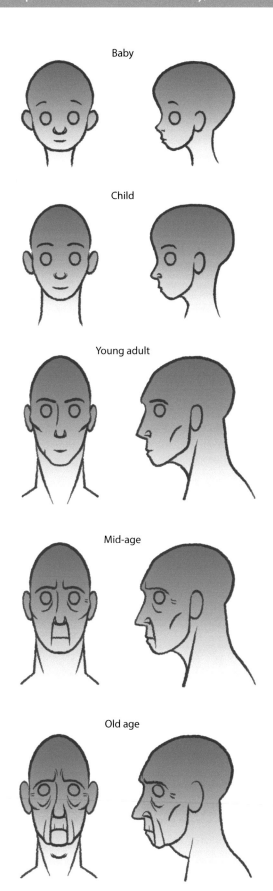

Baby

Child

Young adult

Mid-age

Old age

Figure 28.24

Facial differences in gender

This can obviously only be a crude cliché, but knowing a couple of differences can help to come up with more ideas or be more creative with the characters. There can only be a tendency as all faces are different and have their very own particularities. Do not follow the following information strictly, just use it as a guideline! The following is not race-dependent.

Men

- The overall face is more angular and geometric.
- Jaw and cheeks appear more geometric.
- The brow ridge is more strongly developed and makes the eyes appear deeper set.
- The eyebrows are thicker.
- The eyes are less open (eyelids are closed slightly).
- The nasolabial angle is slightly more obtuse
- The upper lip is less pronounced.
- The nose is slightly longer and wider.

Women

- Features are softer.
- The face is rounder.
- The eyebrows are slightly less prominent.
- The upper lip is more pronounced.
- Eyes are open wider.
- The nose is smaller.

Different age groups

Baby

- The head is larger in proportion to the body and there is a larger cranium.
- The face is shorter.
- Eyes are below the midsection of the skull.
- Overall, the face is much rounder with plumper cheeks and more fat.
- The brow ridge is less pronounced and eyes are bigger.
- The nose is shorter, pointing upward and more stubby.

Child (around 6 years of age)

- Eyes are slightly below the midsection of the skull and face is getting a bit longer.
- The ears are larger.
- The nose is getting slightly longer, but is still small and short, pointing slightly upward.
- The face is still round overall, but cheeks are less plump.
- Eyebrows are more pronounced.

Young Adult (around 24–30 years of age)

- The face is now longer and eyes are at the midsection of the skull.
- Features are pronounced and more angular.
- Muscular structure is more pronounced.

- Even distribution of subcutaneous fat makes features appear smooth.
- Eyes appear smaller and the brow ridge is much more dominant.

Middle age (around 50 years of age)

- There is an overall thinning of the skin.
- The face looks slightly rounder due to skin starting to sag around the chin and jawline.
- Overall loss of subcutaneous fat makes the face look less full.
- Loss of collagen and elastic fibers causes the skin to go downward.
    - Slight sagging at the chin and jawline making the face appear more round and less pronounced; the sagging also starts to develop jowls.
    - Eyebrows tilt slightly and tear bags appear.
- Cartilage in ears and tip of the nose still grow, making those parts appear slightly larger.
- The tip of the nose starts to go down slightly.
- A pronounced nasolabial fold is developing.
- Wrinkles appear around the eyes and neck.
- There is irregular pigmentation and the appearance of small blood vessels.

Old age (about 70 years of age)

- The nasolabial fold is much more pronounced.
- A general sagging of the skin around the mouth drags down the corner of the mouth causing a slight frown in the expression.

- The skin in the cheeks sags inferiorly and results in further development of jowls.
- Folds develop around the neck, causing skin to droop down under the jawline.
- The cheekbones tilt slightly downward as the bones deform which also causes the eye sockets to tilt down on the outside.
- The cartilage of ears and nose still grows and the tip of the nose also goes down.
- A small hump can develop on the back of the nose.
- More wrinkles appear.
- Upper and lower eyelids sag downward.
- The skin of the forehead also sags inferiorly, creating wrinkles and pushing the eyebrows down.
- There is more pronounced irregularity in the pigmentation and more blood vessels appear.
- Age spots appear on the skin.

More on facial expressions:

Faigin G. (2008). *The Artist's Complete Guide to Facial Expression*. New York: Watson-Guptill.

Plutchik R. (July/August 2001). The nature of emotions. *American Scientist* 89(4): 344–350.

Yonan M. (2009). The man behind the mask. Looking at Franz Xaver Messerschmidt. *Eighteenth-Century Studies*, 42(3): 431–451.

CHAPTER 29

Extroverted and Introverted Pose

Introverted or extroverted poses deal with openness or closedness and the resultant energy that flows out of a pose or that is kept within the pose. Aristide Maillol's (1861–1944) sculpture *La Nuit/The Night* (1909) shows the form of a woman depicted in a very clear composition that shows emotional restraint and silence (Figures 29.1 and 29.2). The title *La Nuit* is expressed through the lack of strong movement, but quiet relaxation and inwardly flowing energy. Emotions are limited to the pose as we cannot see her face and only through interpretation rather than the expressive storytelling of the woman can one experience the meaning of the sculpture. Most of the energy from the body is kept within. Every element of the composition tries to keep the energy from leaving the pose (red). There are however some parts, like the feet, that allow energy to be released (blue arrow), but it is not affecting the overall inwardly flowing energy of the pose. This creates a flow in the composition that never leaves the body, but always flows back into the body creating a pose that rests in itself, is calm, and seems to draw the viewer into its very depiction of reflective thoughts, rest, contemplation, and sleep.

Where *La Nuit* is a sculpture whose energy is going inwards and is limited in the occupation of space, the opposite would be to spread out in space and open up into the environment. In this option, the hands are often reaching outwards, opening up, and connecting with the world surrounding it; the energy of the character flows into the negative space. In the Roman sculpture of Emperor Augustus, called *Augustus Prima Porta* dating from the first century AD (Figures 29.3 and 29.4), Augustus, the imperator, is shown in the *adlocutio* pose with raised right arm addressing his troops. The pose speaks of self-confidence, power, and might worthy of the head of an army; he is barefoot, the sign of a hero or even a god. Despite his military strength, his pose still contains subtlety in its movement, like the way the right foot (his left) is slightly bent outward or his right hand holds a consular baton almost casually. Augustus addresses his subjects in front of him in an open and confident pose, quite the opposite of introverted poses, of, for instance, Rodin's *The Thinker*, whose energy, like Maillol's *La Nuit*, also flows back inward. Augustus' index finger being the endpoint of the arm has lots of strength as a vector. It is the culmination of the movement of the whole body: forward.

Figure 29.1

Figure 29.2

Aristide Maillol *La Nuit* (1909) (Courtesy of Wikimedia Commons).

DOI: 10.1201/b22147-29

Figure 29.3   **Figure 29.4**

Augustus Prima Porta (~ 1st century AD) (Courtesy of Wikimedia Commons).

One might see a clash between introverted poses in animation and a well-designed silhouette. In a good and well-designed silhouette, the limbs are supposed to spread out in space, not be in front of the body for easy readability, so an introverted pose in traditional animation is per se a bit more difficult to find. However, Maillol's sculpture has an easy-to-read silhouette and is still introverted. An introverted character does not necessarily have to have introverted poses throughout the character animation; however, they should have one in the character design to express their personality clearly.

Negative and Positive Space

Positive space is the space that the character itself occupies, and negative space is the area around the character (Figures 30.6 and 30.7). Positive and negative space have different purposes, as aids of drawing the characters or their effect on storytelling.

First, positive and negative space help the draftsman to see not only the shapes the character consists of but also the space that surrounds the character. Both need to be seen while drawing. Constantly keeping positive and negative space in mind makes it much easier to fully understand the character's dimensions and how they are imbedded into the spatial environment. One does not only draw the character but also "draws" the negative space by leaving the character out. There is a constant back and forth between positive and negative space and one cannot be without the other. The spaces in-between and around the character are as important as the character themselves. Clarity in the negative space benefits silhouette and legibility.

The contrast between negative space and character is what separates the two. The lighter the negative space is in comparison to the object, the more that object parts from its background and vice versa (Figure 30.1). With little contrast, negative space blends into positive space (Figure 30.1c) and it becomes difficult to separate the two whereas a strong contrast improves the separation (Figure 30.1a).

Positive and negative space live through their contrast to each other. The stronger the contrast, the stronger the silhouette, and the better its legibility. The character in Figure 30.2 cannot be read clearly as the busy background is dragging the attention, there is contrast in shapes, but very little contrast in tone which makes the silhouette disappear. Figure 30.3 has very little emphasis on the background, so the surrounding has the least importance; however, the silhouette of the character is the clearest (there is the greatest contrast in all three images between positive and negative space, but the definition of the background is gone). Figure 30.4 suggests a comfortable

Figure 30.2

Figure 30.3

Figure 30.4

(a)   (b)   (c)

Figure 30.1

DOI: 10.1201/b22147-30

Figure 30.5

Jan Matejko: *The Battle of Grunwald* (1878) (Courtesy of Wikimedia Commons).

in-between where the character is the focus, the background does not drag too much attention, and thus, the silhouette is clear enough. A character is also in need of breathing space surrounding it not just to read well but also to have a comfortable physical space to be in. Too much negative space can make it feel needlessly empty, too little and the character feels claustrophobic. There has to be tension between filled space (character) and empty space (negative space) which of course goes back to the needs of the story. A tension is often needed for compositional reasons to accomplish a dynamism between empty and filled. If both areas are filled, the composition is busy. If both are empty, the image can feel plain. The tension between empty and filled is what accentuates both. The filled area feels more important with an empty area next to it and therefore attracts the eye because it points out its otherness. This concept of the tension between negative and positive space

is crucial for the success of the composition. As mentioned, this obviously depends on the effect one wants to achieve based on the story that is being told. Sometimes it is the very point of the image to have a busy composition and therefore the idea of tension between the two spaces is obsolete, and both negative and positive space are busy. Jan Matejko's painting from 1878 *The Battle of Grunwald* (Figure 30.5) is one example of the composition being so overcrowded that there is literally no negative space other than the clouds on the top of the frame and even they are busy. Everything is extremely vibrant. The characters have no space in-between and feel stacked on top of each other. The composition boils with movement and one can feel the battle going on and the noise and action pouring out of the frame. In this case, the elimination of the negative space and the lack of balance to create contrast between negative and positive is one of the reasons for its success: to depict utmost

Figure 30.6

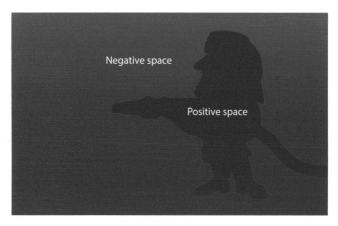

Figure 30.7

Figure 30.8

Caspar David Friedrich (1774–1840): *Der Mönch am Meer/The Monk by the Sea* (1808 or 1810) (Courtesy of Wikimedia Commons).

Figure 30.9

Figure 30.10

action in battle. In stark contrast stands Caspar David Friedrich's (1774–1840) painting *Der Mönch am Meer/The Monk by the Sea* (1808 or 1810) (Figure 30.8). The negative space is empty and leaves so much breathing space that the surroundings are what is important, not the monk. It is the grandeur of the sea, the beach, and the sky that takes the stage and we are in the same position as the monk: feeling small and insignificant. Friedrich silently pushes us to contemplate on nature, existence, and spirituality.

Negative space can also intensify the impact of the story. The negative space between the man and the bottle on a leash (Figure 30.9) is enhanced by the placement of the shadow of the bottle that connects the bottle with the man. The negative space is a slightly curved triangle (Figure 30.10) that continues the movement of the upper body of the old man down to the bottle. Positive and negative space create one shape that leads toward the center of attention: the bottle.

CHAPTER 31

Body Ratio

The body ratio is the division of the human body into head lengths (HL) in order to create an easy system for drawing and designing the body.

Body ratio has or can have various purposes:

- Define the age and height of the character (only in relationship with all the other characters if the design is cartoony or unrealistic)
- Define a style
- Be part of the composition of the pose
- Assist in 2D animation in drawing the character

Define age, height, and style

Figure 31.1 shows how the body ratio can be successfully used in giving variation to a character. The different body ratios not only suggest a different type of character, but also a different age and style. Once the body ratio is established for one character

(of the same species), it should be applied roughly to all the other characters in the character lineup to keep the characters consistent throughout. Each character in the lineup in Figure 31.1 has its own age and height, but that age can be altered if the character is placed next to another character that then pushes the age range further. It is always the range in a lineup that defines the specific determinants of age, height, gender, etc.

Figure 31.2a through d have the same characters in different size relationships (different HL). The character on the left has always the same body-ratio, the character on the right has a smaller head in Figure 31.2a and c, and a slightly bigger head in (b) and (d). In example (a), the bigger character looks like a bigger sized adult next to a shorter adult, whereas in example (b) the bigger one looks like an adult next to a smaller one that now appears to be a younger youth. The head size of the bigger character on the right makes the smaller either look just shorter (a) or shorter and younger (b). Examples (c) and (d) have the same characters, but now the right character is shrunk in size, but still has the

Figure 31.1

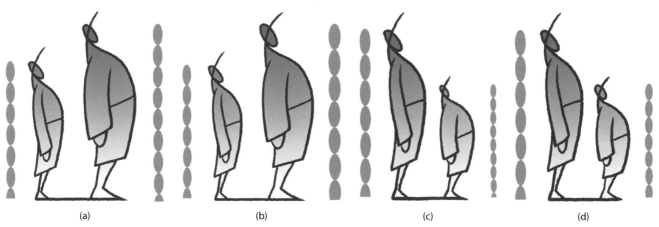

| (a) | (b) | (c) | (d) |

Figure 31.2

DOI: 10.1201/b22147-31

same body ratio. Both (c) and (d) have now an adult next to a child. However, the child in (c) looks a bit odd with his tiny head, but the right characters have a higher body ratio and still look younger next to the taller character. Body ratio therefore is valid only in realistic or semirealistic characters. It loses its validity if the characters are stylized, then the correct body ratio can be omitted in favor of convincing design. This only goes to a certain extent and then falls apart.

Advice for body ratios and character variations

In the lineup in Figure 31.1, the change in body ratio and also the change in the length of the limbs, the height of the belt line, the length of arms, and size of head or feet, give one many different style directions that can change the character from a typical, rather normal ratio, to a more interesting and unique design with tension and inventiveness. Some of the characters in the lineup appear older or younger than the first boy.

Once you have thumbnails or sketches with shapes that might work for your character and that give the character an idea of a personality, try to push your shapes and squash and stretch them to exaggerate the character's body ratio. With some changes in

the proportions, you can get very good results if your character design seems to lack some tension or appeal and feels a little plain. The legs could be much longer than the upper body, the arms shorter, the head smaller or bigger than usual. Changing the proportions is sometimes a good way of making your character more unique.

Be part of the composition of the pose

The body ratio is not just the division of the body into HL segments, but the overall disposition of all those points that are of significance aesthetically or anatomically. Various points in the body are of importance and always drag the attention: the head of course, chest with the separation line of the lower chest muscle in men and children and the breasts in women (the breasts however sit slightly lower than the muscle); the belly button, crotch, knees and elbows, hands and feet. In a naked character (Figures 31.4 and 31.5) the section of the pubic bone or crotch serves as a noteworthy part of the body's composition, because it is the point where the legs separate from the torso and where the body is usually cut in half; legs on the one and torso plus head on the other side having the same or similar length. Then the chest is halfway from head to crotch and the knees halfway from crotch

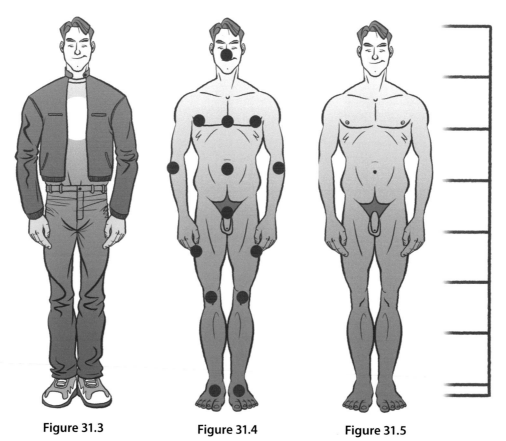

Figure 31.3   **Figure 31.4**   **Figure 31.5**

In this illustration I used a random photo of a man as reference to get the most realistic body ratio. One can see that even the most randomly picked picture that does not have the perfect ratio still follows to an extent the significant points in the composition and body ratio of the human body.

to feet. Those points can serve as important compositional and aesthetic marks when approaching the design of the body. Even in a character that has cartoony and unrealistic body proportions these points are significant.

The same character in clothing has the same points as being accentuated through folds or often through clothing and fashion that emphasize those body points (Figure 31.3).

The two wooden sculptures from the Japanese artist Unkei (1150–1223) (Figure 31.6) and the German sculptor Tilman Riemenschneider (1460–1532) (Figure 31.8) have in common that each relates the composition to its body ratio. Unkei's sculpture *Asanga* from 1208, the Kamakura period of Japanese sculpture, is a realistic depiction of a monk that is about 6 heads high, which makes him a shorter adult. What is however interesting in the sculpture is how the body ratio is intertwined with the composition and how Unkei has used the head length as a tool to arrange the important points of the sculpture and therefore give it structure and clarity. The head is usually the center of attention and its height can be used to balance the parts underneath, creating a structure which is based on the whole body being divided into sections that repeat the head's length. In Unkei's sculpture, the hands that hold up the box are exactly one HL down from the chin. This is significant insofar as the box serves as the balance in shape and position to the head. The sleeves of the robe are draping down left and right and forming a negative space column with the head and feet in its center. The box being in this column and being much closer to the head, pulls the eye upward. Another HL further down from the box is one significantly dominating fold serving as another balance point. The distance from the top of the head to the shoulders, which is a considerable break between the shape of the head and the shape of the cloaked body (red oval and blue triangle in Figure 31.7) is juxtaposed on the bottom of the sculpture by the height of the second, higher cloak. The composition in the top of the sculpture is reflected in the bottom.

The very same idea can be seen in Tilman Riemenschneider's sculpture of Saint Jakobus (Figure 31.8) from around 1505. However, here the HL can be determined with beard and hat (Figure 31.9a), or just the skull (Figure 31.9b).

Figure 31.6

Figure 31.7

Unkei: *Asanga* (1208) (Courtesy of Wikimedia Commons).

Figure 31.8

Figure 31.9

Tilman Riemenschneider: *Saint Jakobus* (1505) (Courtesy of Wikimedia Commons).

Both give us interesting compositional arrangements. Figure 31.9a has the same idea as Unkei's sculpture as the right hand of Jakobus is exactly two HL down, again balancing out the length of the head *with* hat. Also the length of the hat (blue square) having the same height as the cloak is short, again juxtaposing the top with the bottom. Two sculptures from very different cultures and backgrounds, coming up with the very same compositional idea. Figure 31.9b has Jacobus' left bent wrist exactly two HL down, accentuating the break of direction in the lower arm to the hand. Both hands also stay in the imaginary column from the head downward, the very same as in the Japanese sculpture.

Body ratio and character

The most pleasing and "attractive" body proportion seems to be about 7.5 heads in height, which is the average height of classical Greek sculptures. They range from 7.5 to 6 HL or less in adult characters, which does of course not mean that this is the ratio to go with! Whatever is pleasing to you or fits the story is right. The body ratio that we usually draw is what we are used to. We tend to repeat that ratio over and over as we feel it is the "right" one. We have to make an effort to actually change the ratio in order to open up our character range; otherwise, the result is the same type of character. What a character designer has to be able to do is draw a character in every style needed. A big part of this is being able to freely play with the body ratio.

Each comic or animation genre can have its own ratio to attract a specific audience. American superhero comics usually use an exaggerated ratio of 7.5 or even 9 HL in their heroic characters. The huge chest and long legs (Figure 31.10) combined with the small head make the hero even mightier and heroic. He becomes a truly *überhuman* man. A chest seems bigger if the head is smaller and small facial features make him manlier. The higher the body ratio, the taller someone appears; the smaller the ratio, the shorter. The other extreme would be a ratio where the head is bigger than the body, which would push the ratio to the other end of the spectrum, to that of a baby. The Power Puff Girls have a body that is so small that it is little more than half the height of the head. A new born baby's body ratio is about 4 heads, which is much more than the ratio of the Power Puff Girls. But it obviously works and makes them look very cute, young, innocent, and obviously funny as they are fighting crime. The body ratio is not always consistent in the same or similar species: in Shrek and Fiona's case, their ratio is very different from each other. Shrek's head is about 1.5 times bigger than Fiona's, which makes him actually look shorter on his own, because he has the ratio of a baby. In relationship to Fiona, whose ratio is like a short, stocky realistic human, Shrek looks somehow awkward because of his huge head and hands. The characters don't seem to come from the same universe. Finding the right body ratio for one character isn't enough. All the characters of the character lineup have to fit to each other, so having a completely different ratio for

some characters of the same species might look odd, like in the case of Shrek and Fiona (yes, Shrek is an ogre and Fiona is only half-ogre, still when they interact with each other it does look awkward). But of course this depends as always on the story and the style. Different species can have different ratios, but still have to follow the same or a similar extreme to which the characters are pushed. In DreamWork's *Bee Movie* (2007), the main character Barry Bee Benson, obviously a bee, is about 4 heads in height whereas Vanessa, the human flower shop keeper, is a somewhat realistic 7 heads tall. Barry needs to have a bigger head so that he feels smaller in comparison to humans; otherwise, he would just appear as a little fairy with wings (which he slightly does anyway).

There is not much of a difference between the style in anime, American, or European animation in terms of body ratio. It depends more on the genre and who the animation wants to attract. An extremely rough rule is: the younger the audience, the bigger the heads, and the older the audience, the smaller the heads.

Figure 31.10

Body ratio, design, and 2D animation

In 2D-traditional or 2D-digital animation, the head length serves one very important purpose which is to aid in keeping the characters consistent in their body ratio and providing points of reference that are important for the design.

Figure 31.12

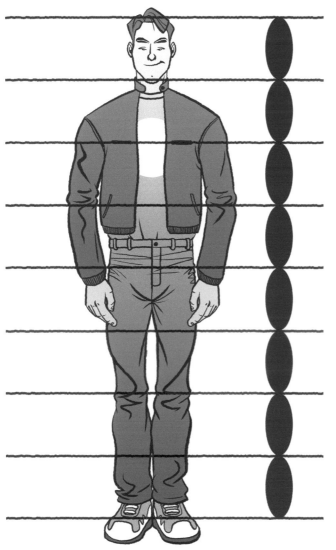

Figure 31.11

Because the character is always drawn first in its shapes as they serve as the foundation of the character, the HL give points of reference to keep a consistency within the character poses or the rough animation. Without keeping the HL in mind and constantly paying attention to the reference points, the character easily falls apart and lacks a dependable foundation. For instance in the character in Figure 31.11, the reference points are the chest pockets on the jacket, elbows, wrists, crotch, and knees. All of those points fall onto the horizontal lines of the HL or could be, like the belt line being between 2 HL. For 2D animation, very often the HL are used for the design to make it easier for the animator to draw the character, but if done too bluntly, the character will look simple and plain and the HL that hit certain design elements are too obvious. The character in Figure 31.12 has all the important elements at the HL, half HL, or quarter HL. This makes the character very even, but also rather plain because the character design lacks tension within the distribution of the elements. The task therefore is to on the one hand make it easy to draw and have a grid that is based on the HL, but on the other hand to also have tension within the design to make the distribution interesting. Because these two tasks are actually contradicting each other, a comfortable balance needs to be found.

CHAPTER 32

Contrast

The term contrast here stands for the difference between two elements.

Contrast separates and points out the otherness of two elements next to each other. The difference in shape is the most significant in character design, but there is contrast in many other aspects of the design.

The otherness in color or tone, for example, separates these two elements and sets them apart.

There is contrast in direction.

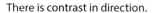

Contrast in texture or material.

Contrast can also be achieved in light and shadow, size, shape, form, but also line quality, brush stroke (thick versus thin; textured versus smooth), texture (smooth versus rough), sharpness, and even movement (fast versus slow).

Contrast separates two elements and either keeps them on one level or pushes the various elements forward or backward, which in turn can then create perspective.

The left two colors above have less perspective as they appear to be on the same level compared to the right pair in which the light turquoise, because it is much brighter, appears to be further back. The difference in the right pair is greater and thus the two separate from each other much more. So the magnitude of the contrast is what determines the intensity of the separation.

Contrast is a continuously important aspect that needs to be considered at all times when drawing and designing, because each line drawn and each shape mentioned need to either separate or connect to the one next to it.

The character in Figure 32.1 has very little contrast as all the elements that would be determined by texture, material, direction, tone, and color are only described by one line, which has its limitations in this case. The character feels flat.

Direction
Material
Tone

| Figure 32.1 | Figure 32.2 | Figure 32.3 |

DOI: 10.1201/b22147-32

either separates from the one next to it or is connecting with it. So each addition that is put on the canvas needs to be chosen for its ability to connect or separate. Contrast is thus the very element that determines the qualities of each brush stroke (hue, saturation, brightness, and texture). As long as those two elements clearly state that they are not one, but two elements on either the same or a different perspective level, the goal of separation is achieved. The more contrast is applied the more the elements state that they are disparate.

Contrast between characters

Different-looking characters point out that they are different in every part of their body. This line of shapes below is much less interesting compared to the line of shapes underneath where each shape is easily recognizable and has its own character.

Contrast is the play between two extremes to avoid sameness and repetition in either the character's personalities or their habitus. Stan Laurel is long, and thin, and cerebrally slow, whereas Oliver Hardy is big, round, and thinks highly of his subpar brain function. Roger Murtaugh from *Lethal Weapon* (1987) is black, older, and safety-conscious whereas Martin Riggs, his cop-buddy, is suicidal, temperamental, younger, and white. Because they are visually different they also point out each other's differences and specific personality traits. Contrast here is needed to emphasize on the character's significant and personality traits, often important for the story development. In literature, the diverging character from the protagonist is called the foil, who is either significantly different from the protagonist and thus amplifies their traits, or is very similar to the protagonist but differ in one key trait which is important for the story to be resolved. The foil has a key trait that the protagonist might lack, but needs in order to approach and solve the problem. The contrast between the characters makes it much easier for them to play off each other and use their differences as an advantage and a source for storytelling ideas. In animation, because of the emphasis on exaggeration, the difference can be pushed to the extreme and every single character can have their own body shape that contrasts with the other characters significantly. In Disney's *The Emperor's New Groove* (2000) Pacha is big, round, and down to earth whereas King Kuzco is slim and in every aspect the exact opposite of Pacha. Izma on the other hand is evil, skinny, smart, and ugly whereas her henchman Cronk is lovely, kind, strong, handsome, and simple. Contrast creates opposites which in turn is the basis for interesting conflicts

Figure 32.4

The character in Figure 32.2 has contrast between all of the various elements and thus has more body and perspective. Figure 32.3 shows which parts show contrast either in tone, direction, or material.

Every part of the drawing or painting deals with contrast and the separation of two different elements, so contrast is needed at all times to create a readable image that can be understood in all its elements.

In Figure 32.4, the goal is not full dimensionality (the rendering with light and shadow is kept to a minimum to give an idea of form but not to render it photorealistically) but a rather graphic flatness that only suggests dimensionality. To separate the foreground from the background, there are different hues used in the snake that do not appear in the background and that already provides a contrast between the two. What really makes the difference however is the contrast in direction and pattern where the background has stripes which, through the overlap of the snake, are proof that there is perspective. The goal is to show that there are two elements, snake and background, separated from each other. The difference is not just in the foreground and background but in every little part of the image. Everywhere there are two elements that stand next to each other and have to separate. Each brushstroke that is placed onto the canvas

Figure 32.5

between the characters. The personality is visualized in different shapes and forms; oftentimes, contrast is developed by having one character fill the gaps in personality and/or ability the other character lacks, and then, it is visualized in distinct body shapes. The more contrast there is the more each character presents their individuality. In Figure 32.5, the two characters differ in many aspects and not only have opposite clothing, but also opposite shapes, personalities, textures, etc. However, the opposites are

pushed too far in the face styles that don't seem to be from the same realm anymore. The left character is more cartoony than the right character, and thus, the difference and contrast are too strong in the facial elements to fit. A more stylized face is needed for the character on the right to match. This is where contrast has its limitations as style is usually homogenous and should not have any contrast if it is not the very point of the show's style like in *The Amazing World of Gumball*.

CHAPTER 33

Texture

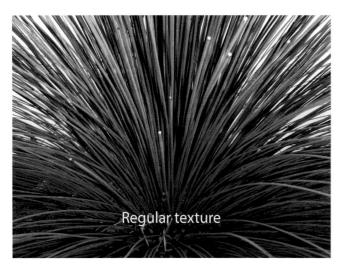

Figure 33.1

Figure 33.2

The character's surface is more than just skin, but has surface properties that specify what kind of skin it is. Is it dry, wet, moist, dusty, shiny, oily, smooth, rough, or wrinkly? The surface properties are what give the character details. In a character, the texture covers skin, hair, nails, teeth, eyes, clothing, and accessories, and all need to be visually explained. That can be either done with just a highlight in the eyes, to point out that they are smooth and wet, or it can be a fully photorealistic rendering of the skin with hair, blemishes, and all. However, it is not always about being fully realistic; texture has not only a visual quality to it but also a tactile and a metaphorical quality.

All three types of textures can again be subdivided into *regular* (organized) and *stochastic* (irregular and disorganized) textures (Figures 33.1 and 33.2).

Different types of textures:

Natural textures
any organic and inorganic matter that exists in nature

Artificial textures
any texture that is man-made

There is a gap on purpose as artistic textures are not part of reality, which the first two textures are.

Artistic textures
any texture that is artistically produced
and interprets or invents textures

Natural textures

- *Organic:* All materials that are based on carbon and are, or derived from, a living organism. In a character that means skin, hair, fur, leather, horn, bone, teeth, fabric based on organic matter, leather, wood, pearls.
- *Inorganic:* Materials that do not contain carbon but appear in nature, like stone, metal, gem stones.

Artificial textures

Man-made textures are fabrics made of artificial fibers (can be based on organic materials), tiles, paints, all kinds of makeup, plastics (most plastics are based on carbon, so technically they are organic materials, but their surface texture isn't organic in their look and feel), artificial hair, and artificial fur.

Artistic textures

Artistic textures can be divided into four types[1]

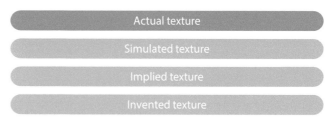

---

[1] http://en.wikipedia.org/wiki/Texture_(painting) (retrieved May 19, 2015).

DOI: 10.1201/b22147-33

Artistic textures are obviously endless and there is no limit of how to interpret textures with different painting or drawing techniques, or even use collage techniques. Additionally, the actual texture of the painting surface, what the painting is painted on: rough burlap, smooth wood, polished metal, affect the texture. The extraordinarily smooth texture of a painting by Jean-Auguste-Dominique Ingres (1780–1867) is very different from the rough texture of a painting by Lucian Freud (1922–2011) whose thick impasto brushwork is an important part of the painting and the emotional effect it has on the viewer. In both drawings and paintings, the materials used affect the outcome.

Actual texture

The actual texture refers to the texture of the object itself. In a painting, it would be the texture of the burlap base or the paint. In a sculpture, the texture of the surface of the stone, the clay, the metal, or in sculptures that use objects for its body (Nam June Paik, for example, who uses various objects in his sculptures whose textures give the pieces a slick and modern feel).

Simulated texture
This is texture that pretends to be something that it is not. For example, in drawings or paintings the brush or pencil mimicking

the actual texture in a realistic way is simulated texture. The rich fabric in a painting by Jan Vermeer van Delft is not the actual rippled texture of the fabric but a smooth surface on the canvas. The painted texture is only giving the impression of it being the actual texture.

Implied texture
This texture is not directly mimicking the actual texture but finds other representations that are close to it and follows the direction of the original, staying in the vicinity of its visuals.

Invented texture
Invented texture is object unrelated and creates texture that has no basis in reality; therefore, it often appears in abstract works that do not mimic reality or interpret reality, but develop its very own visual space.

Visual magnitude of texture
The visual magnitude deals with the strength of the texture and how much it attracts attention. Figure 33.3a has a rather busy texture in the fabric that feels heavy and it does therefore

(a)   (b)   (c)   (d)

Figure 33.3

attract attention. In Figure 33.3b, the dress is lighter and evokes a texture of sand, which gives it a "dry" feel and also attracts attention due to it juxtaposing the smoothness of the girl's skin. The character in Figure 33.3c and d has, for instance, the same texture in the dress, but in Figure 33.3c the texture is reduced and has a much lower magnitude than in Figure 33.3d, where the dress draws more attention, but it also creates more tension between body and fabric. High magnitude textures step visually forward, whereas low magnitude ones usually do not. The character in Figure 33.3c, for instance, has freckles in the face and on the arms which attracts more attention visually than the texture of the fabric, redirecting the eye toward the skin. In Figure 33.3d, the attention seems to be on both dress and face equally.

What texture in a character conveys

Surface properties
Its visual and haptic qualities.

Emotion and mood
How the texture feels like

Metaphorical quality
The meaning of the texture.

Surface property

This point captures the tactile characteristics of surfaces, which contain the granularity, smoothness or roughness of the surface, moist or dry, sticky or not, surface temperature, soft or hard ... It is the qualities of the character's skin, hair, nails, and outfit that we perceive. A character that lives in a swamp would probably not have dry or perfectly clean skin and clothing (if it isn't part of the character's unique personality exactly that he is clean) but be dirty, possibly always damp, or wet.

Emotion and mood

Every texture has through its tactile qualities an emotional feel to it. How does it feel to touch a damp surface? Is it cold and slimy, or warm and soft? The cold and slimy could be uncomfortable to touch, whereas the warm and soft could be comfortable (that of course depends additionally on all the other surface characteristics). How do we feel when we touch a specific surface and what memories does it trigger? Is it possible to use those emotions and memories in the character design in order to then evoke those very feelings in the audience? This is only possible when the emotions and memories are universal and not subjective (although this depends on the execution).

Figure 33.4

Figure 33.5

The character that lives in the swamp is, for instance, an emotionally cold character. The skin of frogs and fish is cold and wet and so giving the character's skin some of the surface and texture qualities of an amphibian or fish could underline their emotional coldness. If they were a warm and comfortable character, their skin could be resembling the qualities of fuzzy peach that reminds us of a delicious sweet treat (but would that relate to them living in the swamp?).

Care needs to be taken however as every additional surface quality will potentially overwrite or change the existing one if not balanced properly. The delicious qualities of the peach can easily turn into the opposite if the character's skin has too many blemishes or is too old and wrinkly (can, not has to!).

Metaphorical quality

The important aspect is how the chosen textures represent the character's personality. The texture stands as a visual metaphor or placeholder for certain personality traits. For instance, the construction worker's personality in Figure 33.4 is a bit on the rough side, he is not the most sophisticated character and does not pay too much attention to his looks, is a bit sloppy, yet still honest and trustworthy. This could be interpreted by the hair on his skin, the pimples or light skin blemishes, hairy forearms, unclean pants ... all this information isn't precisely "texture" but it is information about the character's surface.

Simplicity of character textures in 2D design

Textures are surface information refining what we are actually looking at: material. In 2D artwork, the texture is, like everything else in 2D, usually very reduced and a *pars-pro-toto* approach is common due to the simplicity of the art. Textures are usually just hinted at through simplified line work rather than actual texture. In Figure 33.4, the hairy shoulders, for instance, are just a couple of short lines that suggest that the skin is not smooth; the simple lines on the face hint at a more rough, unshaved skin; the stitching in gloves and pants clarify fabric, the solidity and practicality of the clothing. Figure 33.5 has none of that and because the surfaces contain much less information, the character is easier to read, but also lacks variation in the materials and feels more plain.

(a) (b) (c)

Figure 33.6

The details do not necessarily show texture per se, but hint at a surface material and thus the viewer can draw a conclusion of what material they are looking at and how it might feel. An actual added texture would style-wise often fall out of place and so a simple hint that describes the texture is plenty and less is usually more. As long as the material and surface portrayed come across as what they are, no more information is needed.

There can only be a limited amount of texture in a 2D drawing as too much information would for the most part clutter the image and the strived-for simplicity would vanish. The most important textures are picked that represent an idea rather than being realistic. In Figure 33.6c, there is so much texture and surface information that the textures start to fight each other for dominance and then the overall readability starts to suffer. However, like always, there is the possibility for this working to advantage: a character that is over the top and combines textures in their outfit that, additionally to the business of the skin and hair, creates a visual mess. This could also underline the character's personality.

Character texture in CG animation

CG animation has, in terms of textures, a much wider and more realistic range than 2D animation. But because in CG anything is possible doesn't mean that everything works. CG animation is about realism in form only (even this will in the future break apart as technology evolves); of course, that doesn't mean that every surface of every character in CG has to be realistic and representational. In CG, any material is possible! The character can be made out of jelly with an inner glow and as long as the interpretation of the story allows a choice like that, it could work.

Artistic choices do not have to be realistic! Simulated textures are the common direction in CG, whereas implied and invented textures can push and exaggerate the metaphorical qualities of a texture. However, this needs to be balanced out with the form. If the texture is broken up and artistically interpreted, the form also has to be adjusted; otherwise, the texture is just slapped onto the form.

Pattern and texture

Pattern are structures that repeat on surfaces in a regular and controlled way, are part of the design, and do not describe the tactile qualities of an object. Texture, on the other hand, defines the surface quality with its tactile properties. In 2D animation, the difference can be a bit confusing as the character's dress in any of the examples in Figure 33.3a through d could actually also be printed onto the surface rather than be the texture of the fabric. The textures are usually so reduced to their core information that they can easily be seen as pattern and vice versa. In Figure 33.6a and b, nevertheless, it is very obvious that a pattern on the fabric is printed, not a texture. Both pattern and fabric will equally drag attention toward themselves if they have a high magnitude. Too much of both is very distracting and can make the character look unrealistic or simply unbalanced.

Textures and patterns that are too small and where the single elements are starting to blur into each other instead of clearly separating start to visually vibrate. A meshed fence, for instance, that you out from at some point changes from a pattern to a texture or even a flat color; in-between the two stages of zoomed in and zoomed out, the pattern can move and very much drag attention to itself. Therefore, avoid pattern and textures that are too small or too busy, and push themselves to the foreground.

Line Quality

What affects the line

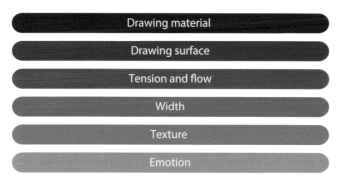

- Drawing material
- Drawing surface
- Tension and flow
- Width
- Texture
- Emotion

What determines the quality of a line? It is first of course the material the line is drawn with, pencil (soft or hard), pen, quill, a mechanical pencil, a piece of charcoal, or how all of these tools and materials are mimicked by digital tools. Also of importance is the material that is drawn on. Soft or rough paper, newsprint or layout paper, panels of wood or parchment, a computer screen or tablet. The drawing surface and tools cannot be separated and always have to be considered as a union as both influence the outcome and how the final drawing "feels" to the viewer. A drawing on a street feels very different from a drawing on soft, white paper. The same character drawn with a different line does not only have a dissimilar feel but also style to it. Figure 34.1 shows a "clean" robot. Figure 34.8 is one that isn't yet sure what it wants to be, even suggesting some movement due to the multiple hands, and Figure 34.9 has the robot in a final illustration that is more organic than Figure 34.1.

In the extraordinary cave drawings of horse heads from the Chauvet Cave in southern France, the material that was used was charcoal on rock wall and it is astounding how realistic and fresh these heads look, considering they are about 30,000 years old. The drawing has an organic feel to it, caused by charcoal already being an organic material, the texture of the stone it's drawn on adds to the natural feel, also the colors of the stone, the smooth flowing line itself, and how the artist uses black and white to render the horses' heads. The artist is not just using an outline, but suggesting form, and used their very hands to create the drawing. There is movement in the rendering which makes the surface move and one can see the textures being created by the hands. The quality of the drawing comes from the interplay between line, smudging the charcoal, and the texture of the stone. This gives the drawing a vibrancy that makes it appear strangely alive. The complete opposite of the horses of Chauvet would be a Disney clean-up drawing of the prince's horse

Samson from *Sleeping Beauty* (1959) for instance. The line quality compared to the Chauvet example is rather plain, as there is not much change in the line's width or pressure; it is however extremely precise. What makes an animation clean-up drawing, that has no texture really and no change in line thickness, feel so alive and most attractive? It's the flow of the line for one thing: the line beautifully curves, describes interesting shapes, and provides a variety of contrasting lines. The drawing is so precise that it gives us a character that has emotion that we can easily identify with. Every line curves organically and the curvature is never boring, but has a tension in itself. Its flow is elegant. Two completely different approaches to drawing a horse, but both have life in them and a strong emotional impact. The emotional impact doesn't just mean that we can read the emotions of the character, like in a Disney clean-up drawing, but also that the drawing evokes emotions in us, like in the drawing on the Chauvet Cave wall. We are emotionally moved because of the beauty of the drawing, the aesthetics of its body, and the incomprehensible age when it was created, which gives us a glimpse into an unknown world of mystery and secrets.

DRAWING MATERIALS

The drawing materials will highly influence the outcome, look, and feel of a drawing. A drawing done with a mechanical pencil will probably not have as much organic feel in the line compared to an unsharpened 4B pencil, because the mechanical pencil produces a much more precise and technical line. It is for technical drawings rather than for free-sketching. Keep in mind that the outcome is controlled by you and you can determine how the final image should look (even when you create it in Photoshop or Painter as digital drawings can you choose from a variety of surfaces and tools). Choose your drawing materials carefully and choose a paper that gives the line the texture it needs. There is a whole range of papers from smooth to rough, each with its own way of keeping the particles of the pencil on its surface differently. The texture and feel of the line is always different on differently textured paper and therefore affects the emotions that the viewer will have. Look through the drawings of artists that you respect and find out what materials they used, then try them out and use them to their advantage.

Assignment: Take several pencils and draw as many textures with the pencil as you can. Make it a challenge to use the pencil to its full capacity. It is not just able to be used for line or for smudging the pencil dust, there are many more textures possible that you can create with a common pencil. This assignment not only teaches you how to mimic textures but also how to make your drawing more interesting by bringing variation into the drawing through line.

DOI: 10.1201/b22147-34

Straight versus curved

There is a well-known and often repeated rule in animation that a straight line should always be balanced out by a curved line in order to make the drawing more interesting, and give the character an organic flow based partly on anatomy. I honestly never really understood the point of this rule, as in my opinion a rule like that reduces the possibilities in design and limits creativity. There is a lot of design out there where this rule doesn't apply and it still looks interesting, convincing, and is aesthetically very pleasing. Take a look at SpongeBob: there is no straight versus curved in his whole design; still, he is a great character, unique and unconventional, which obviously led to his success (apart from being a hoot, of course). A better term for the idea behind straight versus curved is *variation*. Variation is the key in the successful handling of lines and knowing what to do, why to do it, and how it fits the main direction of the work. If you want the arms and legs of your character to have parallel lines like SpongeBob and you have a solid explanation why that decision is important, then there is no reason not to do that, as long as you understand the result and its impact on the character. In SpongeBob's case the reason might be that the character is very cartoony and straight versus curved would make him look more anatomically correct (in a very rudimentary way of course), which defeats the purpose of his rather "silly" look. Straight versus curved is a direction, but it is not a solid rule. It is a design possibility but by no means a necessity. Once we step into the more realistic direction of design, straight versus curved can be a helpful tool for understanding and depicting forces and tension. Mike Mattesi's book series on forces, for example, *Force: Dynamic life drawing for animators*, is a very good example of an extremely helpful approach to figure drawing and understanding how to depict and grasp various types of forces in the human body. But this is just one possibility of many, one that works for this type of animation; it is not a solution for every kind of animation. There are animation designs and interpretations of anatomical forms and movement out there that do very much the opposite of straight versus curved and still work in their own very personal way. Rules are there to be broken!

Variation

Bringing variation into your drawing is the key to create visually interesting drawings that have not just the content of what they are depicting as their body, but are also interesting as drawings themselves, even if abstract. A drawing contains more than just the lines that visually depict an object or character on a two-dimensional plane. It is a record of the artist's movements and emotions during a time frame of the drawing process. For the viewer it is the pleasure of observing how one line affects the one next to it and feeling the line's body, or simply how the pressure of the drawing material changes the thickness or strength of the line. Every line has a personality and a behavior, which can be felt. Once you have two lines next to each other they will relate in one way or another and always tell a story: a curved and a straight line, both being thick on the bottom side and getting thinner toward the top (Figure 34.2) express weight and the obvious fact that both are standing on the heavier side of their "bodies." The curved line bends toward the straight line or away from it, depending on what their relationship would be (though it does appear as if the bend line leans toward the straight one as its standing point is further left than the

Figure 34.1

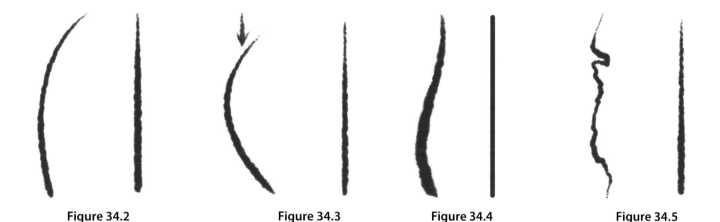

Figure 34.2　　　　　　**Figure 34.3**　　　　　　**Figure 34.4**　　　　　　**Figure 34.5**

head of the line, and also the reading direction from left to right pushes the line to the right). Does the curved line want to get closer to the straight line or does the straight line try to get away from the curved one? Every interpretation of course is possible, depending on the story you see in it. The curved line has tension compared to the straight line and thus movement, and in Figure 34.3, the line appears like a spring and its pressure either comes from above or from within the curve's body. This could also give the line a will, which in turn can create a storyline. Furthermore, the two lines work as opposites: each points out the other's differences. (In this case, the "head" of the curved line in Figure 34.3 is further away from the straight line compared to example Figure 34.2. This in turn makes it feel like the curved line in Figure 34.3 is actually moving away from the straight one).

Two lines always have an interaction and communication between each other. A line's personality always seems much stronger once there is another line next to it that is different. The juxtaposition creates a dialog and therefore a story.

In Figure 34.4 on the right is a still, rigid, and strong line that doesn't seem to hesitate in its direction. It shows a clean and perfect line, that is technical and lacks emotions. A comic that is drawn in this style is *Jimmy Corrigan, the Smartest Kid on Earth* by Chris Ware. The characters in the book often express their difficulties in emotions toward each other and the tone of the book can be sometimes bleak. The clean and aseptic style of the line fits this story perfectly. The line expresses visually the emotional state of the characters, withholding emotions and struggling with communication. Figure 34.4 has a line on the left that is curved and has momentum. Both lines have a strong personality that is not just created by them being either straight or curved, but also by their texture. The straight line's direction and determination is underlined by it being precise and perfect, feeling inorganic. The curved line, on the contrary, is more soft and organic, which fits its movement.

Every line has some kind of personality and you can figure it out once you look at it closely and see what the emotional impact of the line quality could be. Is it a nervous line as in Figure 34.5? An example for this line style is Art Spiegelman's comic *Mouse*, which tells the story of a mouse family in WWII and their misfortune in the holocaust. The delicate topic is brilliantly underlined by the reduced character designs. The facial expressions are mostly nonexistent other than subtly described with eyebrows. This allows for the topic to not be overly emotional in the expressions, which would hurt the story tremendously, but let the emotions evolve through the story itself and the situation rather than the facial expressions. The line quality is very organic and has a bit of a nervous feel to it, which again supports the uneasiness of the situation.

In Figure 34.6, a very heavy and thick line juxtaposed with a subtle and soft thin line. Both have texture though the thick line feels so much heavier than the thin one because of the intensity of the color and also the overall weight and volume of the line.

On the left side in Figure 34.7 is a free-floating line across a rigid and unapologetic line. The traits of easy-going, happy, graceful relate to the line on the left, whereas inflexible, strict, rigid, and compliant are words that come to mind when examining the line on the right. It is up to the artist to give the final drawing or the final animation the line quality that fits the content. If you look at the two lines in Figure 34.5 and don't think about them being straight or wiggly, but look at what the line does on its way—the wiggly line changes its thickness constantly and the straight line just goes from thick to thin. By changing the thickness and using therefore all of the line's qualities, you bring variation into the line work, which makes the drawing more interesting and also more organic. A very good example is the comic book artist Will Eisner and his comic *The Spirit* about a masked crime-fighter. The quality and fluidity of the line is what makes his comic books so stunning. Eisner's drawings all have grace because of this seemingly easy line that is freely moving over the paper. His lines are always flowing, never rigid, and give each page a sophisticated style. The line that varies in thickness becomes a character in itself and looks much more interesting

Figure 34.6   **Figure 34.7**

Figure 34.8

than if it is just a line like in Figure 34.4 on the right, though a statement like that has no meaning if the story and the style of the drawing is not considered. The drawing has to fit the story and therefore has to follow with its line quality the feel and mood of the piece. The character can look much more alive when the line itself is alive, though that doesn't mean that a character with a rigid line cannot feel alive. The line quality is an option and the artist has to choose the one that feels right.

Aside from the line qualities we already observed, every line has direction and rhythm, which is the flow of the line and how it behaves on its way. Every line tells us exactly what the artist's abilities are and is a record of the drawing process. With practice you can clearly see at what point in the drawing the artist was sure about what they were doing and where they hesitated. The line quality, in a drawing is directly connected to the thought process and emotion the artist had at the time. You can see determination and strength in a drawing as much as fear and hesitation, knowledge, and the lack of it. Someone who doesn't know how to draw hands properly or how to simplify them will undoubtedly show that in the drawing and the quality of the line. Therefore, it is of utmost importance to learn how to draw everything in the character: hands and shoes, folds, hair, and all the rest. If you are hesitant about certain parts in your drawing, the well-trained eye will surely detect it. Every part in the drawing is important! Always check each line that you drew and figure out how to improve it the next time to get the most out of your drawings in terms of aesthetics, readability, and information.

2D animation clean-up line examples

Rough animation has a very lively and dynamic line quality to it that expresses the fast drawing process of the experienced animator beautifully. After the clean-up, the rough animation always loses much of its appeal as the line itself isn't the one anymore that the animator was searching for in his animation but is the clean and perfect line chosen by the clean-up artist. This line is very different from the powerful and expressionistic rough animation drawing. In the cleaned-up drawing, the artist is looking for a line that doesn't shake or shiver, that doesn't distract from the movement of the rough character's lines, but provides a clean border for the afterward colored shape. The clean-up does not necessarily have to be all precise and "dead" in terms of the movement of the line itself though, but can also be alive in its own right. The more one frame differs from the next in terms of line quality in the clean-up the more the character on the screen will shake nervously. Chosen with care and in connection with the story this can have a major effect on the final image and can be chosen for its style:

Cordell Barker: *The Cat Came Back* (1988)

In Cordell Barker's *The Cat Came Back*, the story is about a man trying to get rid of a little cute cat that slowly destroys his home. The short is very cartoony in character animation and design, and the character line is constantly moving, adding to the frenzy of the story. It adds much movement to the quirky characters and supports the amusing storyline. The man tries frantically to get rid of the cat and the line seems to express the same nervousness. The extremes in the squash and stretch of the character animation, the tight timing, and the exaggerated shapes of the design make this a very cartoony short, where every aspect follows that one direction.

Koji Yamamura: *Ein Landarzt* (2007)

In Koji Yamamura's *Ein Landarzt,* based on a short story by Franz Kafka, the line quality has even more frenzy than in Barker's short. The story is of a country doctor that has to heal a boy in a farmhouse. The lines are like a storm in the characters that are as disturbing and twisted as the story. The character's shapes change, they squash and stretch, and they lean against gravity. The outline of the characters outside in the snowstorm is shaking violently, addressing the seemingly uninhabitable environment. Yamamura describes with his imagery this uncomfortable situation and disturbance on each level. It very much feels like the characters are shaken up by the storm and the twisted, nightmarish environment. The shaking line adds nervousness and restlessness in characters that try to live through the happenings in the story.

A caricaturist that used the flowing quality of the textureless line in his work extensively is Al Hirschfeld (1903–2003) who is famous for his depiction of celebrities of Hollywood and Broadway. His line work is exquisite and gives the overall drawing, that is just consisting of smooth and organic black lines drawn with a genuine quill, a certain quality and sophistication that very well fits the glitz and glamour of his subjects.

The invisible line and its compositional strength

The line itself has two aspects: the actual body of the line, the part that is seen on the page that has weight, direction, length, width, tension, texture, and a path, but then there is the second aspect that is the unseen part of the line, the one that is felt, but not visible on the page; it is the continuing ghost of the actual line. A line can be seen as being the train on the track that is endless. This unseen part of the line, the track, is extremely important for the aesthetics, arrangement, and the composition of the lines. In Figure 34.10a, the lines relate as they are already close to each other; in their ghost image

however, the vertical line cuts through the tilted line (c). The action comes from the vertical line as it will cut, whereas the tilted line is being cut. The relationship between the two is not as close in (b), where the two lines flow parallel in the upper part and the cutting point is recognized by both lines as their invisible elongations meet in the same point (d). The left line will meet the right one in its lowest point. Both examples, (a) and (b), in their seen and unseen body, also encircle a negative shape (c and d).

The line's flow can relate to any part of the composition, seen or unseen. For example, the line in Figure 34.11a relates its curves, beginning and ending, to two parallel horizontals (Figure 34.11b). If this is ignored, like in Figure 34.11c or d, the lines feel more organic and less organized. In example (d), the lower end runs directly to the higher beginning (Figure 34.11e) in its ghost image and therefore relates to itself. The beginning and end of the line in Figure 34.11c run into infinity, never meeting. Figure 34.11d

Figure 34.9

therefore has a clear negative space that is defined as a shape (e), whereas (c) is open in its negative space.

How much a little detail in a line can affect the flow is shown in Figure 34.12a through d. In (a), the vertical line cuts through the curved line (c). In (b), the vertical line has a little bend toward the horizontal line and thus its invisible elongation will move smoothly into the curved one (d). The little bend has a huge impact on how both lines relate and which direction they move into.

In their invisible strength, two lines can also flow into each other, which is another important aspect that has immense creative possibilities. Example 34.13a has two lines where the lower one clearly seems to flow out of the upper one (Figure 34.13b). The connection between the two in 34.13a is just omitted, but their relationship is still clear and obvious.

All of these line relationships can be used creatively in characters and their design, if this is chosen as a style direction. It is an option, not a need for the design of characters. The line however has an impact on the final artwork, and how the viewer perceives the work and reads it.

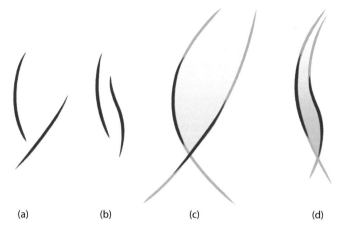

   (a)   (b)   (c)   (d)

Figure 34.10

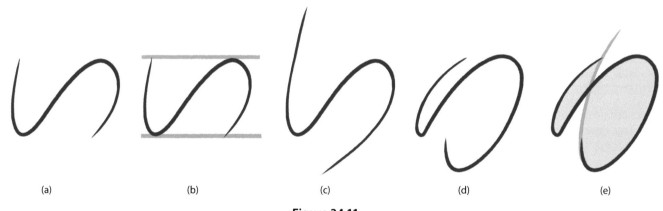

   (a)   (b)   (c)   (d)   (e)

Figure 34.11

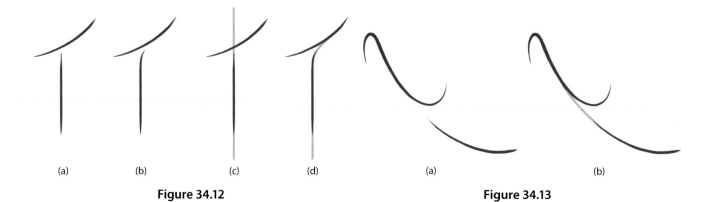

  (a)   (b)   (c)   (d)   (a)   (b)

Figure 34.12   **Figure 34.13**

Figure 34.14

Figure 34.15

The lineup of characters in Figure 34.14 reveals its invisible line relationships in Figure 34.15. The invisible lines have an impact on how the character's line flow creates invisible shapes and connections in which the character is inscribed. These connections are there to take out the business of all the various lines that can occur and also to support the character with a compositional foundation, to arrange its various elements and keeping the character organized. For example, the left character in Figure 34.14 has the feet within the created negative space of the pant's flow down (see left character in Figure 34.15), whereas the next character to the right does not. His feet are shorter. The point here is not to always religiously follow this idea of invisible lines and shapes, but to have yet another option for being creative. If the feet, for example, get shifted forward (Figure 34.16a and b), the character starts to look as if they are arranged out of several parts and then put together like a Lego character instead of consisting of one underlying structure. Of course, all of this is strongly related to anatomy and the character's personality, plus the style of the design. Many aspects contribute to the final look and the line quality/relationships are just one aspect.

(a)   (b)

Figure 34.16

The next more complicated step is to use these ideas in a full illustration and have every part of the character respect each other's flow and importance. Nothing is there without a purpose and everything in the character supports the pose and the overall composition. Figure 34.17 shows in a painted version how far these aesthetic decisions of the

Figure 34.17

line arrangement can be pushed in order to develop a style that takes advantage of those line relationships in a creative way. The line itself is not visible anymore as it is a painted version of the initial line drawing, but still present in the shapes and forms. Every element in the face, for instance (Figure 34.18), has a flow which never exists without succumbing to or leading toward another line. The whole system is balanced and in its stylistic flatness has an aesthetic direction. The colors, textures, and light and shadow can also follow this direction. In Figures 34.19 and 34.20, the character's pose is stylized and slightly artificial to defer to the composition, yet still needs to follow weight, pivot, line of action, etc. to not fall apart. Light and shadow is adjusted artistically in its shape to also support the overall compositional concept of the piece. Light and shadow is therefore not realistic, but meets the compositional needs and the style of the illustration.

The next step in complexity is to find these lines in characters that are three-dimensional. To translate the flat two-dimensional drawing into a three-dimensional sculpture that also incorporates the flow of the lines is yet another matter, as every angle will present a new visual experience. All the important lines need to match to create a sculpture that is

Figure 34.18

Figure 34.19

Figure 34.20

aesthetically pleasing from every perspective. Henry Moore's abstract piece *Reclining Figure* (1951) in the Tate Gallery in London is a good example in this regard as he allows all the lines in the sculpture to recognize each other's direction and flow in a three-dimensional way from one element of the figure to another, creating a figure where all is one, yet clearly distinguishable in its various elements (Figures 34.21 through 34.24, Please be advised that the original sculpture does not contain the purple lines; they are just added here for clarity to demonstrate how the movements of all the lines relate to each other!). Every position one takes to look at this sculpture in

the round reveals yet another perspective of relating lines and form. It is all constant movement and the eye is never resting. The complexity of this is staggering and one can only imagine how difficult it was to create such compositional perfection in a three-dimensional form. Because of the organic roundness of the shapes and forms, it is very easy for the lines to flow and match up with other lines as the eye can pick any point during the line's curvature to match it with another flowing line in the sculpture. This creates an experience when walking around the sculpture that is truly dimensional as every viewing position looks balanced and aesthetically pleasing.

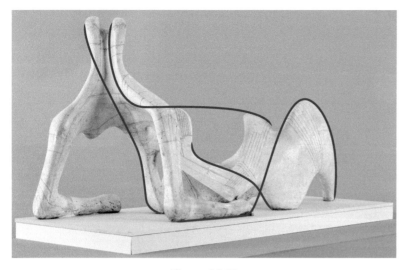

Figure 34.21

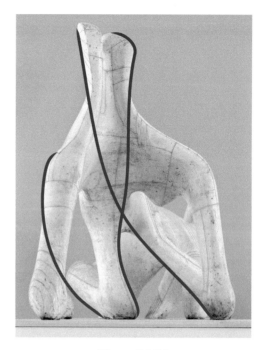

Figure 34.24

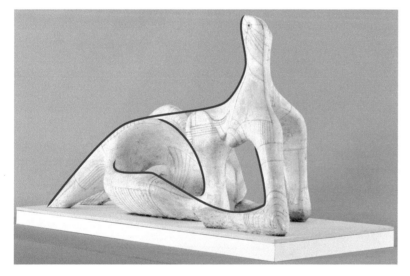

Figure 34.22

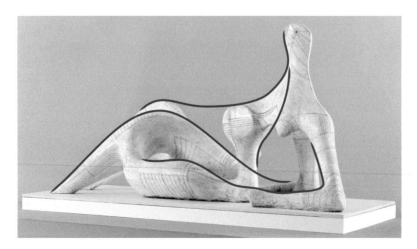

Figure 34.23

More on drawing and line-quality:

Enstice W. (2011). *Drawing: Space, Form, and Expression*. Boston, MA: Pearson.

Robertson S. (2013). *How to Draw: Drawing and Sketching Objects and Environments from Your Imagination*. Culver City, CA: Design Studio Press.

Robertson S. (2014). *How to Render: The Fundamentals of Light, Shadow and Reflectivity*. Culver City, CA: Design Studio Press.

CHAPTER 35

Simplicity and Readability

Simplicity in the image leads to an improved readability and understanding of the content. Too much information is cluttering the image with useless material and thus the audience has difficulties to understand who the character is, what is going on, and where the story is heading. Too much information in the character design is diluting the main point the artist is trying to make, which is the character's personality in relation to his actions. Anything that takes the audience onto another path, a path that steers away from the main direction, needs to be either simplified, adjusted, or eliminated altogether to create a streamlined character design and/or story path that is clear and congruent. For instance, the robots in the *Transformers* series (2007–): Their design is very well done and they look stunning as toys or as concepts. However, as acting characters that have facial expressions and are supposed to cause empathy in a film, the design causes issues. There are so many moving details in the characters, especially their faces, and the design is so intricate and complicated that one has problems knowing where to look when the robots move. This could be acceptable if you only had one robot. But if you have good robots fighting bad ones in fierce battles and fast-paced action scenes, after a while the viewer loses track of who fights with whom and which robot is the good and which the bad. That is the point when the audience starts to detach from the story and loses interest. Fortunately in the *Transformer* series there isn't much story to lose interest in, so it's all still good. Simplicity in the design would have taken away the robot's intricate alien details that make the design quite fascinating, but it would have added readability, which in a feature film is the more important aspect. Pixar's movie *UP* (2009) has explorer Charles F. Muntz's dogs talking due to a device that translates their thoughts and barks into language. This is a funny idea, however does not logically fit into the movie, despite being rather entertaining. Not only does the question arise who actually invented this device in the middle of a cave in South America, but it neither goes along with the world that *UP* is set in nor has it something to do with the actual storyline, even though it's an interesting idea. The overall style of the film could be called contemporary-retro with a lot of 1950/1960s influences and no references to modern inventions at all. Everything in the world of *UP* is semirealistic, exaggerated, and stylized, but actually possible (even flying a house is technically feasible), though a talking dog just does not fit into the world created and thus it is distracting. A cute idea is not always helping the story or solving story problems. Everything needs to follow one goal!

Simplicity and clarity in:
- Story and message
- Character and personality
- Character design
- Composition and positioning
- Action and poses
- Emotion and facial expression

Improved readability

Simplicity in story and message

Usually it is one story path and one message for the protagonist. More, and the audience will be confused and struggle in understanding who and what the story is actually about.

If there is more than one story path, the various paths at least have to share the same goal and message. For example Studio Ghibli's feature *My Neighbors the Yamadas* (1999) has various short stories that are not connected and explain the family members' relationships with each other. The message is clear: the members love each other despite their fights and struggles.

There is also the other possibility of creating animated features that are in complexity more in line with live-action features and present a less traditional storyline, like the work of the late Japanese animation director Satoshi Kon (1963–2010). Animation, because of its production procedure of planning a film through storyboards and editing the film before it is actually animated, has fewer possibilities in cutting a film and shaping it after it's been shot. A live-action film can be edited over and over again because there is usually plenty of shot material to choose from. An animated feature does not have this luxury and thus Kon's work is quite an exception as he created stories that had a mature complexity, that was only possible because of him changing shots and scenes continuously to achieve animation with a live-action sensibility. For instance his feature *Paprika* (2006) is a stunning *tour-de-force* of surreal imagery and a storyline that is presenting puzzle pieces rather than a clear-cut, traditional storyline. This of course makes the viewing a challenge as much of the story will be understood only at a second viewing, but nevertheless it is a valid approach for animation. Simplicity is replaced in Kon's work with complexity, but the complexity has method. "Though this be madness, yet there is method in't."

DOI: 10.1201/b22147-35

Simplicity in character and personality

Clarity in the personality means that the character's journey should have one goal that leads toward success or failure. Those traits of the personality that lead the story points have to be included or pointed out, not the ones that don't push the story forward. Why waste time on presenting traits that have nothing to do with the story? (of course every trait is important and needs to be considered for understanding the character's actions and reactions, but it doesn't have to be dominantly presented on screen). If the character's goal in the story is to learn about their inability to relate to others, which is the reason for their loneliness, then every aspect in the story needs to support this learning curve in order for it to be understood. In the story every element should underline this loneliness. Simplicity here is simply a clarity in personality in relationship with the story.

Simplicity in character design

The character design needs to visualize the primary aspects of the character's personality and it also needs to be congruent and logical within the character's world. Not every single aspect of the character's personality or social standing can be included into the design as this would be a visual overkill and the audience would have no idea who that character is. The main aspects of the personality that relate to the story will be included in the design, but not much more. Additions within the design that make no sense or deviate from the character's primary personality traits distract and make it more difficult to understand who that character is. The character also has to be clear in shape and form. Objects, clothing, attire that dilutes the silhouette, shape and form, need to be taken out. Many game warrior characters are overdesigned and are boasting complex attire and armor, which in turn takes away the emphasis that needs to be on the character and pushes it toward his or her armor and the action. The result is a cold warrior instead of a character the audience can emotionally relate to. We never relate via actions or appeal alone, those are secondary points that make a character attractive and interesting. The audience will always only develop empathy via believable emotions.

Examples of the need of simplification in the design:

- Overly decorated characters
- Color design and textures that attract too much attention and take the focus away from the face
- Too many accessories that clutter the character
- Unclear shapes and forms
- Too much or contradicting information presented
- Visuals so abstract in their meaning the reading is unclear

Simplicity in composition and positioning of the characters

A very clean and clear composition reads well. Overly complicated compositions make the finding of the focal point and the reading of the image more difficult. The relationship between the characters needs to express the story point and visually explain who is submissive and who is dominant in the shot. Who is leading the action and who is following the lead?

Simplicity in action and poses

Action and poses need to express the story point and with it the emotion that is needed in that very moment, otherwise the audience might be led into the wrong direction by interpreting the image differently and the story then is hardly intelligible. This clarity is crucial in the actual character animation as every movement that is not fully committed to the needed action and emotion will be confusing.

Simplicity in emotion and facial expression

A character whose expressions do not match the story points is unclear and incomprehensible. In order to be coherent, every movement, every glance, action, and reaction needs to read well. Time needs to be given for each emotion to be not only seen but fully understood in relation to the story.

Too much squash and stretch, too much cartoony animation for instance can be distracting. In Sony's feature *Hotel Transylvania* the character animation is pushed to an extreme especially in its squash and stretch, and timing. In the overall film it works as the zaniness of the story and characters is reflected in the very cartoony character animation. However, in some scenes this is pushed too far and the distorted faces and especially the timing distract from the actual story. The exaggeration demands more attention from the audience than paying attention to what in fact happens to the characters.

Simplicity in designing for preschool children

When developing characters for preschool (age 2½–5) content, the design has to follow certain rules that take the target age group and their mental development into consideration. The younger the kids the simpler the design should be: for example, toddlers are unable to recognize intricate shapes and colors. The following list gives an idea of what kids at a preschool age are able to grasp.

The simplicity of Guillermo García Carsí's preschool show *Pocoyo* (2004–2009) is a very good example for this kind of design.

- The content is for children that can not yet grasp complex imagery or understand complex story structures. So the simplicity in the visuals and the storyline is crucial.
- Repetition helps children to remember the story.
- Much attention is given to sounds and music.
- Children are constantly stimulated to actively be involved in the program by singing along, dancing, or answering questions that relate to the story.
- Only what strengthens the story and supports the main idea and direction remains: absolute clarity is a must.
- Decoration can strengthen the design, but the decoration should never grasp the attention. It should always be subtle and kept to a minimum.
- The shapes and colors need to be very clear, precise, and easy to read.
- The shapes are roundish and neither have edges nor look overly geometric.
- Children's toys for this age group share similar sizes of the toy's single parts: every part has a certain size that is never really small. Small parts could break off and be swallowed. Also the bigger sizes of the parts makes it easier for the kids to grab them as their motor skills are not yet fully developed. This design style can be used in the design of the show: everything is roundish, there are no sharp edges.
- There are very few folds in the character design that would complicate the design.
- Small additions like a zipper, a bow, or hat give the characters some uniqueness in the design.

- The ratio between head and body is similar.
- The colors are flat and primary colors are given preference.
- The facial expressions are simple and very easy to read, and only a very limited amount of expressions are used which usually only cover the primary emotions—happiness, sadness, anger, disgust, jealousy, and fear; no complex emotions are depicted as they are not understood as of yet.
- The overall emotional direction has to be "happy."

Simplicity and animation technique

The technical advantage of simplicity is the financial feasibility of the project. This relates to the animation technique and how the animation is actually produced (CG, 2D, stop-motion, cutout, experimental technique). There are myriads of techniques and all have their own complexities and requirements. Overly complex characters in a hand-drawn film let the budged skyrocket as every line that is in the character design means money that needs to be spent on drawing and redrawing the character thousands of times. Is the budget allowing for extravagant decoration and elaborate line work, or is simplification required to make the project cheaper and thus feasible? What works in a CG film design-wise might not work for a stop-motion character or a 2D film. The final design needs to be in line with the technique being used and the budget available. Otherwise, the production might run into serious problems half way through and designs need to be changed, which can be a rather pricey decision, affecting the budget and threatening the completion of the project.

CHAPTER 36

Believability

George Lucas said in an interview about aliens and monsters of 1950s movies:

> When you have monsters from outer space or aliens, inevitably when you finally show the monster it's a disappointment. When you try to make that real with film you have to make it exist at some point in some way that the illusion is there, that's what you are seeing. And that's always been a hard problem because its really technical. And from malays on its been how clever are you to trick the audience into believing something that can't possibly exist.[1]

How believable your character is unfortunately not only depends on the character itself and how well it is designed, but also on the audience's reaction to that character. That may include the audience's knowledge of the subject that you are covering and the acceptance of the given subject by the viewer, so the element of disbelief is an additional and rather significant aspect in the success of the story. Believability especially for game characters has a very broad range and they are often designed for a specific audience and target group, which already is more accepting of the design's direction and style in the first place. Many game characters seem visually odd and totally over the top for most people, though for the hard core fan the characters are very much part of the world they love. The viewer's familiarity with the game's world play an important role in the acceptance of the design. If the viewer doesn't have the knowledge of the subculture then the characters might not convince, or do the plain opposite: turning the user away. Friends of mine absolutely did not like the character designs of *The Nightmare Before Christmas*—they considered the characters ugly. This to me was absolutely inconceivable, as those characters were among the most interesting and beautiful that I had seen in stop-motion to that point. My friends were looking for the familiar, for what they expected animation has to look like whereas I was looking for exactly the opposite: unfamiliar characters that suggest a totally different design from what I had seen before. Those are two extreme ends of the spectrum and very difficult or maybe even impossible to combine. At some point in the design process one has to make a decision and settle on a explicit direction otherwise the process of searching for the right design leads nowhere, as there is always another option and another target audience.

The taste and expectation of the audience is difficult to manipulate and not easily addressed. Usually the audience doesn't want to see characters that are very different from what they are used to, but prefer familiar design territory, which usually heightens the believability for the audience (of course exceptions apply).

The main characters in Hayao Miyazaki's films are always believable as they act realistically in accordance to their given personality and always have plausible reasons for their actions. Chihiro from *Spirited Away* for example convinces on every single level. She initially acts like a little girl. She is stubborn, she is homesick, she makes mistakes and is clumsy, she has a fear of heights and is hesitant and shy toward everyone. Nevertheless, she learns quickly and develops throughout the movie a strength that shows her slowly growing up due to all the challenges that she is confronted with. Chihiro does not grow up physically during the movie, but in her behavior and her attitude, her movement and poses, she feels older than the grumpy and stubborn girl from the beginning. Her character is initially very uncomfortable in the environment of the bathhouse she is working in and in the beginning of her task she is not fitting in at all. At the end of her journey her behavior changes and she dresses slightly differently and is more self-confident. She has adjusted to her new home and shows it. The environment is also reacting to her actions, and her capabilities increase with time. She is helping the stink spirit, she is helping Haku, she is helping many others and thus affects the bathhouse with her actions, learns responsibility, and learns above all the lesson that she needs to rescue her parents.

The believability of a character rises and falls with the believability of the story itself in combination with the design, character animation, and of course the character's personality. Believability is the amalgam of various aspects that the character is constructed from. It is not just based on personality or design, but the sum of all of the following:

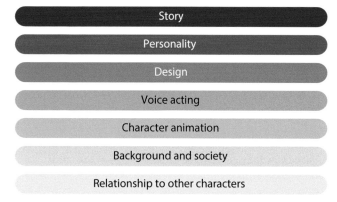

Story
Personality
Design
Voice acting
Character animation
Background and society
Relationship to other characters

[1] Schickel R. (2005). *Watch the Skies!: Science Fiction, the 1950s and Us*. Lorac Productions, Documentary.

DOI: 10.1201/b22147-36

Story, personality, and design

One of the main points for all three aspects of story, personality, and design to create believability is "reason." For everything that is shown on screen and that the characters themselves are doing and experiencing there needs to be a reason. Every single point has to have an explanation for the question "why?" As long as there is an answer to that question and the answer makes sense in this specific world that has been created, the believability will still be maintained (hopefully).

As soon as any of the points are not successfully or satisfactorily answered the believability is at risk. The "why" question is of course a very tricky thing as not everyone for example would buy any given reason for why a fighting woman in a game has to be dressed in a bikini when the fighting man next to her is covered from head to toe in armor that he can barely carry. Reasons satisfy only to a certain point and only satisfy a certain crowd and it is obviously up to the producers and artists to decide which reason is actually valid and which is not. Is it believable that Akira can morph into such an incredibly huge monster, or that Tarzan can skate on bare feet over tree bark, or that a dinosaur is actually harvesting crops? Much in animation is a stretch when one starts to logically think about those stories and most are appealing exactly because they stretch the boundaries of our reality. However, there needs to be a certain logic within the world that is established and that logic needs to be absolutely solid and well thought through. Once the audience starts to think about the stories' flaws, it is very difficult for them to get back into it and actually keep believing the happenings on screen.

Voice-acting (also see Volume 1, Chapter 19, "Sound")

A character's believability rises and falls with the interpretation of the character by the voice actor. A character can be beautifully designed and animated stunningly but if the voice doesn't fit, the character will not be believed in. We connect with the voice of a character more than with its visuals and Chuck Jones proved it to us in *Duck Amuck* (1953) when Daffy Duck's body is erased and only his voice remained. Without the body it was still Daffy, and we felt his personality and insanity coming through, despite his body not being there.

Finding the right voice actor for the character is one of the most crucial aspects in the preproduction phase. An excellent voice actor has the ability to make the character not only come alive, but also to inspire the character animators (and the entire team) to come up with ideas of how that character will act. There is something in the timing and the talent of how the actor emphasizes moments of the voice

track that sparks the imagination of everyone listening to the invented character. If the voice track is weak it is very difficult to nearly impossible to have a good performance in the character animation.[2]

Background and society

Why does Shrek wear a rustic vest and Pinocchio a Tyrolean hat? Why does Ariel wear a bra made of shells and Wallace a knitted pullover? It is their environment that is reflected in the attire and imbeds the characters into their settings. A character is the product of their surroundings and either follows it or sets themselves apart, but there is always a liaison between the two. The environment consists of both the natural and the social setting with its architecture, society, social norms, and morals. The clothing displays the character's social standing, his upbringing, his beliefs and convictions, and stands as a visual reminder for the environment they are living in or coming from. Every environment and society shapes its inhabitants and vice versa. Both are connected and influence each other in their look. The environment can be reflected in the character's clothing, behavior, color, mood, expressions, etc. Neither character nor environment can exist without the other. Even if the character distances themselves from their surroundings, there is still a connection between them as the character actively rejects it. Rejection is a strong emotion that results in a visual impact in the design: the character might ostentatiously dress differently from everyone else in their social circle to show them distancing themselves.

The character on the other hand can be reflected in the environment through their architecture and their shaping of nature. They construct their living quarters and the whole landscape they are living in and use it as their life source. Robinson Crusoe indicates in his attire the island he is living and suffering on. Everything in his habitus tells the story of what occurred to him, how he survived, and still does on his secluded retreat. All materials used in his clothing and accessories he either rescued from the shipwreck or found on the island. Without exception, all elements of his outfit are a representation of his past or current surroundings. Nothing should be randomly chosen for effect. It must all be part of a well-developed concept that creates an overall believable character. Any new tool Crusoe builds is, in shape and purpose, based on a tool that he remembers from his past or he designs it himself based on his current needs. Crusoe is as much the product of his environment as each one of us is the product of our background and present situation. Every outfit we wear reveals something about why we

---

2 More information on voice acting: Winder C, Dowlatabadi Z. (2011). *Producing Animation*. Boston, MA: Focal Press, pp. 198–205.

chose that specific combination in clothes and colors. It exposes what we want to express, consciously or subconsciously. Do we want to appear more conservative, young or hip, smart, or dapper? Many aspects of our personality and how we want to be perceived by our peers can be observed in the way we dress. Many are convinced they dress neutral, but we never do. Our choices are an open book there just to be read. Every outfit is of course strongly connected to the social norms of the environment we are living in or connected to. What seems conservative in one place might not be considered as such in another.

Relationship to other characters

Very few characters are alone in their environment (even Robinson Crusoe at some point has his comrade-in-arms Friday), but those are exceptions and in their specific situation, nature becomes the character they relate to or struggle with. In all other instances, the protagonist deals with other characters and their personality shows and is explained by how they interact with their family, friends, or adversaries. Every action toward another character helps to define who the protagonist is, how they use others, or help them. The relationships a villain has are usually very weak and their lack of friends or functioning relationships is what usually weakens them in the end, whereas the positive relationships of the protagonist is what often leads to their success. What makes this point so important is that most of what is *story* is actually the relationships between the characters: what they do, and why they do it, all goes back to the emotions between the various personalities. Without relationships there is usually no story.

The questions that need to be asked when developing the character's background and vice versa are:

- Where is the character coming from?
- What is the character's background and how does it reflect in their habitus?
- How does the character change their environment and vice versa?
- How do the social norms reflect in the character's habitus and personality?
- How are the character's actions reflecting their social standing?
- How does the environment reflect the character's personality?

Color Design

Color is obviously not just randomly applied to the character to "give it some color" but it has a purpose, has meaning, and speaks on a subconscious level to the audience. Without a well-thought-out color design the character feels random and disorganized.

Color in character design has three points to cover in order to describe the character.

The *descriptive side* of color explains the materials and surfaces, and visualizes textures and lighting. It defines the overall surfaces of character, clothing, and accessories. This for example shows in Figure 37.1 that the kid's skin has a pinkish, healthy hue.

The *emotional side* illustrates the feelings we get when looking at specific colors and what emotions those colors evoke in us. In the illustration this would be for example the purple checkered pants that feel playful and "happy." This side of the color or color combination often reminds us of something; the color is therefore making a connection between two elements. The shirt and pants of the boy remind one of ice cream, fruit, or candy for instance and therefore they look positive and playful.

The *intellectual side* of color design deals with the meaning of colors, the relationship between the elements within the character, or how parts of the character relate to elements in the surroundings of the character. In the illustration for example the flag with the fish is pink which relates to the boy's overall clothing color, thus a relationship between boy and the content on the flag is established.

There is also the social meaning of color established over centuries. The color codes vary in different societies and time frames but are sometimes helpful in defining a character further (please also see Chapter 14, "Color," in Volume 1). Thorough research needs to be done about the meaning of color before they are chosen and used.

Purpose of color design

- To avoid color clutter
- Create a color concept
- Drag attention to the significant elements in the character
- Create an emotion that the viewer can relate to
- Represent the character's personality, age, and social standing
- Represent a time frame and point in history (or not)
- Allow the character to be either in line with the other characters or differ from them
- Assist with the character's appeal
- Create contrast between fore-, middle-, and background
- Define the relationships between parts of the character and the image
- Just a simple background color can define a mood, setting, or environment and place the character from a neutral setting into a suggested setting.

To avoid color clutter

Color design's first purpose is to avoid an image that is difficult to read in its color information. A plan or concept for how and why the color is applied prevents the image from being

Figure 37.1

DOI: 10.1201/b22147-37

too busy and confusing. Randomly applying color has no intellectual basis in storytelling or in the information given. The color needs to support the overall design direction, not go against it. In Figure 37.1 the main information is the boy, so the color of the boy should be dragging the attention, not the background.

Create a color concept

The color concept is needed to organize the various colors and arrange them with a plan. This needs to always have the story and character personality as a basis, because the color needs to explain the character intellectually, emotionally, and descriptively in order to cover all three points that color offers. This then results in a fully rounded color design. Figure 37.2a through c show what this concept could be when it comes to warm and cold colors. Warm colors usually attract the eye, so having the focal point of the illustration, the boy, in mostly warm colors will drag attention (Figure 37.2a). In Figure 37.2b, the warm colors would gradually shift toward cold colors the further the eye moves away from the face, and in Figure 37.2c, the warm colors are on the right, the cold ones on the left. This accentuates the direction of the boy's pose toward the right. There can obviously be further conceptual color ideas that

are layered on top of each other. However, they must always support one idea, not have several ideas that fight each other. If the boy is the focal point, all concepts need to support the boy in their color design. In Figure 37.1, the boy is painted with mostly warm colors and his skin is the brightest element in the design. If the backpack would be brighter than the skin, despite being warm, it would lose its focus and the attention required for the boy to be the focus would shift toward the backpack. The overall concept of the boy being the focal point would be lost.

Drag attention to the significant elements in the character

Color consists of the three components of saturation, brightness, and hue, and all three can be used to highlight parts in the image. The brightness of the boy's skin already pushes the boy forward in importance and highlights his position in the frame. With each of the three elements, saturation, hue, and brightness, each color can either push forward or recede an element in the design, strengthening or weakening its importance. The subtleties within color allows an extremely sensitive interplay between all the colors used and can make it a challenge to balance out all the colors within the character.

(a)

(b)

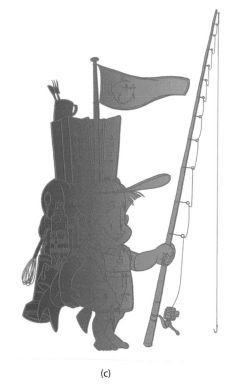
(c)

Figure 37.2

Warm and cold colors are clearly separated.

Warm colors blur into cold colors from the focal point outwards.

Warm colors blur into cold colors from right to left to suggest warm light from the front.

Create an emotion

Single colors or color combinations have the ability to evoke an emotion if used sensitively. What feeling the color has depends on its surrounding colors and its own ability to remind the viewer of a texture, surface, object, or a situation, and thus evoke a memory or create a mood. A peach for instance being soft when touched, the color combination of a peach with soft rose, yellow, orange, and red might evoke aside from reminding of the sweetness of a peach also the softness and fuzzy touch of it, so creating comfort. Any kind of emotion can be represented by a color and thus subconsciously affect the viewer's reading of the character.

Represents the character's personality, age, gender, and social standing

Colors have the ability to refine the character's personality by showing for example someone being jealous by using green, which is just the most simple way of visualizing that the character is "green with envy." Obviously this can be much more complex and can be used with more subtlety to illustrate the character's primary personality traits. The character's age can be shown in the color of their skin, hair, or fashion, gender can also be shown in the subtle use of male or female color combinations. The social standing of the character is easily represented by the use of fashion with a very specific color combination that demonstrates wealth or social power, or outstanding social benevolence. The question is, how to interpret traits like giving, positive outlook on life, dominance, or social boldness with color? Connections can be established by the use of colors that simply connect to an object or place: a more grounded earthen tone connects the character with earth, or dark blue to connect them with the night sky, or with bright colors that remind one of spring and the awakening of "an idea." The choice would have to be the colors that also connect to the story's plot and subplot, the character's personality and their goals and aspirations. It is only the combination of it all that will finally determine which color combination is the correct one for the character.

Represents a time frame and point in history

Any color combination will position the character in a specific time frame as every era has preferred colors for fashion and design. The use of specific color combinations either place the entire style into a historical period or context, or let just the character be positioned in a stylistic period through the use

Figure 37.3

of these colors in their fashion. A character that for example wears 1970s-style clothing with the fitting color combination in a contemporary story has a reason to wear it; either to show the complete lack of sense of fashion, or to show exactly that they are "hip." The subtleties of choosing the right colors to define the character further is not only about the character's personal preferences, but also about the character's role in the story. The representation of this role through the colors evokes a specific period in history and thus connects that time period's ideas, opinions, or politics with the character's goals, aspirations, and their overall personality. The colors black–red–white of the Nazi swastika for example are often used to represent the "evil" side of a political agenda or group, like the emblems and insignias of the First Order in *Star Wars: The Force Awakens* (2015).

Allows the character to be either in line with the other characters or differ from them

The five ovals represent simple characters. One can see that one of them falls out of the group, because its color is significantly different from the others, which is the green. All other colors contain some degree of red which groups them together (Gestalt theory). The odd one out can be easily recognized by lacking red. This obviously needs to be much more complex in a character lineup, but the idea is the same: variation creates separate characters, similarity groups characters together.

Assists with the character's appeal

Well-developed color design will obviously create a character with more appeal for the audience to be drawn toward. A well-balanced and thought out color concept can drag the audience's attention and create a warm and comfortable feeling toward the character or in case of a colder color design, reject it (or vice versa is also possible if done right). The simplest direction for creating attraction is warm colors as they attract the eye and cold colors create more distance toward the character. In Figure 37.4, the left character has warm, the right character more cold colors. We tend to be more drawn to warm colors as they show a healthy character, compared to the cold colored right guy. Attraction however does not mean the character's personality is more attractive! Warm colors just suggest a warm

personality, they are not proof of one. The character's animation, his actions and reactions, his goals and aspirations, are what makes the character attractive to the audience, despite their warm or cold appearance. However, obviously there should be some relationship between the two or at least an explanation for the warmer or colder direction. Jack Skellington or Sally from *The Nightmare Before Christmas* (1993) both have cold colors and are still warm and lovable characters. But because they are from Halloween town they obviously lack a functioning and healthy warm bloodstream.

Creates contrast between fore-, middle-, and background

Color contrast helps to create perspective, separating colors from each other and defining the different levels of information in the frame. In Figure 37.1, the character is mostly painted in warm and brighter colors, whereas the background is either dark green or white/light green. The stark contrast between background and foreground is what sets the character apart from their surroundings.

Defines relationships between parts of the character and the image

Colors that share attributes in their hue, brightness, or saturation establish connections between elements in the design that can be utilized for the story to develop or the personality to be refined. The simplified example in Figure 37.5a shows how the warm color of the orange boy is immediately connecting with the cup and the bottle, whereas in Figure 37.5b the fish is straight

Figure 37.4

(a)   (b)

Figure 37.5

away grouping with the flag and the fishing pole. This can be used in an obviously more subtle and sophisticated method to increase personality, backstory, story, and the relationship to objects or other characters. It can also make a strong connection to ideas outside of the character and their environment and bring for example a character's love for flying into the design, but having him wear a light blue shirt. Then the idea of the sky is constantly prevalent in the character.

Just a simple background color can define a mood, setting, or environment

In Figure 37.3 the subtle green in the background is enough to evoke the feeling of nature. It is unclear what the specifics of that "nature" are and obviously it is unimportant for the purpose of the illustration, which is to present the character in their personality. Nevertheless, the green background not only helps to set a comfortable mood but also helps with the storytelling

and puts the character into a setting, however abstract it might be. It does create a warm and comfortable setting that affects the character positively. Simple color suggestions of settings can have a tremendous influence on how the character is perceived.

More on color:

Burchett K. (2005). *A Bibliographical History of the Study and use of Color from Aristotle to Kandinsky*. Lewiston, NY: Edwin Mellen Press.

Lynch D, Livingston W. (1995). *Color and Light in Nature*. Cambridge: Cambridge University Press.

Itten J. (1970). *The Elements of Color: A Treatise on the Color System of Johannes Itten Based on His Book The Art of Color*. Hoboken, NJ: John Wiley and Sons.

Clothing Design, Folds, and Fabrics

I will not be explaining folds in detail, because there are great books that have already done that and taken on the complex task of folds. They are mentioned in the book list at the end of this chapter.

Clothing design

The clothing of the character is neither just an outer shell that provides protection from the elements, nor just a fashion statement. It is a visual representation of who that character is in their personality. Clothing is also never just one design, but a group of dressed characters that are defined by comparison. A character that wears a pair of ripped jeans and a T-shirt looks more careless and outgoing next to a character in a conservative suit. But put another character next to them that wears beach shorts and flip-flops, the jeans and T-shirt character isn't as outgoing anymore. The clothing needs to be designed with all the other characters in mind. Usually the protagonist is designed first and then all the other characters use that as the reference point.

What makes fashion and clothing design so incredibly difficult is the scope of possibilities. There is literally no end to the design of clothing and to find the right fashion for the character to shine without repeating often-before-seen styles and outfits is a task. Most of the character designers aren't fashion designers or know much about fashion to begin with. The main goal is to create a character that doesn't follow a cliché but is unique enough to stand their ground and expresses their personality through clothing.

The character of Miranda Priestly, the head editor of a fashion magazine in NYC, sums it up so poignantly in the film *The Devil Wears Prada* (2006) when she says to Andy Sachs, her new assistant:

Miranda and some assistants are deciding between two similar belts for an outfit. Andy snickers because she thinks they look exactly the same

Miranda Priestly: Something funny?

Andy Sachs: No. No, no. Nothing's ... You know, it's just that both those belts look exactly the same to me. You know, I'm still learning about all this stuff and, uh ...

Miranda Priestly: This ... stuff? Oh. Okay. I see. You think this has nothing to do with you. You go to your closet and you select ... I don't know ... that lumpy blue sweater, for instance, because you're trying to tell the world that you take yourself too seriously to care about what you put on your back.

But what you don't know is that that sweater is not just blue, it's not turquoise. It's not lapis. It's actually cerulean. And you're also blithely unaware of the fact that in 2002, Oscar de la Renta did a collection of cerulean gowns. And then I think it was Yves Saint Laurent ... wasn't it, who showed cerulean military jackets? I think we need a jacket here. And then cerulean quickly showed up in the collections of eight different designers. And then it, uh, filtered down through the department stores and then trickled on down into some tragic casual corner where you, no doubt, fished it out of some clearance bin. However, that blue represents millions of dollars and countless jobs and it's sort of comical how you think that you've made a choice that exempts you from the fashion industry when, in fact, you're wearing the sweater that was selected for you by the people in this room.[1]

Fashion is not only there to make the character belong to a certain group, but can carry much additional information (can, not must!):

- Group affiliation and social standing
- Purpose of the clothing
- Define the personality
- Emotional effect on the viewer and wearer
- Define the character's task in the storyline
- Visually show the character's goals and aspirations
- Visual representation of the character's current situation
- Visually show the character's past
- Emphasize the body shape
- Position the character in a certain time period
- Define the character's political and social views
- Define the character's sexual orientation
- Separate the characters visually from each other
- Support the initial shape and form language
- Raise questions
- Be logical within the character's world
- Be unique when needed, and plain and common when required

Group affiliation

Clothing tells us the profession of the wearer, the age, sometimes nationality or cultural affiliation, possible gender and sexuality, but also gives us information on hobbies, sports, and health. All of this information is not always proof of the character's actual affiliation, but usually suggests the possibility.

---

[1] *The Devil Wears Prada* (2006), directed by David Frankel, 20th Century Fox.

DOI: 10.1201/b22147-38

For instance not everyone that wears a motorcycle jacket actually rides a motorcycle. It can just be a fashion accessory instead of a practical piece of safety clothing.

Make sure that the character wears clothing and uses accessories that are clearly positioning them in their accurate position on the social ladder. For instance, certain colors are only allowed to be worn by high officials or royalty in historical settings, jobs have specific attires and accessories that cannot be changed, colors always come with a meaning and that meaning often is rooted deeply in society and the time period. Make sure that the colors, fabrics, shapes, and textures used are socially acceptable. A peach-colored silk shirt worn by a farmer working in the fields wouldn't be the most practical thing to wear and also not the most logical one when it comes to the task.

Purpose of the clothing

The purpose of a piece of clothing needs to be obvious and well thought through if the believability is not to be jeopardized. What is the character doing and how does the clothing support that action, job, hobby, etc.? Is the clothing practical and comfortable for that action or job, or is it hindering the character's movements? As fierce fashionista Edna Mode explains: "NO CAPES!" as they might be getting caught in action.

Much clothing and gear of warriors in game characters is utterly impractical as it has so many parts and pieces where one can easily get stuck that the practicality of it tends to go toward zero. It looks tough and manly (to some users) but it lacks believability. That is not necessarily a bad thing if the target audience is already aware of this and still accepts the character's outrageous drag-like fashion for what it is without questioning their believability. A hiker shouldn't wear high-heels in the mountains as much as an Olympic swimmer shouldn't wear blue jeans in a competition. The level of practicality in the clothing shows how much we can take that character seriously in successfully finishing the given task. Someone that rides a bicycle and is obviously overweight, but is dressed like a professional with tight and over-the-top biking gear can come across as a show-off that might not be able to perform as well as they'd like to. But then again, they could outperform our expectations and be incredibly good, and thus our prejudices were already expected by the designer and used as a tool to give the character a twist. Thinking that every overweight character is incapable of performing well in sports is obviously wrong and silly. But the designer can use those prejudices as an advantage and surprise the audience.

Define the personality

Obviously the outfit was chosen by the characters themselves so it expresses their choice of style, colors, and shapes, and how they want to be seen and portray themselves to others. It is not about what the designer wants the characters to wear but about what the characters themselves would choose to wear at that moment. Many questionable fashion choices for the characters derive from not fully grasping who that character is, or choosing outfits that present an established yet overused cliché. Every character has something that is unique and deserves to be visualized in their clothing. If it is the most boring character on earth, plain, and with no fashion taste at all, then this is what makes them special and that needs to be exaggerated. They have to be in the lineup of characters the most plainly dressed, so plain and gray indeed that they suck out the colors from everyone next to them with the gravitational pull of a black hole.

The personality clearly shows in not only what the character is wearing but also how they are wearing it. Are the clothes clean and neat, or dirty and rugged? Does everything fit perfectly and is even custom made, or is it from the supermarket hanging rail and not a fit at all? Is the combination of the clothes well thought out or is it just assembled randomly? All those little decisions that one makes to pick and choose their outfits always go back to the personality of the character (and of course their financial means).

Emotional effect on the viewer and wearer

"Clothes make the man" (and woman) is a well-known saying and most definitely has truth to it. We respond to a doctor in a white lab coat with much more respect than a doctor in jeans and T-shirt. The lab coat seems to express knowledge and expertise, however put some coffee stains and a leaking pen stain on the coat and the trust might vanish rather quickly. But it is not only the other person that is affected by the clothing, but also the wearer's behavior changes when wearing a distinct outfit. A doctor that wears the pristine lab coat is probably carrying themselves with much more confidence and pride than the one that has a dirty lab coat (of course the doctor's personality has an impact on this, too; the clean-cut doctor might know that he is a fake and lacks extensive expertise in his field but he is so pompous and full of himself, that pretending is his road to success).

Define the character's task in the storyline

What is the role of the character within the story and how could the clothing interpret it? A successful banker probably would wear a spotless and custom-made suit. The banker in the story slowly loses their grip on life and goes through some inner turmoil, questioning their job choices and thinking about the pointlessness of their life: they are in a mid-life crisis. Being in the crisis, they have to ever so slightly show in their clothing that they are going through this life-changing process. This is not about a broad sign of the character falling apart, but a subtle hint that things don't work out perfectly at the moment.

In Steven Spielberg's feature *Indiana Jones and the Temple of Doom* (1984) Indiana Jones is an intellectual professor of archeology and also occasional tough guy that can take on any challenge while robbing another archeological site. His outfit says exactly that: it is robust, practical, manly, not at all flashy.

Everything he carries is useful, comfortable, and practical. Mister Short Round on the other hand, Indy's companion, is wearing a worn-out Chinese outfit, also practical, presenting his background and social standing. He also wears a New York Yankees baseball cap which shows that he has a strong fan connection to that American club, which could also show his aspirations of one day going/immigrating to the US. The singer Willie Scott, in the beginning in Shanghai, is wearing a red and golden glitzy evening gown (from Paris) which proves so very impractical later on in the Indian jungle. Then she is dressed at the Indian Pankot Palace in a white and gold dress. Both dresses are utterly unsuitable for the physical tasks ahead. She comes across as slightly simple and spoiled, whereas Jones comes across as mostly in control with the challenges they will face. He will save the day, whereas she is "tagging along." He is the active one with Short Round on his side, whereas she is the passive one, the damsel in distress. Both active and passive shows clearly in the clothing.

In Roman Polanski's film *The Fearless Vampire Killers* (1967) all the main characters that are vampires or will become vampires wear blood-red or a variant of it. The main character Alfred, a vampire hunter, wears a red jacket from the beginning, which puts him— for the acute viewer—closer to the vampires. There is a color connection that cannot be denied and in the end Alfred is the one that will also be turning into a vampire. The beginning, in the color of the character's jacket, therefore already predicted the outcome of his journey.

The character's clothing however also extends to their hair-style, which is part of the overall appearance. The character of Norman in Laika's stop-motion extravaganza *ParaNorman* (2012) is the only character in the lineup with distinct spiky hair. The hair is so stiff that its impossible for Norman to comb it, because it snaps up right away. The idiom of "to make someone's hair stand on end" means to make someone frightened. Norman can see the dead that surround him at all times. His way to school is like a meet-and-greet of his dead acquaintances that he meets every morning. A "normal" kid would be petrified, but not Norman. He is dealing with the situation because he has to. That doesn't mean that it has no impact on him; the hair still shows that he is frightened, but he deals with his anxiety.

Visual representation of the character's goals and aspirations

The character's goals and aspirations are often visualized by pendants that have a significance for the character, by bracelets or objects they carry around to remind the audience of their journey past, present, and future. What the character wants or wishes for can also be visualized in colors, textures, fabric types, clothing cuts, or accessories. A character that wants to become a doctor, because it is their most intense wish for whatever reason, could have some design on their clothing that already reminds one of a doctor. That doesn't mean they wear doctors' clothing, but maybe the clothing could be rather bright instead of dark, or

they wear an earring or chain that has some medical symbol. This should obviously be done in a very subtle way to not make the point too clearly, but enough to be read.

Pinocchio in Disney's feature from 1940 wants to be a boy; that is his aspiration and goal. He is a wooden marionette, but he is already dressed like a boy with the typical Tyrolean hat and shorts. His outfit doesn't look like a puppet's, which would be slightly too decorative and exaggerated, but like a normal boy's.

Young Hercules in Disney's feature of the same name (1997) already wears rather different clothing compared to his parents or everyone else in town. His tunic is worn as a himation, over only one shoulder, whereas his father wore his shirt over both shoulders. This makes Hercules look more athletic and thus different. Also, the white fabric of his tunic makes him look pure and "unspoiled." His parent's clothes, as they are farmers, are brown and ochre. The clothing already shows that Hercules is different and that he is more than "just" human.

Visual representation of the character's current situation

This point is pretty obvious and covers most of the characters. Shrek is dressed modestly as he lives in the swamp and only uses materials that are to be found in his living space. Ariel, the little mermaid, has shells as a bra; Lilo's shirt with a simple Hawaiian print; Princess Mononoke's fur and teeth necklace ...

Visually show the character's past

Objects and accessories can be of significance to the character and a reminder of an incident in the past, an incident that had an impact on the character's personality or their relationship with others. These are usually objects that the character carries around or applies to their clothing, or even the clothing itself, thus reiterating the important incident constantly. The message or theme of the storyline can be expressed in that one single object and thus the main topic of the film is steadily visible. The blue pendant in the film *Titanic* (1997), Luke Skywalker's lightsaber, Indiana Jones' fedora hat, are all not just objects that are part of the character's attire, but are carriers of important information and visualize an idea or a moment of the past that made the character into who they are. Many of these objects don't have a meaning on the surface of the story but reveal their true importance throughout a film series or as a backstory that is not officially told in the main plot.

Emphasize the body shape

The clothing the character wears should not water down the body shape of the character or change it dramatically. It always has to strengthen it and support it, otherwise there would be two different silhouettes of one character which can be confusing. However, if the character has two different versions then the clothing can enhance it. For example in Disney's feature *Aladdin* (1992), Jafar turns even more evil at the end of the film and his clothing style is pushed in the shoulders and headgear to resemble a snake in shape. This is exaggerating the existing shape, but does not create a completely new one.

Position the character in a certain time period

When designing the clothes one should always go to the source material of the original fashion style and study it, instead of relying on other character designs or illustrations, which would only feed an incestuous design direction where character design is born out of other character design instead of going back to the source of the clothing. If for instance the task is to design a peasant from the Middle Ages it is important to look into actual depictions of peasants in visual materials of that time or if those are not available, to study scientific research of how these clothes of peasants might have looked. Do not base your knowledge on existing character design alone!

Proper research is the only way of dealing with the complex topic of fashion and accessories throughout the ages and what people of the various social standings were wearing. This also depends on the scale of the production and how far the accuracy needs to be pushed. Some productions don't care at all about historical accuracy and others do.

Define the character's political and social views

A character that fights in the Russian Revolution for social changes and equality, and supports communist values, should maybe not be wearing a frock and a top hat. The outfit can give a hint about the character's political standing and not every fashion item is free of a political message. Research is the only way of getting clarity.

Define the character's sexual orientation

This is obviously really a pickle because one does really not want to fall into clichés and stereotypes! One of the most remarkable openly gay characters is Hana, from Satoshi Kon's *Tokyo Godfathers* (2003). She is a loud and emotional homeless drag queen that is entertaining but also has a big heart and is the one mostly attached to the baby she finds on Christmas Eve, to whom she wants to become a mother. She clearly comes across as a transsexual and is in her outfit somehow in-between man and woman. She wears men's shoes and a suit, but also wears a woman's coat and other female garb. She is concerned about her makeup, but also has a bit of stubble on her face once in a while. Satoshi Kon is, considering that Hana is one of the first drag queens in animation that is not made fun of and not a gag-target (like for instance Bugs Bunny's drag performances), very respectful toward the portrayal of Hana. Her character is well researched and, even though some of her facial expressions

and poses are a bit over the top compared to the other two main characters, Kon is never insensitive toward her. Hana comes across as a strong woman that wants to do right what her mother missed: being a mother.

The only character that has been portrayed as openly being gay in American animation is Mitch in *ParaNorman* (2012). He is not at all being outed as gay until the very end of the film, which makes him just a normal guy and one assumes that he is straight. This is the very point of the entire film that deals with tolerance. The audience catches themselves stereotyping and being caught in the assumption that of course Mitch is straight. The only sign of him being gay might be the tight shirt, but then again straight guys that work out also want to show their muscles, so this isn't at all a "sign." What is extremely important here is to not fall into the trap of supporting a stereotype that is hurtful and inappropriate, but still gets the message across and in some cases is also funny and entertaining. Mitch was everything but a stereotype, but a character that loves fixing cars, loves to work out, is a typical unassuming guy, a bit on the simple side, that just happens to be gay. His outfit doesn't show that he is gay, but when looking back at the end of the film, one gets the "message."

Separate the characters visually from each other

Make sure that the characters separate from each other in their fashion. Every character should have a unique outfit that is only for them and clearly expresses that one character. The characters need to have their own color-, shape-, and style language to define each of them for who they are without a doubt and thus distinguish them from the others.

Support the initial shape and form language

The clothing always has to accentuate the character's body shape that was initially given to the character. Having a unique shape language but then covering it up with a long coat would defeat the purpose of the shape language in the first place.

Raise questions

There are characters that are mysterious and their function is to not clearly show what their purpose in the story is or will be. Those characters don't want to be clearly recognized in their attire and are therefore leading the audience in the wrong direction with their outfit, or keeping it vague as an option. Not everything has to make perfect sense to the audience. Some information can be kept hidden to make the audience think and guess, supporting the suspense.

Be logical within the character's world

What the character is wearing and using as accessories needs to make sense in the character's world, not necessarily in ours.

Be unique when needed, and plain and common when required

Not every character needs to be flashy and loud in their clothing, because not every character is loud. Some like to be quiet and invisible, and present their unassuming personality in their plain clothing. Having a plain and common sense of fashion is for some characters an important visual aid to not let them stand out from the crowd. A very shy character could wear clothing that covers up more than it should to be comfortable, because they want to hide.

Accessories

Accessories complement an outfit and also very often complete the character. They are secondary to the main clothing but always have the important task to strengthen the specific look. There is two types of accessories:

- *Worn:* shoes, scarves, jackets, gloves, glasses, jewelry, socks, ties, watches, hats, caps, belts, holsters, pouches, ponchos, bandanas, hard-hats
- *Carried:* bags, umbrellas, fans, suitcases, walking sticks, weapons, cellphones, armor ...

Additionally, in designing the character the accessories need to have a purpose that connects to the story and again the character. What would be the point of a character carrying around a heavy sword if he never really needs to use it in the story (but then again it would be rather funny if the character carries around that heavy sword and everyone in the story comments on it and questions it). Every accessory has a meaning and refines the character in their personality, history, and goal. Only the accessory with a strong purpose should be used, not one that is only there as decoration.

What would Indiana Jones be without his whip, what Lara Croft be without her guns, Luke without his lightsaber, Princess Mononoke without her dagger, or Ashitaka without his bow and arrows, Kiki without her broom, or Lilo without her scary doll Scrump. All these objects and accessories have a very strong meaning, not only for the development of the story, but also in refining a crucial side of the character's personality. Before assigning a character an accessory or an object, one needs to be very clear on what it stands for and how it is a representation of a character's inner life, history, or goal. Without that meaning, just randomly choosing an accessory for a character makes it banal and the audience won't understand how the object connects with the story.

Fabric

Fabric is a tricky thing to draw considering it has a unique behavior and if not understood from a physical perspective seems utterly random and without logic, and thus impossible to draw and get right. So studying fabric is crucial to not only understand it, but also to be able to artistically interpret it. What makes fabric easier to visualize is understanding what actually happens when fabric is draped around a form in terms of forces, weight, and material.

The danger with folds is that one wants to "get it right" and render them to a precision that can actually be seriously mind-numbing. Simplicity therefore is the key, and grasping what actually happens with the fabric with logic helps to "invent" correct-looking folds. It doesn't have to be 100% correct as long as it is convincing and the folds describe the forces the fabric is exposed to. If everything in the character design is stylized, the folds also need to be stylized to the same degree. The simplification of folds helps a great deal in not only making the forces clearer by eliminating all the distracting information, but also improving the readability of the entire character. Folds that push themselves visually into the foreground are destroying the focal point of the image and drag too much attention. Busy folds drag attention, but plain folds lack the information needed to convince.

The surface of fabric wrinkles and creates folds when there is stress on the material. This can happen through a force that tugs on the fabric, or is caused by the body underneath moving, or through the weight of the fabric itself. Once the fabric folds in one area, the areas around that section have to react too, as there is always the same amount of fabric and when one area wrinkles, the other area has to stretch: action and reaction. It is again all about forces and how they act on the fabric. However, there is also the artistic use of fabric and using its flow or folds as vectors for the reading direction of the pose. The following points help to use folds and fabric in the designs:

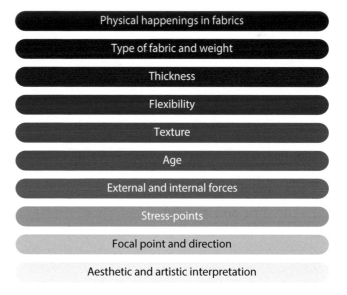

- Physical happenings in fabrics
- Type of fabric and weight
- Thickness
- Flexibility
- Texture
- Age
- External and internal forces
- Stress-points
- Focal point and direction
- Aesthetic and artistic interpretation

Physical happenings in fabrics

Fabric needs to succumb to the forces it is exposed to, which means that if you pull on one side of the fabric, the other side will react either by stretching or by shifting. If a square of fabric is on a table (Figure 38.1a) and one corner is pulled, the distance

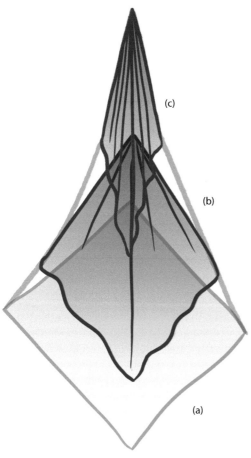

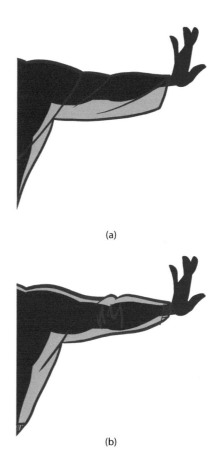

Figure 38.1

Figure 38.2

pulled is equal to the distance it will travel. All points of the fabric are following the point of the pull (Figure 38.1b). The stronger the pull the more accentuated the folds are; all follow the source of the force (Figure 38.1c).

What is pulled in one direction has to give in another area of the fabric. If the fabric is able to stretch, then the percentage of the rule's impact depends on the amount of stretch the fabric is able to achieve.

Type of fabric and weight

This point is pretty obvious. Silk falls very differently compared to a thick corduroy. The weight of the corduroy will create very different folds, will be much rougher and more cumbersome in its behavior than silk.

Thickness

Every fabric has its own specific way of creating folds which is what gives it personality and uniqueness. It is not just that the folds themselves have a different appearance, but also

the body underneath shows more of its surface curvature under silk and other delicate fabrics than under a thick and heavy blue denim. The thicker and heavier the fabric, the more rough and big are the folds and the less visible is the body underneath (obviously depending on the tightness of the cut of the clothing). The thinner and more delicate the fabric is, the smaller and thinner are the folds and the more can be seen from the body's form (Figure 38.2a). Also the weight of the fabric itself has a tremendous impact on how it behaves and how it creates folds. However, thick fabric can be so rigid that it holds itself up (Figure 38.2b). A thick jacket is less prone to the forces of gravity because the fabric's stiffness can be greater in its forces than the weight of the fabric itself, which causes the fabric to create its own shapes. Stiff fabrics can alter or intensify the wearer's body shape. Japanese warriors were wearing the kataginu, a vest that accentuates the shoulders with massive protruding wings, historically worn for combat's need of high mobility. The wide shoulders are made of stiff fabric that widen the shoulders immensely and thus exaggerate the human form underneath, making the warrior appear bigger.

Flexibility

The flexibility of a fabric affects the ability of it to have folds and also the number of folds happening. A regular white man's dress shirt made of cotton is quite soft and creates many folds; the same fabric heavily starched might not create any. The more rigid the fabric, the less it will budge and change its own shape, and replicate the surface underneath. The more flexible the fabric is, the more it is able to wrinkle and show the body's surface.

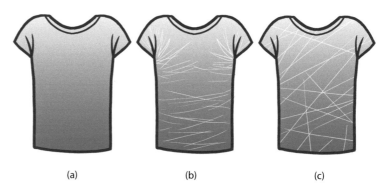

(a)   (b)   (c)

Figure 38.3

Texture

How does the fabric feel to the touch? How is its surface: soft or rough, wet or dry, long hair or short hair, dense or loose, transparent or opaque?

How does the texture of the fabric represent the character's personality or the story point? How does the texture represent the character's environment? An 18th century mine worker in South Yorkshire for sure did not wear an expensive brocade jacket for his mining work, but a robust outfit with a practical fabric, which can withstand the heavy wear and tear of his daily job.

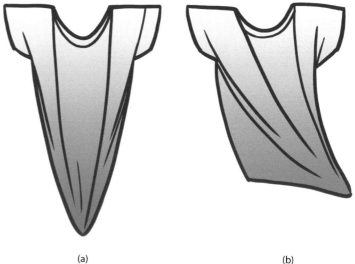

(a)   (b)

Figure 38.4

Age

The age of the fabric is of importance as new fabric behaves differently from old fabric. New fabric has not yet adjusted itself to the body underneath, the elbows have not yet stretched out, the knees not bulged, the bottom of the pants hasn't yet sagged (Figure 38.5). Figure 38.6 shows where there are significant stress points that will always show bulges or wrinkles in aged clothing. Where there are wrinkles in the front, there will be a bulge in the back and vice versa. Again, the rule applies: action causes reaction. In used fabric the surface does *actually* bulge and the area is often permanently stretched. It is not merely a situation where the fabric gets stretched but as a matter of fact it expands to imitate the forms underneath.

Additionally, fabric can be cared for and ironed (Figure 38.3a) or be slightly wrinkly in its surface texture (Figure 38.3b). The wrinkly texture can show the signs of wear, where the wrinkles are caused by the body's movement. Wrinkles then appear in stress points. Or, wrinkles can randomly appear which would show that the fabric was for example just lying around, not being folded (Figure 38.3c). The wrinkles then are not caused by the body's shape. The wrinkly surface texture has a feeling of carelessness or a happy-go-lucky attitude. A banker with

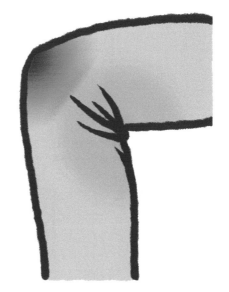

Figure 38.5

Figure 38.6

a perfect suit, but a wrinkly shirt, shows an interesting aspect in their outfit that doesn't seem to fit, but might give them a unique addition to their personality.

External forces

There are two external forces: pulling and pushing forces. Wind for example creates a force that pulls the fabric into one general direction, within which is randomness that is caused by the weight and stiffness of the fabric fighting the wind's pull. Other pulling forces create a distinct direction where the created folds clearly strive toward the stress point (Figure 38.4a and b). Every point in the fabric is exposed to the pull and will be dragged toward the stress point.

Internal forces

The movement of the body underneath is what creates the strongest internal forces the fabric is succumbing to. As mentioned before, tension and compression are two forces that often happen opposite each other and thus act in unison. If the knee bends, the fabric in the front of the knee gets stretched, whereas the fabric in the hollow of the knee gets squashed, creating folds. These folds appear where there is stress on the fabric caused by the movement of the body (Figure 38.5).

However, there is a second incident when folds appear which is caused by the cut of the clothing itself. Those folds

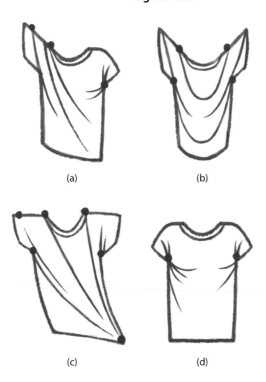

(a)   (b)

(c)   (d)

Figure 38.7

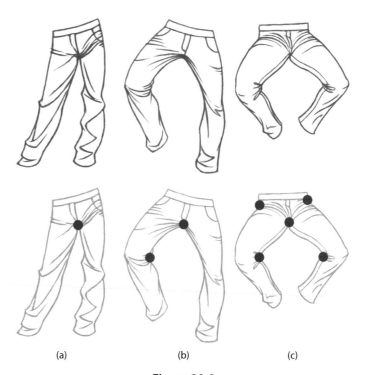

(a)   (b)   (c)

Figure 38.8

Figure 38.9

Figure 38.10

are either there for a reason and the cut of the clothes was specifically designed to create folds in that very same spot, or they are caused by stress points, points in the body that will always cause wrinkles and folds. Stress points occur where there is significant movement (armpits, elbows, crotch, knees …) or where the clothing has significant seams (Figure 38.6).

Stress points

Tension and compression is the main cause of the creation of stress points. The fabric is exposed to forces that the body underneath creates. Figure 38.7a through d shows stress points in a T-shirt and where they happen by a body moving underneath, or when tucked in Figure 38.7c. In Figure 38.8a through c, the stress points are happening depending on the pose of the body underneath: (a) standing, (b) halfway sitting, and (c) sitting. In the standing pose, the fabric is creating folds merely because of its own weight, plus one stress point in the crotch where some folds go forward due to the hip tilt. The folds in the legs become more and more intense the closer they get to the ground, as the fabric's own weight drags it down and causes it to cascade. In the middle pose (Figure 38.8b), the character is sitting halfway on a barstool; the fabric's weight is partly held up by the upper legs, it's only the lower part of the pants that hang down freely, though

still affected by the position of the knees. This pose creates a stress point in the crotch, because of the legs spreading. We can see one more thing happening at the knee: the fabric creates folds that wrap around the knee and define its three-dimensionality. In Figure 38.8c, the fabric is stretching over the legs, so the shape of the legs is now dominating, not the folds. Even in the lower part of the legs, the fabric is stretching around the calves, showing much more of the anatomy than in Figure 38.8b.

Focal point and direction

We have already discussed Figures 38.9 and 38.10 in the section on vectors. Folds can be of great help to point toward the focal point in the image if planned right. The folds can be designed more freely in a drawing because we can "decide" which folds are helping the composition and which are not, and then exaggerate them accordingly. The flow in the design is the priority and the folds need to follow its direction. The statue of Urania (Figures 38.11 through 38.13), a Roman copy from the fourth century Greek original, shows how the folds do two things:

- Define the body underneath the fabric and clearly show the contrapposto of hips and shoulders (Figure 38.12)
- Guide the eye toward the focal point, the globe, and Urania's head (Figure 38.13)

| Figure 38.11 | Figure 38.12 | Figure 38.13 |

Urania (4th century BC) (Courtesy of Urania).

She is the muse of astronomy and obviously the globe that she is presenting is her insignia, alongside the staff that she is holding in her right hand. The folds accentuate the movement and connect the points of importance.

Aesthetic and artistic interpretation

Folds are the most convincing when they show some organic flow. Once they lose that organic feel, the fabric can feel rigid and stiff. However, the style of the design might require a look that is not following an organic flow, so an artistic interpretation needs to be found that covers both the style and the feel of the fabric.

Mike Mignola's comic *Hellboy* is in some illustrations pushing its geometry and graphic style heavily into the style of the folds and creates a "feel" rather than mimicking the actual realistic fabric. The feel and flow of the fabrics is always in relation to all the other materials portrayed, but once movement comes into

the image the fabric doesn't only have to look convincing in its stylization, but also move convincingly. The Japanese feature *Tekkonkinkreet* (2006) proves successful in both stylization and movement and has folds that are reduced and stylized without jeopardizing the style of the character design or the character animation.

It is important that the fabric feels right in relation to all the other materials in the world created. A fabric that is soft can be much harder or softer depending on the style and the direction of the entire project.

Figure 38.14 has two approaches. In Figure 38.14a, the fabric feels soft due to the organic flow of the line and has a convincing weight to it. In Figure 38.14b, the line is more inorganic and rigid, so the fabric does feel harder and more inflexible. Both (a) and (b) however give out the same information about the fabric. The line quality changes the feel and the solidity of the fabric.

Gender, sexuality, religion, and culture

One that designs characters needs to consider the portrayal of gender, race, culture, sexual orientation, and any other group that easily leads itself to stereotyping. Because we have to design so many characters and we cannot possibly be knowledgeable in every aspect of every culture, clichés are often coming handy to quickly define a character. A stereotype is helping the character to be instantaneously understood, yet one has to be aware of the portrayal becoming negative and the character coming across as inferior. Is a space heroine comfortable in her sexy bikini and is it the proper outfit to wear to fight aliens? Probably not ... the question one needs to ask is if the male counterpart would also be shown in a speedo or is it more the fantasies of a male audience to peek at the leading lady in a sexual way instead of showing the woman's strength through other means? Is every military man a emotionless tough guy that can just fight anything and anyone? That's pretty doubtful. The leading man in many first shooter games are overly masculine and tough, overly muscular and huge, focusing on the gender's sexual stereotypes. Sex appeal or steroid muscles are often a tool that can help the attraction and believability of a character; however, it should never be the single aspect that leads to the final design. A character is more than just their sex appeal or physical strength. Sexism, racism, and stereotyping are never just negative. There is also positive racism that are a misrepresentation of the truth (however, what is the truth?). So how can one avoid stereotypes that are insulting? By asking questions and having answers to those questions that are satisfying, and that are not avoiding risky topics. Questions that help avoiding stereotyping a group are as follows:

Culture

- Is that culture properly and positively represented?
- Is the positive representation tiptoeing around some negative points that are avoided?
- If it is negatively represented is there a valid reason for that? Can some positive aspects also balance out the negative?

Gender

- How is the gender represented in the attire?
- Is it too cliché and thus lacks a unique interpretation?
- Is the female character as strong in her personality and outfit as the male character and vice versa?
- Are gender clichés avoided or if used, have a solid reason within the story?

Religion

- Is the religion portrayed in a respectful way avoiding stereotypes?
- Is the portrayal knowledgeable or just covering the basics?
- Are the details of the religious garment correct?

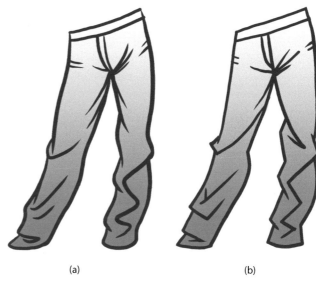

(a)   (b)

Figure 38.14

Sexual orientation:

- Is a straight hero the only option of having a strong male or female character?
- Is the gay character represented in a positive way or only serves as a sidekick assisting the hero or heroine in their journey?
- Is the sexual orientation of the character used to make him or her appear subordinate to the straight characters?
- What is the reason within the story for the character to actually be gay? Does there need to be a reason?

Balance

What makes this topic always a bit tricky is the lack of balance in the film. If there are ten white characters with another white character that comes across as a fool, then there are still the ten other white characters that intellectually balance out his simplemindedness. If there are ten white characters but the fool is Asian, then this would obviously be racist. If there are ten Asian characters but one white fool, then this is obviously also racist. If there is only one female character that is the sexy sidekick (like the character of Willie Scott in Indiana Jones), then this is sexist. If her clichéd passive behavior is balanced out by another strong and active female character, then sexism can be avoided and the two female characters are two different personalities rather than only one woman being the representation of an entire gender. Clichés and stereotypes are not untrue and they are not a lie either, but they are also not the full truth. It is the range of traits, looks, and behaviors that need to be portrayed. "French food is delicious" is a broad statement that does not mean that all French food is delicious. It means that some is good and some not as much. But it most definitely does not mean that French food is the best on earth. By having the rat in Pixar's *Ratatouille* (2007) be a French chef obviously caters the cliché of French food being the best food there is. Why not have the rat be a Thai chef or a Turkish chef? Because it would not follow the cliché of French cuisine being seen as the epitome of global cuisine, which is obviously a ridiculous statement.

More on folds and fabrics:

Hogarth B. (1995). *Dynamic Wrinkles and Drapery: Solutions for Drawing the Clothed Figure.* New York: Watson-Guptill Publications.

On Props:

Hayes D, Webster C. (2013). *Acting and Performance for Animation.* Burlington, MA: Focal Press, p. 99.

CHAPTER 39

Style Pass

The character design task of a feature film production stretches from a couple of months to a year or sometimes even longer. Additionally, there is not necessarily only one designer that contributes character suggestions, but often more designers and they all have a slightly different style; even though they might follow the design direction already established, there are always differences in their work. The final character lineup has to consist of only characters that look like they actually populate the same world and are a cohesive group that share the authorized design. In order to achieve this needed cohesiveness, all characters that have been chosen by the director and art director have to undergo a "style pass" during which all characters are redesigned and fine-tuned to precisely fit the final design language. Often, a suggested character is approved because of a certain quality the drawing has, a specific look or personality that is the perfect direction for the character, which doesn't mean the design itself is final or perfectly fits the style of the film. The style pass makes sure that all design rules are integrated into every character. Usually, the main character/s is/are finished first and all the others are then adjusted in style to fit their lead. In this stage, care needs to be taken to not lose the initial look and personality of the approved sketch. You just want to adjust the style, not change the character's personality and attitude. The design rules for the characters also have to follow the design of the background as both always go hand in hand and cannot be seen separately. The characters are part of their surroundings and the design needs to respect that. Keep your design strong and don't dilute it by weakening design elements that you initially considered important for the character, nor add elements just because they "look good." It is very easy to go overboard in this stage and lose the initial look and personality. Appeal is the goal, not an overloaded look that distracts.

Ask yourself these questions:

- What is the film's technique? (different animation techniques require different design technicalities.)
- What shape language are you using?

- How cartoony or realistic do you want your characters to be, and are all characters following the same level on the design scale?
- How can you achieve consistency in their design without repeating the same look? Variation is the key!
- What body ratio are you using for the characters, and does it work in relation to their age and height?
- What color represents each character's personality, and how do the characters relate to each other in their color design?
- How do the main characters relate to each other in their shapes and forms? Do they represent in their shapes, forms, and silhouettes their defined personalities in the story?
- Does the final design still have the personality and appeal of the sketch?

Your rules also determine which characters are pushed the most in their design and which characters are more subtle. There needs to be a certain tension between the characters to keep the lineup interesting. Not every character needs to drag attention and neither does every character have to be exaggerated to the extreme!

Explore a wide range in your character lineup and vary size, silhouette, color, attitude, personality, behavior, clothing, shapes, hairstyle etc. Variety makes the lineup much more interesting and helps distinguish the characters from each other. But don't forget that the variety shouldn't clash with the style direction you established for your movie. If the characters vary too much in style from each other the result could make it hard for the audience to believe that the characters inhabit the same world. Variation is important in the difference in "character," not the difference in design. However, there is always the exception, and in this case, it is the successful TV show by Cartoon Network *The Amazing World of Gumball* (2011–). The characters are all over the place and there doesn't seem to be any direction at all. There are different animation techniques from puppets, CG, 2D, and cutout. There seems to be no rule in the character design, or if there is one it is "anything goes." The result is a highly creative and exciting show because it does exactly the opposite of what animation design has been teaching for decades and thus has invented something totally unique.

DOI: 10.1201/b22147-39

CHAPTER 40

Character/Model Sheets

The final character's design ends with the model sheets. These are the blueprints for the characters and clearly define them in their entirety with all the information that is needed to successfully translate the designs into moving characters on screen. A successful character is always based on a strong communication between the various artists and the model sheets are the tools to transfer the information from one department to another. Shapes and forms, poses and personality studies, turnarounds, facial expressions, anatomical drawings, design specifics, and details are all part of those model sheets in order to translate the drawings into a different medium in 3D or stop-motion, or to use the drawings for traditional or digital 2D character animation. It is crucial for these character sheets to be as accurate and precise as possible to avoid any mistakes in the implementation in the film. A mistake in the turnaround in a 2D production opens the character up for interpretation by the artists and that leads to mistakes that can be rather costly. Describing the design of the character meticulously and accurately avoids problems down the line and reduces the range of interpretability. What information those sheets includes depends of course on the animation technique being used and the studio.

The turnaround is by no means just a technical turn of the character, but a turn that maintains the aesthetics of the character drawings and its complex interplay of the right shapes and forms, lines, and "feel." Without keeping the balance of shapes and the tension and forces within them, the character will ultimately fall flat. The character needs to still have those elements that made the drawing attractive in the first place, not to exaggerate them, but translate them into the character turn so that those elements are to be seen in every view of the turn.

Character sheets

Character sheets can include:

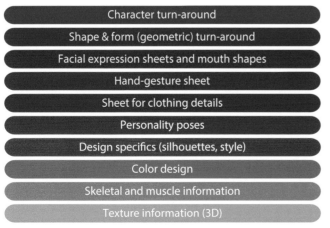

- Character turn-around
- Shape & form (geometric) turn-around
- Facial expression sheets and mouth shapes
- Hand-gesture sheet
- Sheet for clothing details
- Personality poses
- Design specifics (silhouettes, style)
- Color design
- Skeletal and muscle information
- Texture information (3D)

Character turnaround

Turnarounds are the most important drawings among the model sheets and are rather technical drawings that are not the most creative part of character design; however, they are crucially important. Turnarounds explain the character in its forms and shapes. The actual purpose of a turnaround depends on the technique of the film if it's 2D, 3D, stop-motion, or any other animation technique. Each medium requires a slightly different approach because the information in the drawings has different purposes and the point of the turnaround is transferring information from one artist to another.

There are two different turnarounds: the final character as it is being seen on screen (Figure 40.1), and the shape and form turnaround (Figure 40.2) that describes the character's underlying structure and explains which shapes and forms are used to create that very character. Both are of the same importance!

There is however a different approach in the animation techniques as each requires different information about the character.

2D hand-drawn animation

The model sheets in 2D animation need to present the character as it is to be seen on screen, whereas in 3D animation the character is just based on the model sheet's forms as it is still to be translated into a digital character and thus undergoes yet another translation into a different medium.

In 2D animation, the line quality and simplicity of the characters are obviously the most important technical aspects the model sheets should follow. Everyone who works from the designs interprets the character drawings in a slightly different way. Animators work from the model sheets, clean-up artists use them for their final drawings, and all artists need to adhere to the model sheets meticulously. They need to exactly demonstrate the character's shape language and details, its overall style and use of line (with the width, the thickness, and weight of the line etc.). Therefore, the character in the turn has to have the final aesthetics and a precision that is accurate enough to not expose the character to interpretation. The less precise the drawings are, the more room there is for personal styles from the artists to creep in. If there are 20 people working on a character based on your drawings, there will be 20 slightly different versions of the same character if the turnaround isn't accurate (there is always the personal drawing style of

DOI: 10.1201/b22147-40

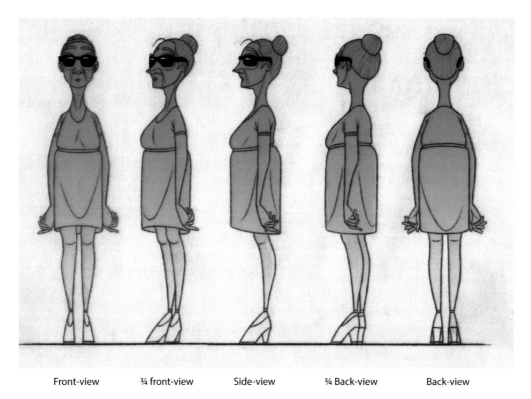

| Front-view | ¾ front-view | Side-view | ¾ Back-view | Back-view |

Figure 40.1

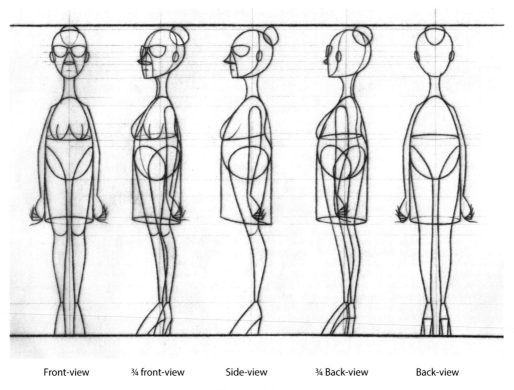

| Front-view | ¾ front-view | Side-view | ¾ Back-view | Back-view |

Figure 40.2

the artists coming in, but you can reduce that by providing correct artwork).

Not all the turns in 2D animation are proper turns that are based on an actual three-dimensional form in space. Some shows want the characters to have a graphic and flat look and the turnarounds have to clearly express that. *The Simpsons*, for instance, don't turn perfectly at all, but there is a unique way of showing the flatness of the characters. The mouths of *The Simpsons* characters are a unique shape that only works from a certain angle. If turned perfectly as a 3D shape, the iconic silhouette would be lost. A turnaround has to be developed and designed insofar as that it contains the specific look in either every angle, or the character can only be shown from specific angles to keep the silhouette intact.

To draw a character turnaround without the proper geometry and shape/form, language imbedded into the character is rather pointless. Animation characters have that reduction and simplification in their design specifically for the purpose of every animator being able to draw the character easily from various angles and this is where the shape and form turnaround comes in, to help the animator know which shapes and forms the character is based on and how to easily construct it. This can be of tremendous help for the animator to understand the character in its geometric architecture. The shapes and forms suggested should however always be as simple as possible and be built up from primary shapes/forms to secondary ones. Avoid overly complex shapes and forms!

3D animation

The turnaround for the 3D character only goes into the model department in a CG production and is then used by the modeler for sculpting the character. What is crucial though for a 3D turn is its accurate 3D forms. In a 2D turn, one can graphically cheat and make the character look good with a couple of mistakes that don't make sense in a geometric way, but work in a 2D graphic drawing. In 3D, the character has to have a correct spatial expansion and cheating doesn't work (as yet). There are some parts that the modeler can fix and figure out that are not fully thought through in the turnaround drawings (it is rather difficult to figure out all the form issues in a drawing), but the overall shape language of the character's structure should be correct. The same is important for a stop-motion turnaround.

In 3D animation, the character sheets are accompanied by digital paintings that show the final character with light and shadow, texture, and with clothing; those paintings more or less present the character as it is going to look in the final movie, but all of course painted in Photoshop and/or Painter. The more precision there is in those paintings, the easier it is to communicate the goal.

Generally, a turnaround is not a drawing that one just does in one go: it is a drawing that has to be refined and refined again, redrawn, and corrected; problems need to be solved and mistakes eliminated; a turnaround has to be improved until it is "good enough." Very often a certain shape/form looks good from one angle, but from another angle it does not fully represent the character and has to be changed or adjusted. It is a continuous process of improvement to get each angle in the turn to represent the character.

Types of turnarounds

There are obviously as many types of turnarounds as there are studios, as much of animation isn't a precise science but a creative expression. So, whatever kind of turnaround defines the character's look, its shape language, and its accuracy in its details is a valid turn.

What all turns have in common is the positioning of the different views next to each other on the same height. Horizontal lines then help to see which elements of the character's body are on the same level.

There is the typical turn of the character being rather stiff and rigid. This turn shows the character in a neutral pose without any expression or body movement other than the straight standing position (in CG animation often with arms stretched out in a T-pose). Aesthetically, this turn isn't very appealing and does look technical and plain; nevertheless, it is the easiest turnaround to draw and has all the information needed.

Then, there are the more complicated character turns where the character is in motion or strikes a pose that expresses their personality additionally to the turn. The character is presented in a sculptural way, though this is rather difficult to achieve. It is more appealing and shows an interesting side of the character with an expression from various perspectives and thus makes the character easier to like. What type of turn is appropriate is defined by the studio's needs and preferences.

A turn of five different angles is usually sufficient. Front, three-quarter front, side, three-quarter back, and back views are plenty to know how the character looks three-dimensionally.

Simple turn (Figure 40.3)

1: The form is a ball with a simple vertical line on the ball's surface, A being the side view of the line and B the front view. In order to get the in-between of A and B (the three-quarter view) we need to construct it.

2: What we want is the in-between of A and B in perspective. If we would just cut the distance between A and B in half, we get an in-between line, which however is not in perspective, so it needs to be constructed.

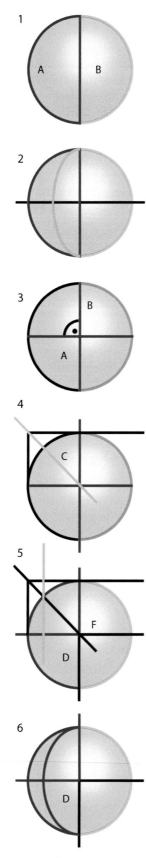

Figure 40.3

3: We can easily find the perspective middle between A and B if we see the same form with the two lines A and B from the top, then A is the horizontal and B the vertical. The angle is obviously 90°.

4: Construct the middle between lines A and B. The connection between the circle and the middle line creates the point C.

5: Drop a perpendicular from that point C onto the horizontal of the ball which determines the middle point D between points E and F (which are positioned on the lines from drawing 1; E is on A, and F on B). D is now one point on the horizontal curve between E and F in perspective.

6: Connect D with the beginning points on the top and bottom of the form of the ball and you will get the in-between of the side view A and front view B. By comparing the correct position of point D in drawing 6 with the wrong point in drawing 2, D is slightly off to the left.

Turning of a more complex shape (Figure 40.4)

Many shapes in a turnaround are rather complex and do not always just represent a simple circle or a cube. In those cases, the turn needs to be approximated in order to quickly come to a solution. Take the front and side view and overlap them. Create an in-between that is right in the middle between the two, and then just shift it slightly toward the side view, which gives you a simple and quick (not fully correct, but correct enough) three-quarter view.

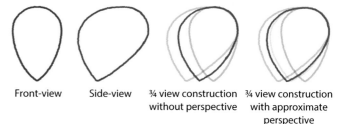

| Front-view | Side-view | ¾ view construction without perspective | ¾ view construction with approximate perspective |

Figure 40.4

The turn of a head (Figure 40.5)

The simple turn of a head is exactly the same procedure as the turn of the shape on the section, Simple turn. The only difference is that it's more complex as there is a combination of shapes and forms involved which need to be stacked on top of each other.

(a) Always start out with the sketch first and how you "think" the character should look or how you would like the character to look. This is an extremely important step as it determines how you see the character. The rest of the process is you trying to translate that look and feel into a working geometric turn. However, you constantly need to

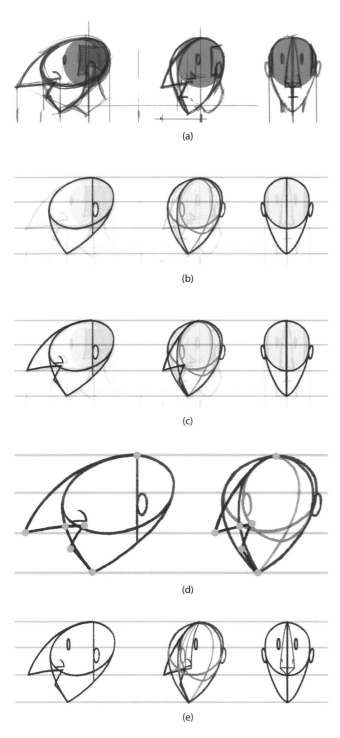

(a)

(b)

(c)

(d)

(e)

(f)

Figure 40.5

go back to that sketch and see if your turn is still expressing that initial personality!

(b) Add the silhouette of the side view and construct it into the three-quarter view by using geometric shapes and forms to build up the foundation of the character. Without the correct foundation the rest will be out of line. Obviously all of those shapes and forms need to be based on the initial sketch, so always work on top of the sketch! Use horizontal lines to keep everything accurate.

(c) Add the silhouette (blue) of the side view and construct it into the three-quarter view by using points that are created as can be seen in drawings D and E.

(d) Follow the line flow of the silhouette and create reference points that help to construct the same silhouette in perspective. The distance from the tip of the nose to its origin is more than half its length in the three-quarter view (as we have seen in the example turn on section, Turning of a more complex shape). Do that with every line! The more shapes and forms you add the more horizontal lines need to be drawn to keep everything in line.

(e) Add more details and define the width of the nose, which defines the position of the eyes in the three-quarter view.

(f) Fix elements that look odd in the three-quarter view and add parts that give you a more convincing dimensionality. You cannot turn each single shape and form perfectly in space, that would take too much time. So, some of the elements are guessed and approximated; too much accuracy can make the turn overly rigid. In the end, it is a character, which is an organic being.

Line of action and tension in the turnaround

When drawing the turnaround pay a lot of attention to the tension in the entire body and where the core of that tension lies. See the whole body and not just its various parts! This tension needs to show in the final drawing weight, strength, and overall posture of the character. The bulge of the belly, the lifting of the chest, the bend of the spine, the tension in the legs are all crucial for the pose and stand of the character to be read. Especially in the character turnaround, this is important so that the final character does not look stiff and rigid, but alive and organic.

It is much easier to control the standing figure in its three-dimensionality and its line of action when you pay attention to the flow of belly, chest, and spine first and use that as a basis for the character's basic shapes and forms. If you do not pay attention to the line of action, the character easily looks rigid and stiff, lacking the feel of a living and breathing character. It looks flat and weightless, lacks structure within itself, and feels robotic. All the other added parts are built around the tension of the character's basic shapes and forms.

Figure 40.6

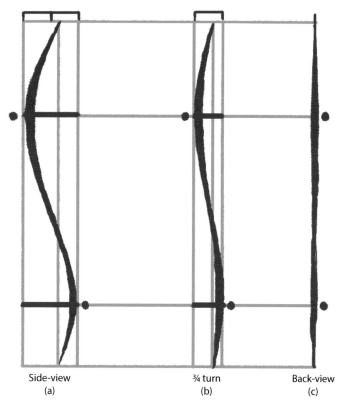

Side-view (a)   ¾ turn (b)   Back-view (c)

Figure 40.7

Every perspective turn has to contain this same tension in the limbs and arms, spine and belly, chest and neck. You need to feel the weight of the character and show it in every angle. The example shows how the line of action or the tension in the body (Figure 40.6) can be used in the turn to give each angle this needed underlying solid structure. It is important to keep the tension in mind especially in the three-quarter front and three-quarter back view as the perspective is more difficult to draw and judge compared to the easier side view, in which the tension is much more obvious.

The simple turn of the line of action

Figure 40.7a has the line of action in the side view. The blue lines determine the width of the line of action. Turning the line by three-quarters in (b) means to cut the width approximately in half by keeping the blue lines on the same height. The back view in (c) is obviously just a straight line; however, the blue dots are still important as they determine the points closest or furthest away from the viewer. The tension in the back view still needs to be felt in order for the forces to be seen and avoiding the back or front view to feel flat. The forces that keep the body upright still need to be considered!

Different types of turns

Graphic turn

The graphic turn (Figure 40.8a) does not follow the character's true form, but finds graphically pleasing shapes instead of accurate geometrical forms that turn in space. The office guy, for example, has a very similar silhouette in each turn and the front and side view are kind of mixed together to create the three-quarter view. The hat never changes position and the legs and shoes don't change either in their shape, they are in each perspective shown in the side view. What part of the character changes in which view depends on the design and character animation style. The graphic turn follows a strong shape and silhouette—those are its main focus—and it omits all information of perspective and dimensionality. It always aspires flatness and always lives on a two-dimensional plane. Examples here are many characters from 1950s and 1960s TV shows, like Hanna-Barbera shows but also many Cartoon Network shows, which reference the design of modern cartoons.

The graphic turn does not use any vanishing points for its construction.

Parallel turn

In the parallel turn (Figure 40.8b), all parts match up horizontally and all forms are accurate in their spatial expansion. This simple

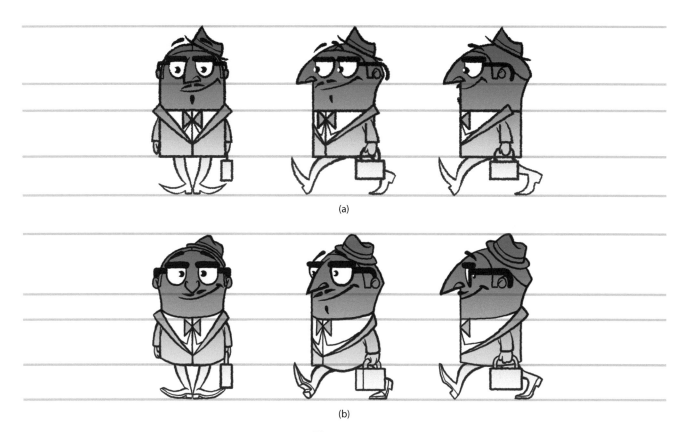

(a)

(b)

Figure 40.8

turn lacks perspective, but is the most accurate depiction of the character in three dimensions as it precisely shows the correct sizes without any perspective distortion. This turn also does not use any vanishing points for its construction.

One-point perspective turn

In this perspective turn (Figure 40.9), the character's forms are constructed on a one-point perspective that changes the sizes of certain elements as they are diminishing toward the vanishing point. The closer the element to the viewer, the bigger it appears, the further away the smaller (e.g., an arm would be slightly bigger in the side view than in the front view). This turn is less practical as it is rather time-consuming to accurately construct and it shows the character distorted through the perspective. In Figure 40.9, the feet are now looked down on and the rim of the hat can't be seen due to the perspective; the arms of the glasses are also tilting toward the vanishing point.

Facial expression sheets and mouth shapes

These clarify the character's personal expressions and unique mouth shapes for the dialog. Make sure that in some animation styles with lots of squash and stretch, the changing mouth shape also affects the entirety of the face; the whole head can also squash and stretch dramatically.

Hand gesture sheet

Drawing the hands of the character (or modeling them in CG) can be an extremely important part of the character's style. To define hands and the character's gestures through additional clarifying sheets is often a must. For instance, Hogarth's hands in *The Iron Giant* shows various examples of his hands the animator can use as references (Figure 40.10).

More on dialogue and mouth shapes:

Richard Williams, *The Animator's Survival Kit.* Faber & Faber: London UK, 2009, p. 304.

Sheet for clothing details

These pages define how certain clothes are worn and how the fabric drapes. This is not only important for traditional clothing but also for personalized clothing. For instance, a character with a seventeenth-century pair of pants is not likely to have a similar cut or look as a contemporary pair. Details are needed not only to mimic it but to get it accurate.

Additional pages need to explain all the accessories of the character in detail and design.

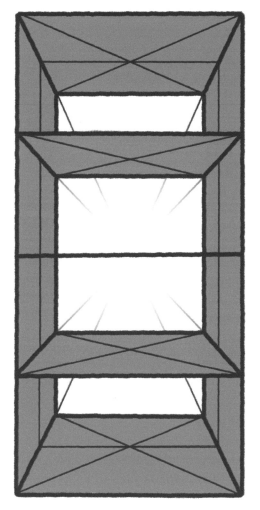 

Figure 40.9

Personality poses

How does the main character in DreamWorks' *Kung Fu Panda* (2008), for instance, pose in his own Kung Fu style, and how can those poses be used to additionally define parts of his personality? How does every other character use their specific Kung Fu style in their poses and do they differentiate from each other?

Design specifics

The character of Count Dracula in Sony Pictures Animation's feature *Hotel Transylvania* (2012) had a very strong silhouette in his cape and body language. One needs to describe this important information on the count in the character sheets as t is being used in many shots as a significant design element that defines the character and supports composition.

Color design

This point is pretty obvious. However, the different times of day color designs are optional and depend on the production.

Skeletal and muscle information

For instance, the character of Tarzan in Disney's animated feature from 1999 had a very detailed anatomy for a 2D character. In order to explain his complexity, more information about the character's anatomy needs to be provided to the artists to learn how that specific character is being drawn.

For more realistic and complex CG characters, a detailed anatomy explanation is a necessity, which can include muscle and skeletal information.

Texture information

What kind of texture is being used for all the different fabrics, materials, and also the character's skin, hair, teeth, or nails is obviously important. Leather is not just "leather" and skin can come in myriad colors and textures. Is the skin smooth or shaved, does it have freckles on the nose or cheeks, have a reddish hue on the cheeks, or is it dry on the elbows is all defining the character further. The scope of the texture information on one CG character can be extensive to say the least as every texture that is used for the character needs to be defined in detail to ensure that they all follow the same concept and idea. Images found online and linked to the specific area on the character design can visually explain which texture needs to be mimicked.

THE IRON GIANT   REFERENCE

Final Ruff -- Hogarth Hands

Figure 40.10

Brad Bird: *The Iron Giant* (1999); hand-gesture sheet

CHAPTER 41

Refinement

We always only see the final piece of art and never the development work or the different stages it went through to arrive at that final piece with all its complexities and dimensionality. This is obviously misleading as it looks like the artist "just" did it without thinking too much about it; just sat down and drew it. This is clearly not happening especially with programs like Photoshop or Painter where many different layers are compiled for the final piece to evolve. Every artist starts out with sketches and small thumbnail drawings to develop an idea. Few artists just sit down and create a piece from scratch without any preliminary sketches. Do not underestimate the importance of thumbnail drawings and the exploration of shapes and forms. Figure 41.1a through c is showing the progression of the character from the first thumbnail to the final sketch. However, there are many more stages in-between that develop the character and their personality further. The beginning (a) is just a thought, a quick thumbnail that expresses a simple idea; the drawing is obviously tiny; refining the thumbnail during the drawing process (b) makes one think and feel about the character and who they are. This will then lead to changes that refine the type—in this case, determination and aggressiveness (c). From the first to the last character, there might be 20 different ones that are tossed away, but they are necessary to "find" the final one and being confident about it. Changing the shapes and forms, and exaggerating them

has an impact on the expression, pose, and overall stature. His mustache was bent downward in the thumbnail drawing, but having the end of the mustache point upward gave him a slight smirk and less of a grumpy demeanor. Character design is not a straightforward process, but a trial and error procedure that can be messy.

The next step is to refine the drawing and clean it up to achieve forms that work, and lines and contrast that are balanced (Figure 41.2). Then, a color sketch that contains the basic direction of the final, followed by the final illustration (Figure 41.3). It is the logical step-by-step approach that helps to maintain a quality throughout.

There is always the question of when to stop and at what point is the piece finished aside from its artistic needs. One can of course render forever and refine it more and more. But at what point is it done, fitting what is actually needed? The level of completeness for a feature or TV company usually depends on the company and the needs of the project. Some artists or directors like to see finished work, others like to see sketches and then go from there. However, one should always ask themselves if the time spent on one image is more about pleasing oneself and creating polished artwork rather than supporting the needs of the project, which is sometimes done with a simple sketch to get the point across and discuss it first, then refine it.

(a)

(b)

(c)

Figure 41.1

DOI: 10.1201/b22147-41

Figure 41.2

Figure 41.3

For freelance work, some questions might help to decide if the art created is finished:

- What is the piece for?
- Who is the client?
- How much am I getting paid?
- How much time am I given for the job?
- What are the arrangements in the contract?

What is the piece for?

If it is a presentation piece, then the final artwork needs to be polished and perfect (polished does not necessarily mean highly rendered, but means presentable and publishable). Or is the final a sketch that will be developed further after some feedback? Then, a sketchy direction would be sufficient for the job. The purpose of the piece often determines its details and level of refinement.

However, many clients want to see a final design from the first sketching phase onward until the final piece, which is obviously not possible due to time constraints. Not every sketch can be finished and polished. Many clients do not fully understand the time it takes to develop characters, which can be an issue. But as always, there are exceptions. Some character designers are being hired exactly because of their ability to produce sketches that do

have a very polished and illustrative look to them that also look "finished."

Who is the client?

The work submitted should always have a high standard and professional look to it; one should not work harder for a high-end client, but work less for a small company. Always try to do the best you can in the time frame given.

How much am I getting paid?

If the client doesn't have the money to pay for a high-end photorealistically rendered piece, then the final needs to be reduced in its scope and detail. In the end, being a designer is a job and one needs to be aware of timing, finances, and how much work can be put into a job so in the end it still pays the bills. If the job isn't paid much from the beginning for whatever reason, one should stay away from highly complex designs that take forever to render (if of course one chooses to work in a time frame that makes financial sense; there is always the job here and there where one does not want to consider the low pay but does it for the fun anyway).

How much time am I given for the job?

Usually, jobs are supposed to be finished yesterday and more often than not there is not enough time to finish the piece in a relaxed time frame. Do plan ahead and know how much time a certain technique will take, and make sure that the client does allow you that time to finish the piece. It is embarrassing and unprofessional if the given time frame is not sufficient and one needs to get an extension. Make sure that you spend the right amount of time on each section of the job and always leave enough time for the final piece (including changes).

The time is usually split into the following:

- Sketches
- Refined sketches (with additional time for changes)
- Final drawing (with additional time for changes)
- Final illustration/painting/design (with additional time for changes)

What are the arrangements in the contract?

What does the contract require? Stick to that contract because it is what you agreed on in the first place! If there are changes to the artwork, make sure that you follow the number of changes mentioned in the contract as changes can get out of control. Usually, it is okay to have one or two additional small changes and not charge the client for it, but at some point if the changes are coming constantly it needs to be discussed.

The main difficulty is to decide when the piece is technically finished. One can go on and on with refining it and slowly ruining it. It takes practice and a sensibility for one's personal style to know when the piece "feels" done. This solely depends on the style. There is absolutely no rule that might help as a guideline.

Additional Reading

Animation history

Balakirsky Katz Mayaa, *Drawing the Iron Curtain: Jews and the Golden Age of Soviet Animation*, Rutgers University Press, New Brunswick, NJ, 2016.

Barrier Michael, *Hollywood Cartoons: American Animation in Its Golden Age*, Oxford University Press, Oxford, 2003.

Bendazzi Giannalberto, *Animation: A World History: Volume I—III*, Focal Press, Waltham, Massachusetts, 2016.

Bendazzi Giannalberto, *Cartoons: One Hundred Years of Cinema Animation*, Indiana University Press, Bloomington, IN, 1995.

Cohen Karl F., *Forbidden Animation: Censored Cartoons and Blacklisted Animators in America,* McFarland & Co, Jefferson, NC, 2004.

Crafton Donald, *Before Mickey: The Animated Film 1898–1928*, University of Chicago Press, Chicago, IL, 1993.

Culhane Shamus, *Talking Animals and Other People*, Da Capo Press, Boston, MA, 1998.

Ghez Didier, *Walt's People: Volume 1–19: Talking Disney with the Artists Who Knew Him*, Theme Park Press, 2014–2017.

Giessen Rolf, *Animation Under the Swastika: A History of Trickfilm in Nazi Germany, 1933–1945*, McFarland & Co., Jefferson, NJ, 2012.

Klein Norman M., *Seven Minutes: The Life and Death of the American Animated Cartoon*, Verso, New York, 1996.

Koyama-Richard Brigitte, *Japanese Animation: From Painted Scrolls to Pokémon*, Flammarion, Paris, 2010.

Laqua Carsten, *Wie Micky unter die Nazis fiel: Walt Disney und Deutschland*, Rowohlt Taschenbuch Verlag, Berlin, 1992.

Lehman Christopher P., *The Colored Cartoon, Black Representation in American Animated Short Films, 1907–1954*, University of Massachusetts Press, Amherst, MA, 2007.

Neupert Richard, *French Animation History*, Wiley, Hoboken, NJ, 2014.

Pointer Ray, *The Art and Inventions of Max Fleischer, American Animation Pioneer*, McFarland & Co., Jefferson, NC, 2017.

Animation theory

Furniss Maureen, *Art in Motion, Revised Edition: Animation Aesthetics*, John Libbey Publishing, Barnet, UK, 2008.

Leslie Esther, *Hollywood Flatlands: Animation, Critical Theory and the Avant-Garde*, Verso, New York, 2004.

Wells Paul, *Animation and American Society: Cartoons to Computers*, Keele University Press, Keele, UK, 2002.

Wells Paul, *Understanding Animation*, Routledge, London, 1998.

Visual perception

Arnheim Rudolf, *Art and Visual Perception: A Psychology of the Creative Eye*, University of California Press, Berkeley, CA, 2004.

Arnheim Rudolf, *Visual Thinking*, University of California Press, Berkeley, CA, 2004.

Composition

Arnheim Rudolf, *The Power of the Center: A Study of Composition in the Visual Arts*, University of California Press, Berkeley, CA, 2009.

Film history

Monaco James, *How to Read a Film: The World of Movies, Media, Multimedia: Language, History, Theory*, Oxford University Press, Oxford, 2009.

Drawing

Enstice Wayne, Melody Peters: *Drawing: Space, Form, and Expression*, Pearson Education Inc., New York, 2013.

Hampton Michael, *Figure Drawing, Design and Invention*, Michael Hampton, 2013.

Mattesi Mike, *Force: Animal Drawing: Animal Locomotion and Design Concepts for Animators*, Focal Press, Waltham, MA, 2011.

Mattesi Mike, *Force: Dynamic Life Drawing*, Focal Press, Waltham, MA, 2006.

Robertson Scott, *How to Draw: Drawing and Sketching Objects and Environments*, Design Studio Press, Culver City, CA, 2013.

Robertson Scott, *How to Render TP*, Design Studio Press, Culver City, CA, 2014.

Stanchfield Walt, *Drawn to Life: 20 Golden Years of Disney Master Classes: The Walt Stanchfield Lectures—Volume 1 & 2*, Focal Press, Waltham, MA, 2009.

Storyboarding

Katz Steven, *Film Directing Shot by Shot: Visualizing from Concept to Screen*, Michael Wiese Productions, Studio City, CA, 1991.

Katz Steven, *Film Directing: Cinematic Motion: A Workshop for Staging Scenes*, Michael Wiese Productions, Studio City, CA, 2004.

Editing

Murch Walter, *In the Blink of an Eye, A Perspective on Film Editing*, Silman-James Press, West Hollywood, CA, 2001.

Cinematography

Alton John, *Painting with Light*, University of California Press, Berkeley, CA, 1998.

Kenworthy Christopher, *Master Shots Vol 1–3: 100 Advanced Camera Techniques to Get an Expensive Look on Your Low-Budget Movie*, Michael Wiese Productions, Studio City, CA, 2003.

Mascelli Joseph V., *Five C's of Cinematography: Motion Pictures Filming Techniques*; Silman-James Press, West Hollywood, CA, 1998.

Mercado Gustavo, *The Filmmaker's Eye: Learning (and Breaking) the Rules of Cinematic Composition*, Focal Press, Waltham, MA, 2010.

Animation techniques

2D animation

Culhane Shamus, *Animation: From Script to Screen*, St. Martin's Griffin, New York, 1990.

Gilland Joseph, *Elemental Magic, Volume I & II: The Art of Special Effects Animation*, Focal Press, Waltham, MA, 2009 & 2011.

Thomas Frank and Johnston Ollie, *Illusion of Life: Disney Animation*, Disney Editions, Glendale CA, 1995.

Webster Chris, *Action Analysis for Animators*, Focal Press, Waltham, MA, 2009.

Whittaker Harold, Halas John and Sito Tom, *Timing for Animation*, Focal Press, Waltham, MA, 2009.

Stop-motion animation

Gasek Tom, *Frame-By-Frame Stop Motion: The Guide to Non-Puppet Photographic Animation Techniques*, CRC Press, Boca Raton, FL, 2017.

Lord Peter, Sibley Brian and Park Nick, *Cracking Animation: The Aardman Book of 3-D Animation*, Thames & Hudson Ltd., London, 1998.

Pettigrew Neil, *The Stop-motion Filmography: A Critical Guide to 297 Features Using Puppet Animation, Volume I & II*, McFarland & Co., Jefferson, NC, 2007.

Purves Barry J.C., *Stop-Motion Animation: Frame by Frame Film-Making with Puppets and Models*, Fairchild Books, London, 2014.

Shaw Susannah, *Stop Motion: Craft Skills for Model Animation*, Focal Press, Waltham, MA, 2017.

Ternan Melvyn, *Stop Motion Animation: How to Make & Share Creative Videos*, Barron's Educational Series, Hauppauge, NY, 2013.

Experimental animation

Russett Robert and Starr Cecile, *Experimental Animation*, Da Capo Press, Boston, MA, 1988.

Computer animation

Kerlow Isaac V., *The Art of 3D Computer Animation and Effects*, Wiley, Hoboken, NJ, 2009.

Special effects

Duignan Patricia Rose, *Industrial Light and Magic (Into the Digital Realm)*, Del Rey Books, London, 1996.

Smith Thomas G., *Industrial Light and Magic*, Ballantine Books Inc., New York, 1992.

Game design

Schell Jesse, *The Art of Game Design: A Book of Lenses*, CRC Press, Boca Raton, FL, 2008.

Matte painting

Cotta Vaz Marc, *The Invisible Art: The Legends of Movie Matte Painting*, Chronicle Books, San Francisco, CA, 2004.

Now that you have learned all of this complicated "stuff" and suffered through the whole book, I'd suggest to push that new knowledge all the way back into your brain right into a small cupboard behind some shelves where it doesn't cause too much havoc. Then relax, get a cup of hot chocolate and just draw. Above all rules is the one rule that says to break all the other rules and see what that does to your work. Draw, have fun, and be creative!

Index